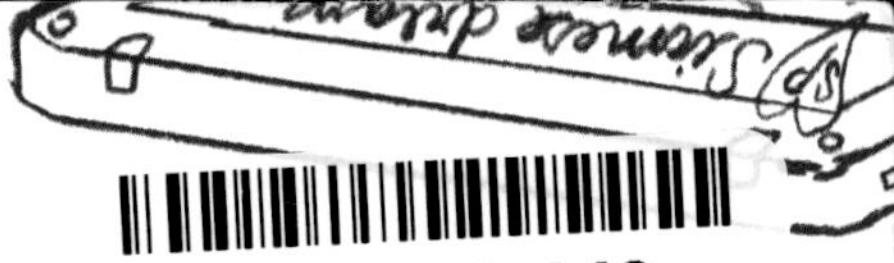

"DO YOU KNOW THE FEELING WHEN YOU'RE VISITING SOMEWHERE AND YOU WANT TO GO HOME? THAT FEELING, ALL THE TIME, THE WHOLE DAY, UNINTERRUPTED AND ABOUT YOUR OWN BODY."

— DANIËLLE WAGEMAKERS – FADING GENDER

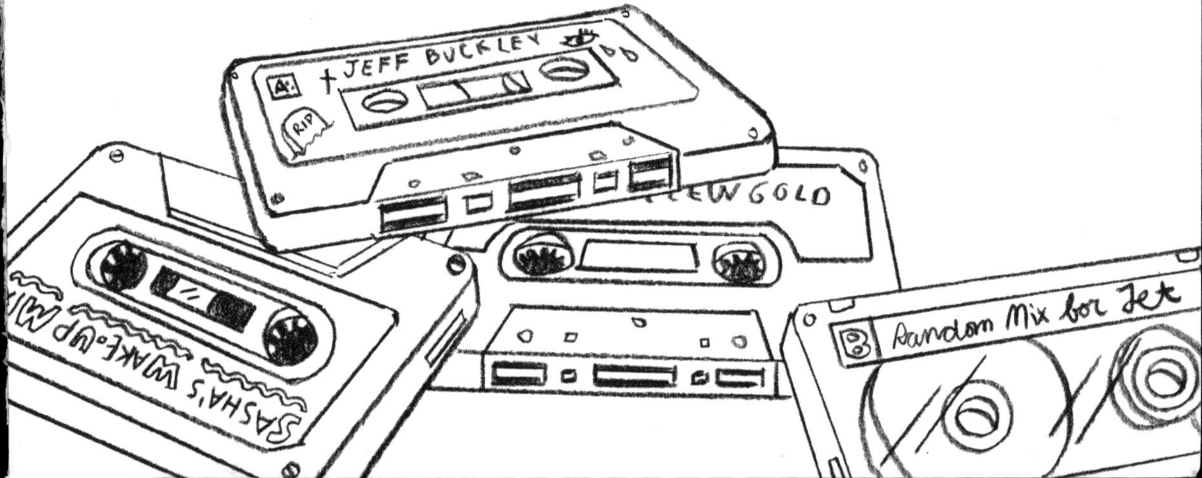
A
JEFF BUCKLEY
RIP
SASHA'S WAKE-UP MIX
B
Random Mix for Jet

fondskwadraat

Created with the kind support of family, unemployment benefit, and the artist loan from Fonds Kwadraat.

First published in 2022 by Nobrow Ltd.
27 Westgate Street, London E8 3RL.

Translation: Ameera Rajabali

10 9 8 7 6 5 4 3 2 1

Published in the US by Nobrow (US) Inc.

FSC www.fsc.org MIX Paper from responsible sources FSC® C002795

Printed in Latvia on FSC® certified paper.
ISBN: 978-1-913123-03-1

www.nobrow.net

JORIS BAS BACKER

KISSES FOR JET
A COMING-OF-GENDER STORY

TRANSLATED BY AMEERA RAJABALI

NOBROW
LONDON | LOS ANGELES

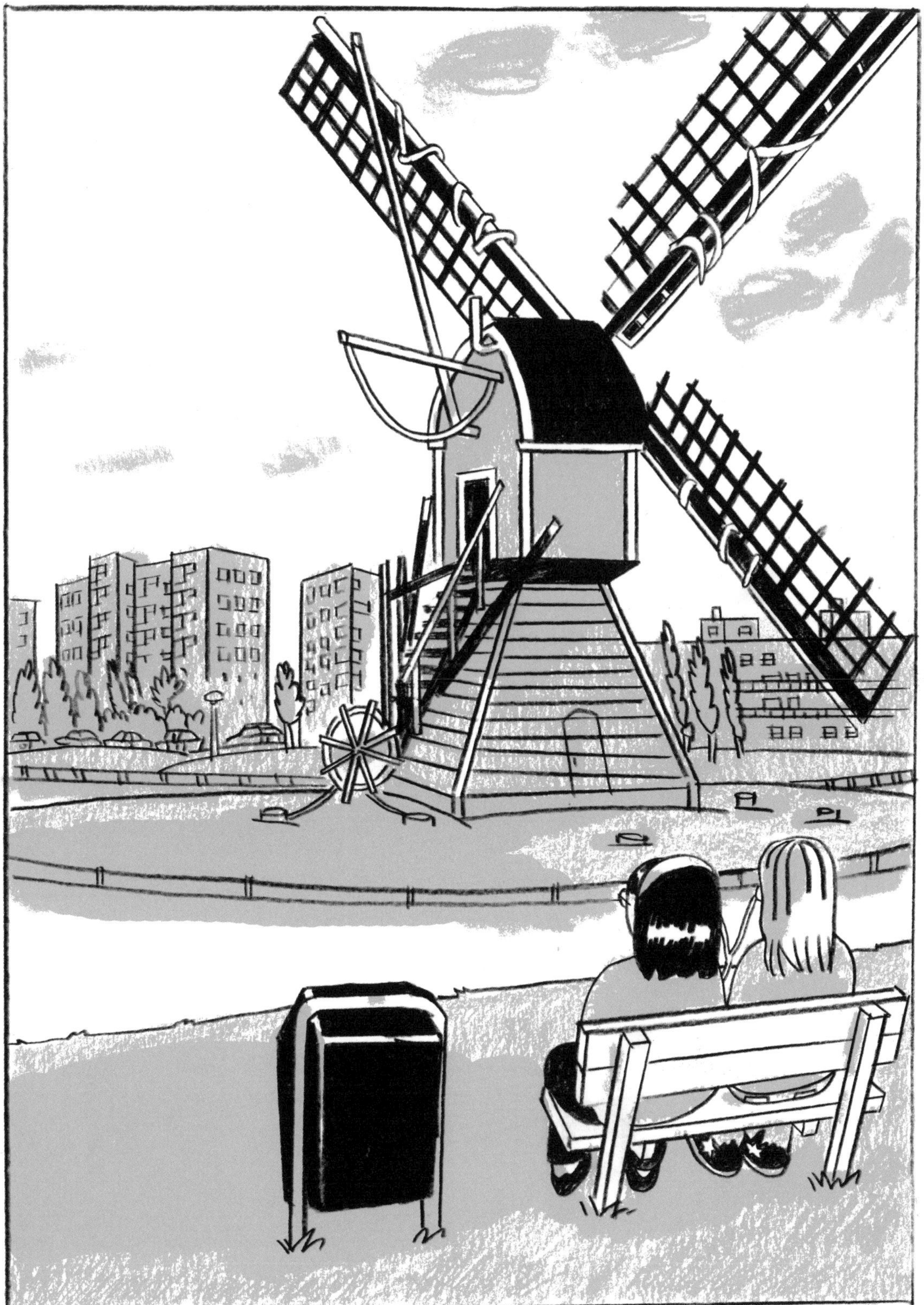

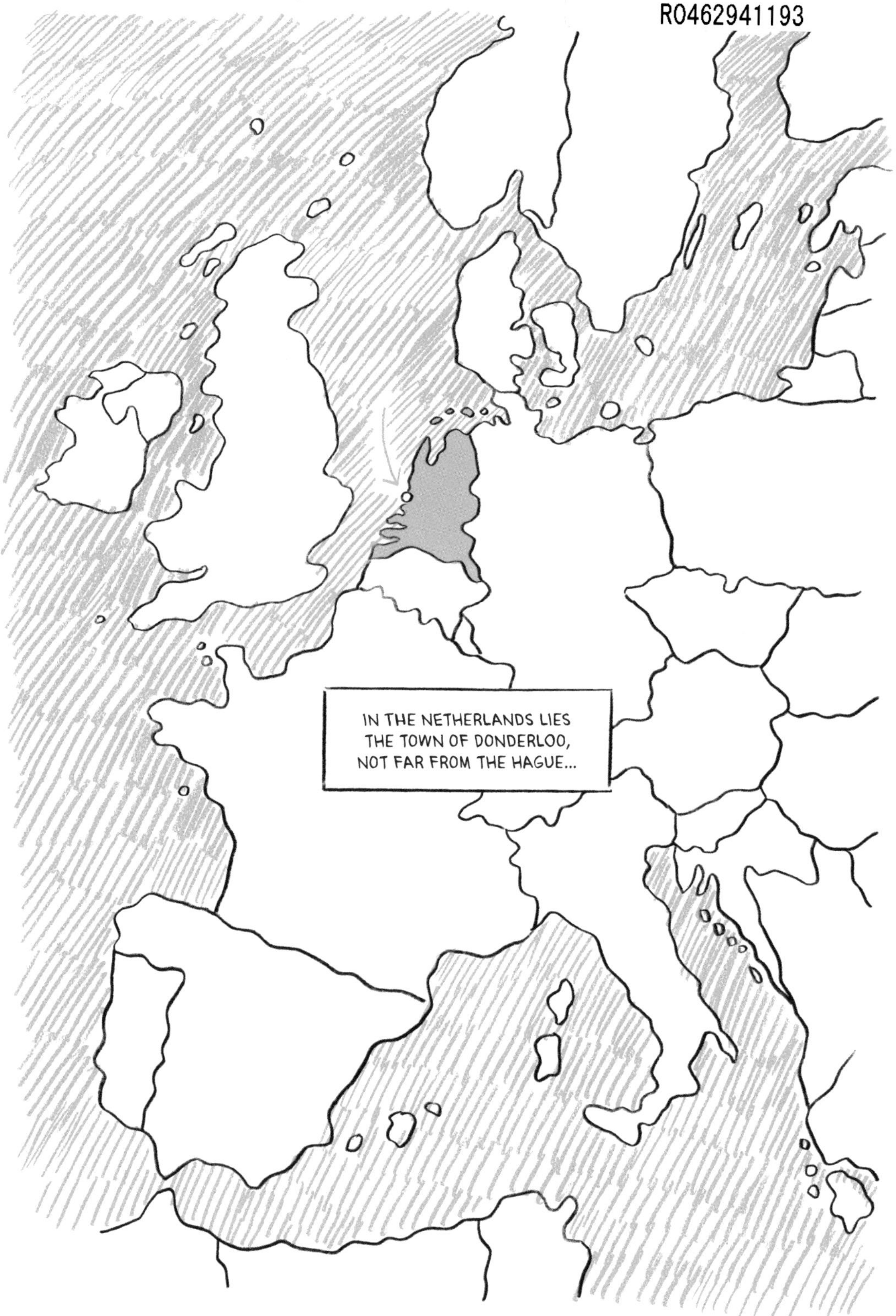
IN THE NETHERLANDS LIES
THE TOWN OF DONDERLOO,
NOT FAR FROM THE HAGUE...

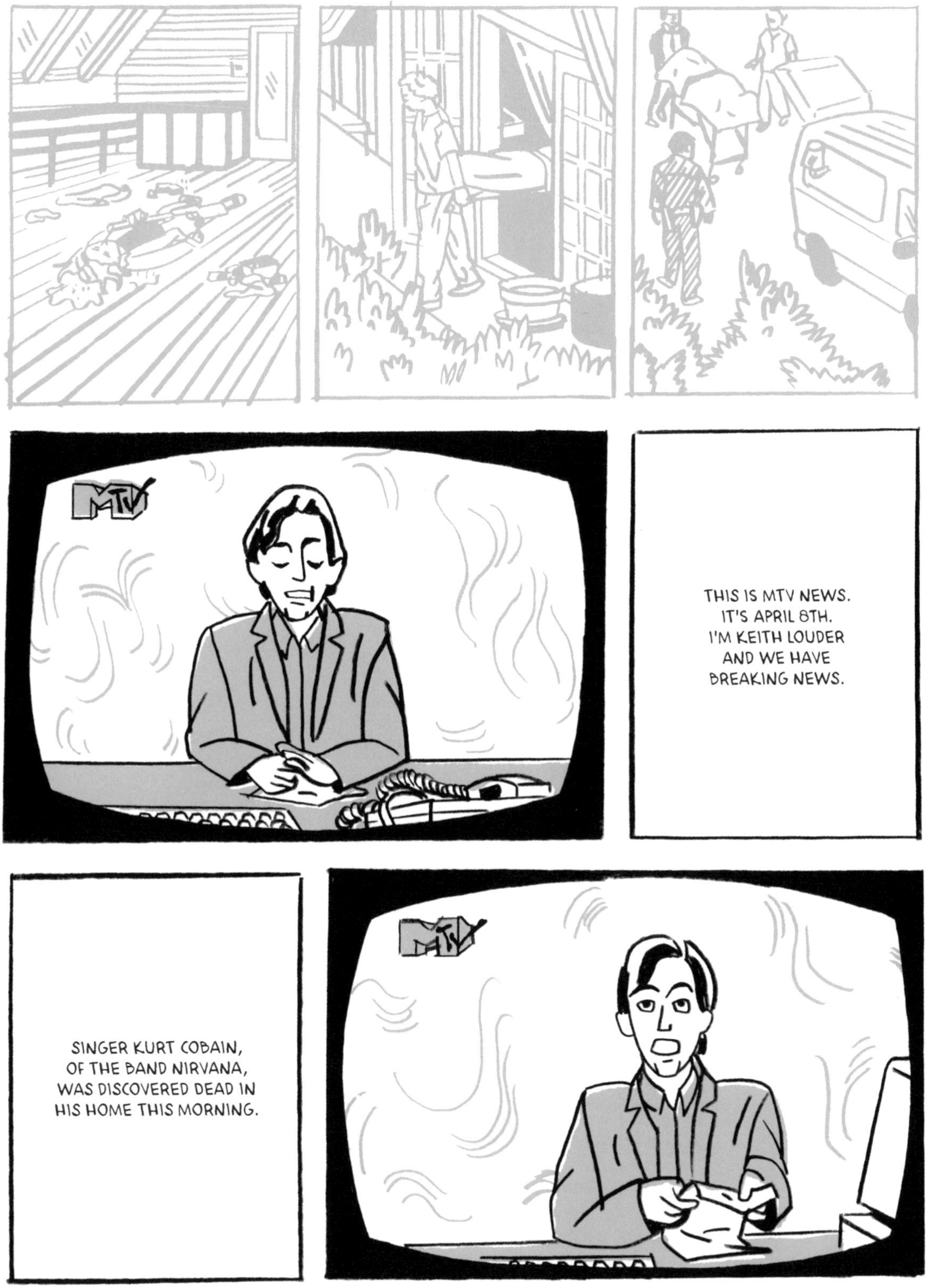
THIS IS MTV NEWS. IT'S APRIL 8TH. I'M KEITH LOUDER AND WE HAVE BREAKING NEWS.
SINGER KURT COBAIN, OF THE BAND NIRVANA, WAS DISCOVERED DEAD IN HIS HOME THIS MORNING.

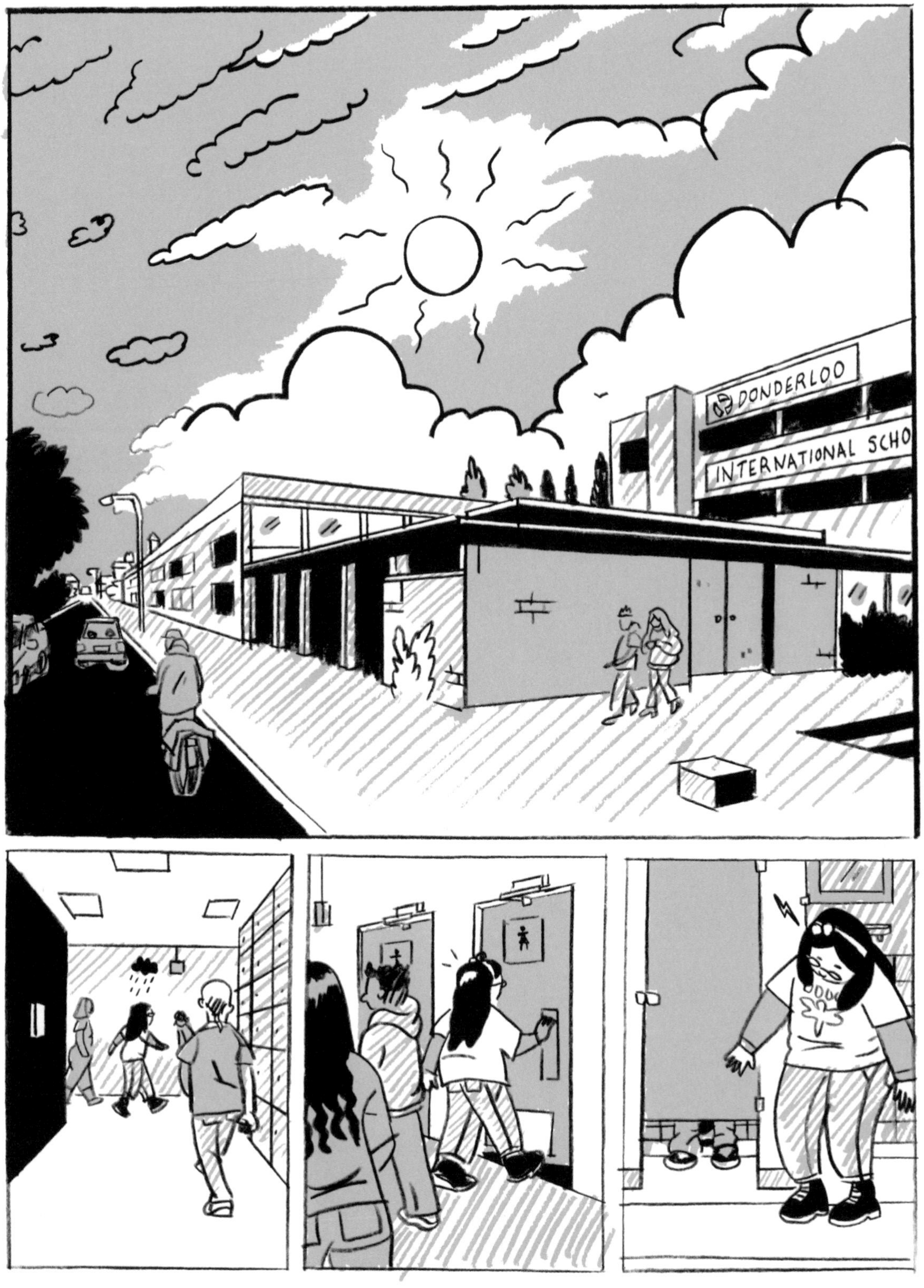
DONDERLOO
INTERNATIONAL SCHO

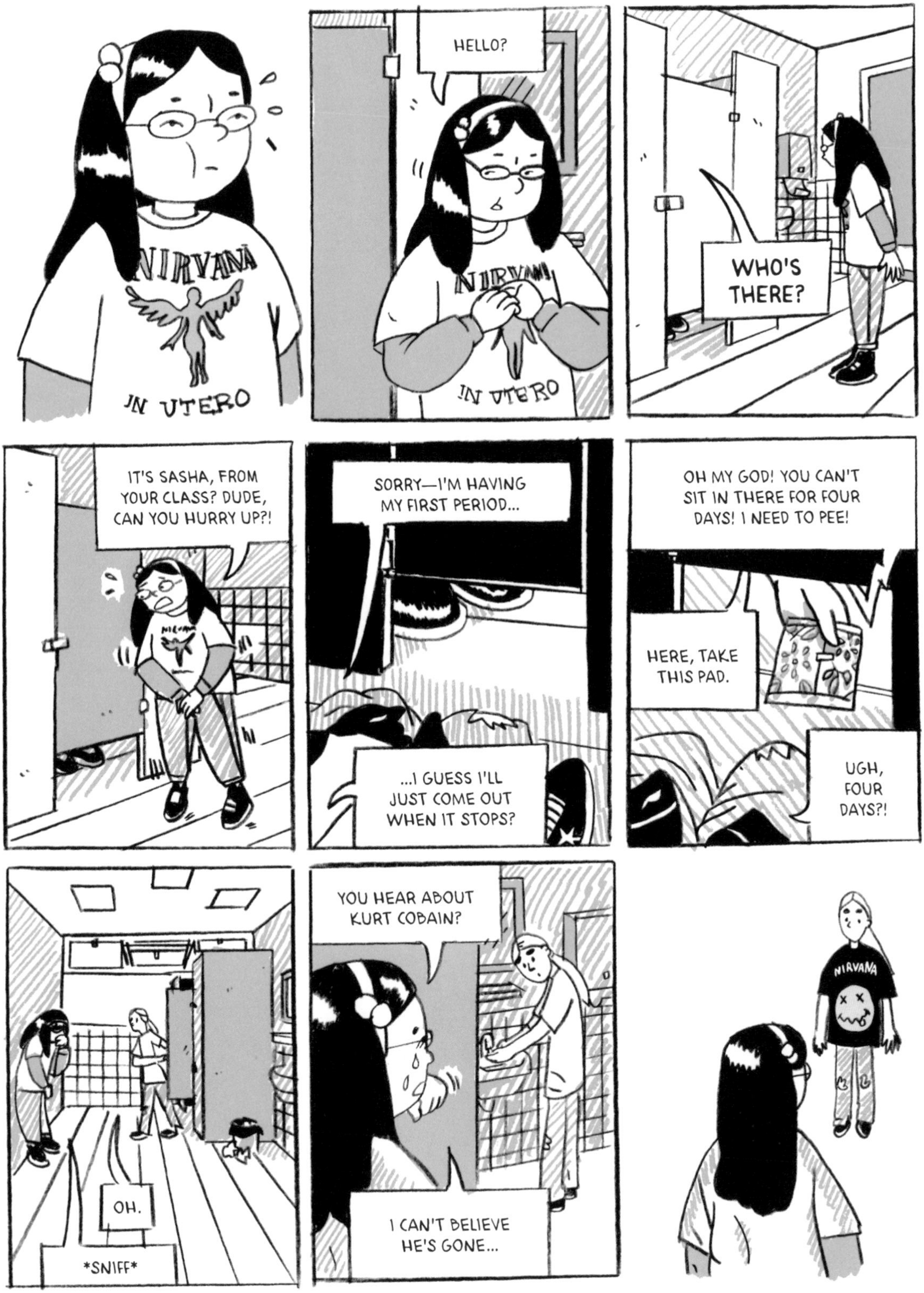
NIRVANA
IN UTERO
HELLO?
WHO'S THERE?
IT'S SASHA, FROM YOUR CLASS? DUDE, CAN YOU HURRY UP?!
SORRY—I'M HAVING MY FIRST PERIOD...
...I GUESS I'LL JUST COME OUT WHEN IT STOPS?
OH MY GOD! YOU CAN'T SIT IN THERE FOR FOUR DAYS! I NEED TO PEE!
HERE, TAKE THIS PAD.
UGH, FOUR DAYS?!
OH.
SNIFF
YOU HEAR ABOUT KURT COBAIN?
I CAN'T BELIEVE HE'S GONE...
NIRVANA

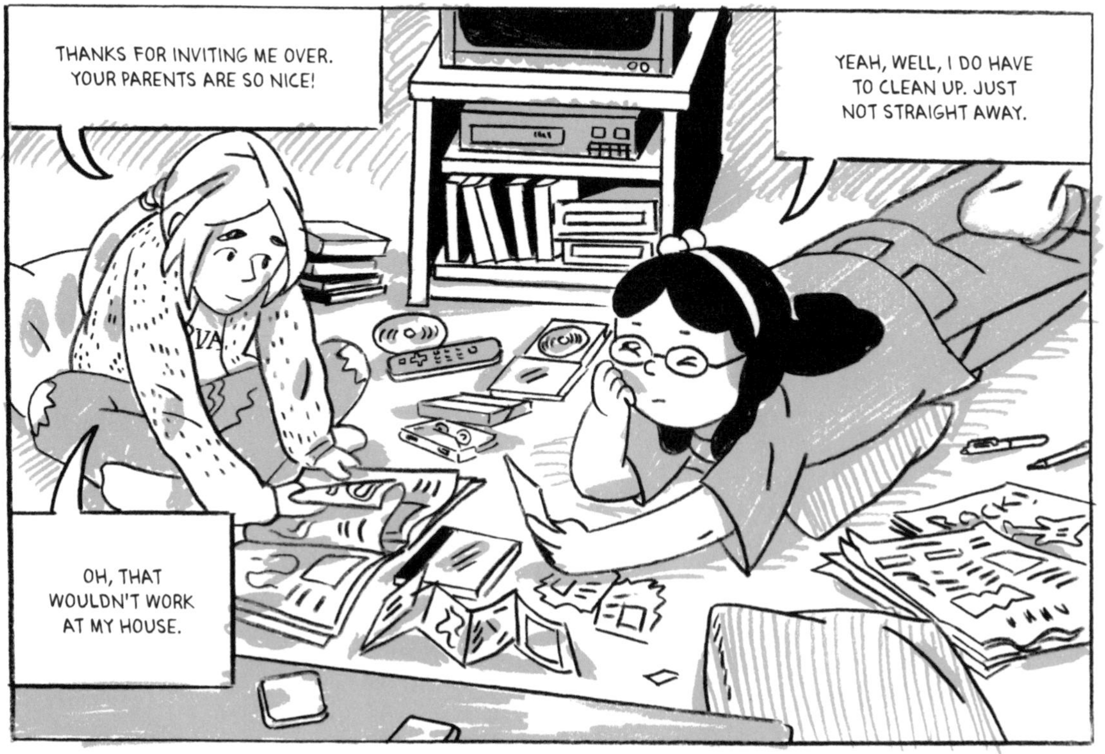
THANKS FOR INVITING ME OVER. YOUR PARENTS ARE SO NICE!
YEAH, WELL, I DO HAVE TO CLEAN UP. JUST NOT STRAIGHT AWAY.
OH, THAT WOULDN'T WORK AT MY HOUSE.

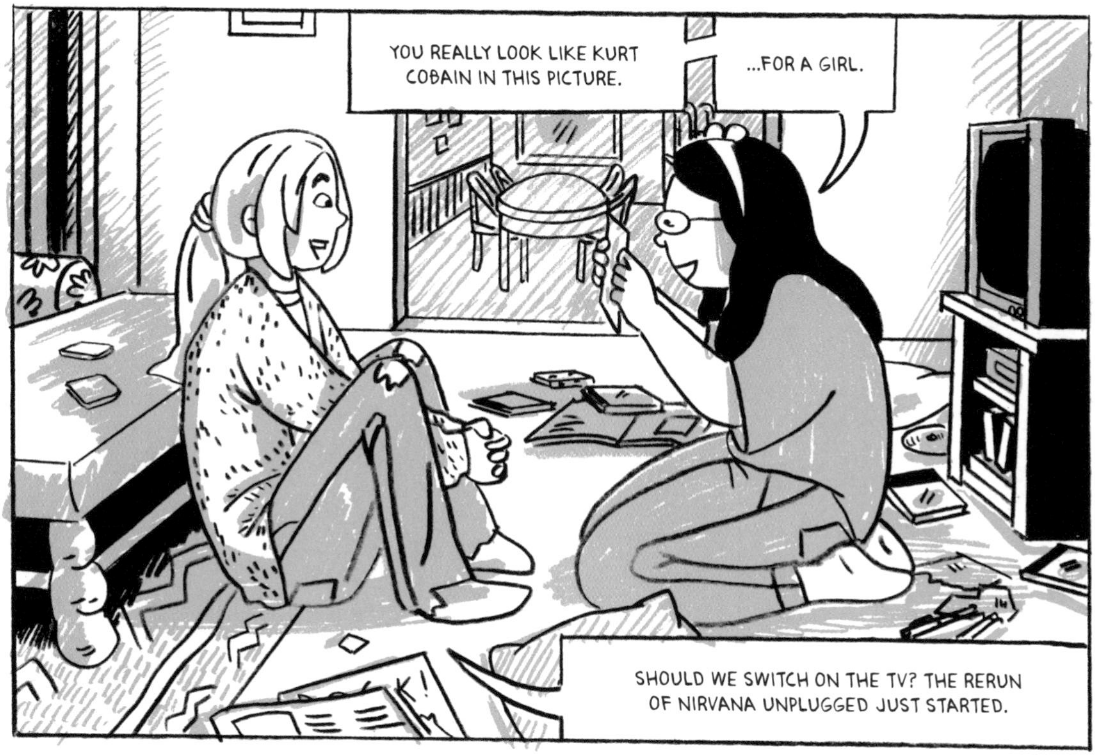
YOU REALLY LOOK LIKE KURT COBAIN IN THIS PICTURE.
...FOR A GIRL.
SHOULD WE SWITCH ON THE TV? THE RERUN OF NIRVANA UNPLUGGED JUST STARTED.

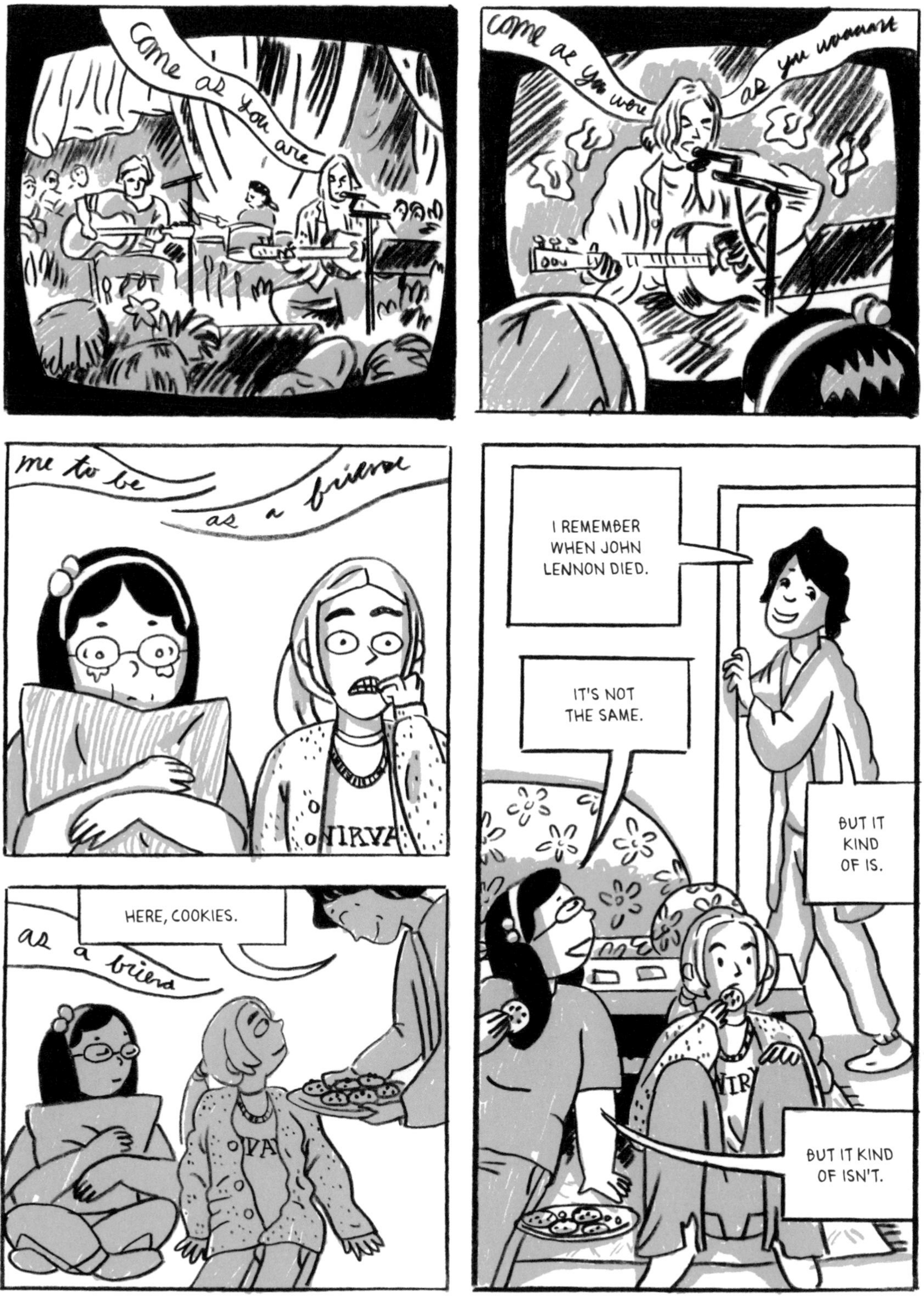
come as you are
come as you were
me to be
as a friend
I REMEMBER WHEN JOHN LENNON DIED.
IT'S NOT THE SAME.
BUT IT KIND OF IS.
as a friend
HERE, COOKIES.
BUT IT KIND OF ISN'T.

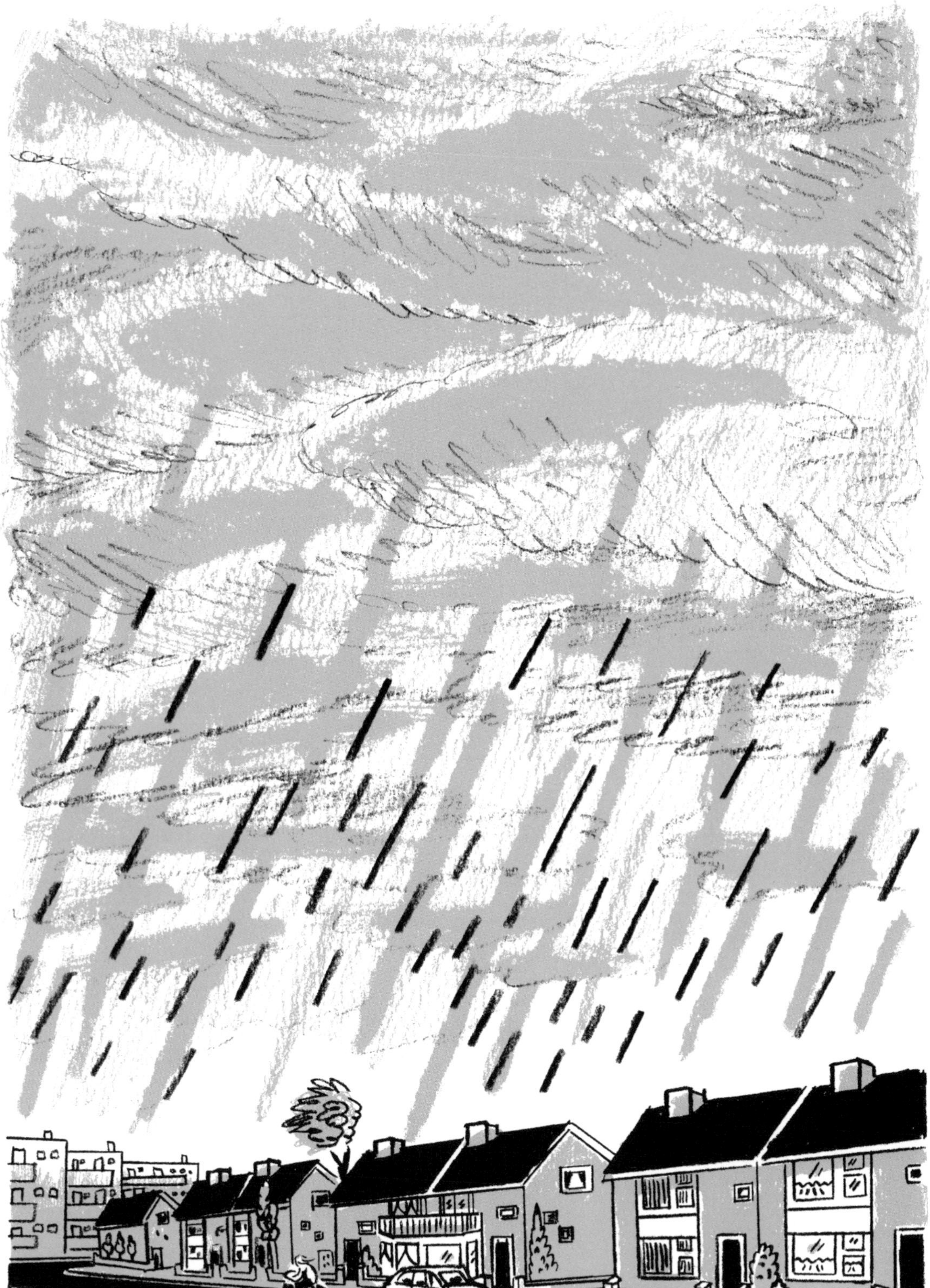

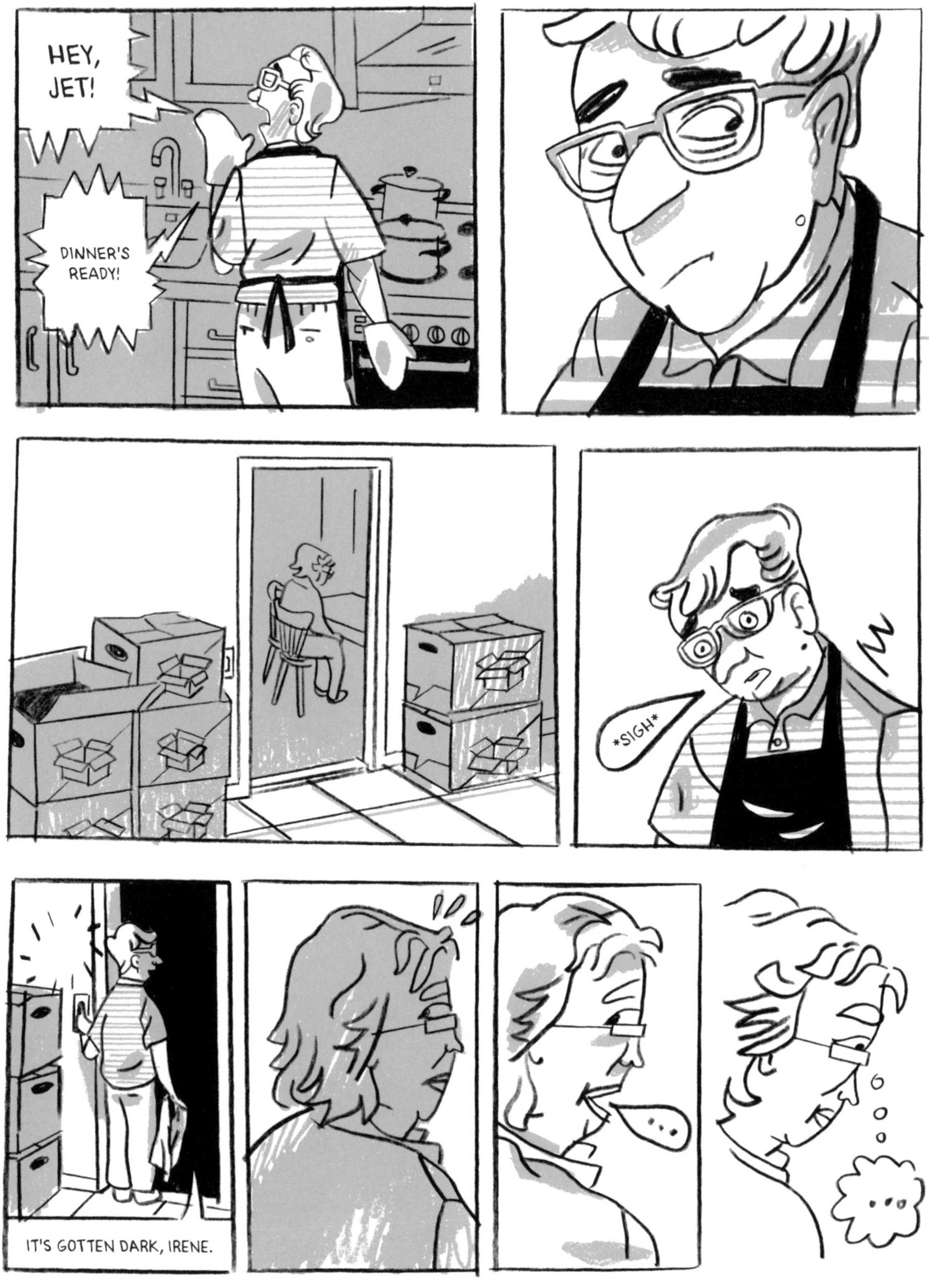
HEY, JET!
DINNER'S READY!
SIGH
IT'S GOTTEN DARK, IRENE.
...
...

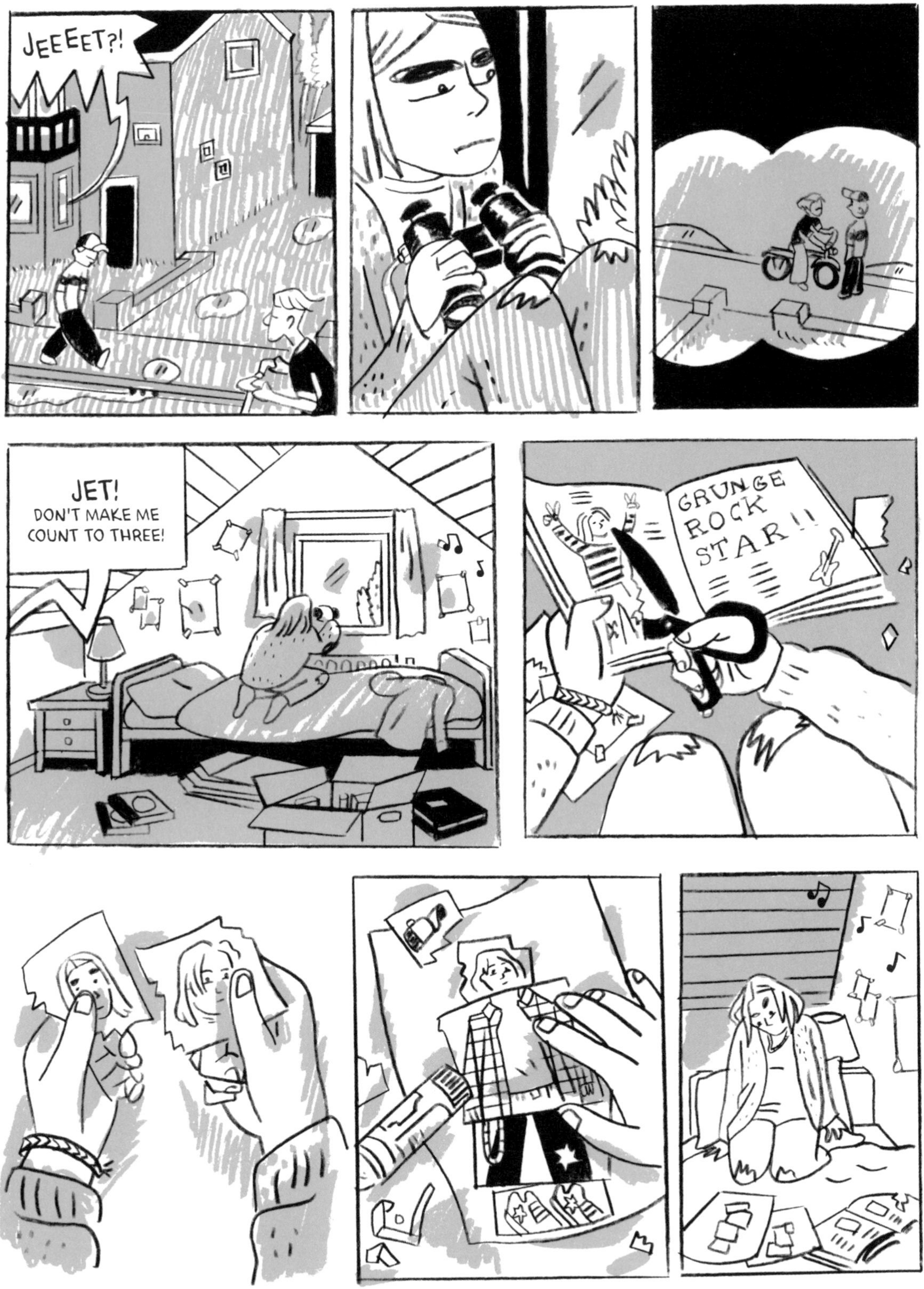
JEEEET?!
JET! DON'T MAKE ME COUNT TO THREE!
GRUNGE ROCK STAR!!

*"DISARM" BY SMASHING PUMPKINS

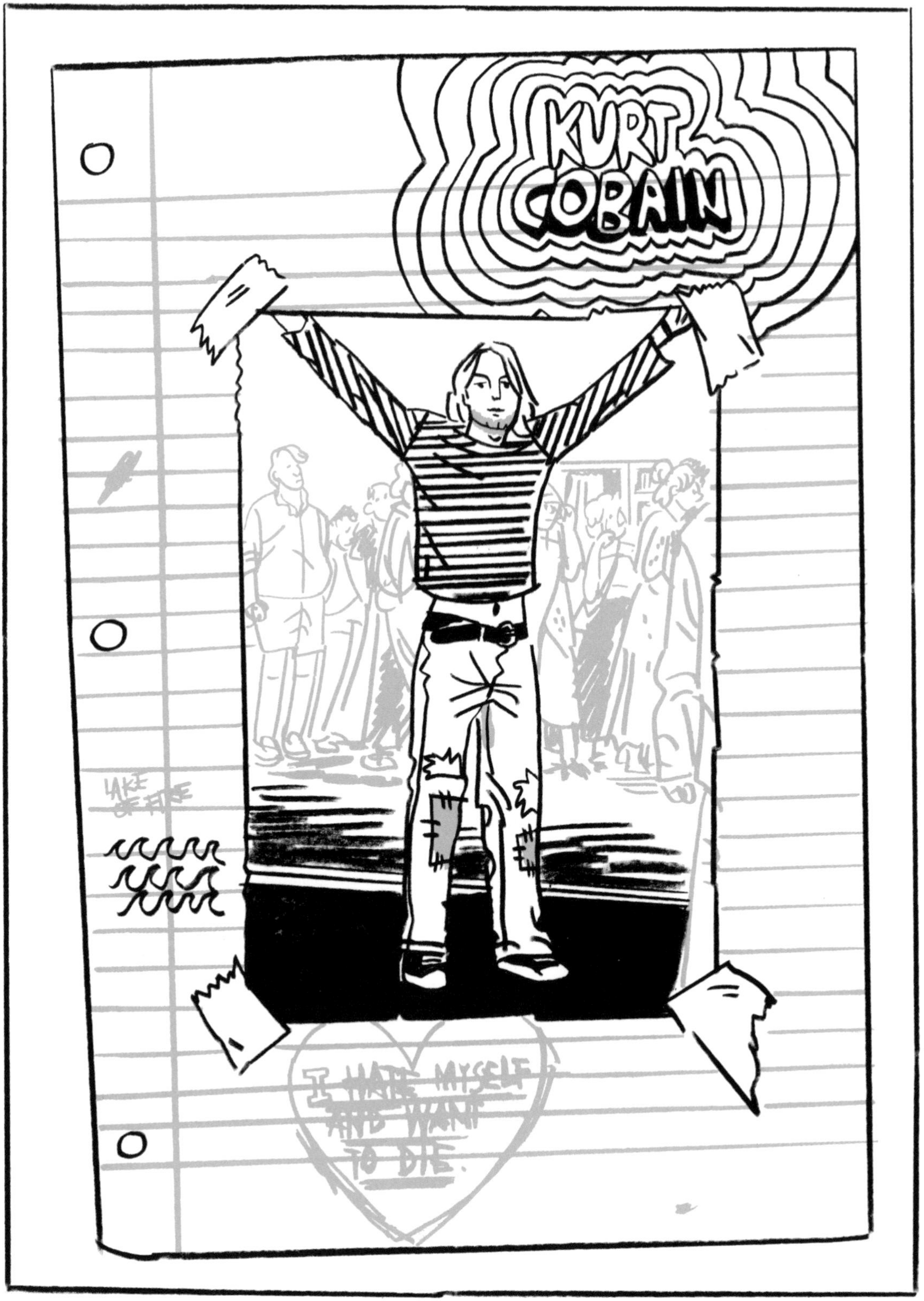
KURT COBAIN
LAKE OF FIRE
I HATE MYSELF AND WANT TO DIE.

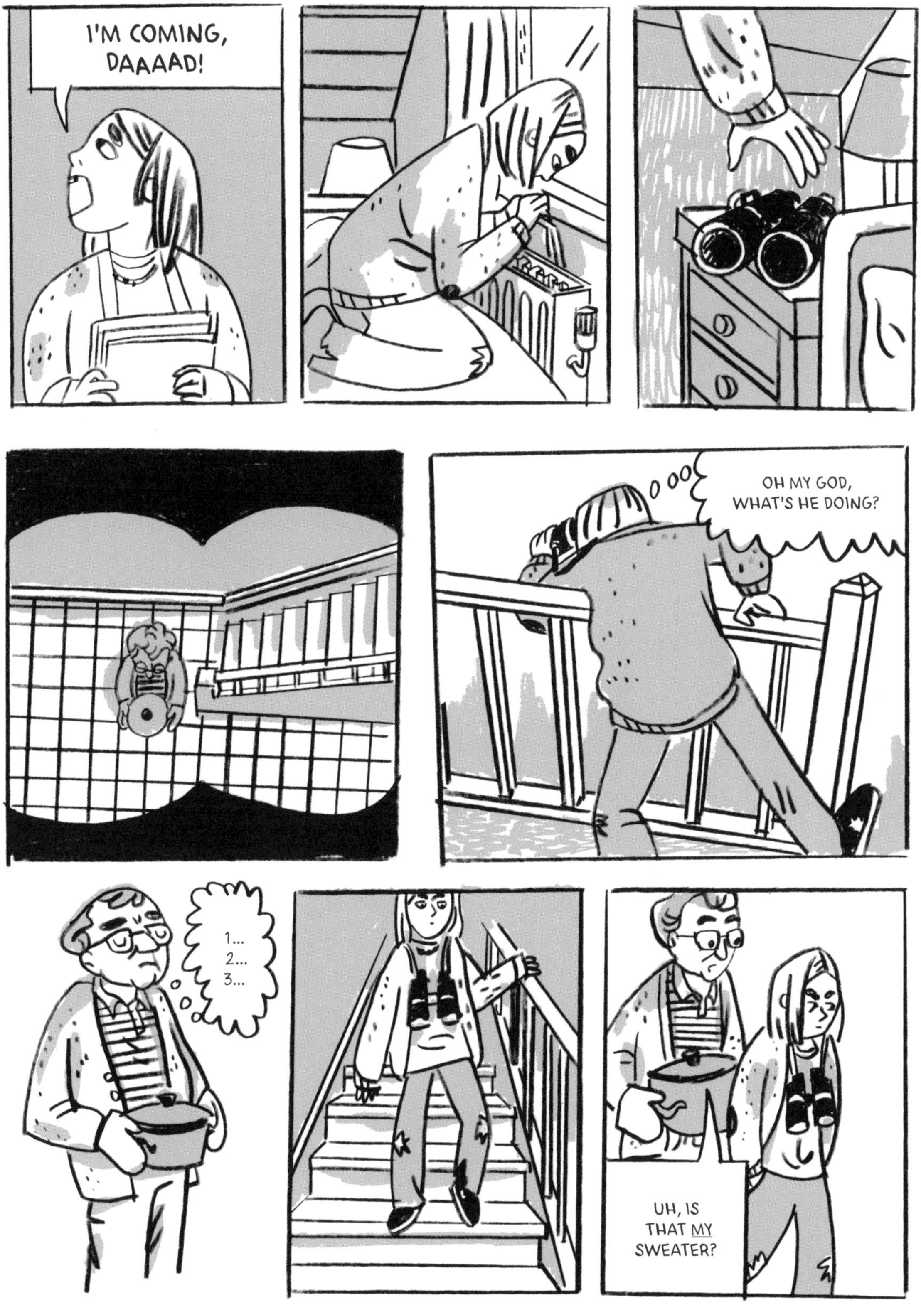
I'M COMING, DAAAAD!
OH MY GOD, WHAT'S HE DOING?
1... 2... 3...
UH, IS THAT MY SWEATER?

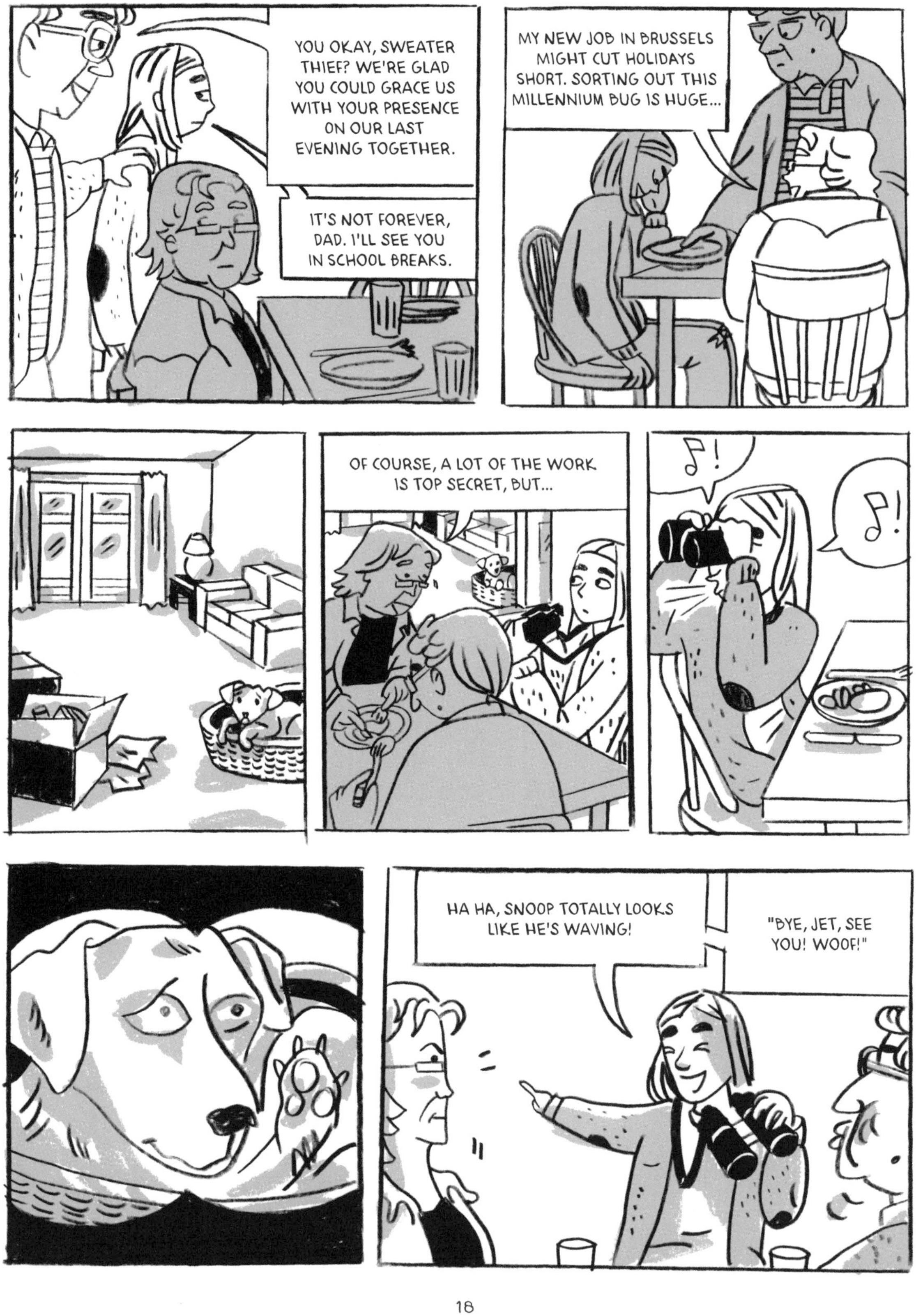
YOU OKAY, SWEATER THIEF? WE'RE GLAD YOU COULD GRACE US WITH YOUR PRESENCE ON OUR LAST EVENING TOGETHER.
IT'S NOT FOREVER, DAD. I'LL SEE YOU IN SCHOOL BREAKS.
MY NEW JOB IN BRUSSELS MIGHT CUT HOLIDAYS SHORT. SORTING OUT THIS MILLENNIUM BUG IS HUGE...
OF COURSE, A LOT OF THE WORK IS TOP SECRET, BUT...
♪!
♪!
HA HA, SNOOP TOTALLY LOOKS LIKE HE'S WAVING!
"BYE, JET, SEE YOU! WOOF!"

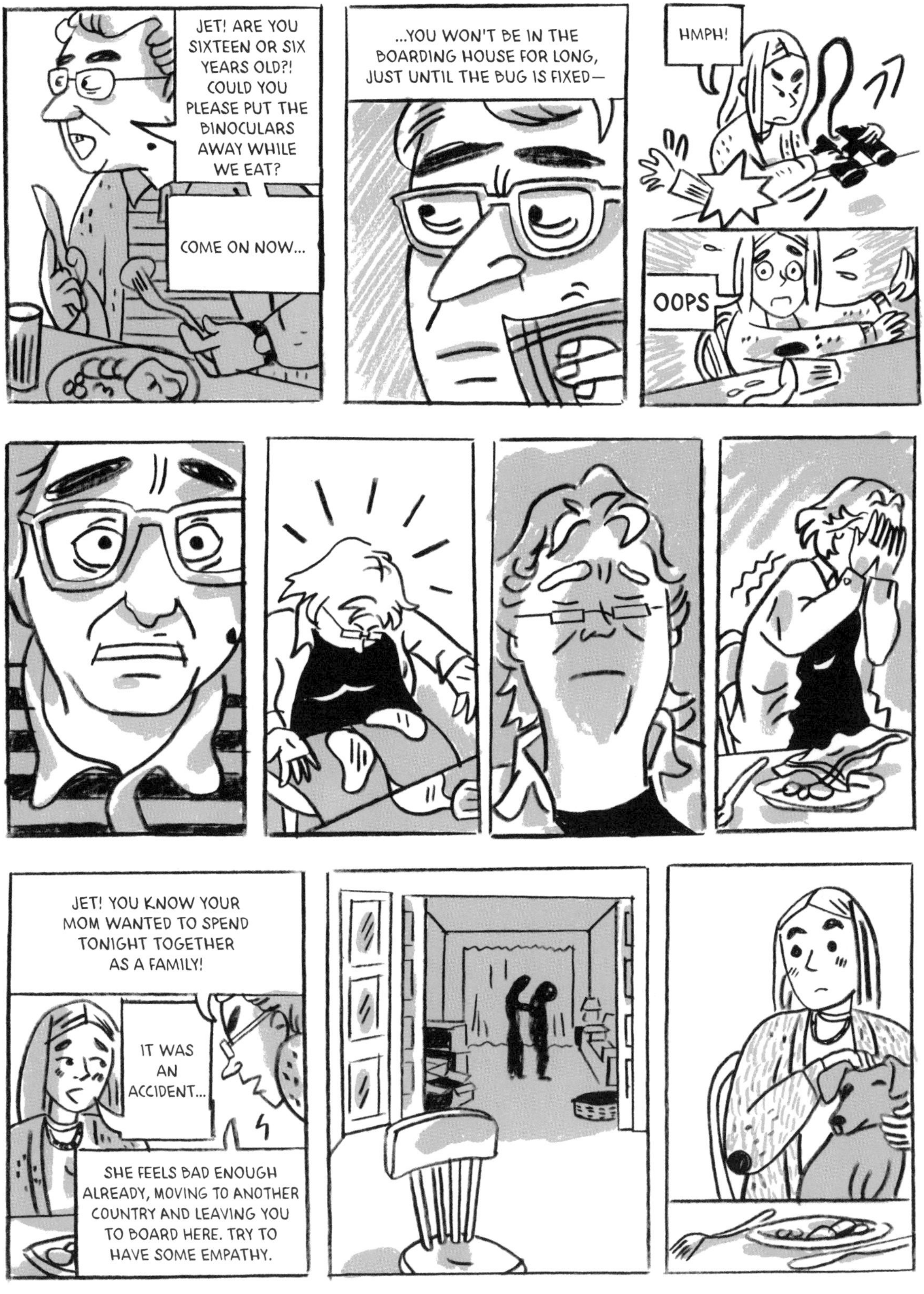
JET! ARE YOU SIXTEEN OR SIX YEARS OLD?! COULD YOU PLEASE PUT THE BINOCULARS AWAY WHILE WE EAT?
COME ON NOW...
...YOU WON'T BE IN THE BOARDING HOUSE FOR LONG, JUST UNTIL THE BUG IS FIXED—
HMPH!
OOPS
JET! YOU KNOW YOUR MOM WANTED TO SPEND TONIGHT TOGETHER AS A FAMILY!
IT WAS AN ACCIDENT...
SHE FEELS BAD ENOUGH ALREADY, MOVING TO ANOTHER COUNTRY AND LEAVING YOU TO BOARD HERE. TRY TO HAVE SOME EMPATHY.

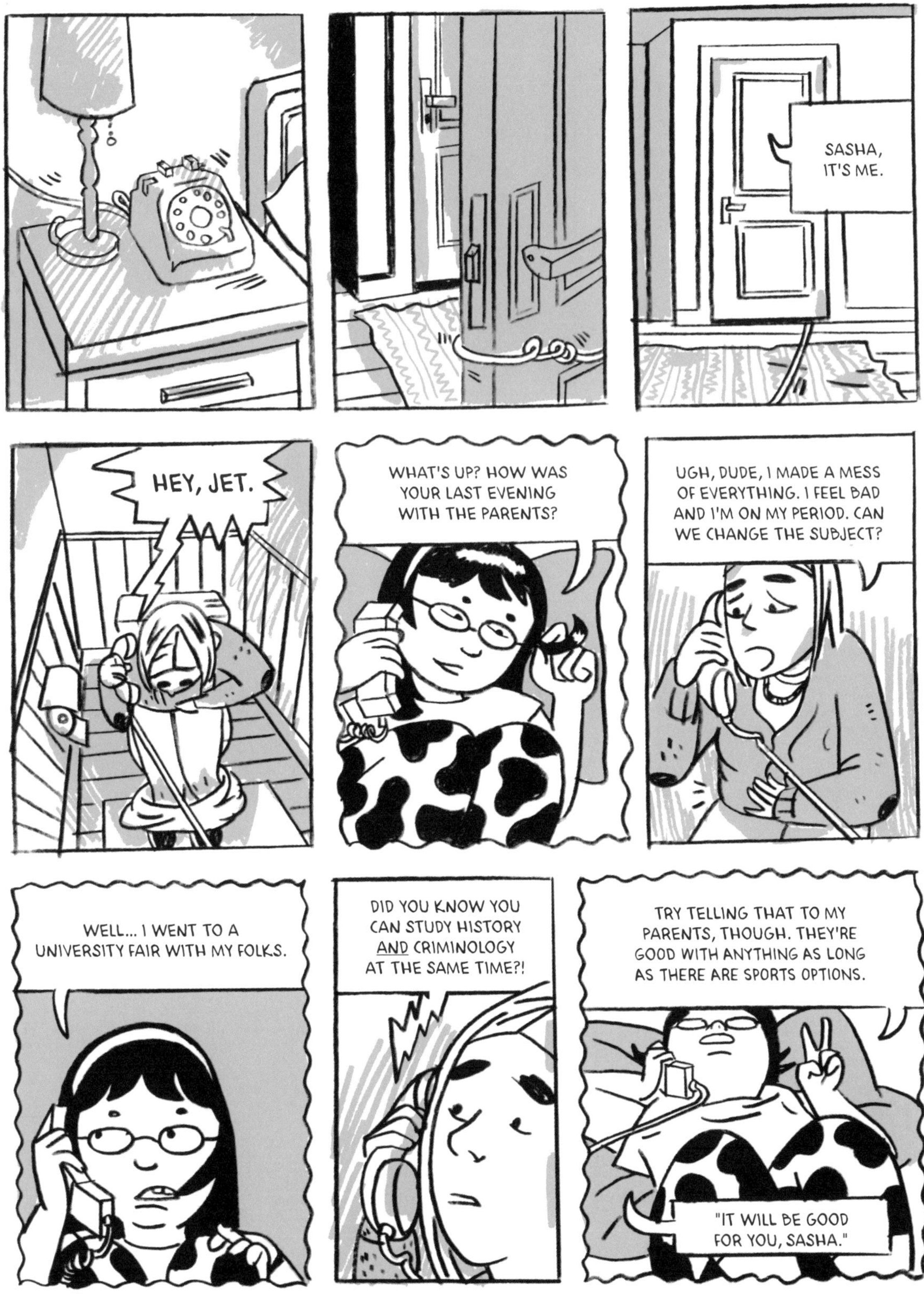
SASHA, IT'S ME.
HEY, JET.
WHAT'S UP? HOW WAS YOUR LAST EVENING WITH THE PARENTS?
UGH, DUDE, I MADE A MESS OF EVERYTHING. I FEEL BAD AND I'M ON MY PERIOD. CAN WE CHANGE THE SUBJECT?
WELL... I WENT TO A UNIVERSITY FAIR WITH MY FOLKS.
DID YOU KNOW YOU CAN STUDY HISTORY AND CRIMINOLOGY AT THE SAME TIME?!
TRY TELLING THAT TO MY PARENTS, THOUGH. THEY'RE GOOD WITH ANYTHING AS LONG AS THERE ARE SPORTS OPTIONS.
"IT WILL BE GOOD FOR YOU, SASHA."

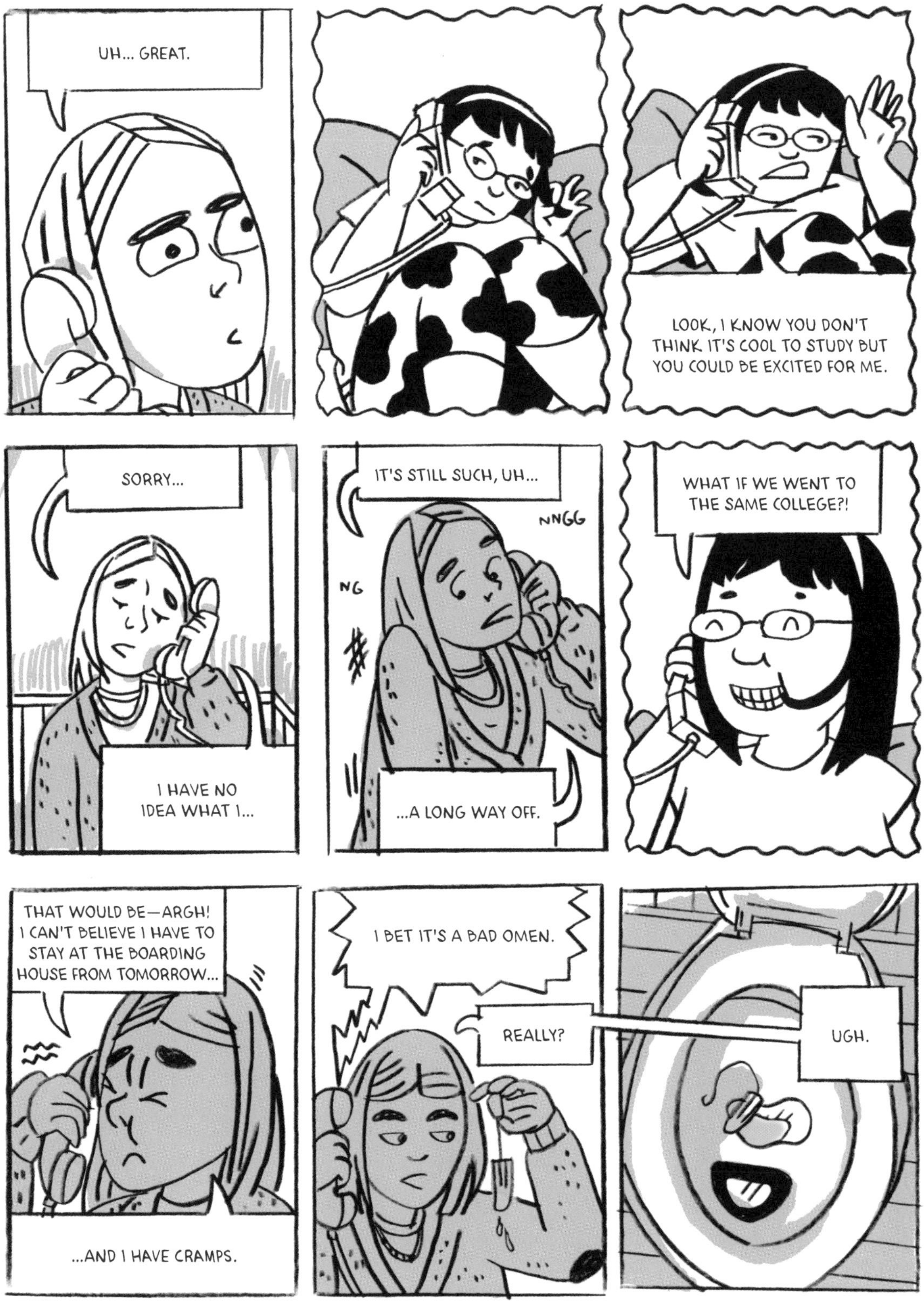
UH... GREAT.
LOOK, I KNOW YOU DON'T THINK IT'S COOL TO STUDY BUT YOU COULD BE EXCITED FOR ME.
SORRY...
I HAVE NO IDEA WHAT I...
IT'S STILL SUCH, UH...
NNGG
NG
...A LONG WAY OFF.
WHAT IF WE WENT TO THE SAME COLLEGE?!
THAT WOULD BE—ARGH! I CAN'T BELIEVE I HAVE TO STAY AT THE BOARDING HOUSE FROM TOMORROW...
...AND I HAVE CRAMPS.
I BET IT'S A BAD OMEN.
REALLY?
UGH.

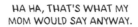
HA HA, THAT'S WHAT MY MOM WOULD SAY ANYWAY.

...BUT SHE THINKS EVERYTHING IS A BAD SIGN.

AT LEAST YOU DON'T HAVE TO CHANGE SCHOOLS, THOUGH!

AND YOUR BOARDING HOUSE IS CLOSE TO WHERE I LIVE.

YEP. SURE IS.

SO... WHAT SUBJECTS ARE YOU TAKING?

DUDE, I DON'T KNOWWWWW!

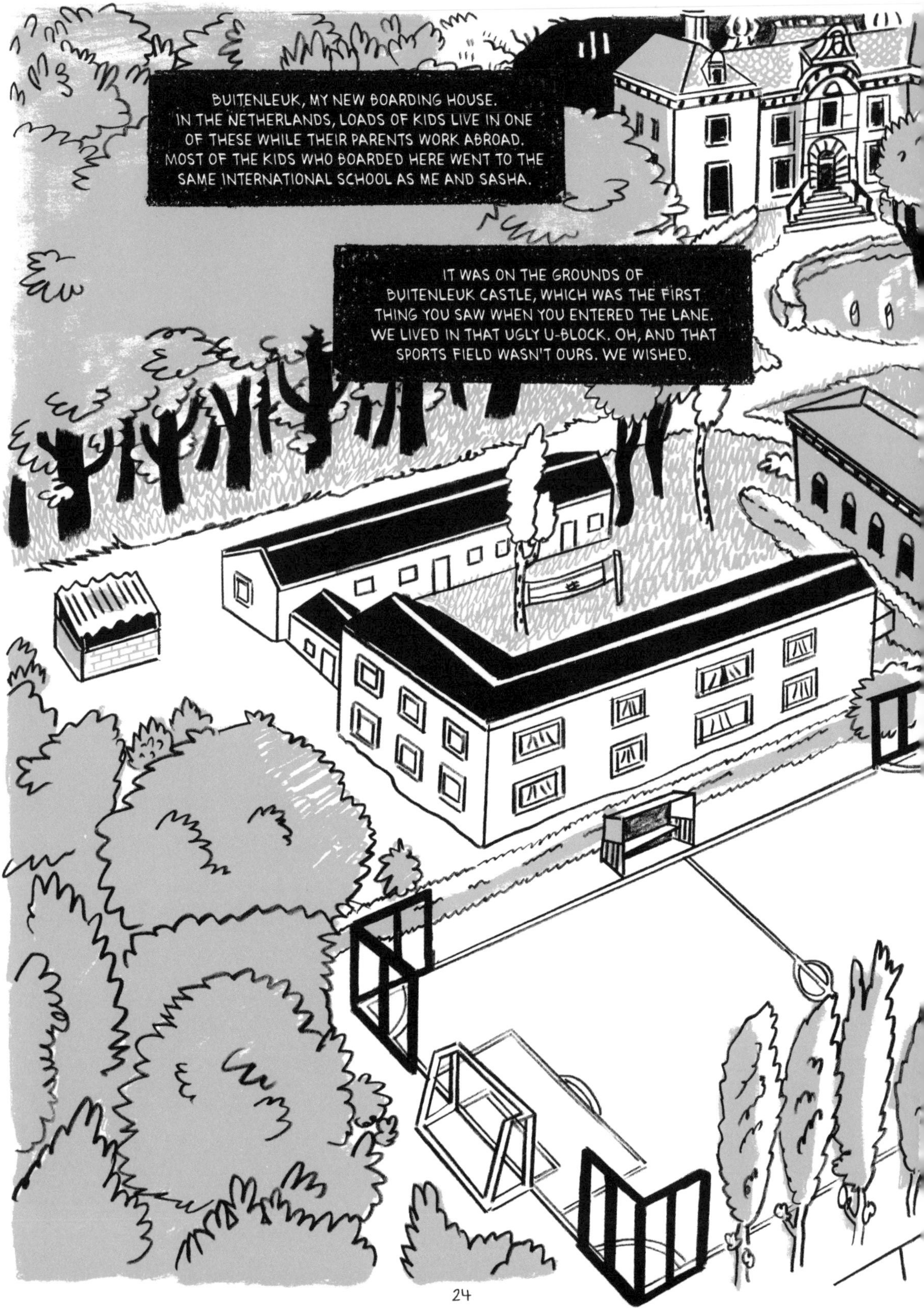
BUITENLEUK, MY NEW BOARDING HOUSE. IN THE NETHERLANDS, LOADS OF KIDS LIVE IN ONE OF THESE WHILE THEIR PARENTS WORK ABROAD. MOST OF THE KIDS WHO BOARDED HERE WENT TO THE SAME INTERNATIONAL SCHOOL AS ME AND SASHA.
IT WAS ON THE GROUNDS OF BUITENLEUK CASTLE, WHICH WAS THE FIRST THING YOU SAW WHEN YOU ENTERED THE LANE. WE LIVED IN THAT UGLY U-BLOCK. OH, AND THAT SPORTS FIELD WASN'T OURS. WE WISHED.

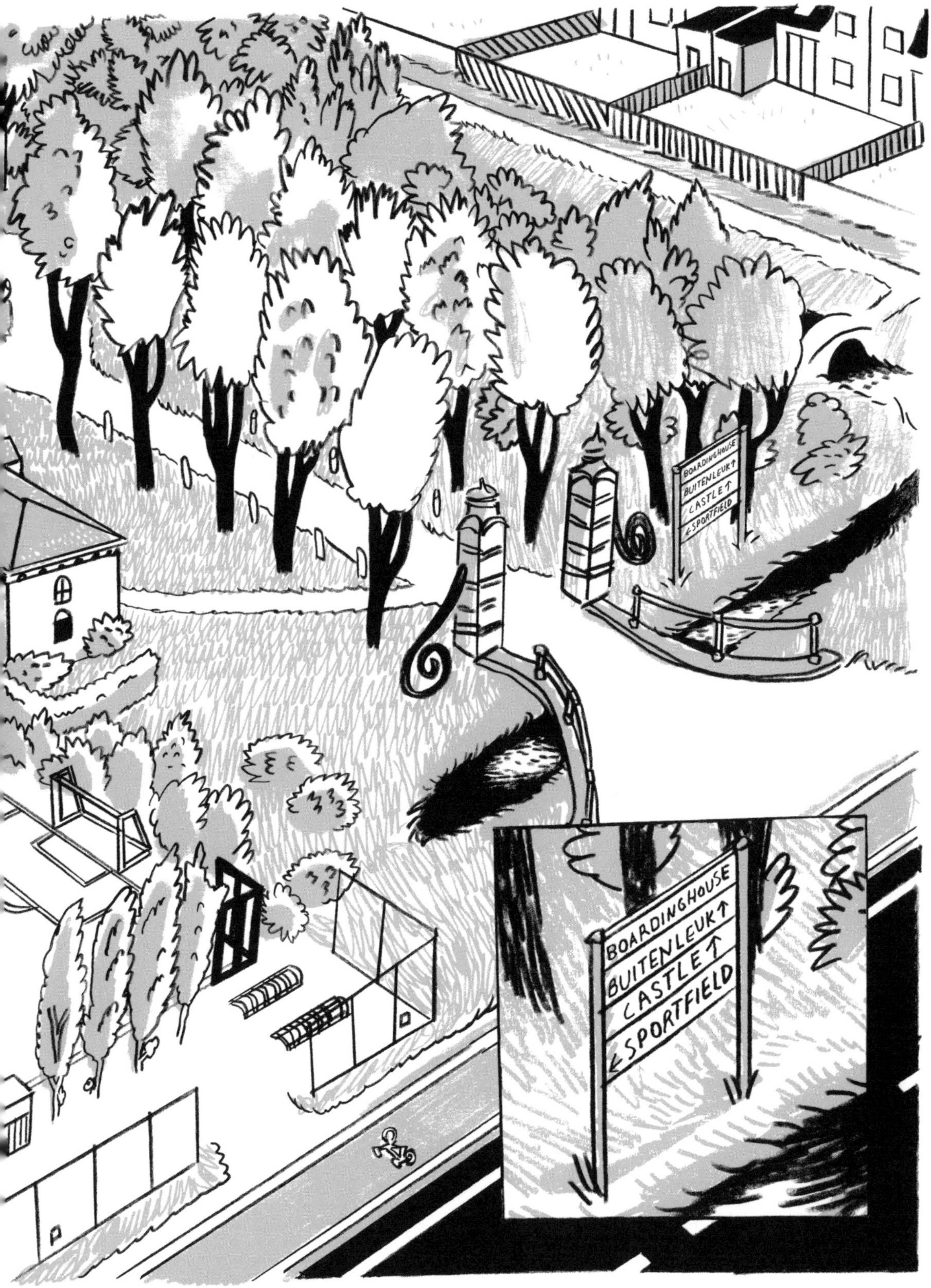
BOARDINGHOUSE
BUITENLEUK↑
CASTLE↑
←SPORTFIELD

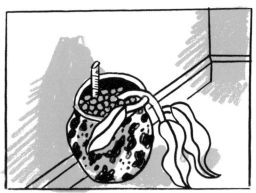

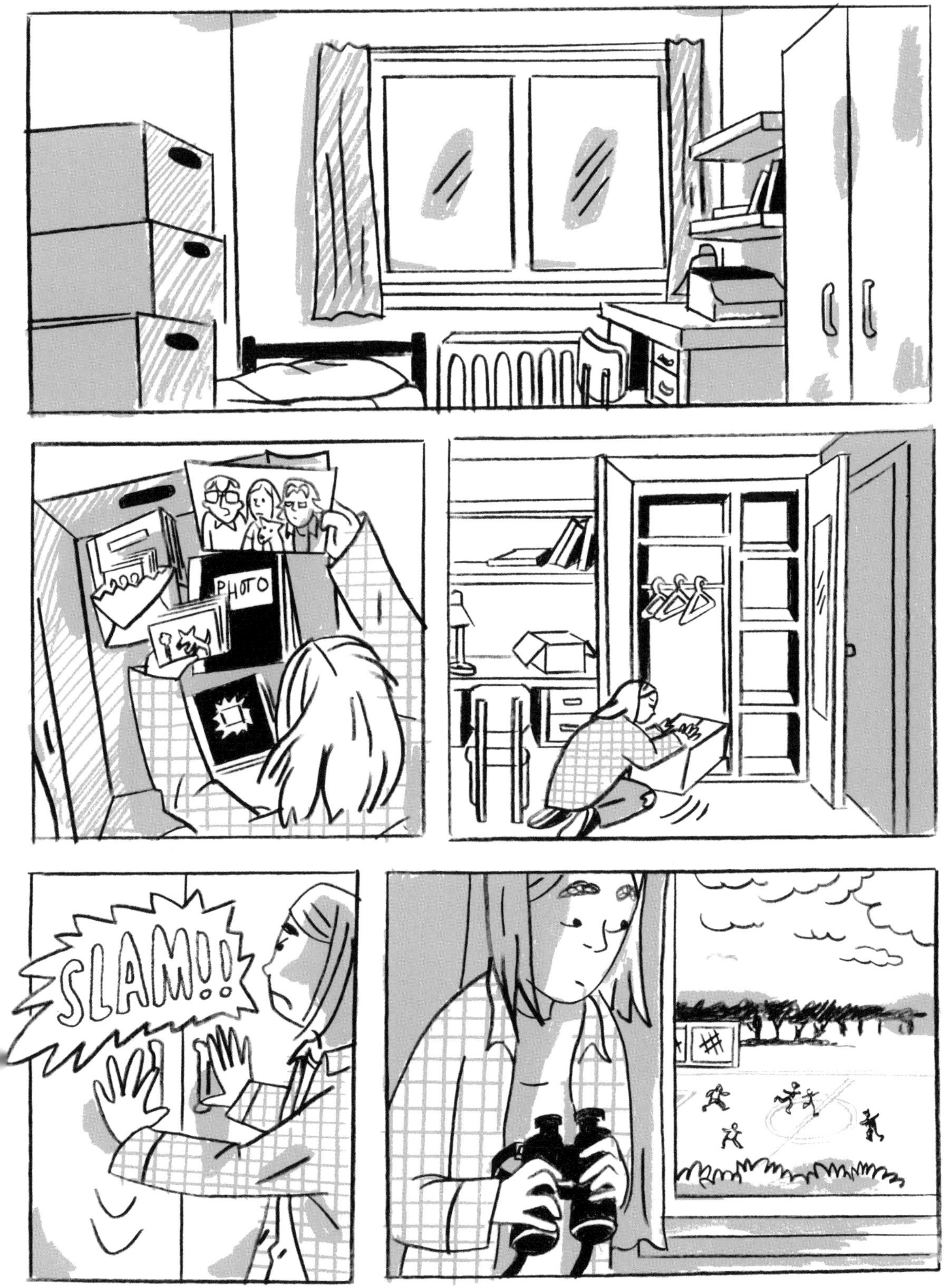
PHOTO
SLAM!!

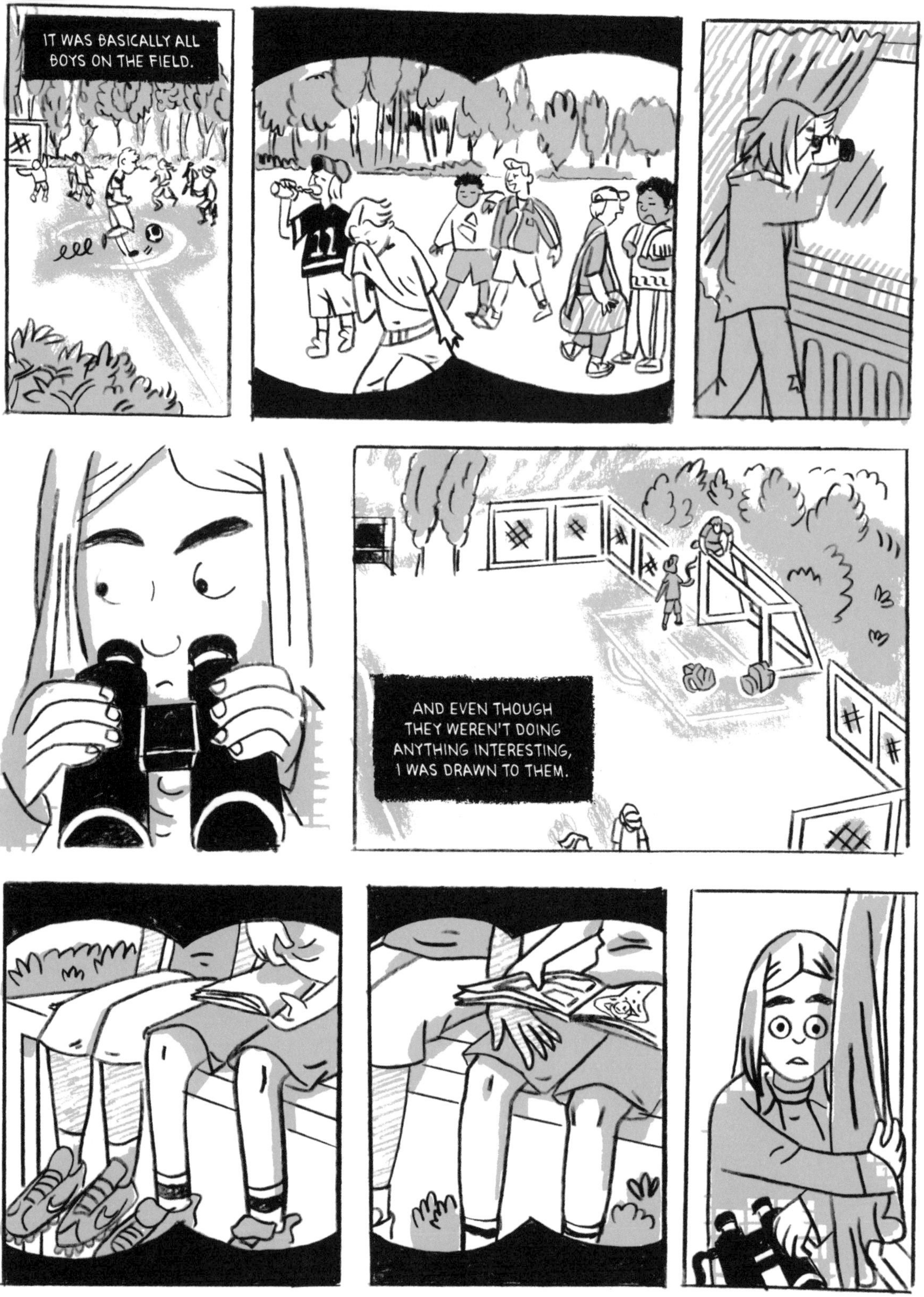
IT WAS BASICALLY ALL BOYS ON THE FIELD.
AND EVEN THOUGH THEY WEREN'T DOING ANYTHING INTERESTING, I WAS DRAWN TO THEM.

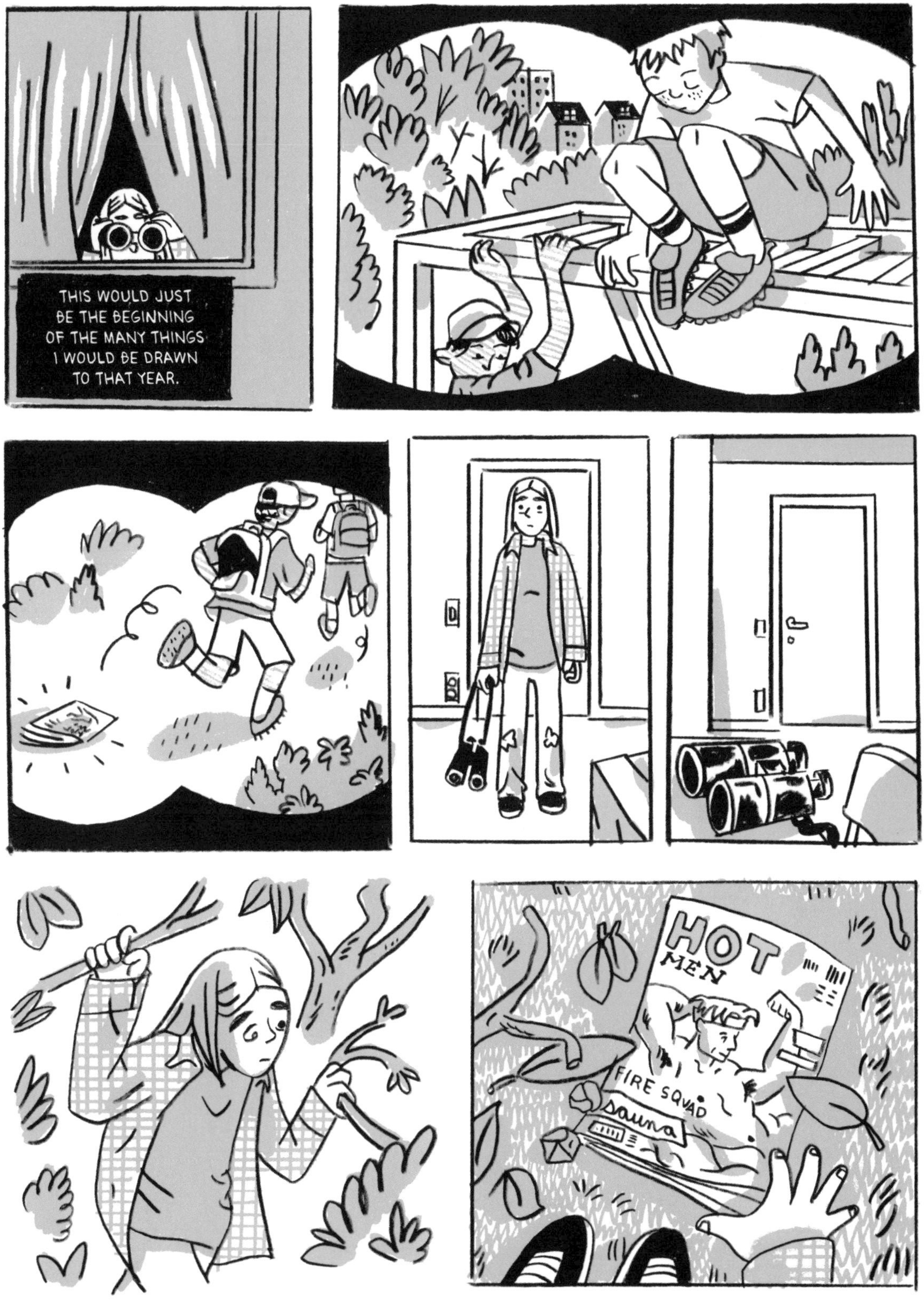
THIS WOULD JUST BE THE BEGINNING OF THE MANY THINGS I WOULD BE DRAWN TO THAT YEAR.
HOT
MEN
FIRE SQUAD
sauna

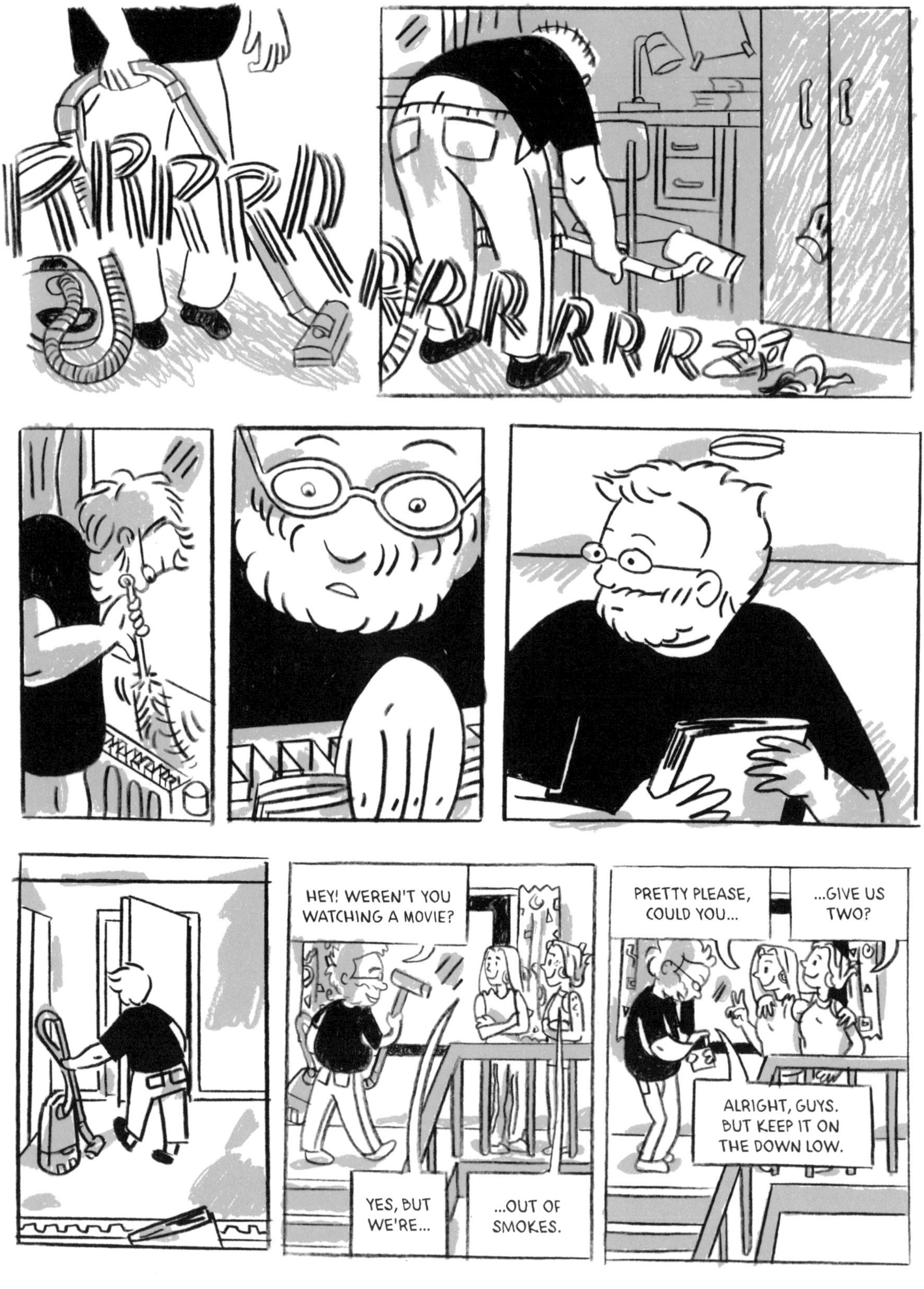
RRRRRRR
RRRRRRR
HEY! WEREN'T YOU WATCHING A MOVIE?
YES, BUT WE'RE...
...OUT OF SMOKES.
PRETTY PLEASE, COULD YOU...
...GIVE US TWO?
ALRIGHT, GUYS. BUT KEEP IT ON THE DOWN LOW.

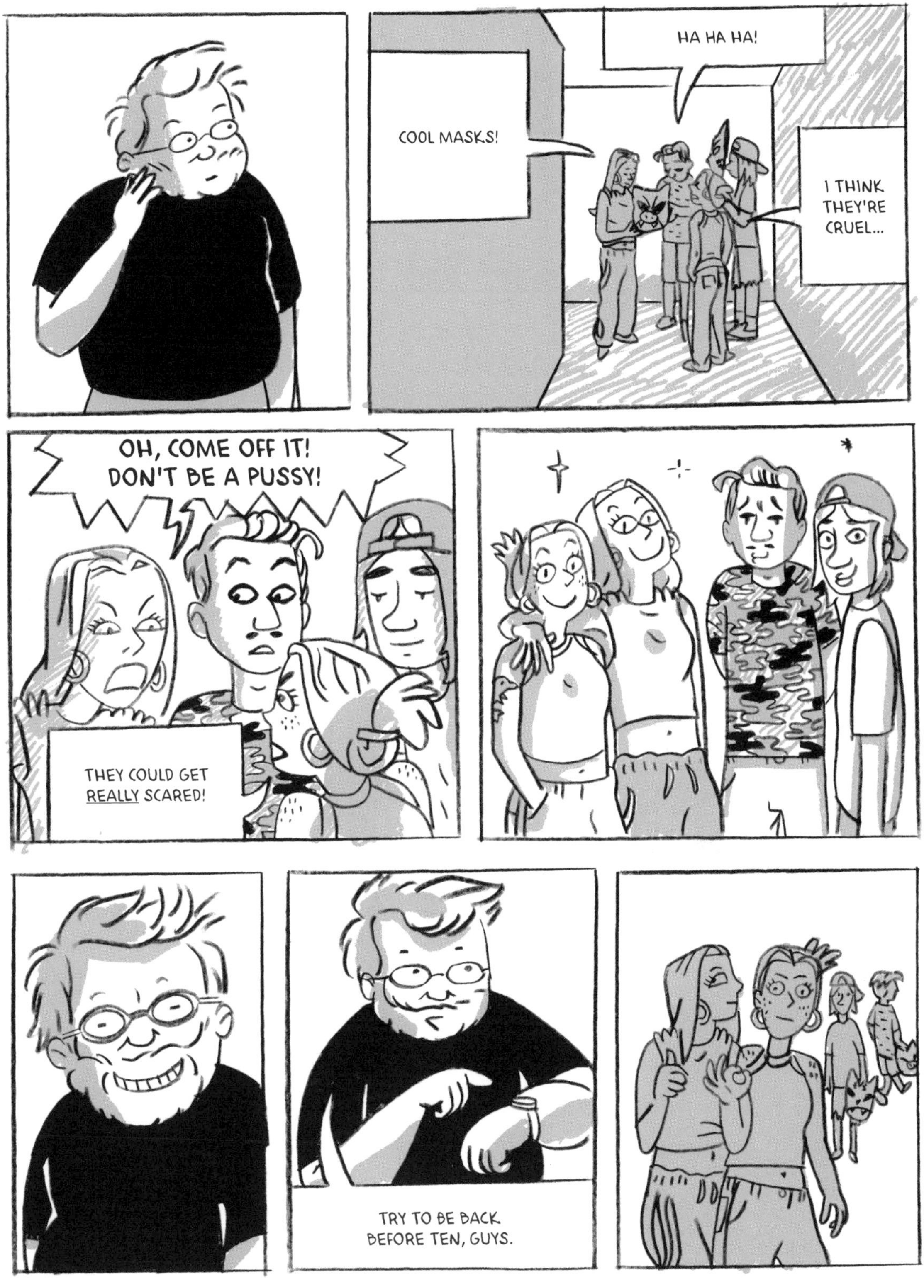

HA HA HA!
COOL MASKS!
I THINK THEY'RE CRUEL...
OH, COME OFF IT! DON'T BE A PUSSY!
THEY COULD GET REALLY SCARED!
TRY TO BE BACK BEFORE TEN, GUYS.

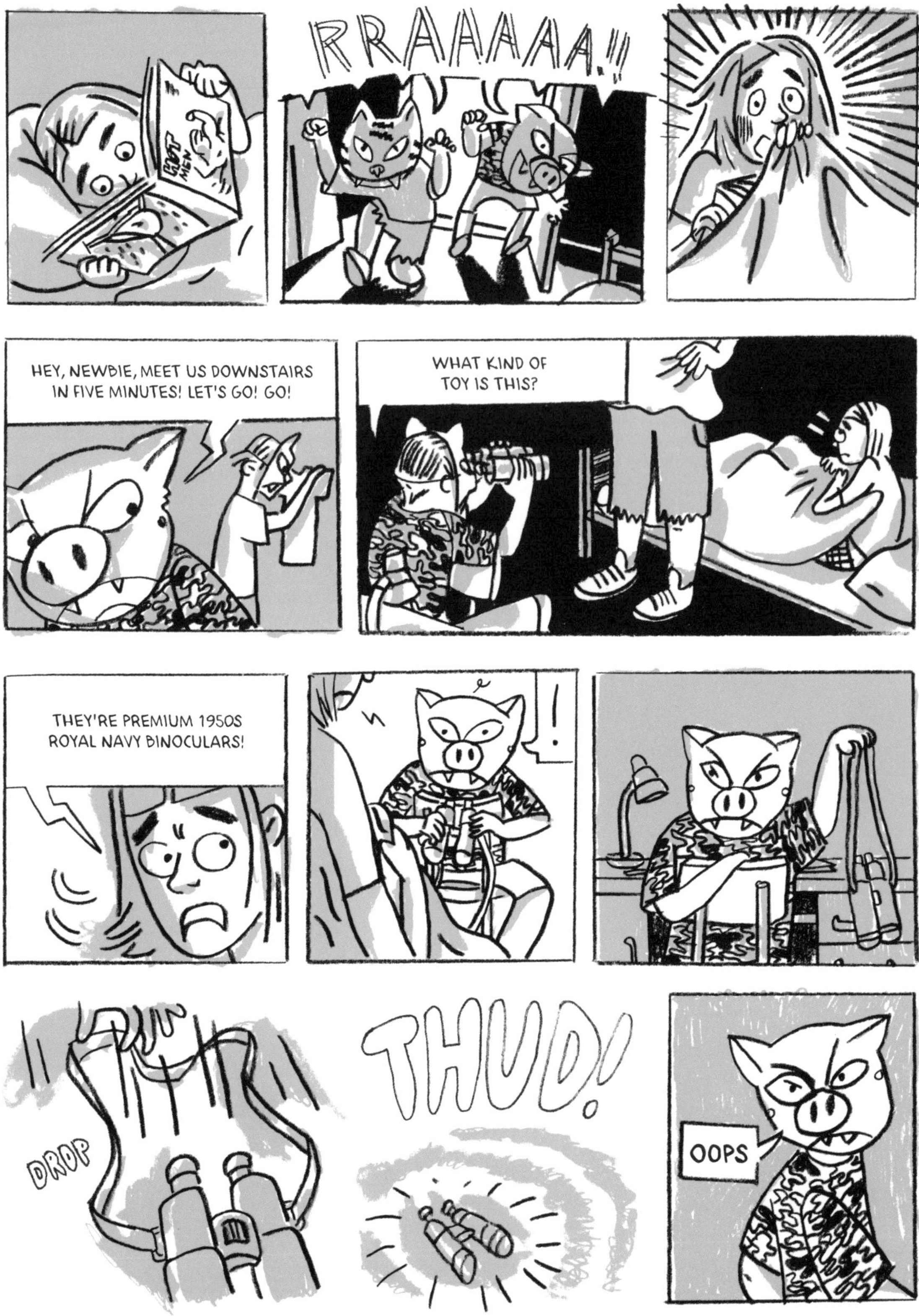

ROOF MEN
RRAAAAAA!!
HEY, NEWBIE, MEET US DOWNSTAIRS IN FIVE MINUTES! LET'S GO! GO!
WHAT KIND OF TOY IS THIS?
THEY'RE PREMIUM 1950S ROYAL NAVY BINOCULARS!
!
DROP
THUD!
OOPS

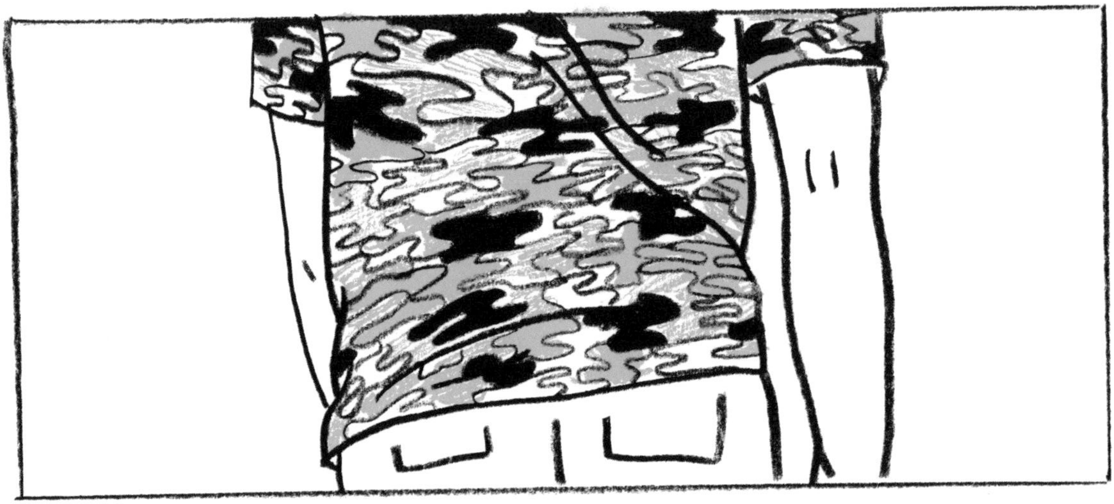
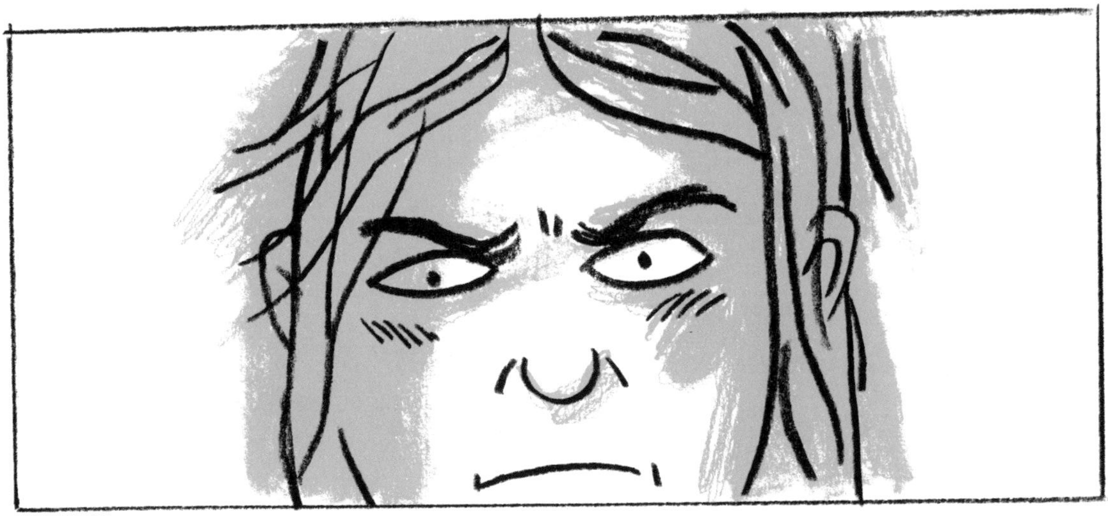
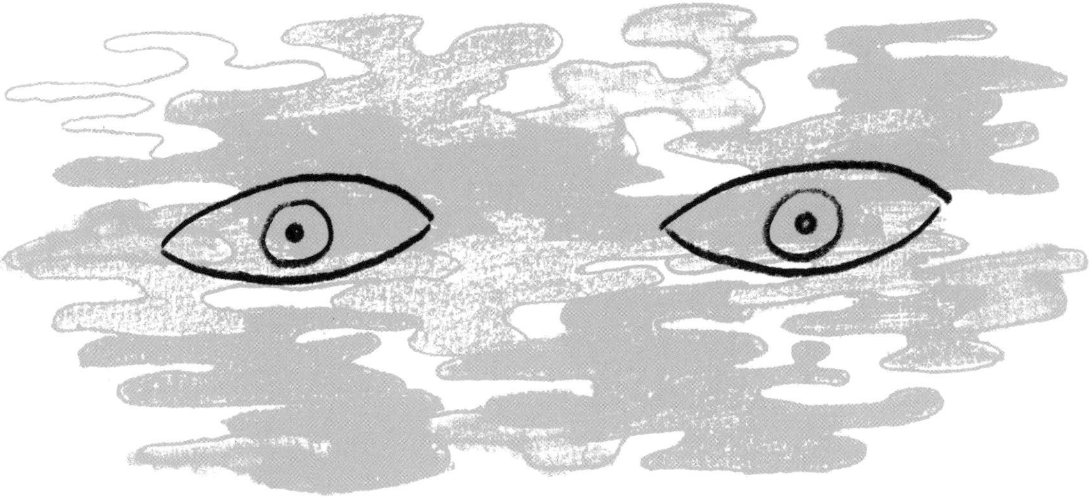

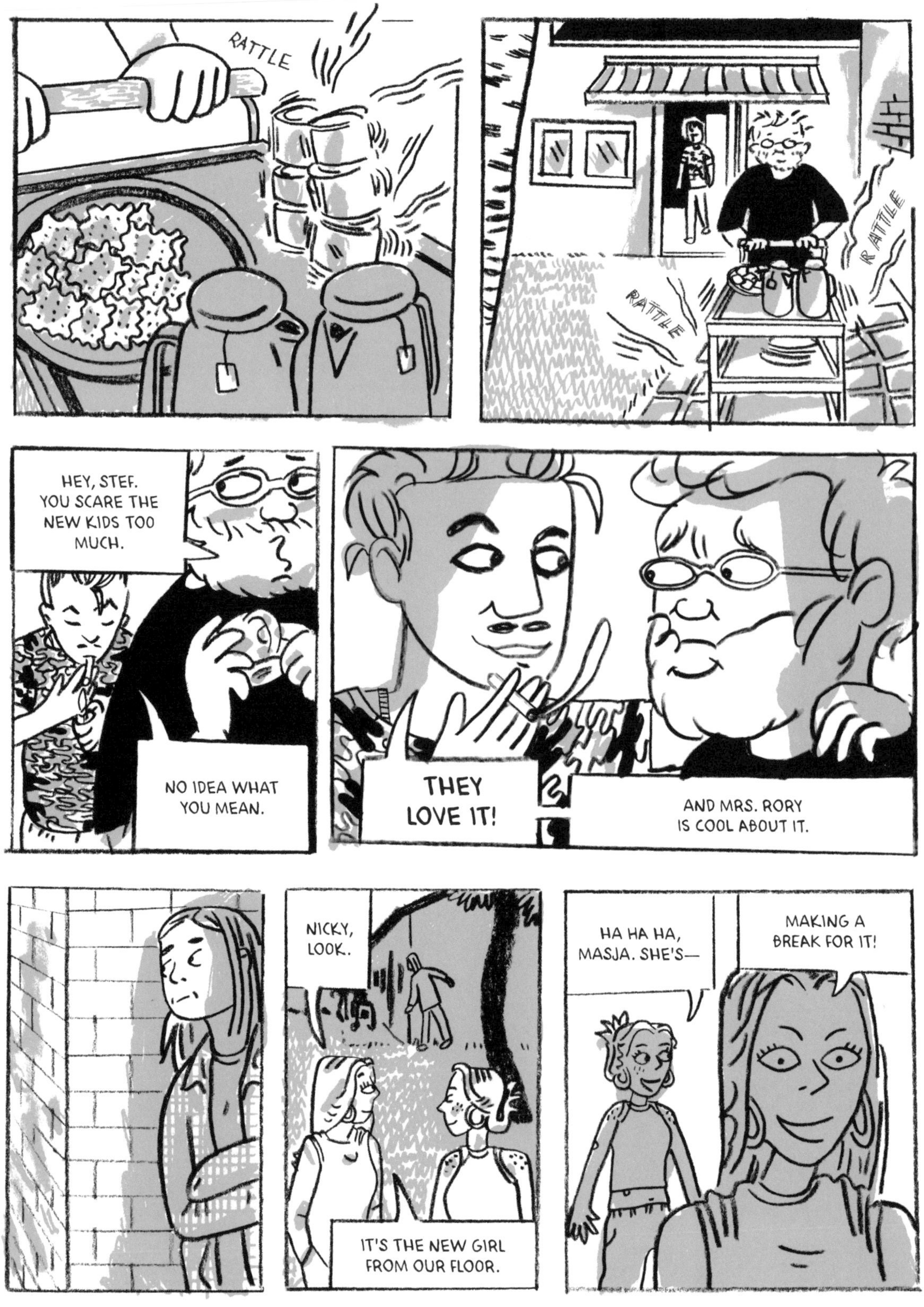
RATTLE
RATTLE
RATTLE
RATTLE
HEY, STEF. YOU SCARE THE NEW KIDS TOO MUCH.
NO IDEA WHAT YOU MEAN.
THEY LOVE IT!
AND MRS. RORY IS COOL ABOUT IT.
NICKY, LOOK.
IT'S THE NEW GIRL FROM OUR FLOOR.
HA HA HA, MASJA. SHE'S—
MAKING A BREAK FOR IT!

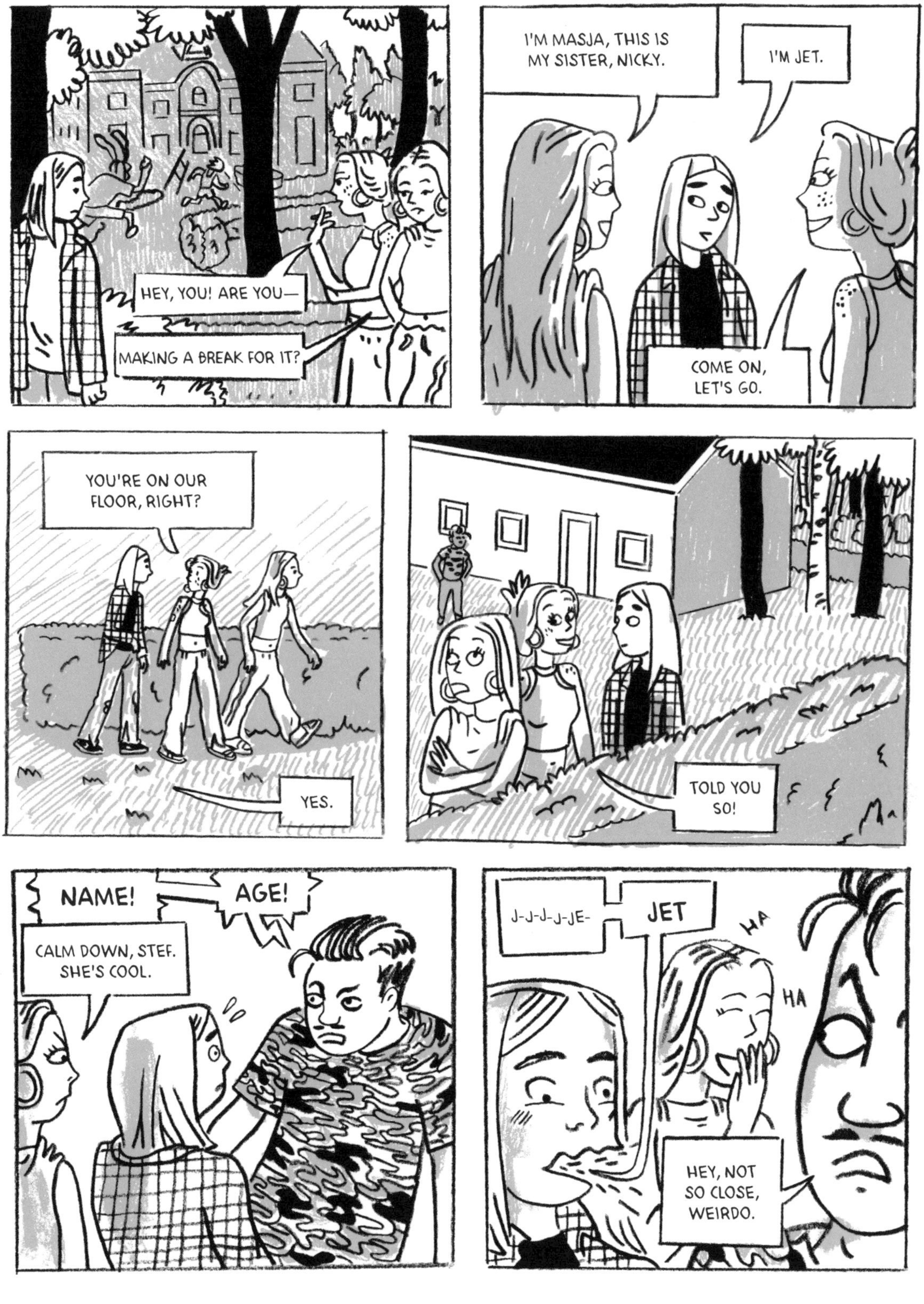
HEY, YOU! ARE YOU—
MAKING A BREAK FOR IT?
I'M MASJA, THIS IS MY SISTER, NICKY.
I'M JET.
COME ON, LET'S GO.
YOU'RE ON OUR FLOOR, RIGHT?
YES.
TOLD YOU SO!
NAME!
AGE!
CALM DOWN, STEF. SHE'S COOL.
J-J-J-J-JE-
JET
HA
HA
HEY, NOT SO CLOSE, WEIRDO.

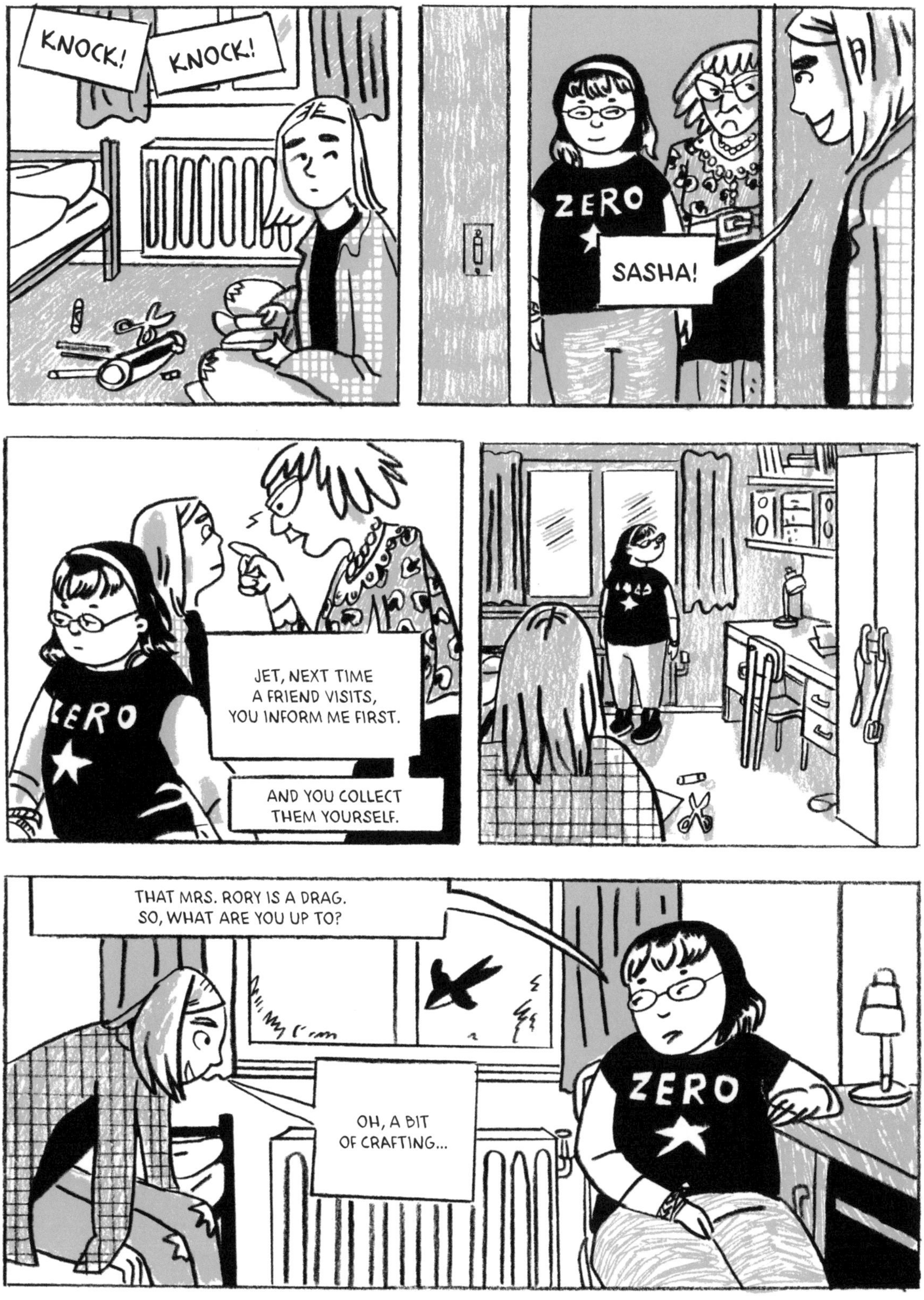
KNOCK!
KNOCK!
SASHA!
JET, NEXT TIME A FRIEND VISITS, YOU INFORM ME FIRST.
AND YOU COLLECT THEM YOURSELF.
THAT MRS. RORY IS A DRAG. SO, WHAT ARE YOU UP TO?
OH, A BIT OF CRAFTING...

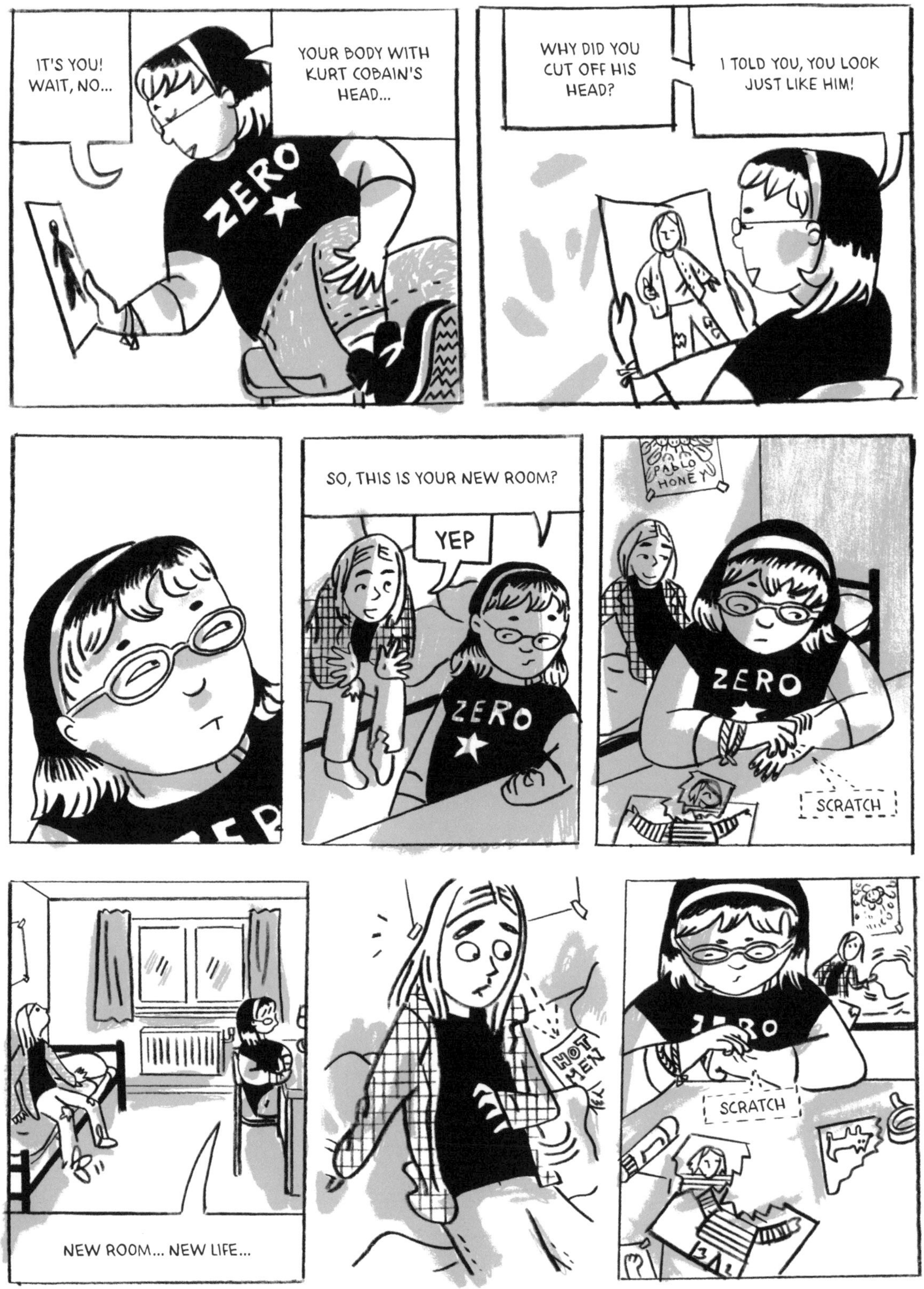
IT'S YOU! WAIT, NO...
YOUR BODY WITH KURT COBAIN'S HEAD...
ZERO
WHY DID YOU CUT OFF HIS HEAD?
I TOLD YOU, YOU LOOK JUST LIKE HIM!
SO, THIS IS YOUR NEW ROOM?
YEP
ZERO
PABLO HONEY
ZERO
SCRATCH
NEW ROOM... NEW LIFE...
HOT MEN
SCRATCH

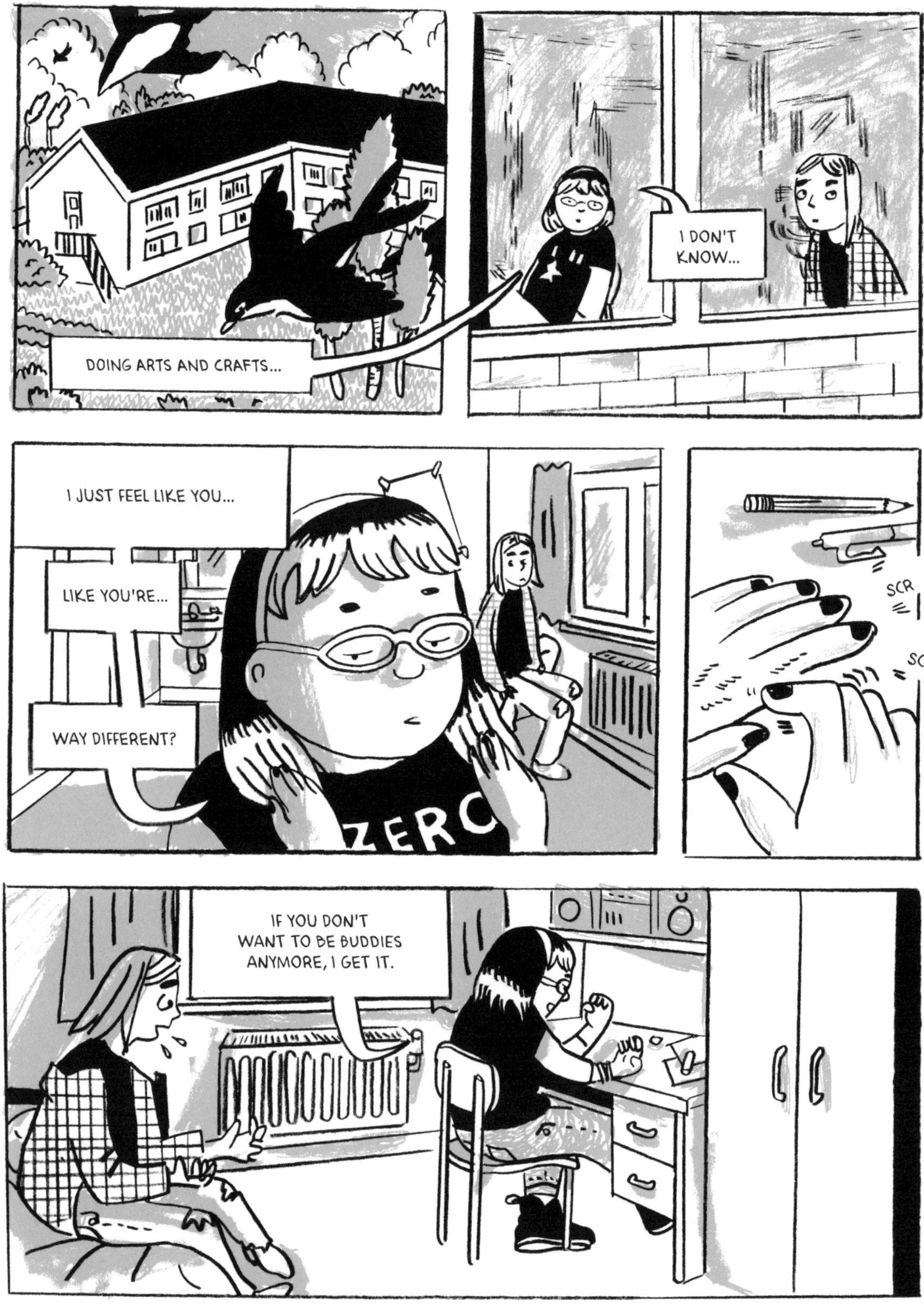

DOING ARTS AND CRAFTS...
I DON'T KNOW...
I JUST FEEL LIKE YOU...
LIKE YOU'RE...
WAY DIFFERENT?
SCR
SCR
ZERO
IF YOU DON'T WANT TO BE BUDDIES ANYMORE, I GET IT.

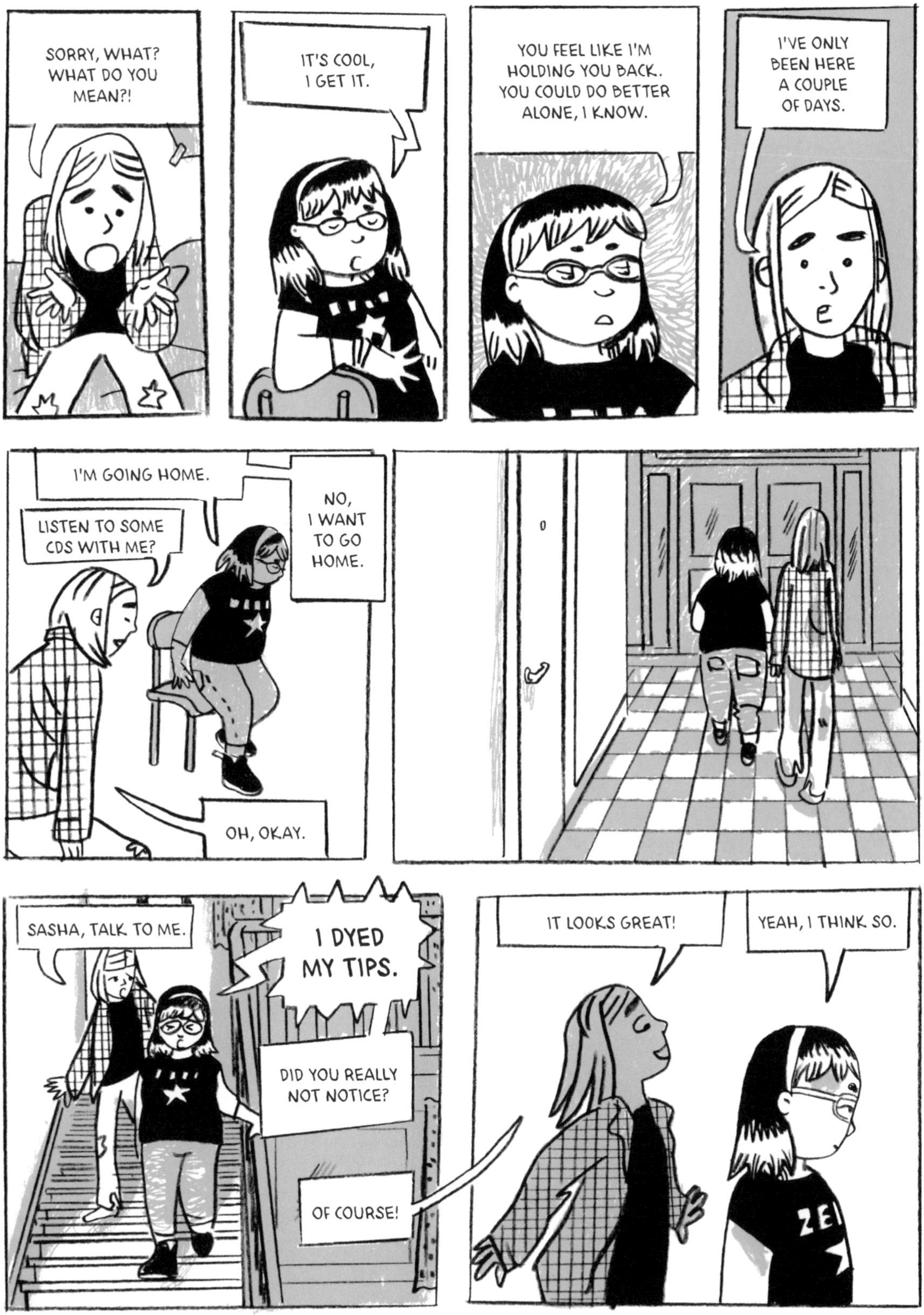
SORRY, WHAT? WHAT DO YOU MEAN?!
IT'S COOL, I GET IT.
YOU FEEL LIKE I'M HOLDING YOU BACK. YOU COULD DO BETTER ALONE, I KNOW.
I'VE ONLY BEEN HERE A COUPLE OF DAYS.
LISTEN TO SOME CDS WITH ME?
I'M GOING HOME.
NO, I WANT TO GO HOME.
OH, OKAY.
SASHA, TALK TO ME.
I DYED MY TIPS.
DID YOU REALLY NOT NOTICE?
OF COURSE!
IT LOOKS GREAT!
YEAH, I THINK SO.
ZE

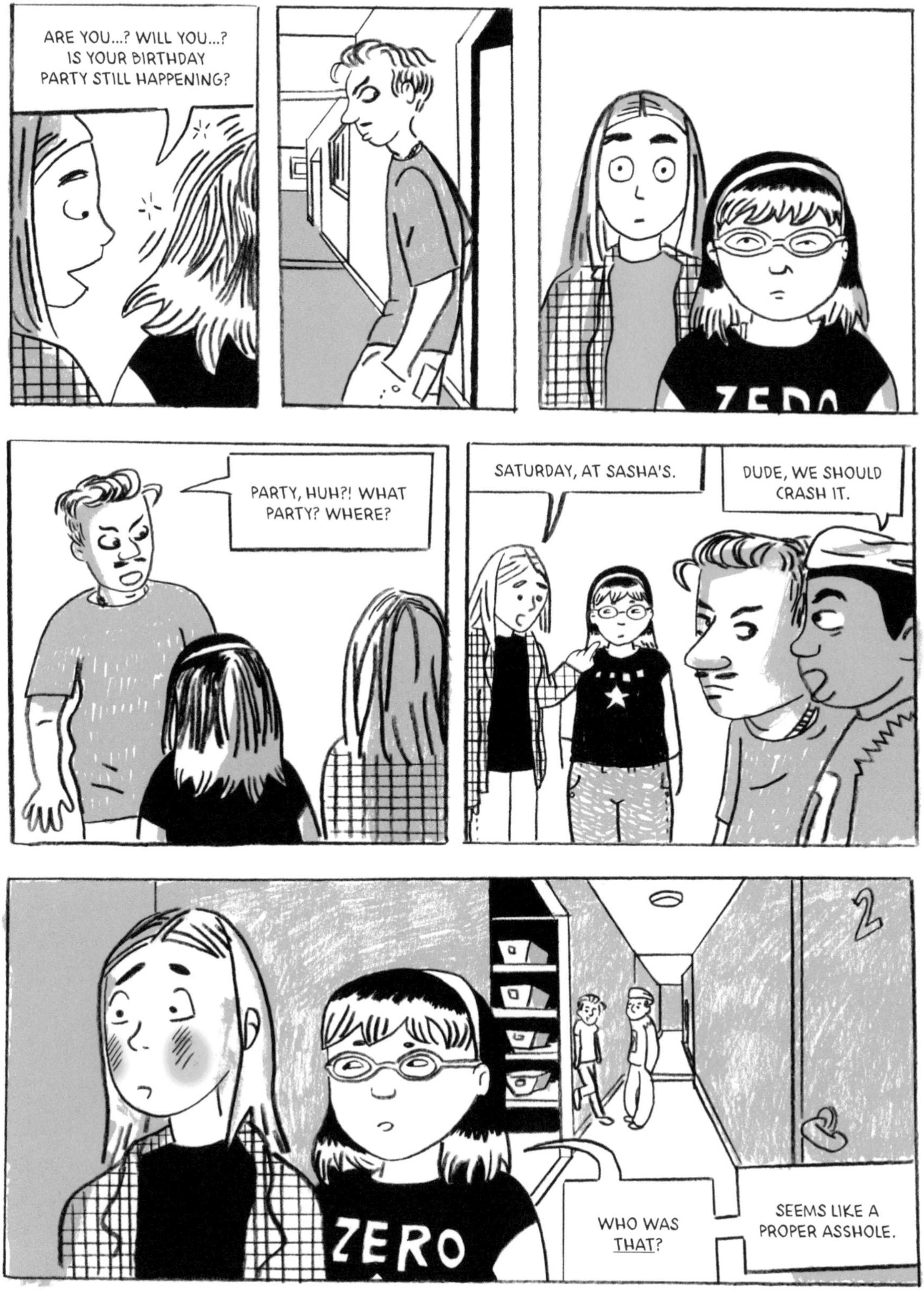
ARE YOU...? WILL YOU...? IS YOUR BIRTHDAY PARTY STILL HAPPENING?
ZERO
PARTY, HUH?! WHAT PARTY? WHERE?
SATURDAY, AT SASHA'S.
DUDE, WE SHOULD CRASH IT.
2
ZERO
WHO WAS THAT?
SEEMS LIKE A PROPER ASSHOLE.

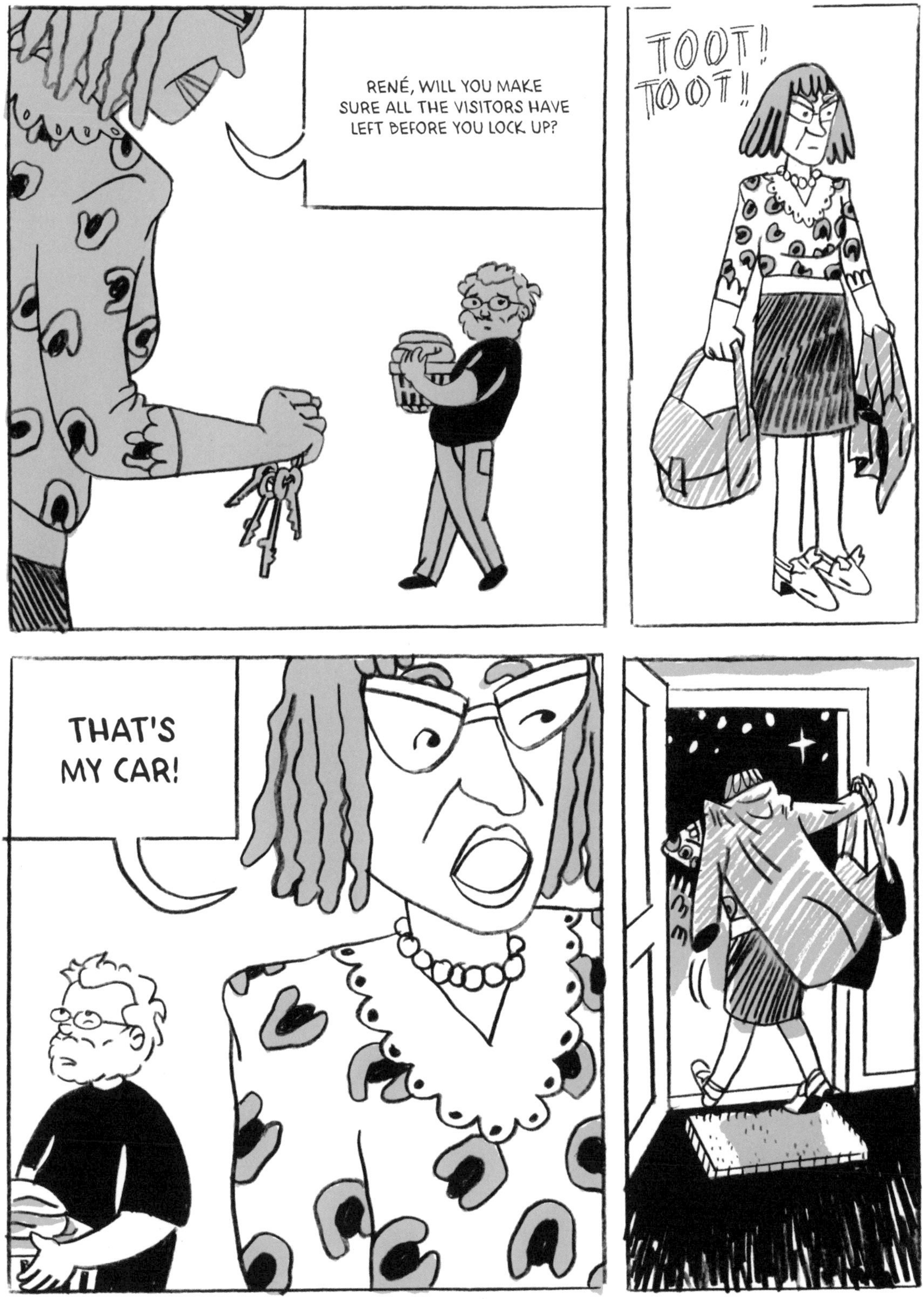
RENÉ, WILL YOU MAKE SURE ALL THE VISITORS HAVE LEFT BEFORE YOU LOCK UP?
TOOT! TOOT!
THAT'S MY CAR!

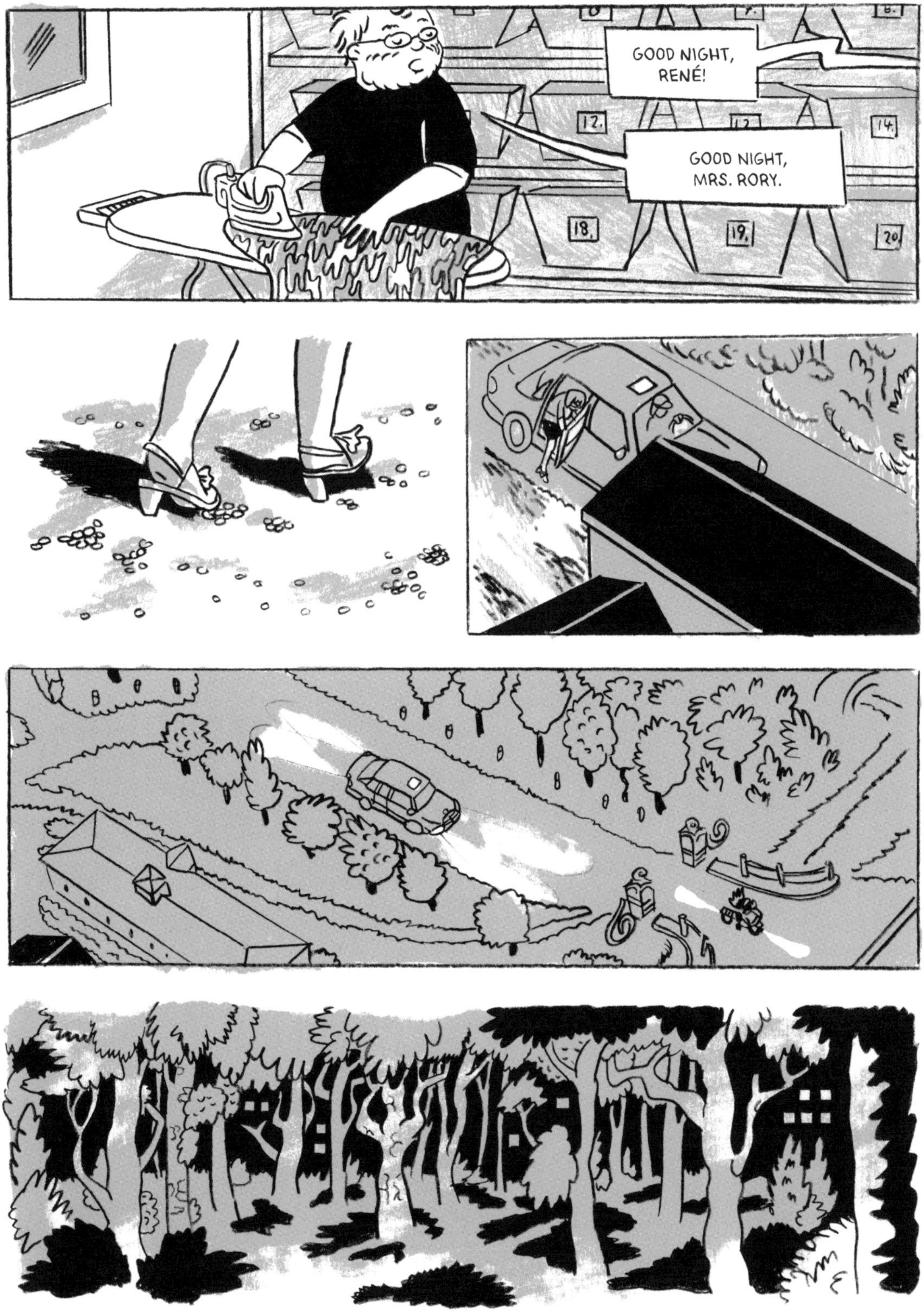
GOOD NIGHT, RENÉ!
GOOD NIGHT, MRS. RORY.

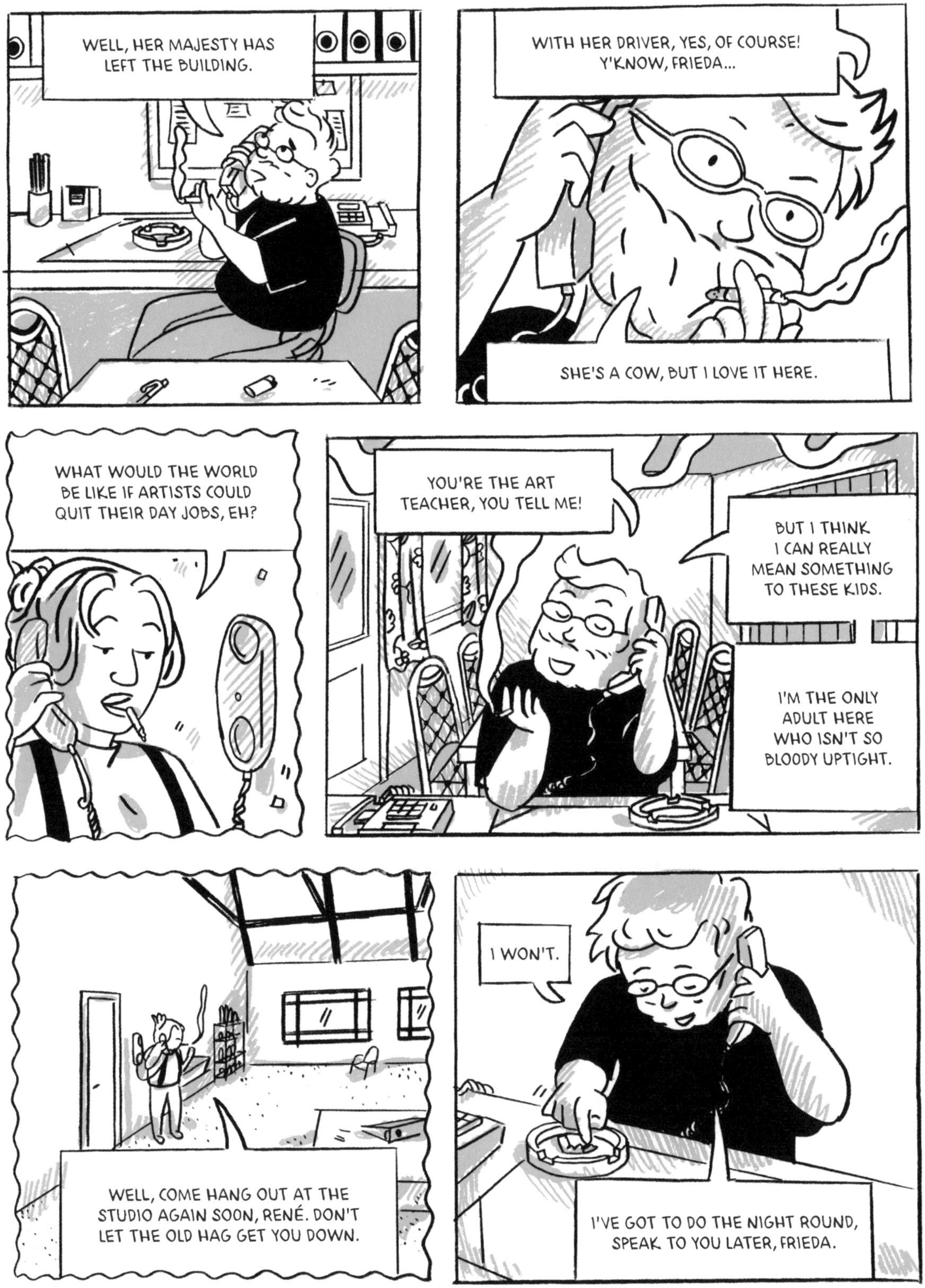
WELL, HER MAJESTY HAS LEFT THE BUILDING.
WITH HER DRIVER, YES, OF COURSE! Y'KNOW, FRIEDA...
SHE'S A COW, BUT I LOVE IT HERE.
WHAT WOULD THE WORLD BE LIKE IF ARTISTS COULD QUIT THEIR DAY JOBS, EH?
YOU'RE THE ART TEACHER, YOU TELL ME!
BUT I THINK I CAN REALLY MEAN SOMETHING TO THESE KIDS.
I'M THE ONLY ADULT HERE WHO ISN'T SO BLOODY UPTIGHT.
WELL, COME HANG OUT AT THE STUDIO AGAIN SOON, RENÉ. DON'T LET THE OLD HAG GET YOU DOWN.
I WON'T.
I'VE GOT TO DO THE NIGHT ROUND, SPEAK TO YOU LATER, FRIEDA.

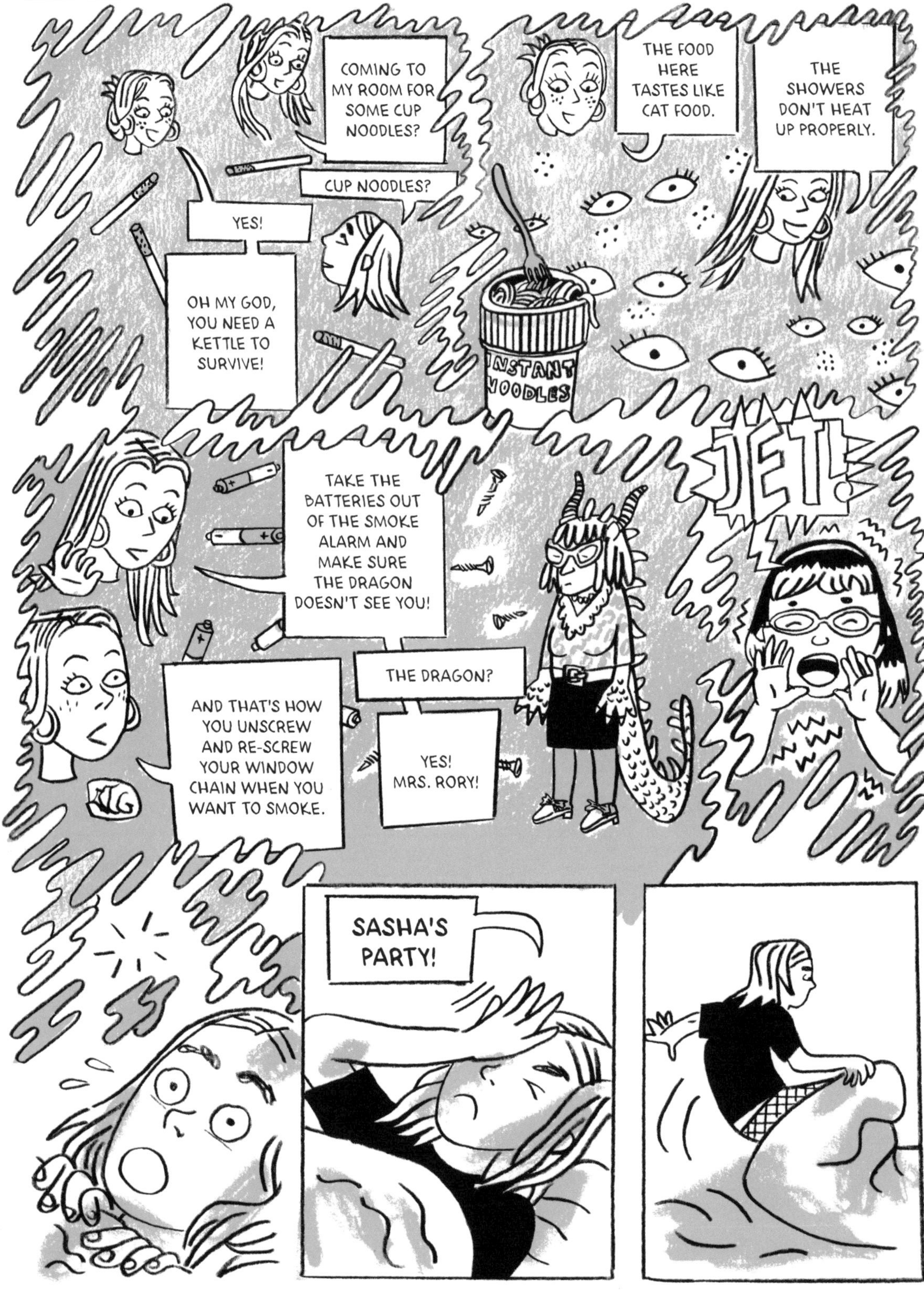
COMING TO MY ROOM FOR SOME CUP NOODLES?
CUP NOODLES?
YES!
OH MY GOD, YOU NEED A KETTLE TO SURVIVE!
INSTANT NOODLES
THE FOOD HERE TASTES LIKE CAT FOOD.
THE SHOWERS DON'T HEAT UP PROPERLY.
TAKE THE BATTERIES OUT OF THE SMOKE ALARM AND MAKE SURE THE DRAGON DOESN'T SEE YOU!
THE DRAGON?
AND THAT'S HOW YOU UNSCREW AND RE-SCREW YOUR WINDOW CHAIN WHEN YOU WANT TO SMOKE.
YES! MRS. RORY!
JET!
SASHA'S PARTY!

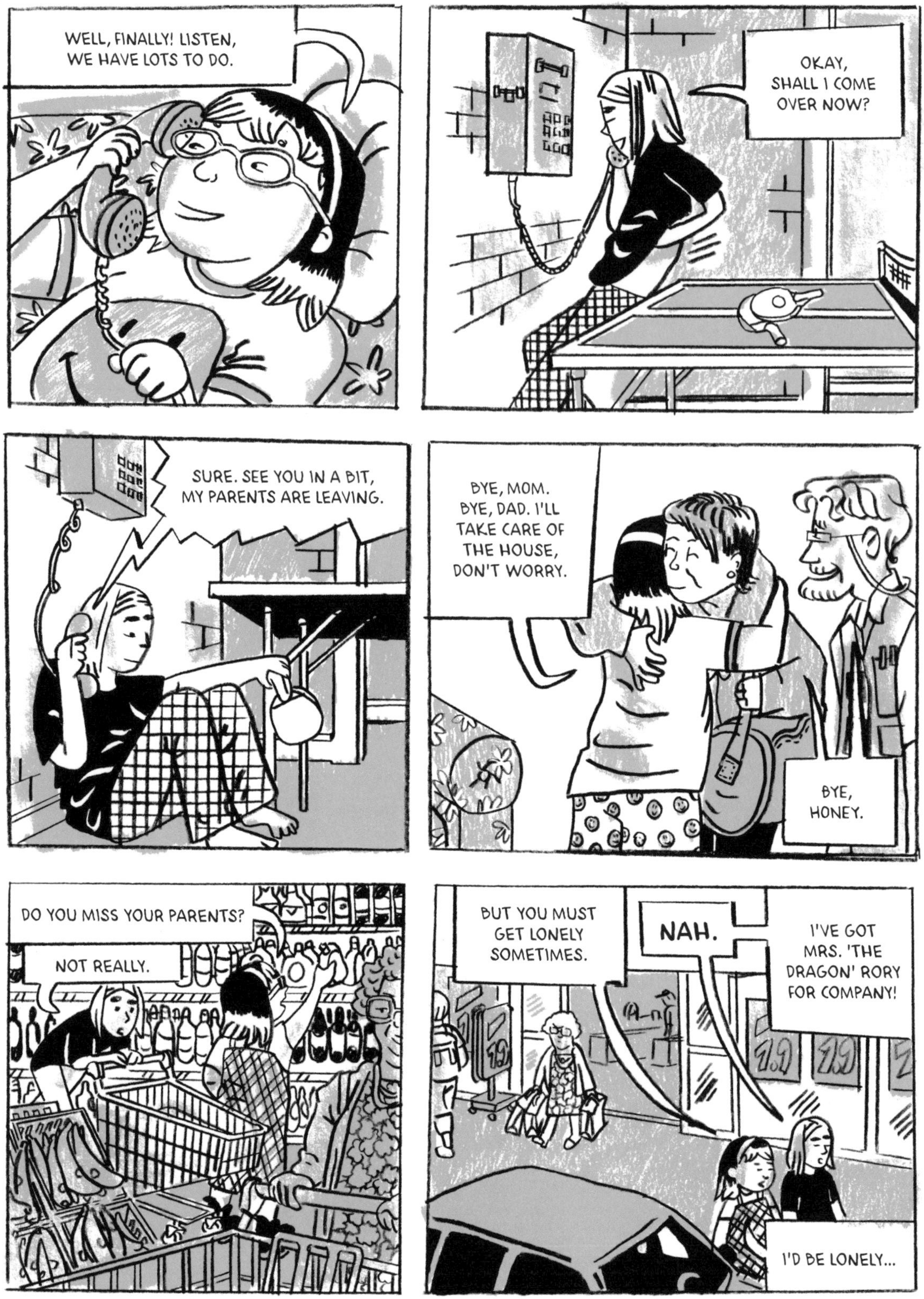
WELL, FINALLY! LISTEN, WE HAVE LOTS TO DO.
OKAY, SHALL I COME OVER NOW?
SURE. SEE YOU IN A BIT, MY PARENTS ARE LEAVING.
BYE, MOM. BYE, DAD. I'LL TAKE CARE OF THE HOUSE, DON'T WORRY.
BYE, HONEY.
DO YOU MISS YOUR PARENTS?
NOT REALLY.
BUT YOU MUST GET LONELY SOMETIMES.
NAH.
I'VE GOT MRS. 'THE DRAGON' RORY FOR COMPANY!
I'D BE LONELY...

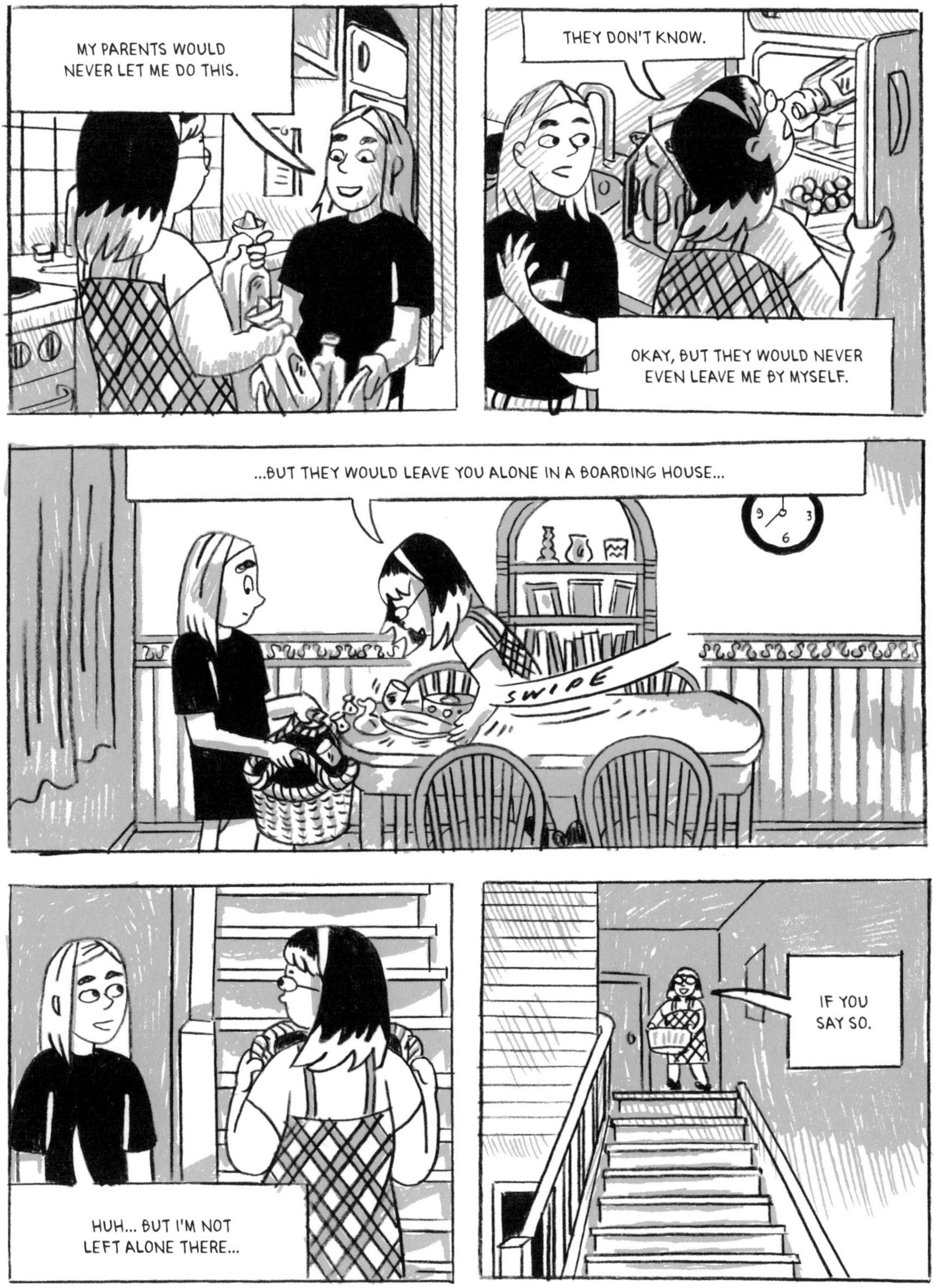
MY PARENTS WOULD NEVER LET ME DO THIS.
THEY DON'T KNOW.
OKAY, BUT THEY WOULD NEVER EVEN LEAVE ME BY MYSELF.
...BUT THEY WOULD LEAVE YOU ALONE IN A BOARDING HOUSE...
SWIPE
HUH... BUT I'M NOT LEFT ALONE THERE...
IF YOU SAY SO.

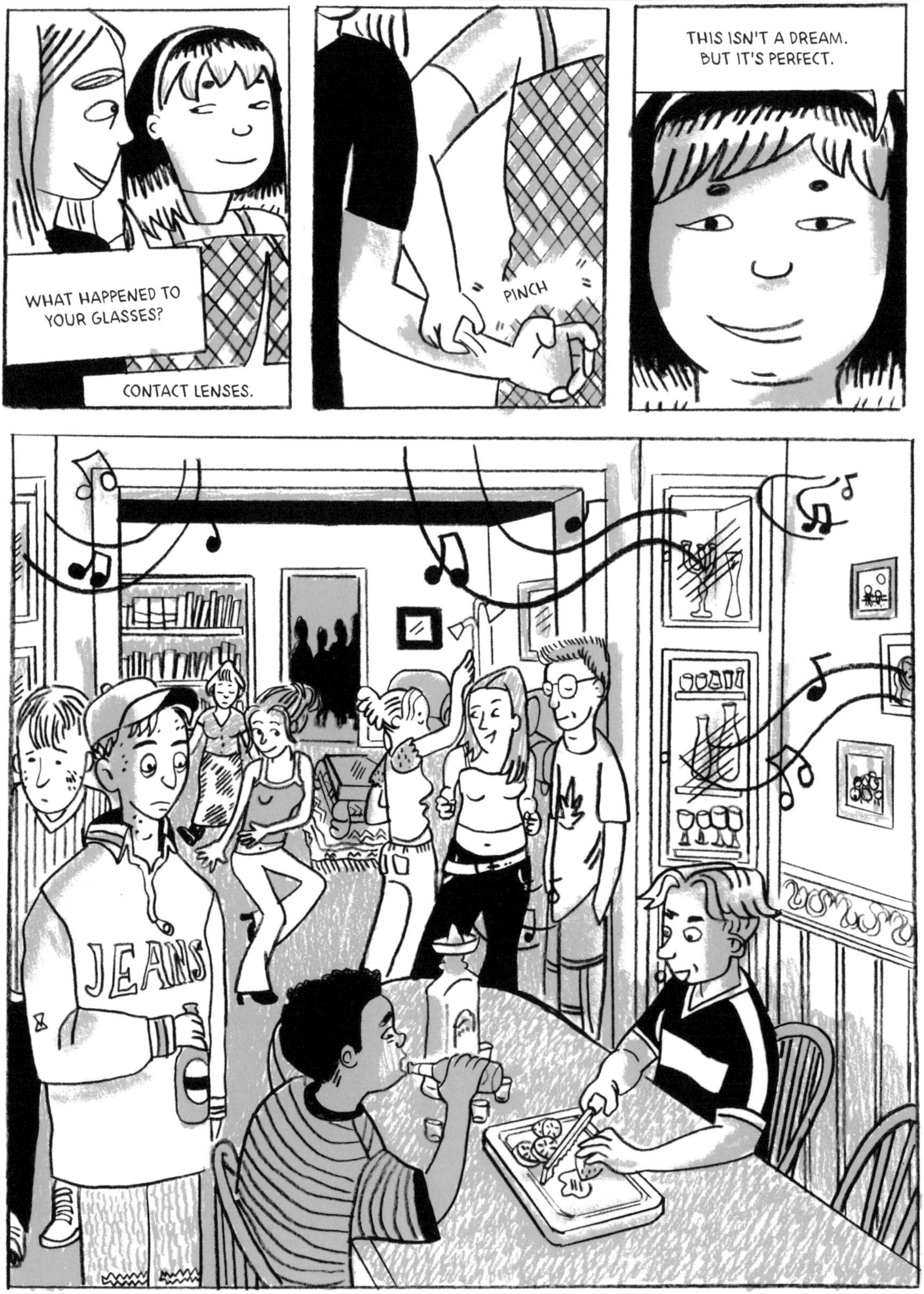
WHAT HAPPENED TO YOUR GLASSES?
CONTACT LENSES.
PINCH
THIS ISN'T A DREAM. BUT IT'S PERFECT.
JEANS

*"CREEP" BY RADIOHEAD

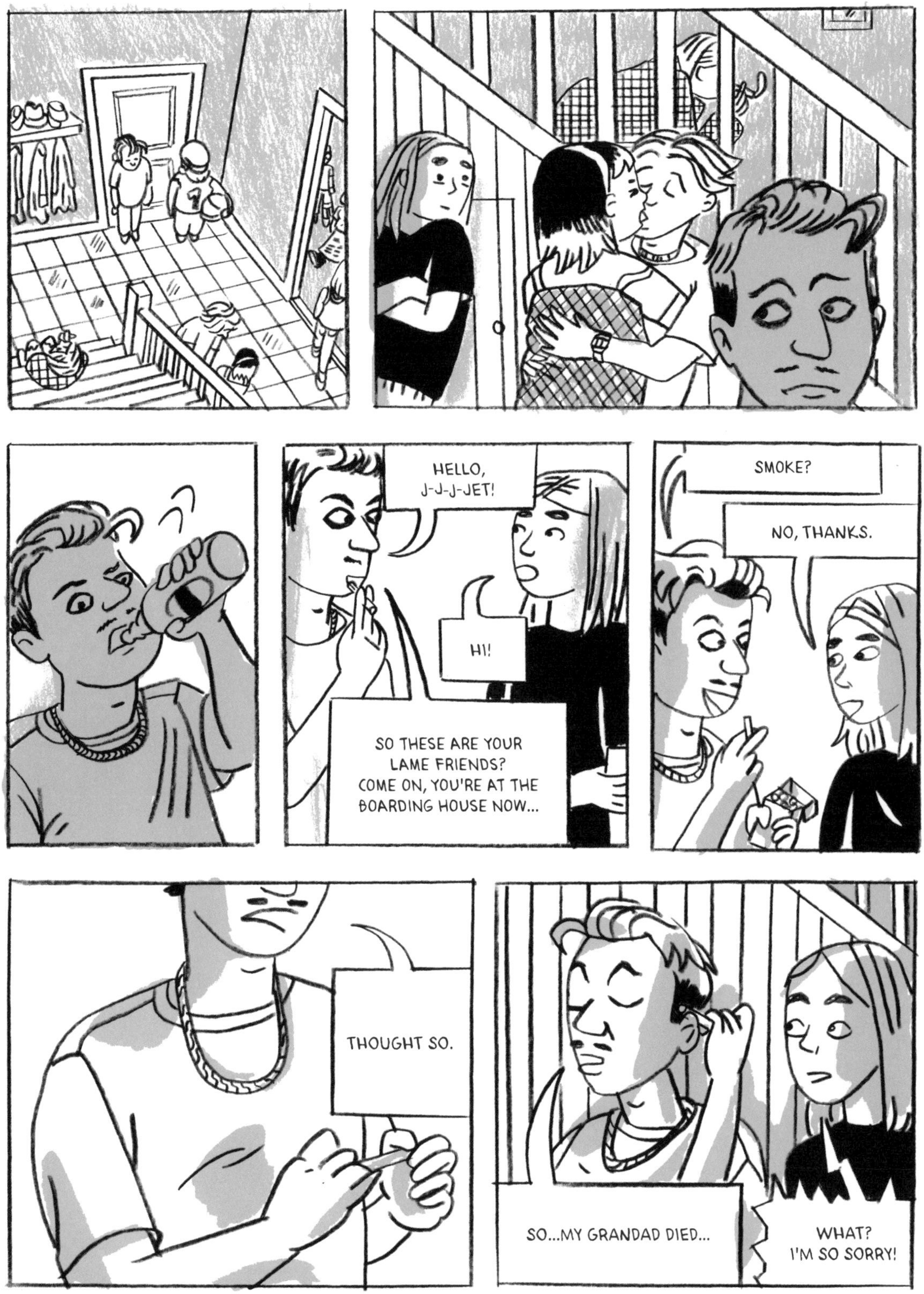
HELLO, J-J-J-JET!
HI!
SO THESE ARE YOUR LAME FRIENDS? COME ON, YOU'RE AT THE BOARDING HOUSE NOW...
SMOKE?
NO, THANKS.
THOUGHT SO.
SO...MY GRANDAD DIED...
WHAT? I'M SO SORRY!

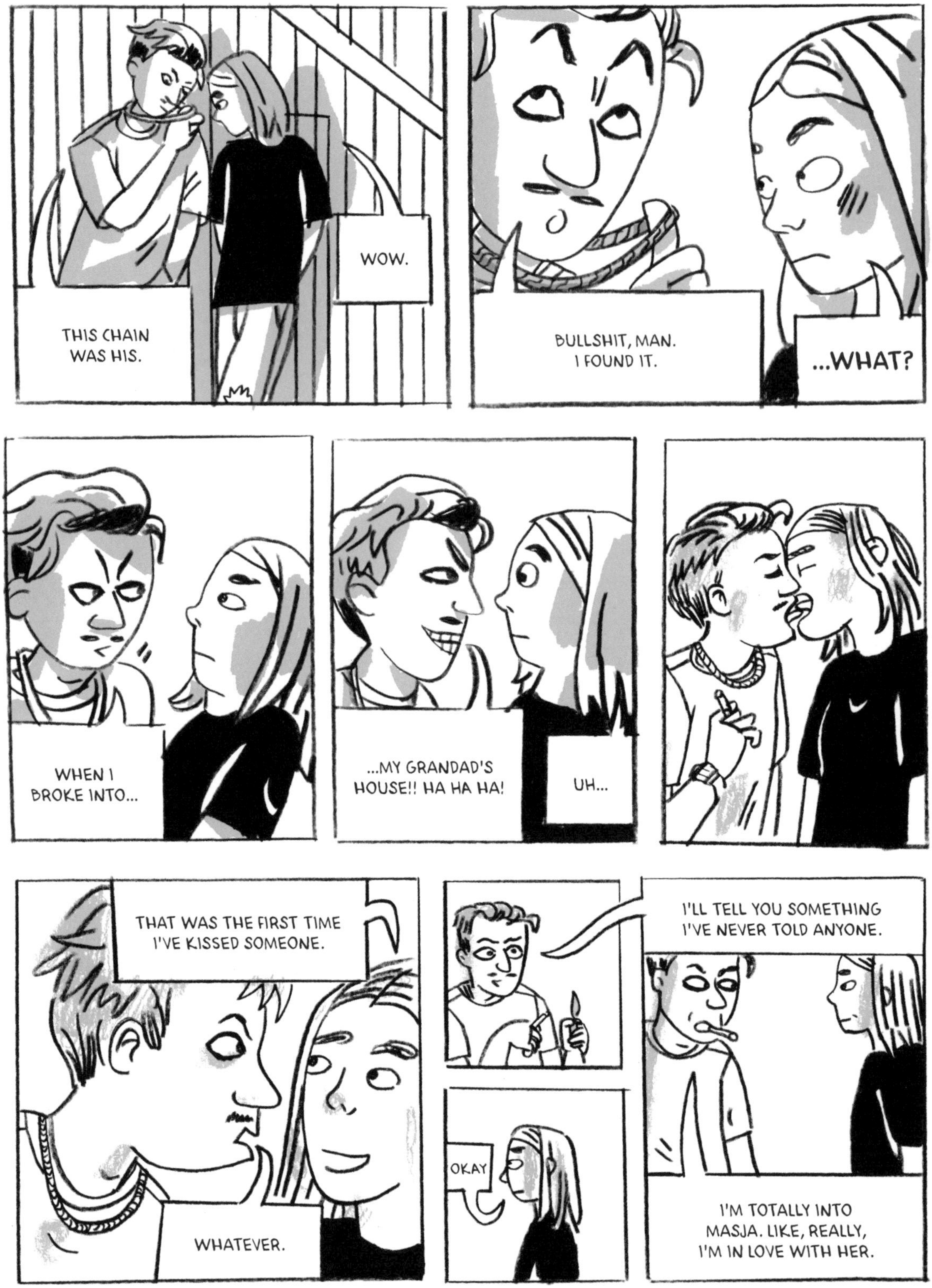
WOW.
THIS CHAIN WAS HIS.
BULLSHIT, MAN. I FOUND IT.
...WHAT?
WHEN I BROKE INTO...
...MY GRANDAD'S HOUSE!! HA HA HA!
UH...
THAT WAS THE FIRST TIME I'VE KISSED SOMEONE.
WHATEVER.
I'LL TELL YOU SOMETHING I'VE NEVER TOLD ANYONE.
OKAY
I'M TOTALLY INTO MASJA. LIKE, REALLY, I'M IN LOVE WITH HER.

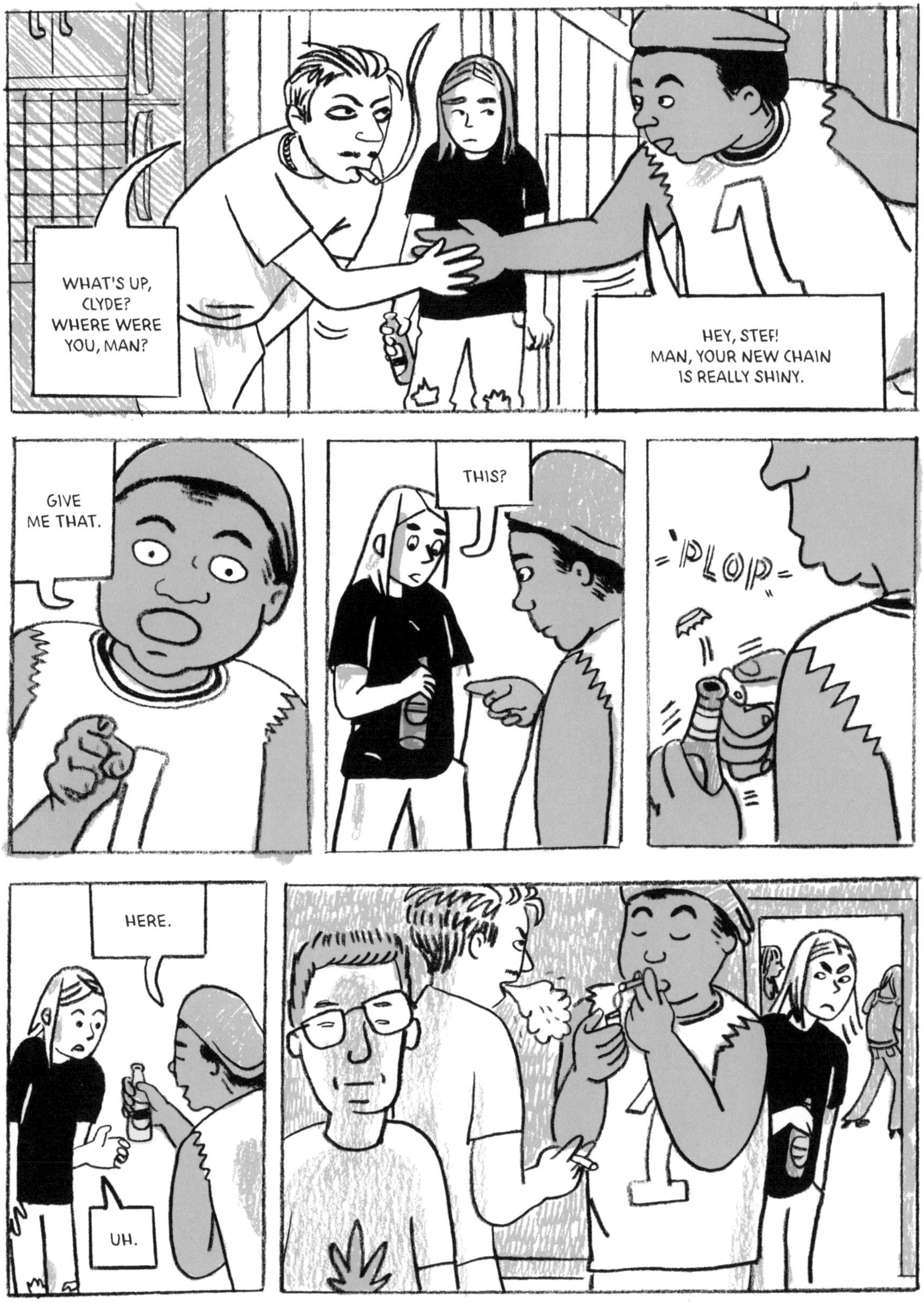
WHAT'S UP, CLYDE? WHERE WERE YOU, MAN?
HEY, STEF! MAN, YOUR NEW CHAIN IS REALLY SHINY.
GIVE ME THAT.
THIS?
PLOP
HERE.
UH.

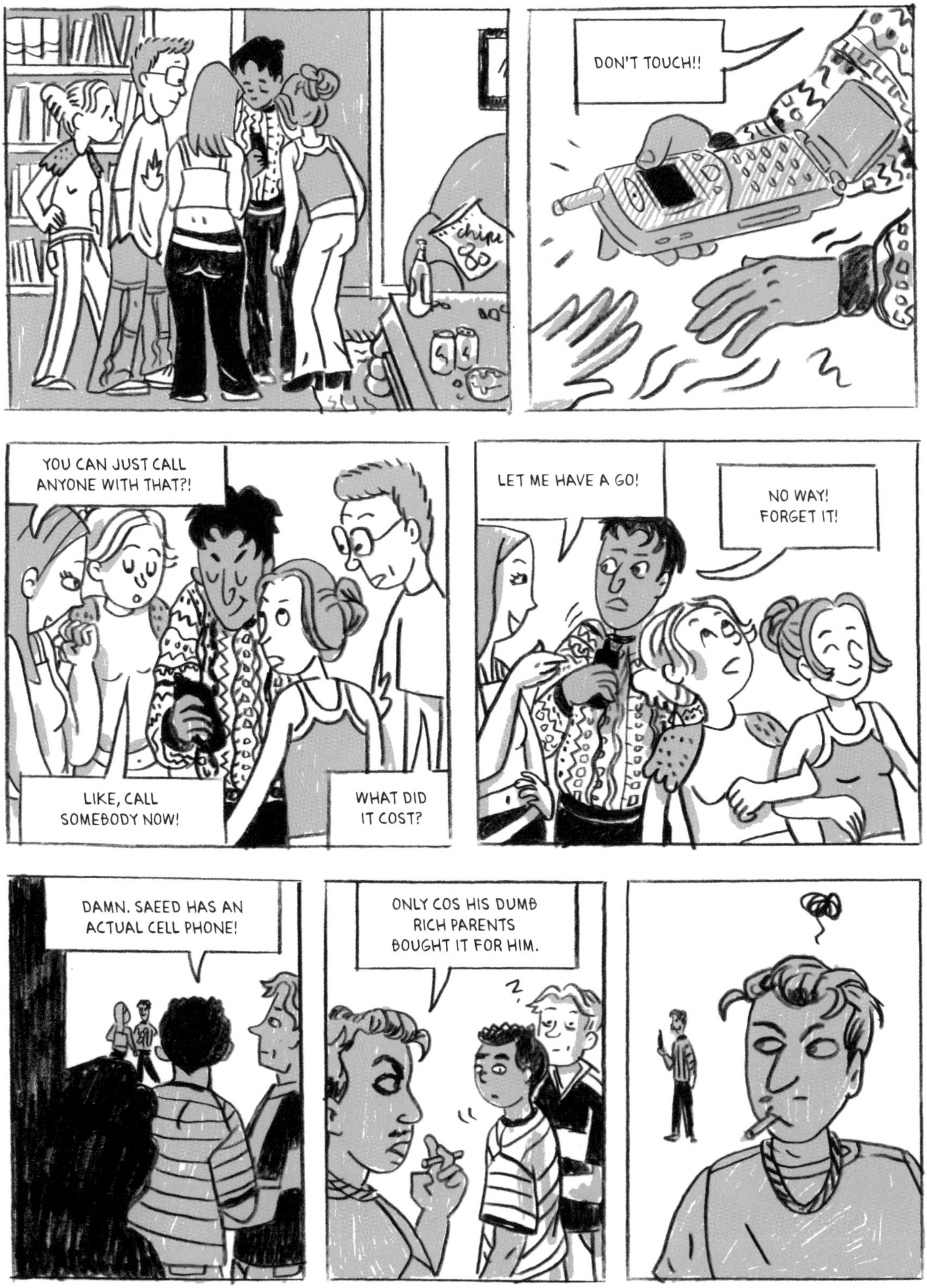
chips
80
DON'T TOUCH!!
YOU CAN JUST CALL ANYONE WITH THAT?!
LIKE, CALL SOMEBODY NOW!
WHAT DID IT COST?
LET ME HAVE A GO!
NO WAY! FORGET IT!
DAMN. SAEED HAS AN ACTUAL CELL PHONE!
ONLY COS HIS DUMB RICH PARENTS BOUGHT IT FOR HIM.

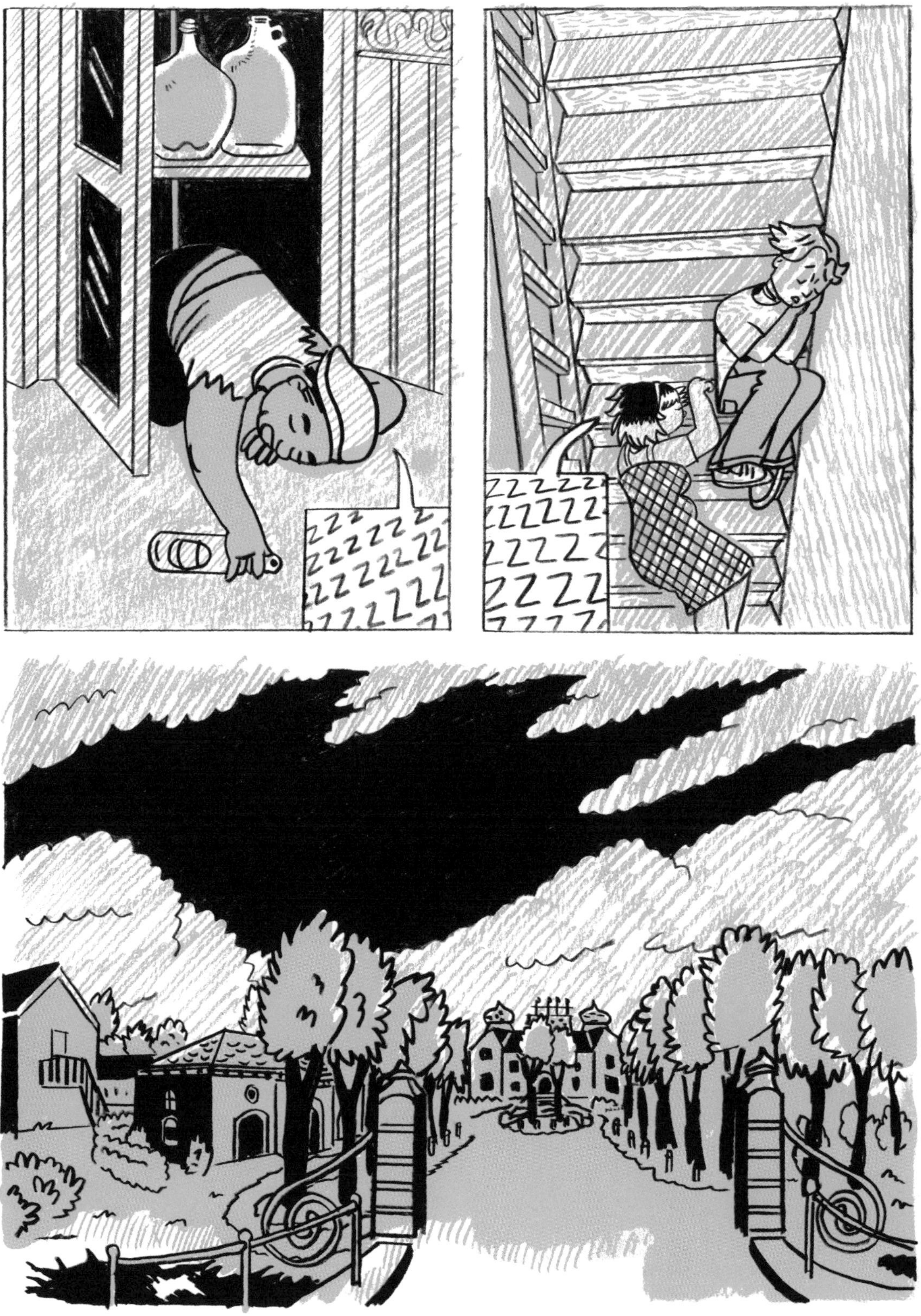

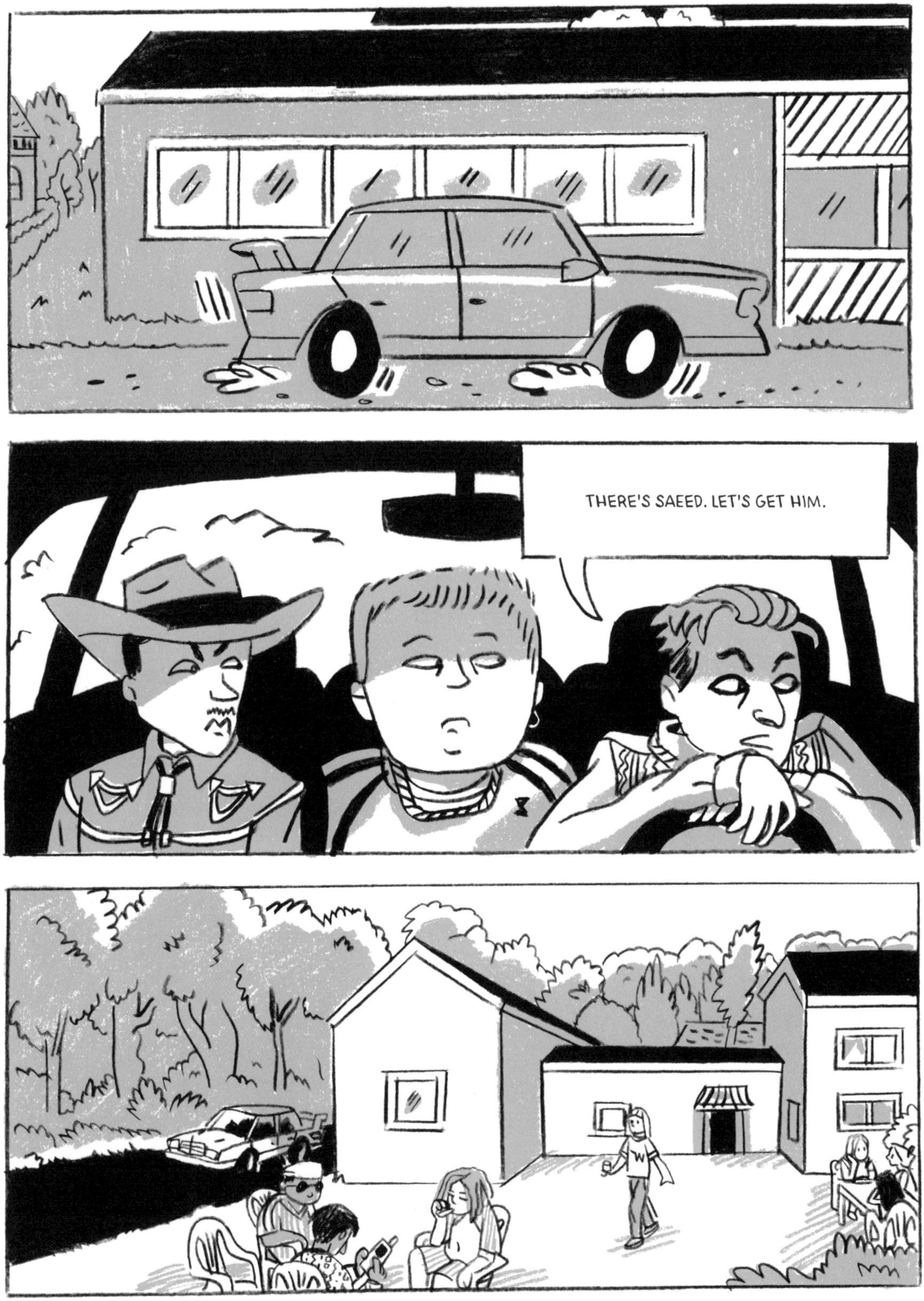
THERE'S SAEED. LET'S GET HIM.

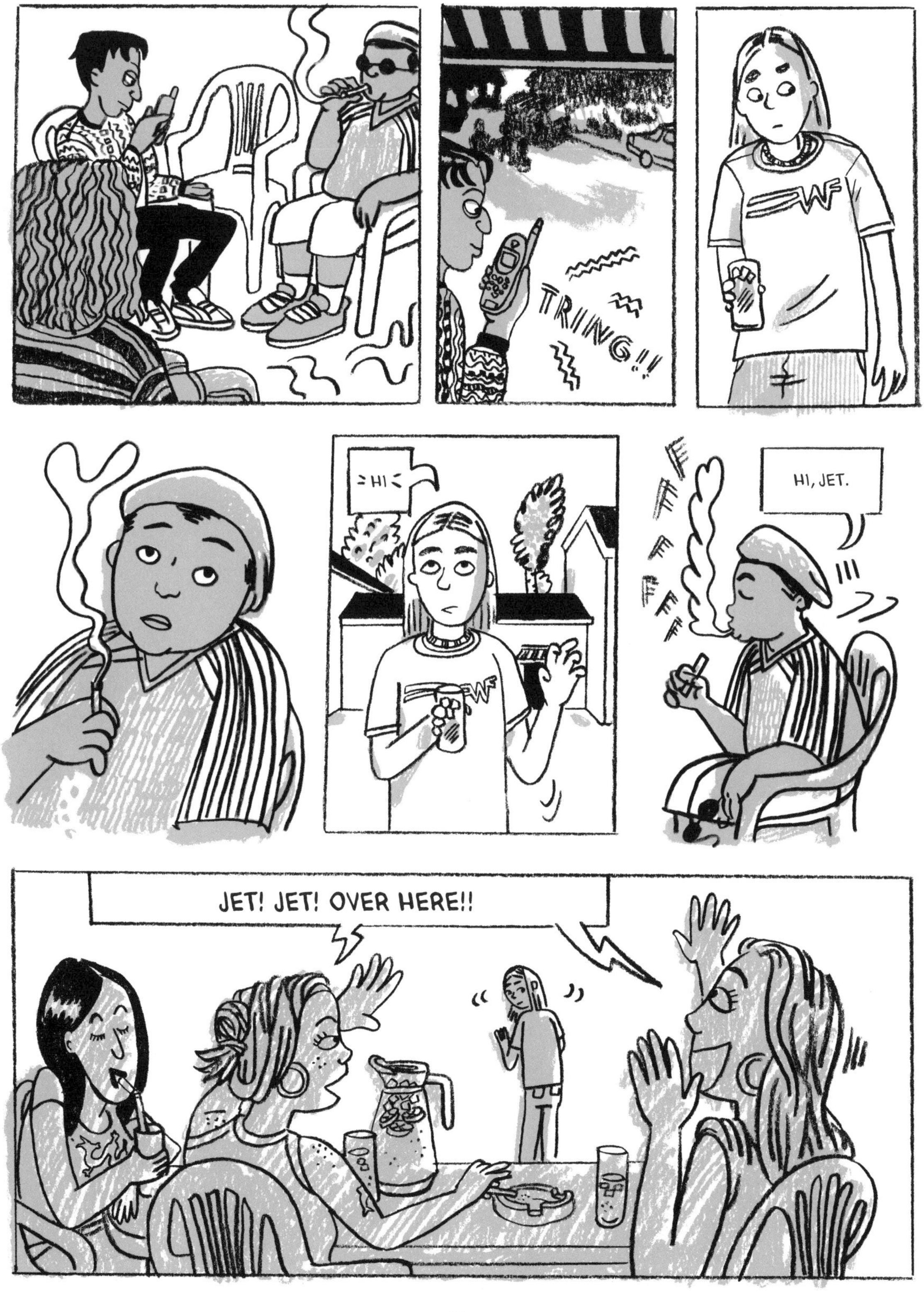
TRING!!
HI
HI, JET.
JET! JET! OVER HERE!!

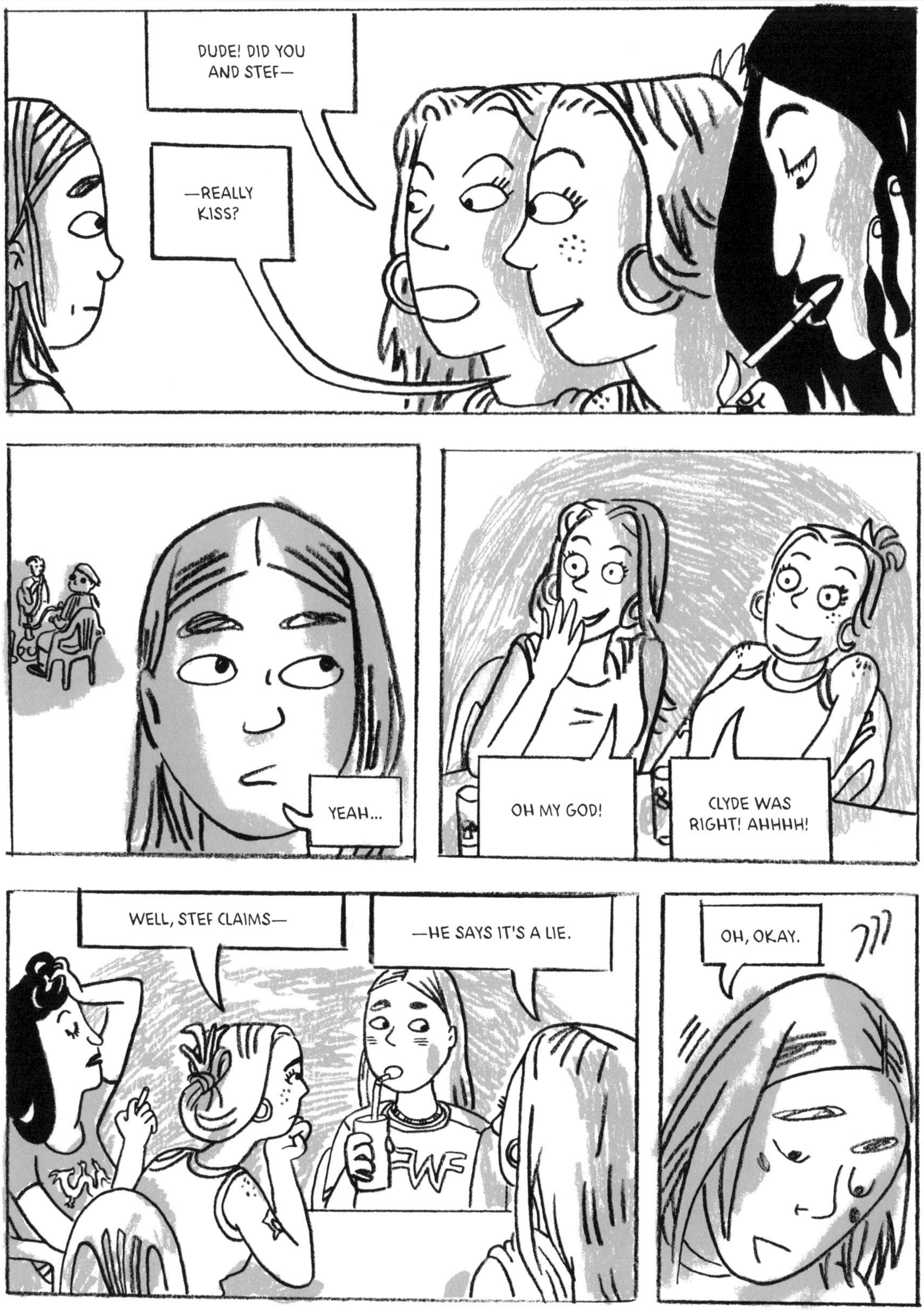
DUDE! DID YOU AND STEF—
—REALLY KISS?
YEAH...
OH MY GOD!
CLYDE WAS RIGHT! AHHHH!
WELL, STEF CLAIMS—
—HE SAYS IT'S A LIE.
OH, OKAY.

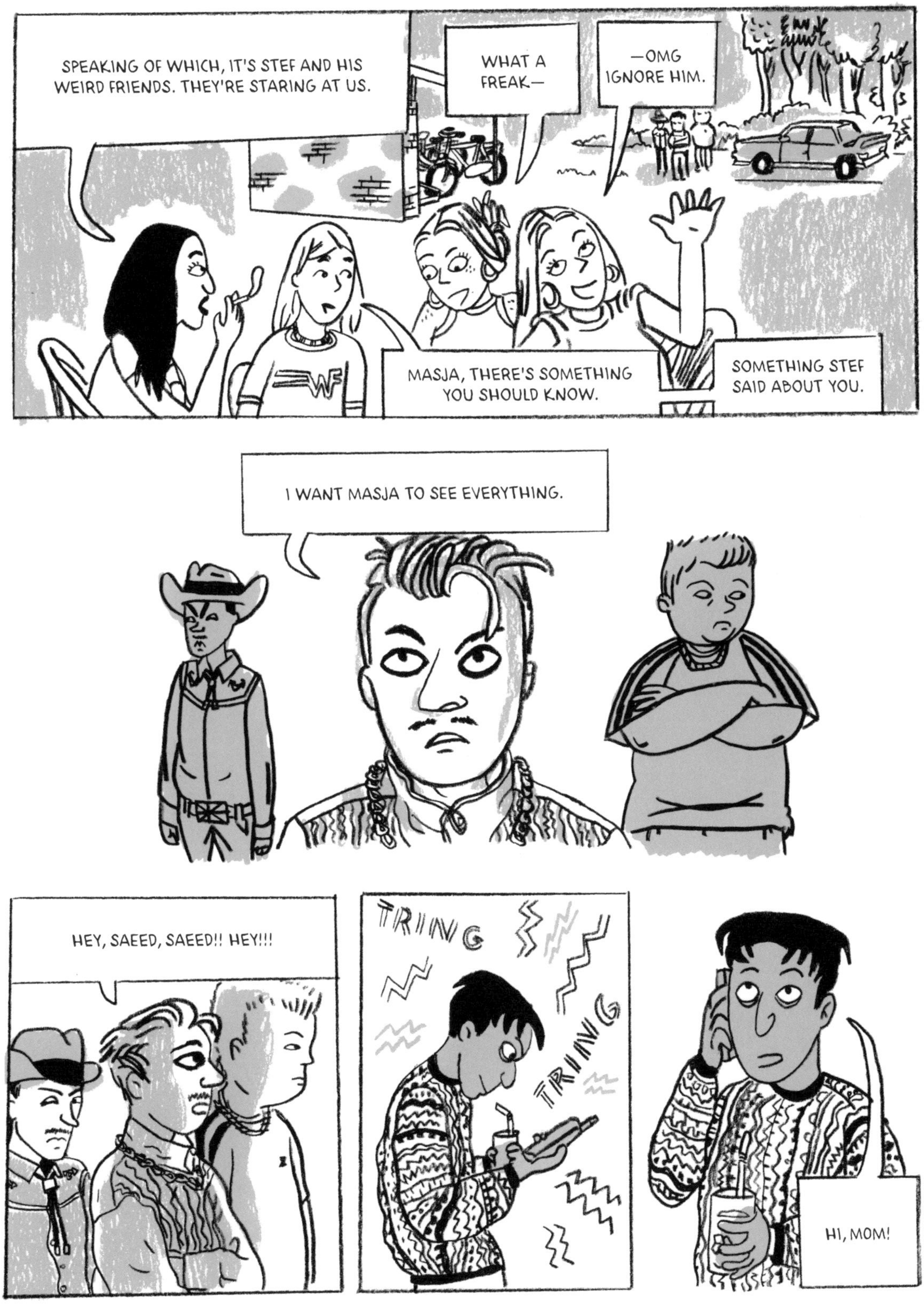
SPEAKING OF WHICH, IT'S STEF AND HIS WEIRD FRIENDS. THEY'RE STARING AT US.
WHAT A FREAK—
—OMG IGNORE HIM.
MASJA, THERE'S SOMETHING YOU SHOULD KNOW.
SOMETHING STEF SAID ABOUT YOU.
I WANT MASJA TO SEE EVERYTHING.
HEY, SAEED, SAEED!! HEY!!!
TRING
TRING
TRING
HI, MOM!

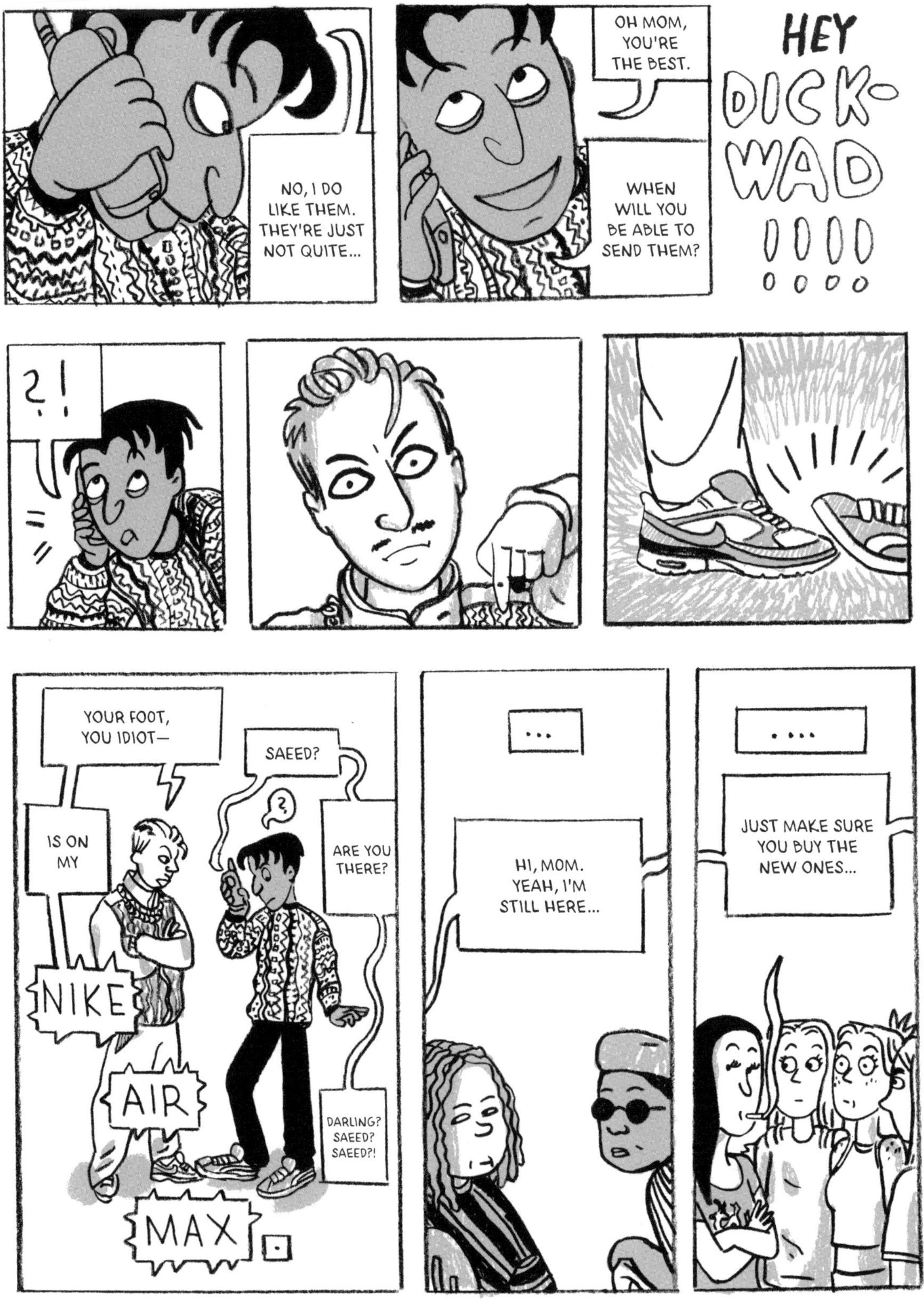
NO, I DO LIKE THEM. THEY'RE JUST NOT QUITE...
OH MOM, YOU'RE THE BEST.
WHEN WILL YOU BE ABLE TO SEND THEM?
HEY DICK-WAD !!!!
?!
YOUR FOOT, YOU IDIOT—
IS ON MY
NIKE
AIR
MAX.
SAEED?
?
ARE YOU THERE?
DARLING? SAEED? SAEED?!
...
HI, MOM. YEAH, I'M STILL HERE...
....
JUST MAKE SURE YOU BUY THE NEW ONES...

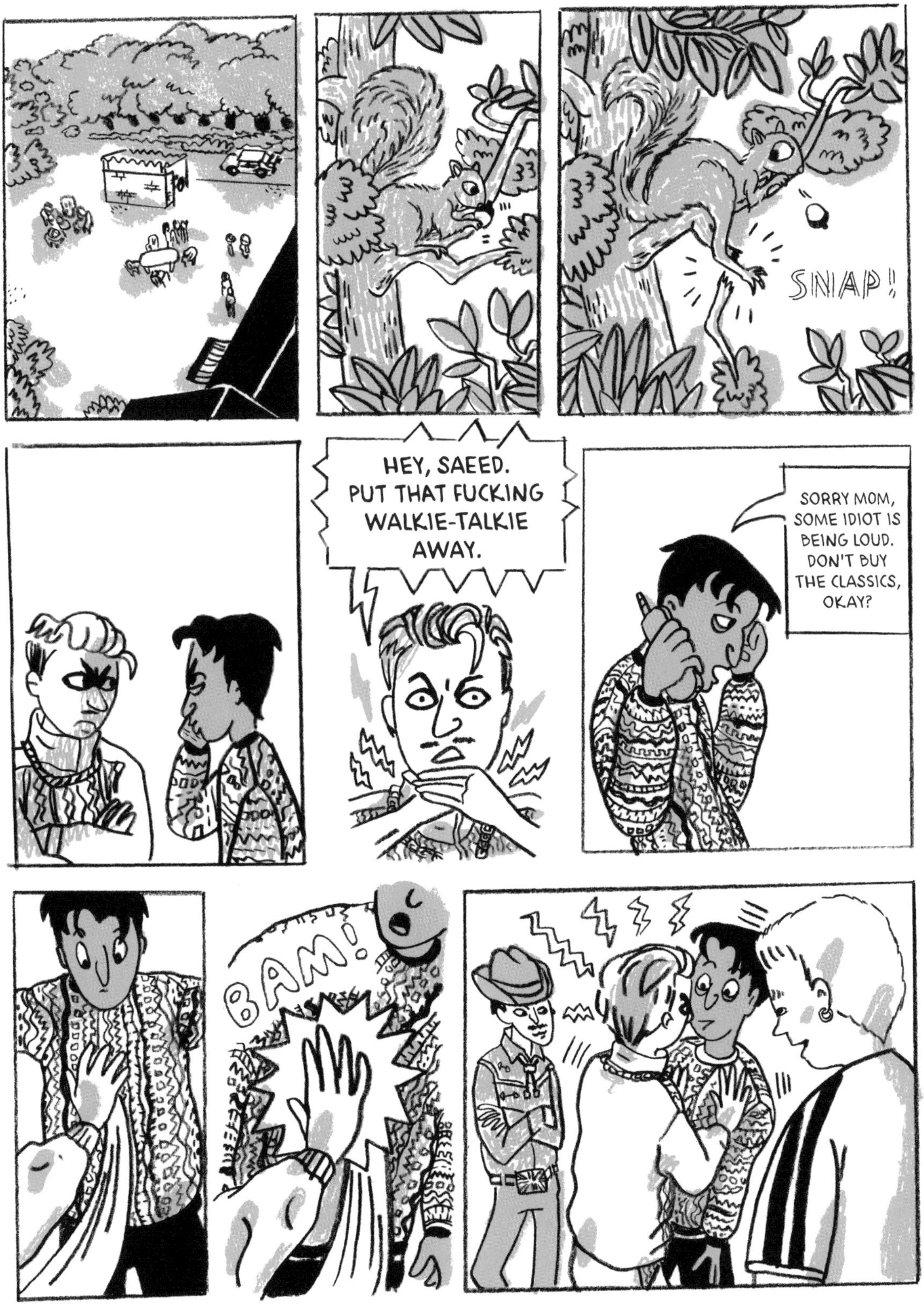
SNAP!
HEY, SAEED. PUT THAT FUCKING WALKIE-TALKIE AWAY.
SORRY MOM, SOME IDIOT IS BEING LOUD. DON'T BUY THE CLASSICS, OKAY?
BAM!

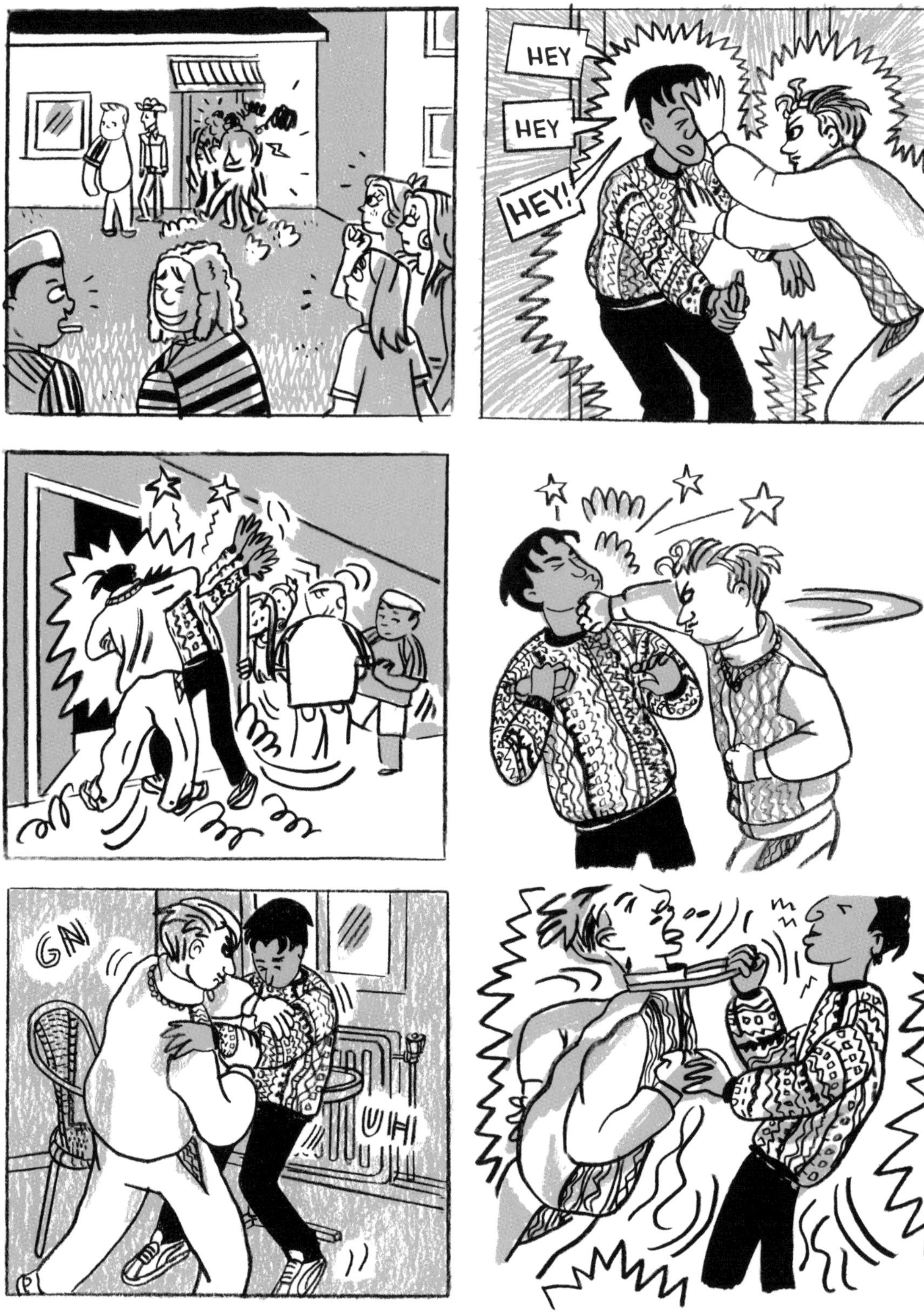
HEY
HEY
HEY!
GN
UH

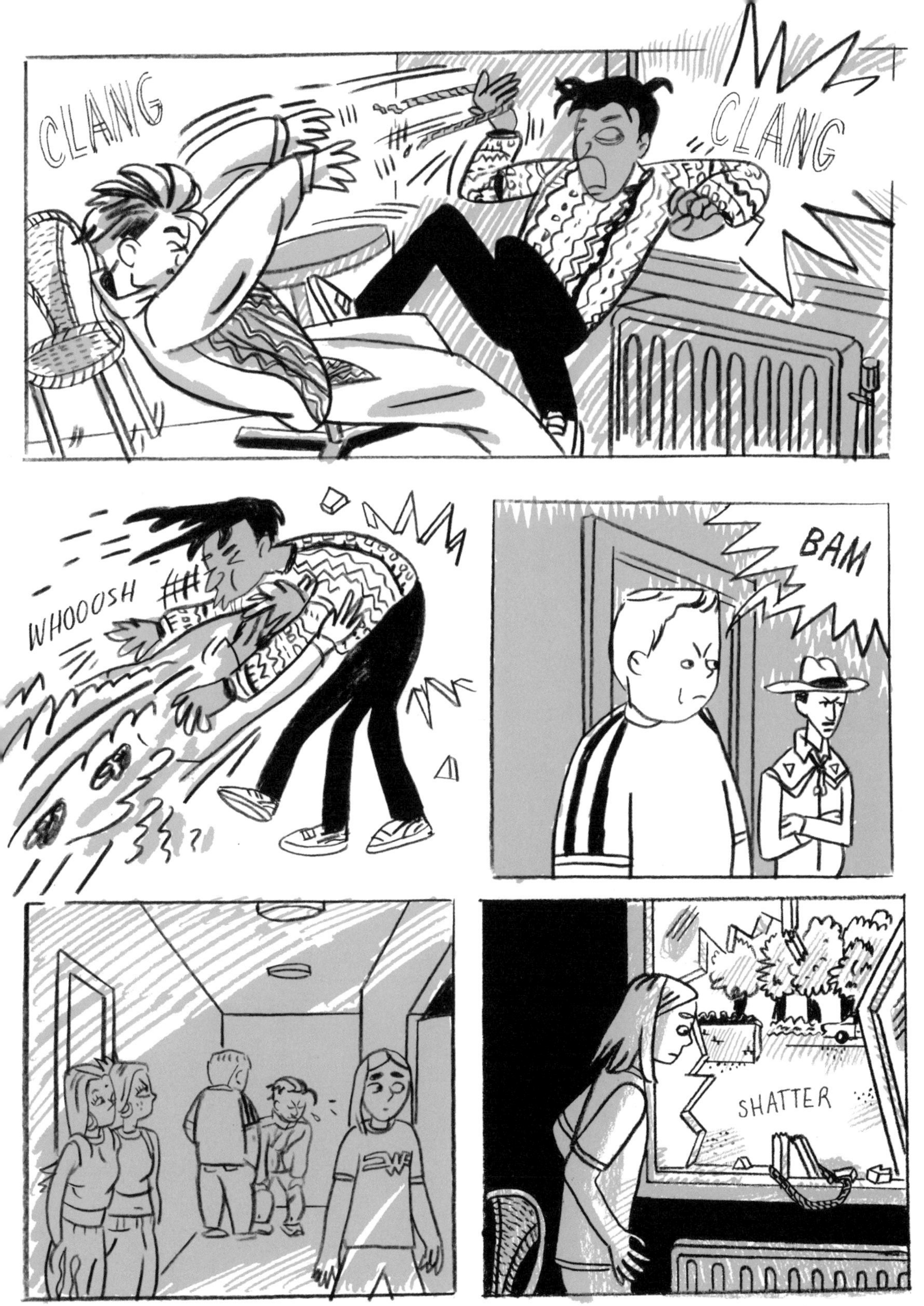
CLANG
CLANG
WHOOOSH
BAM
SHATTER

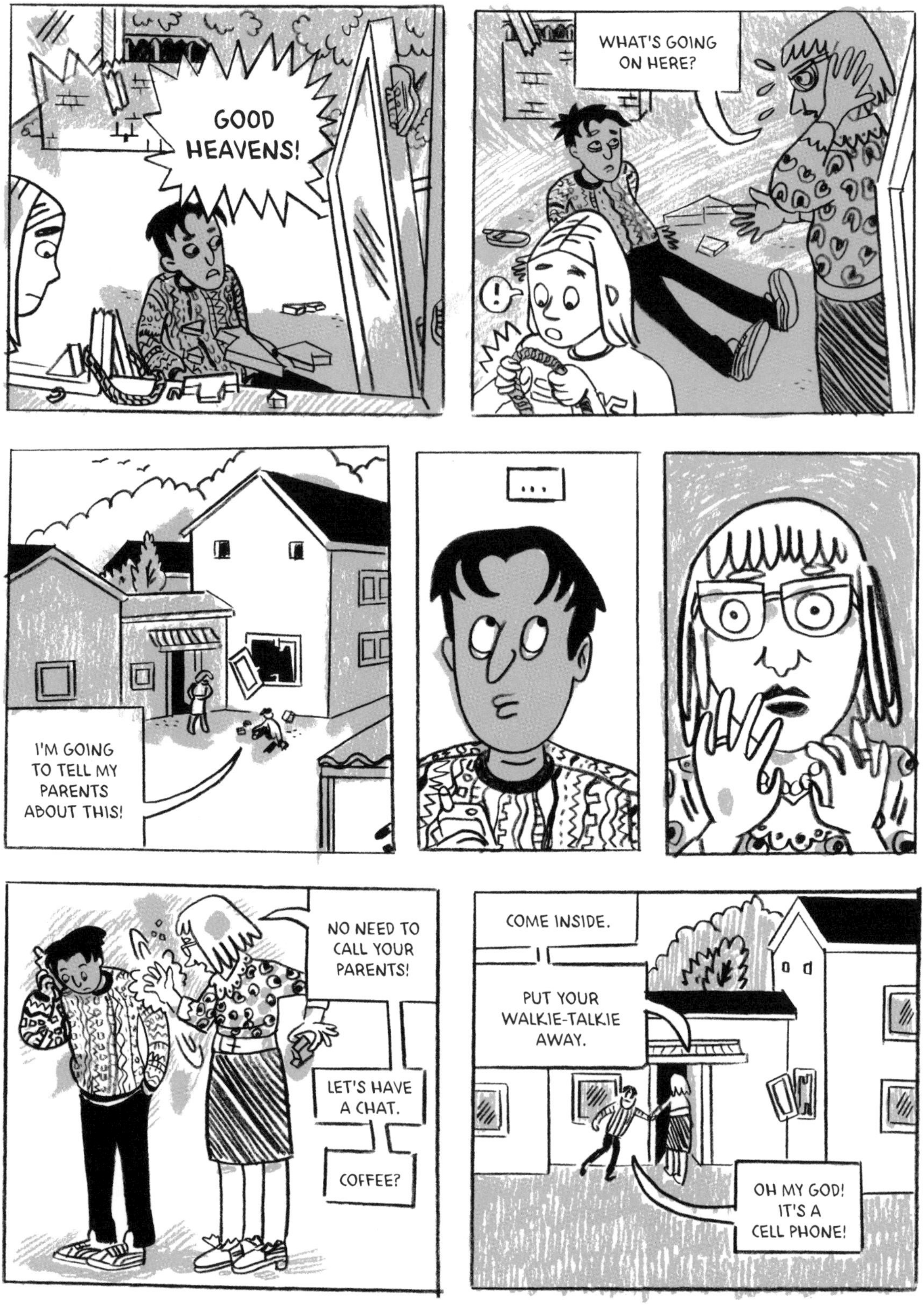
GOOD HEAVENS!
WHAT'S GOING ON HERE?
I'M GOING TO TELL MY PARENTS ABOUT THIS!
...
NO NEED TO CALL YOUR PARENTS!
LET'S HAVE A CHAT.
COFFEE?
COME INSIDE.
PUT YOUR WALKIE-TALKIE AWAY.
OH MY GOD! IT'S A CELL PHONE!

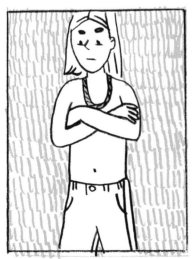

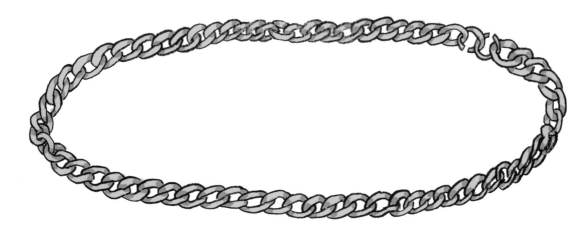

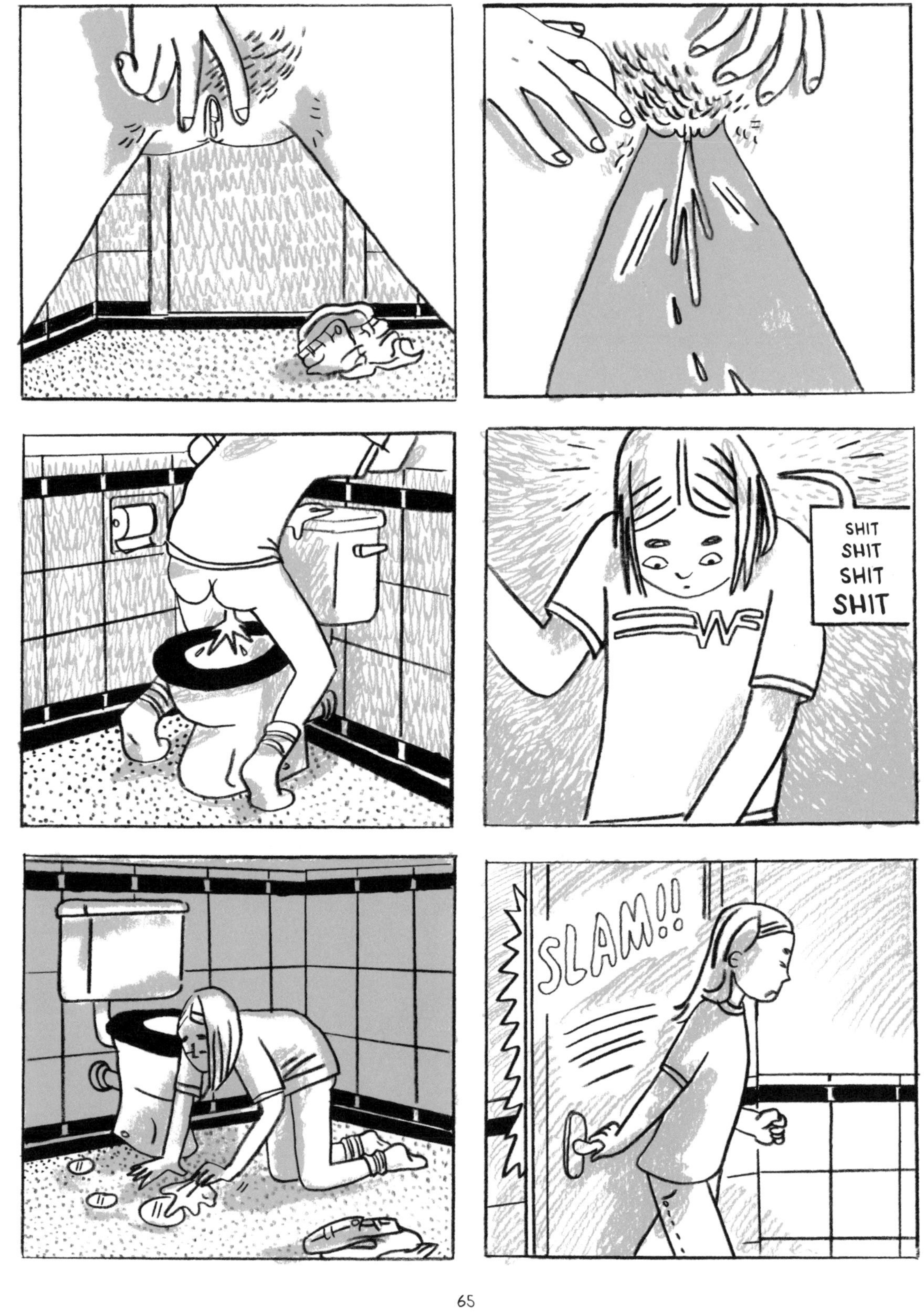
SHIT
SHIT
SHIT
SHIT
SLAM!!

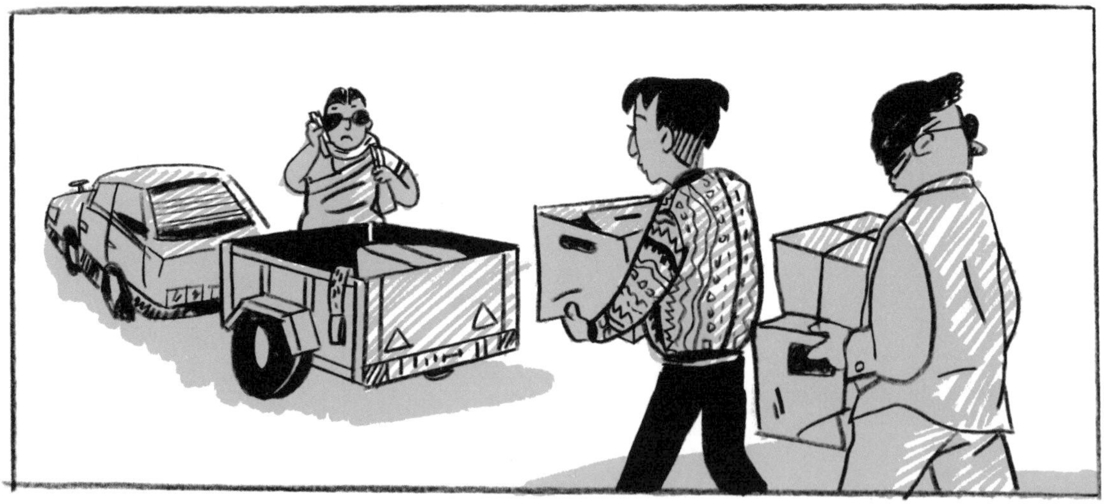

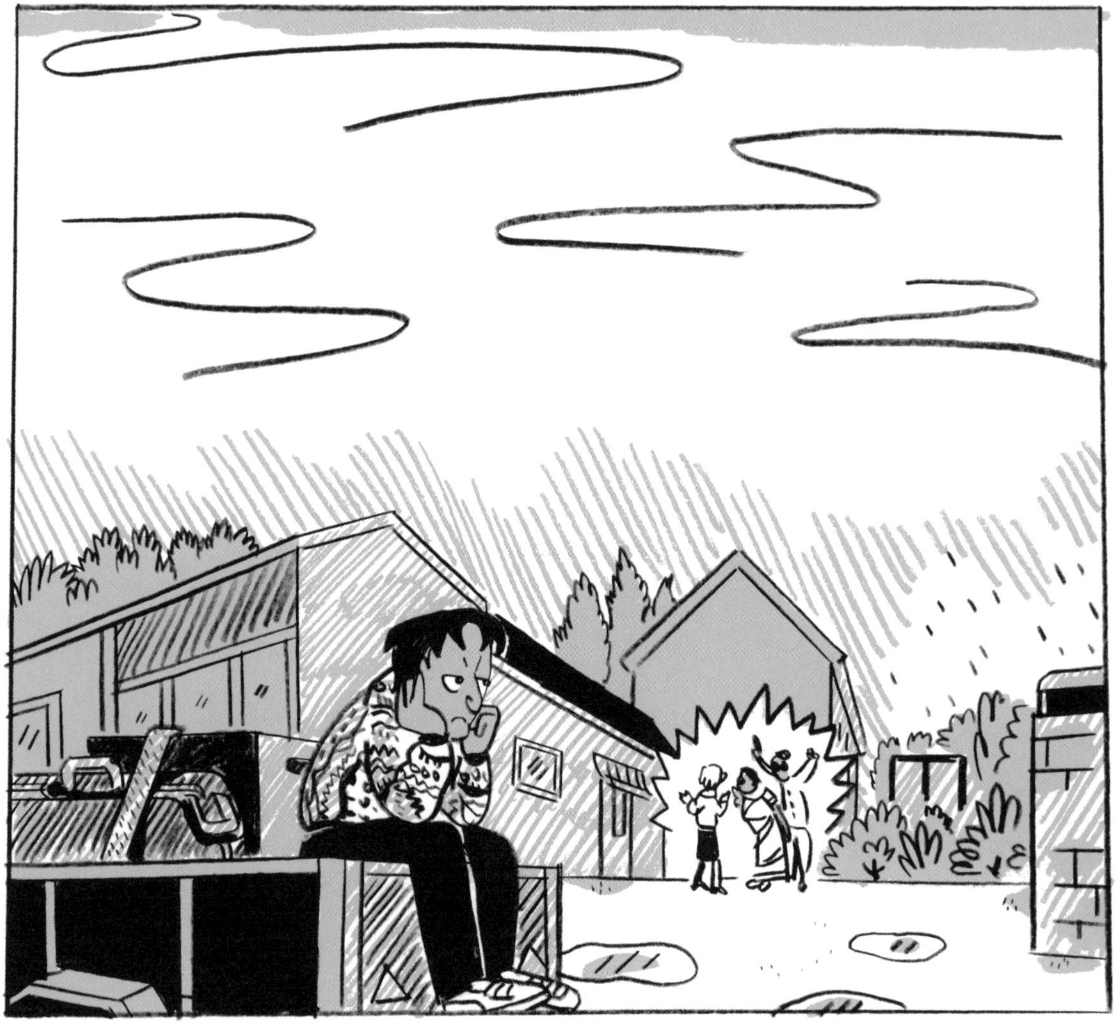

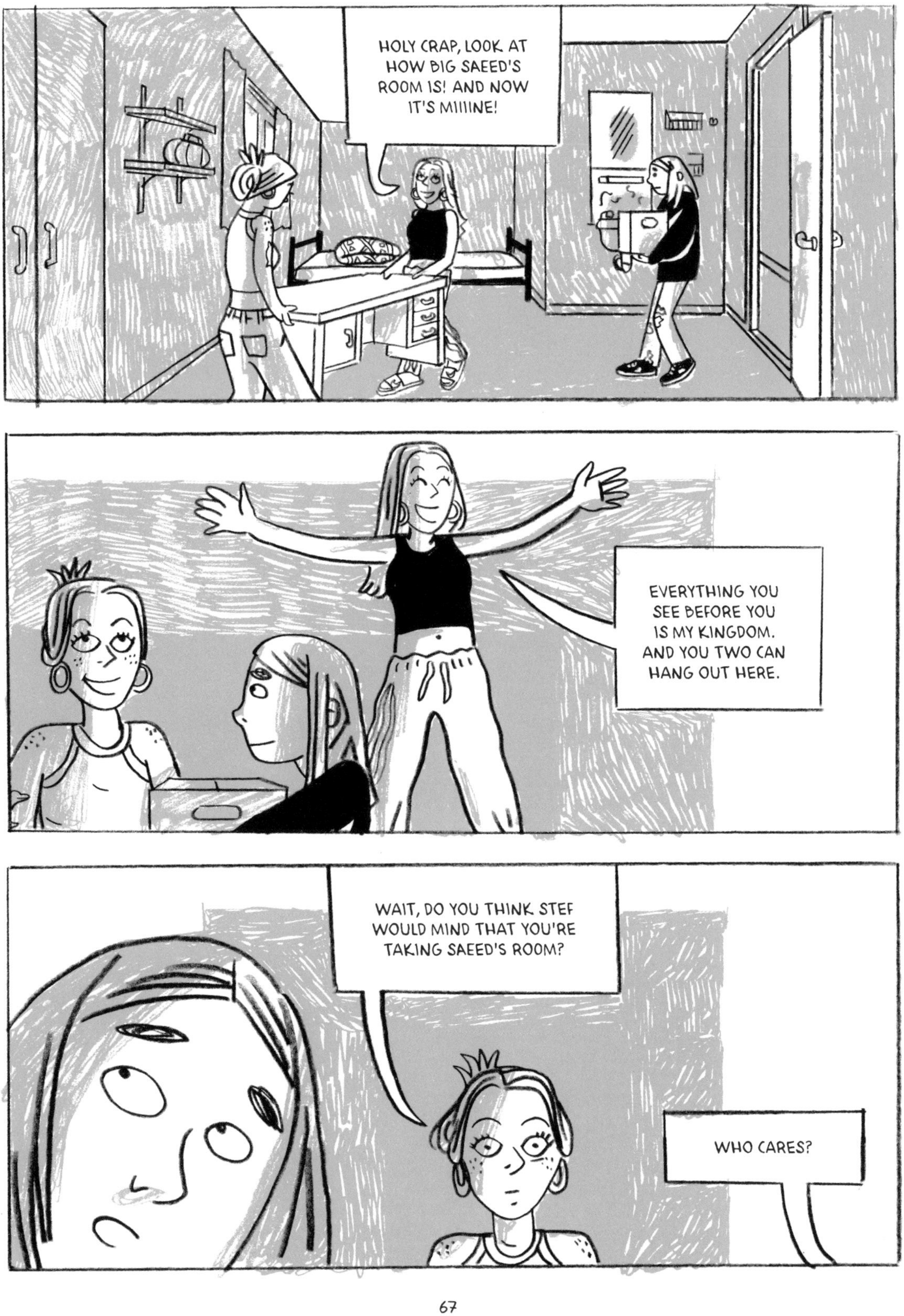
HOLY CRAP, LOOK AT HOW BIG SAEED'S ROOM IS! AND NOW IT'S MIIIINE!
EVERYTHING YOU SEE BEFORE YOU IS MY KINGDOM. AND YOU TWO CAN HANG OUT HERE.
WAIT, DO YOU THINK STEF WOULD MIND THAT YOU'RE TAKING SAEED'S ROOM?
WHO CARES?

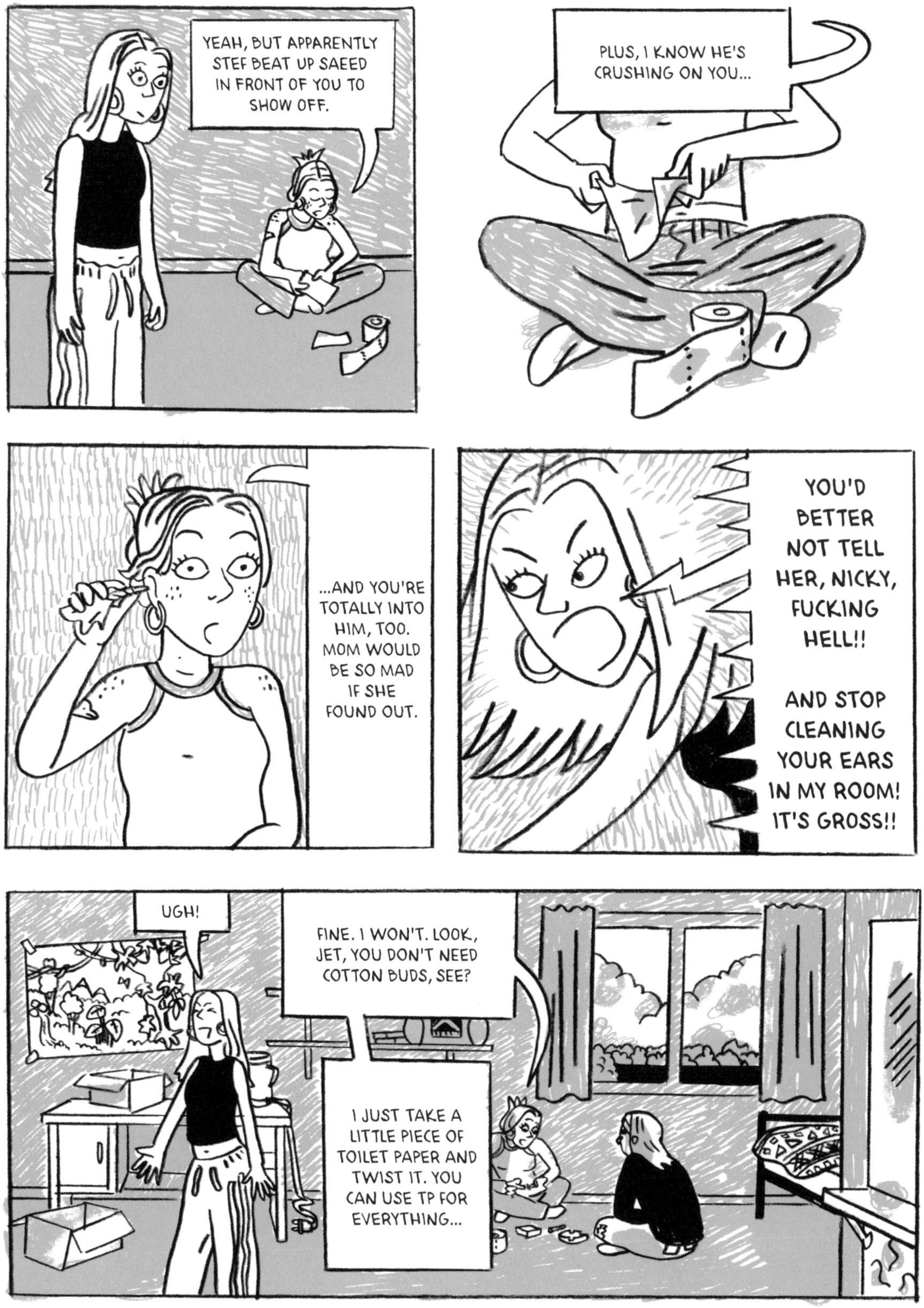
YEAH, BUT APPARENTLY STEF BEAT UP SAEED IN FRONT OF YOU TO SHOW OFF.
PLUS, I KNOW HE'S CRUSHING ON YOU...
...AND YOU'RE TOTALLY INTO HIM, TOO. MOM WOULD BE SO MAD IF SHE FOUND OUT.
YOU'D BETTER NOT TELL HER, NICKY, FUCKING HELL!!
AND STOP CLEANING YOUR EARS IN MY ROOM! IT'S GROSS!!
UGH!
FINE. I WON'T. LOOK, JET, YOU DON'T NEED COTTON BUDS, SEE?
I JUST TAKE A LITTLE PIECE OF TOILET PAPER AND TWIST IT. YOU CAN USE TP FOR EVERYTHING...

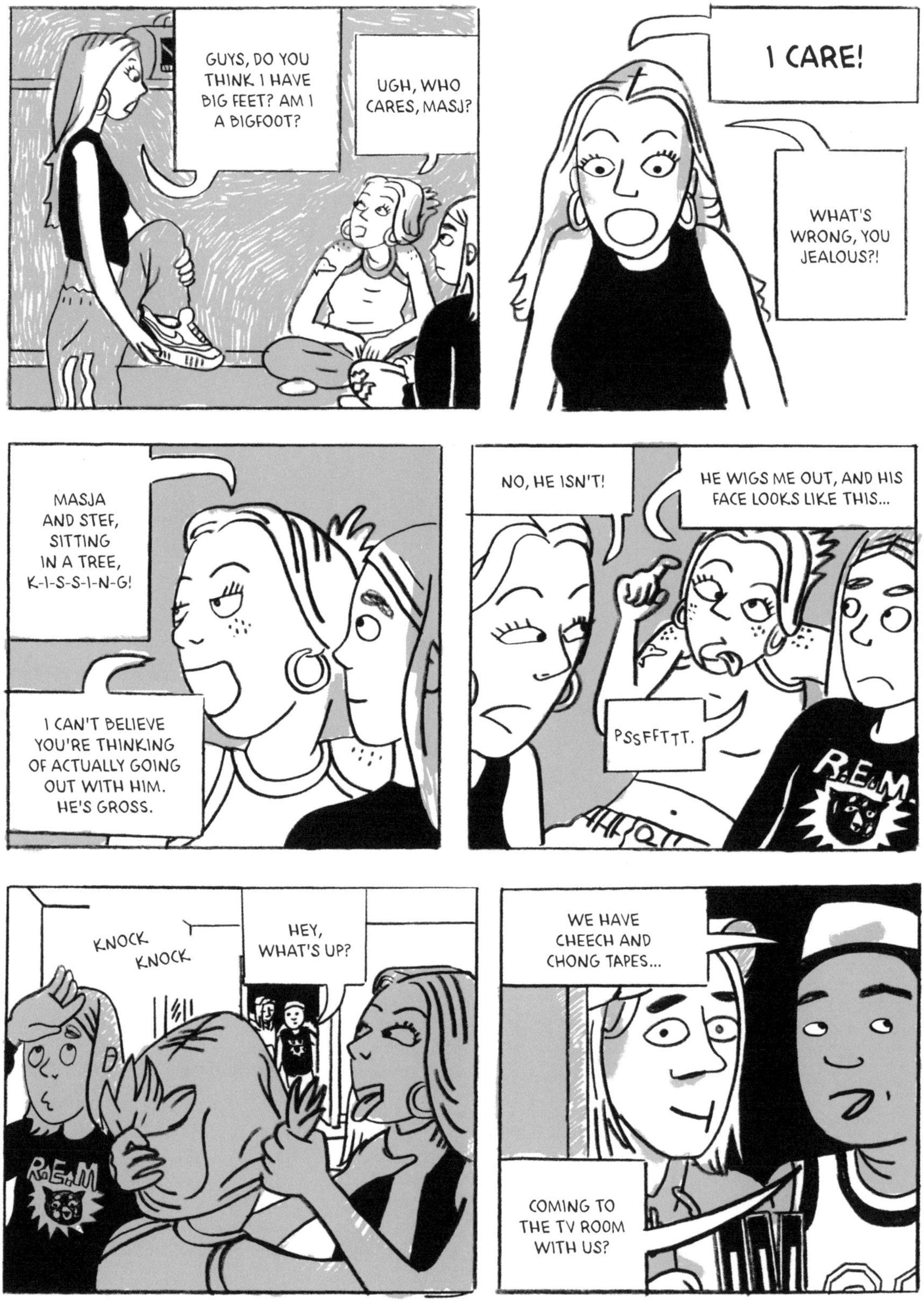
GUYS, DO YOU THINK I HAVE BIG FEET? AM I A BIGFOOT?
UGH, WHO CARES, MASJ?
I CARE!
WHAT'S WRONG, YOU JEALOUS?!
MASJA AND STEF, SITTING IN A TREE, K-I-S-S-I-N-G!
I CAN'T BELIEVE YOU'RE THINKING OF ACTUALLY GOING OUT WITH HIM. HE'S GROSS.
NO, HE ISN'T!
HE WIGS ME OUT, AND HIS FACE LOOKS LIKE THIS...
PSSFFTTT.
R.E.M.
KNOCK KNOCK
HEY, WHAT'S UP?
R.E.M
WE HAVE CHEECH AND CHONG TAPES...
COMING TO THE TV ROOM WITH US?

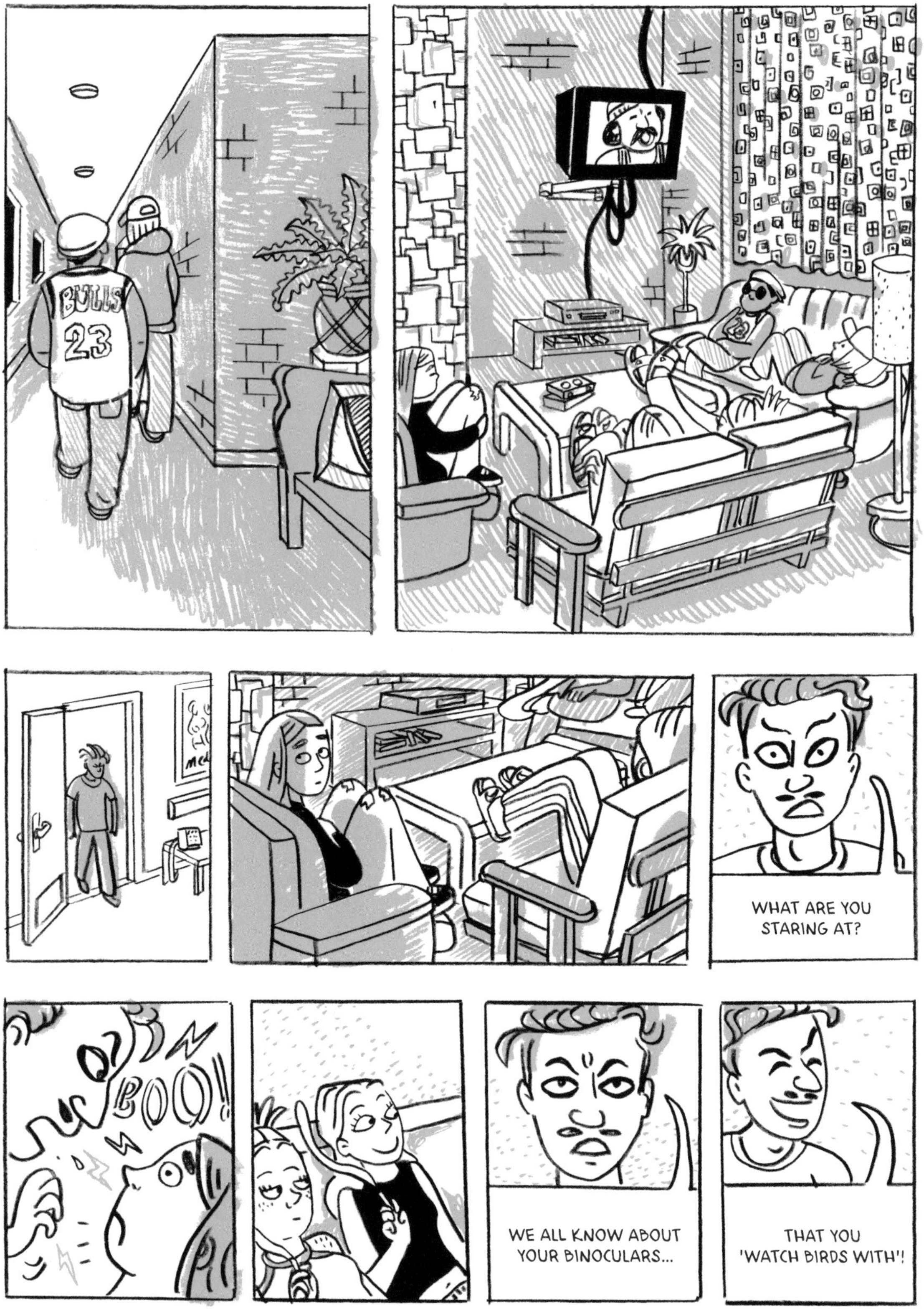
BULLS
23
WHAT ARE YOU STARING AT?
BOO!!
WE ALL KNOW ABOUT YOUR BINOCULARS...
THAT YOU 'WATCH BIRDS WITH'!

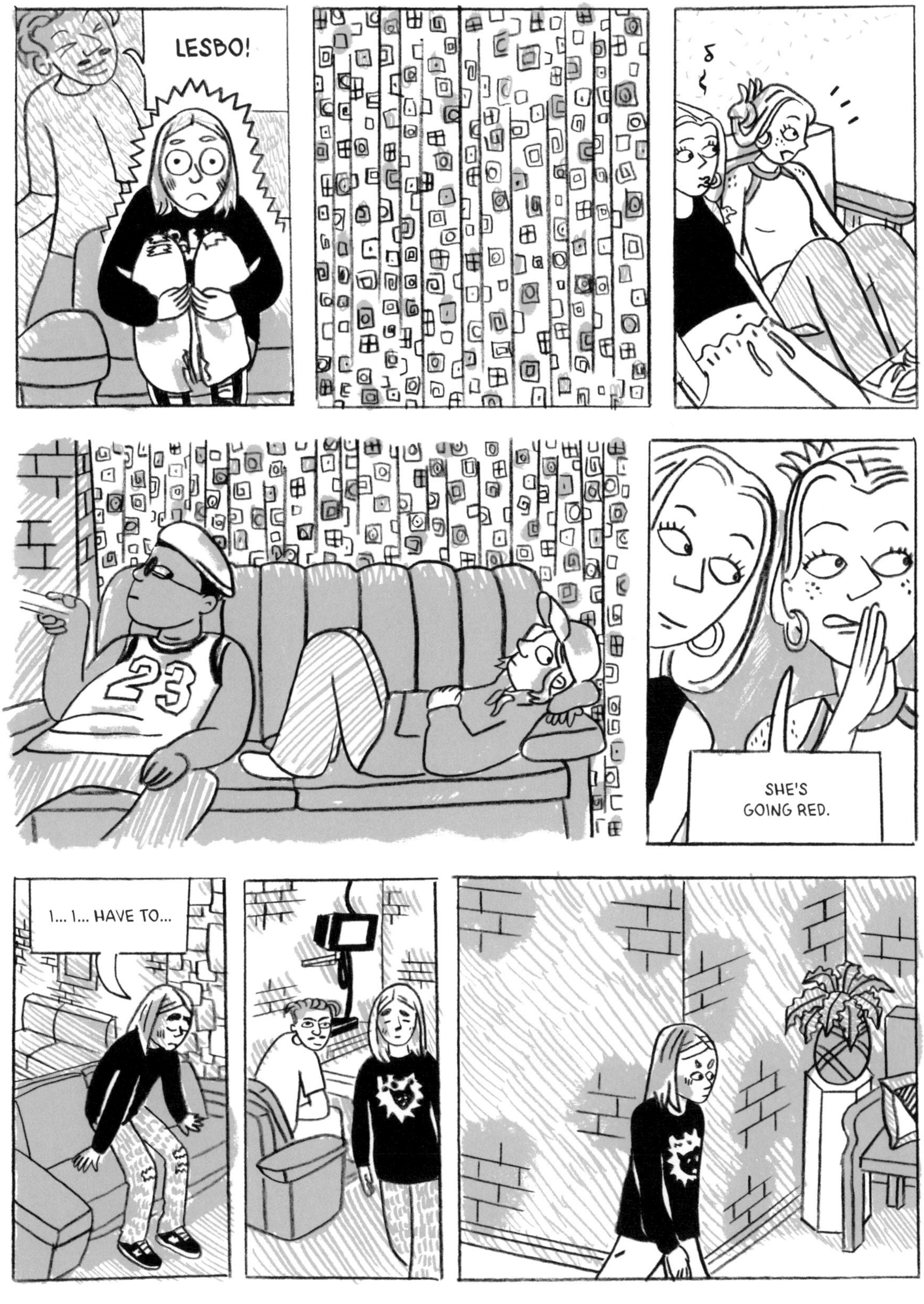
LESBO!
SHE'S GOING RED.
I... I... HAVE TO...

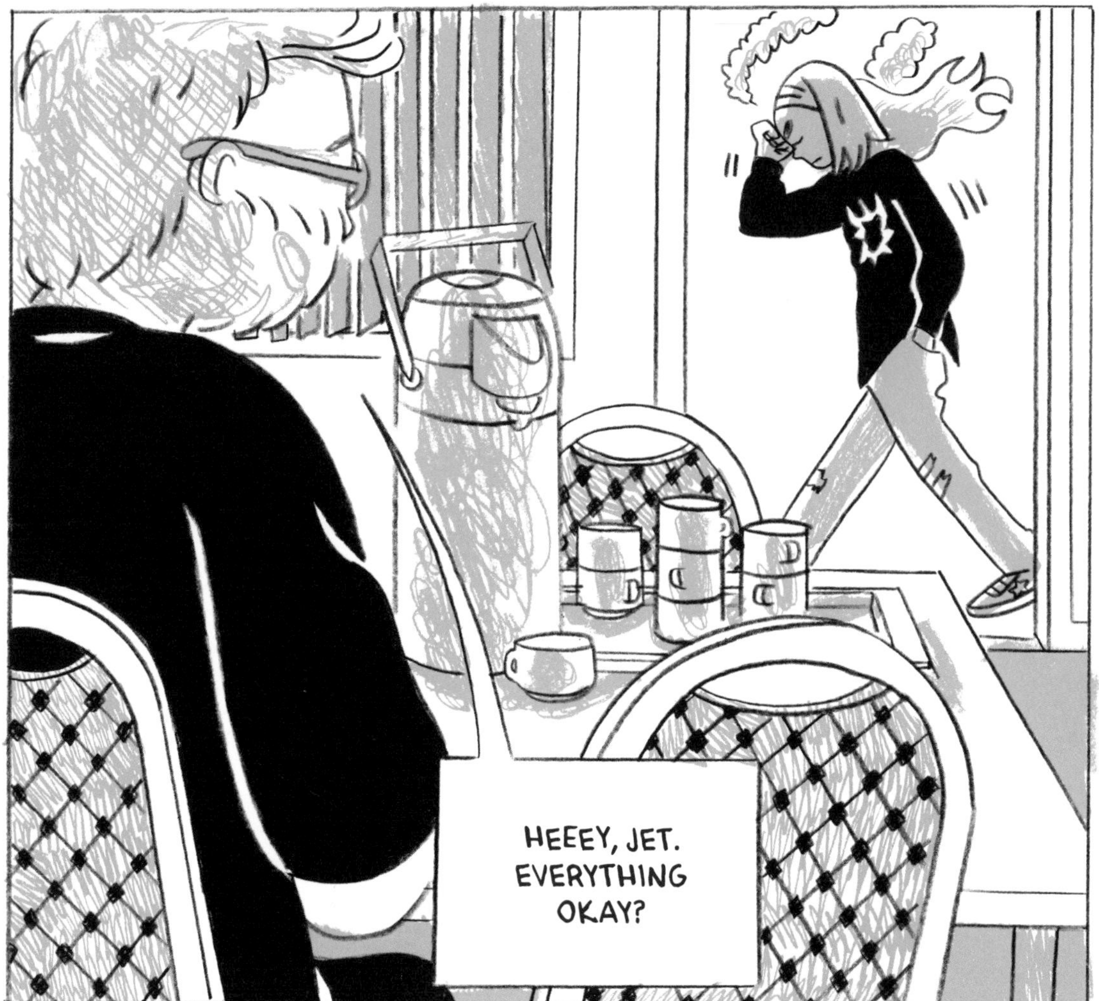
HEEEY, JET.
EVERYTHING
OKAY?

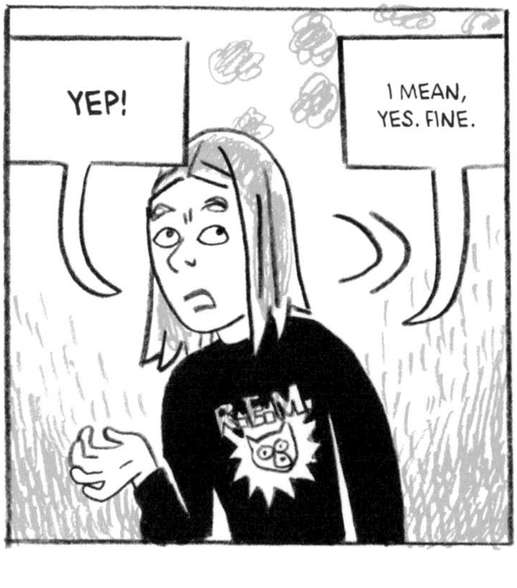
YEP!
I MEAN,
YES. FINE.
R.E.M.

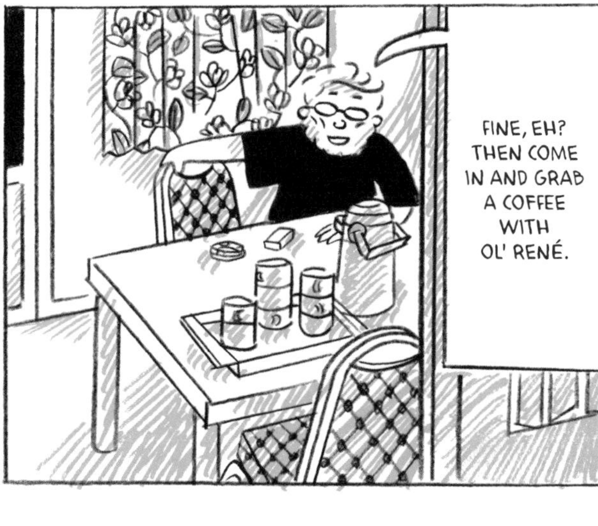
FINE, EH?
THEN COME
IN AND GRAB
A COFFEE
WITH
OL' RENÉ.

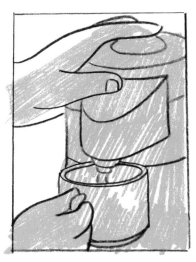

MY MOM USED TO SAY THAT IF EVERYTHING IS SUDDENLY COMING AT YOU...

THEN YOU'RE DRIVING ON THE WRONG SIDE OF THE ROAD.

I DON'T KNOW...
...SOMETIMES—

RENÉ?

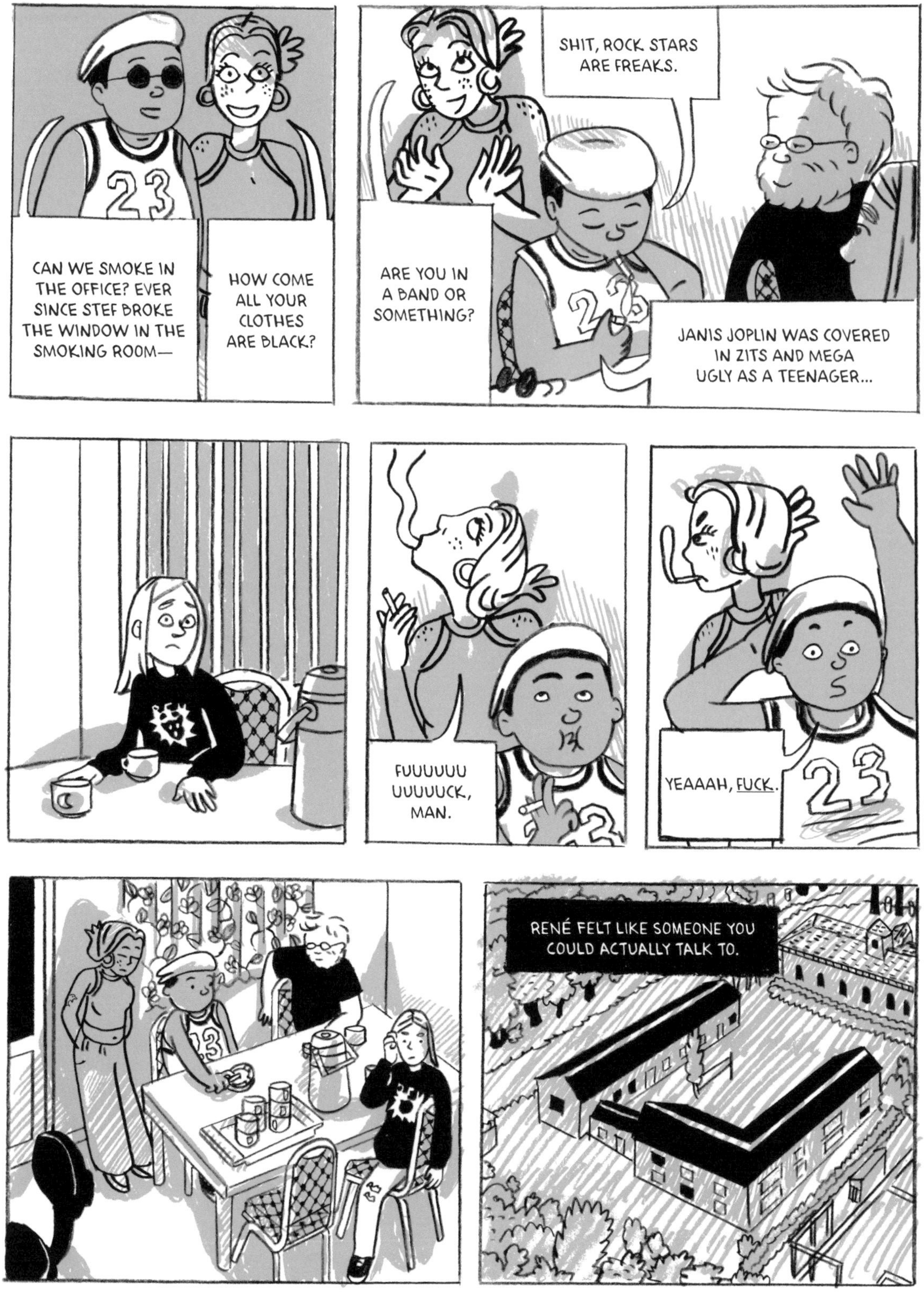
CAN WE SMOKE IN THE OFFICE? EVER SINCE STEF BROKE THE WINDOW IN THE SMOKING ROOM—
HOW COME ALL YOUR CLOTHES ARE BLACK?
ARE YOU IN A BAND OR SOMETHING?
SHIT, ROCK STARS ARE FREAKS.
JANIS JOPLIN WAS COVERED IN ZITS AND MEGA UGLY AS A TEENAGER...
FUUUUUU UUUUUCK, MAN.
YEAAAH, FUCK.
RENÉ FELT LIKE SOMEONE YOU COULD ACTUALLY TALK TO.

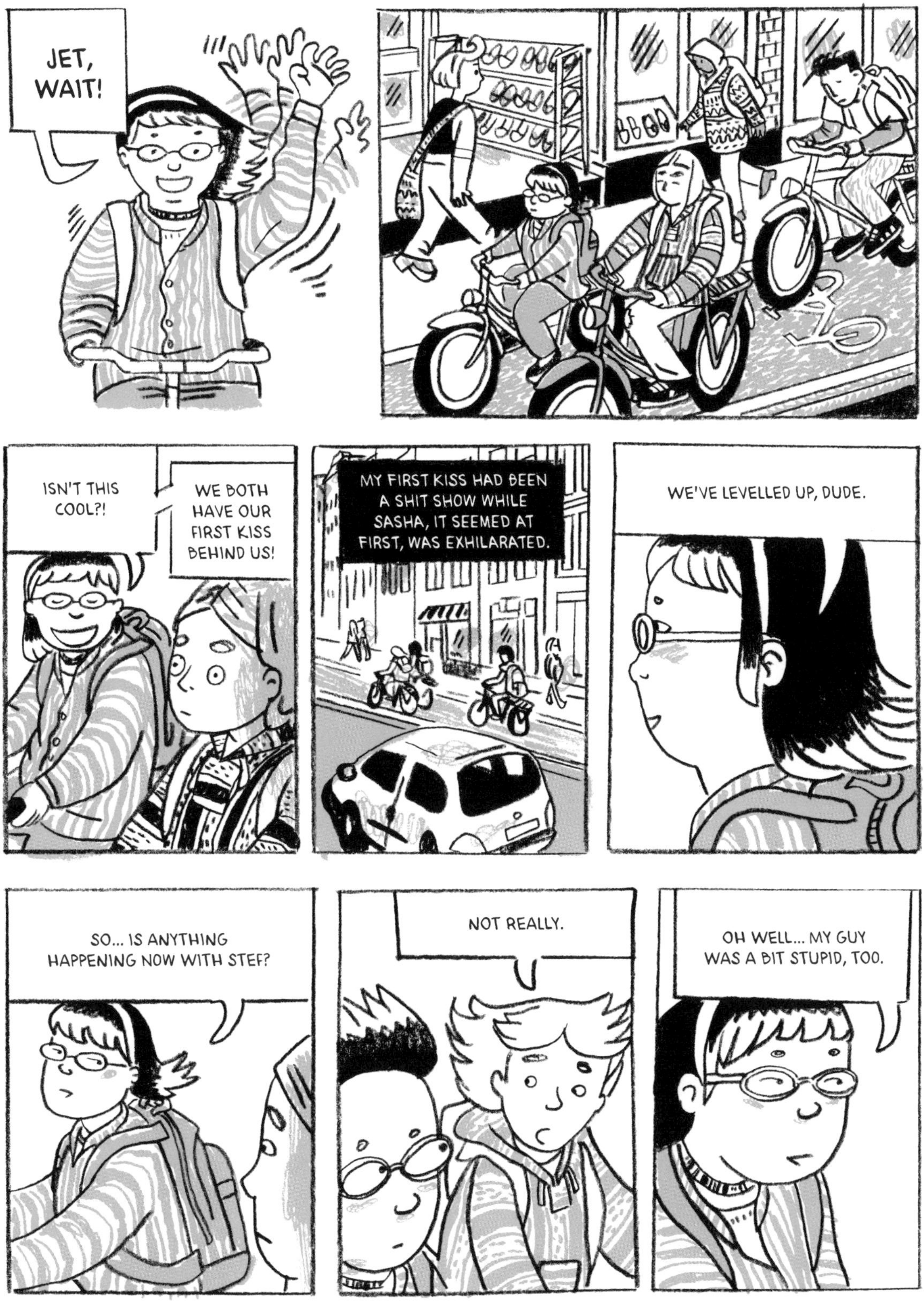
JET, WAIT!
ISN'T THIS COOL?!
WE BOTH HAVE OUR FIRST KISS BEHIND US!
MY FIRST KISS HAD BEEN A SHIT SHOW WHILE SASHA, IT SEEMED AT FIRST, WAS EXHILARATED.
WE'VE LEVELLED UP, DUDE.
SO... IS ANYTHING HAPPENING NOW WITH STEF?
NOT REALLY.
OH WELL... MY GUY WAS A BIT STUPID, TOO.

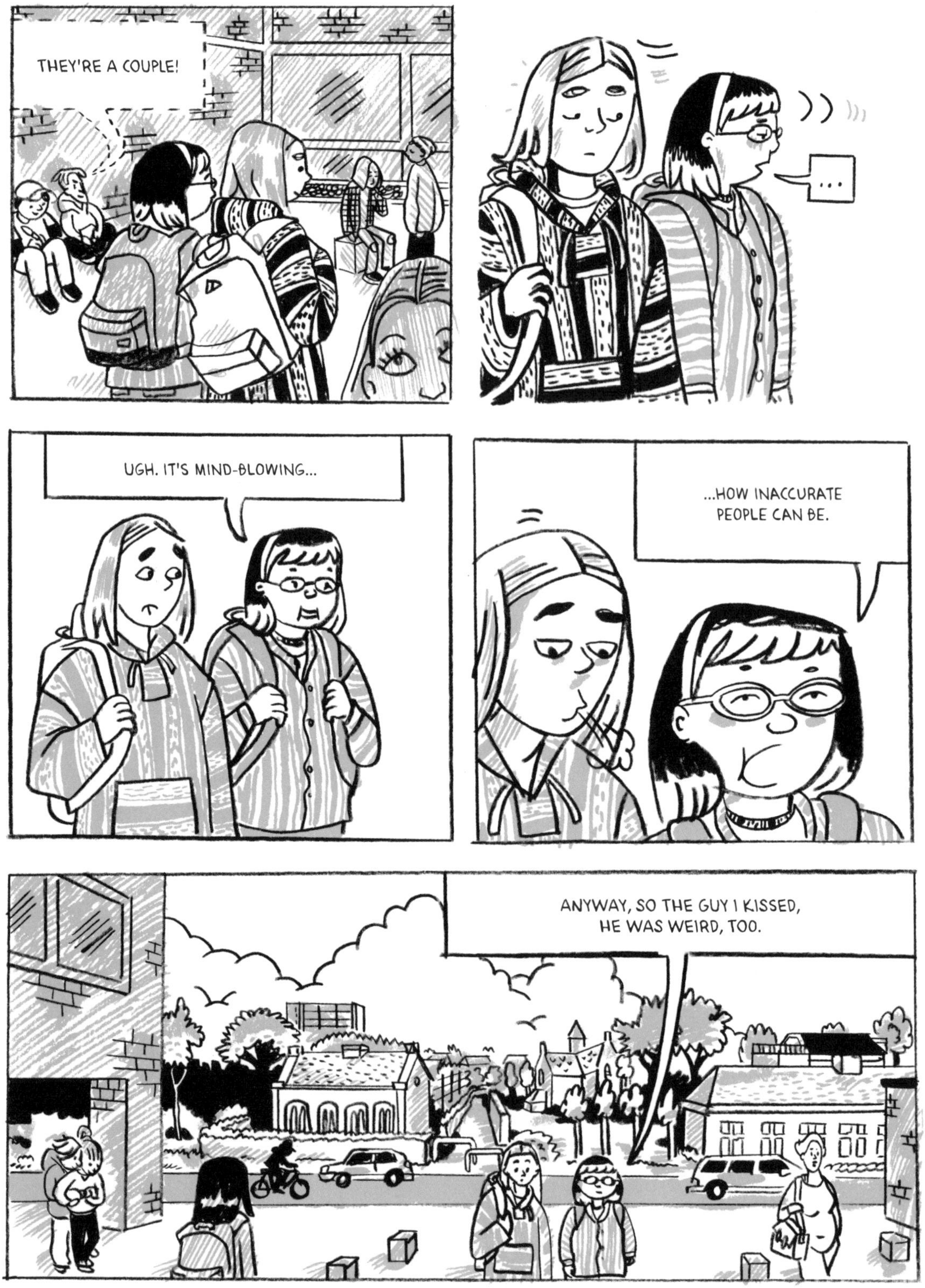
THEY'RE A COUPLE!
...
UGH. IT'S MIND-BLOWING...
...HOW INACCURATE PEOPLE CAN BE.
ANYWAY, SO THE GUY I KISSED, HE WAS WEIRD, TOO.

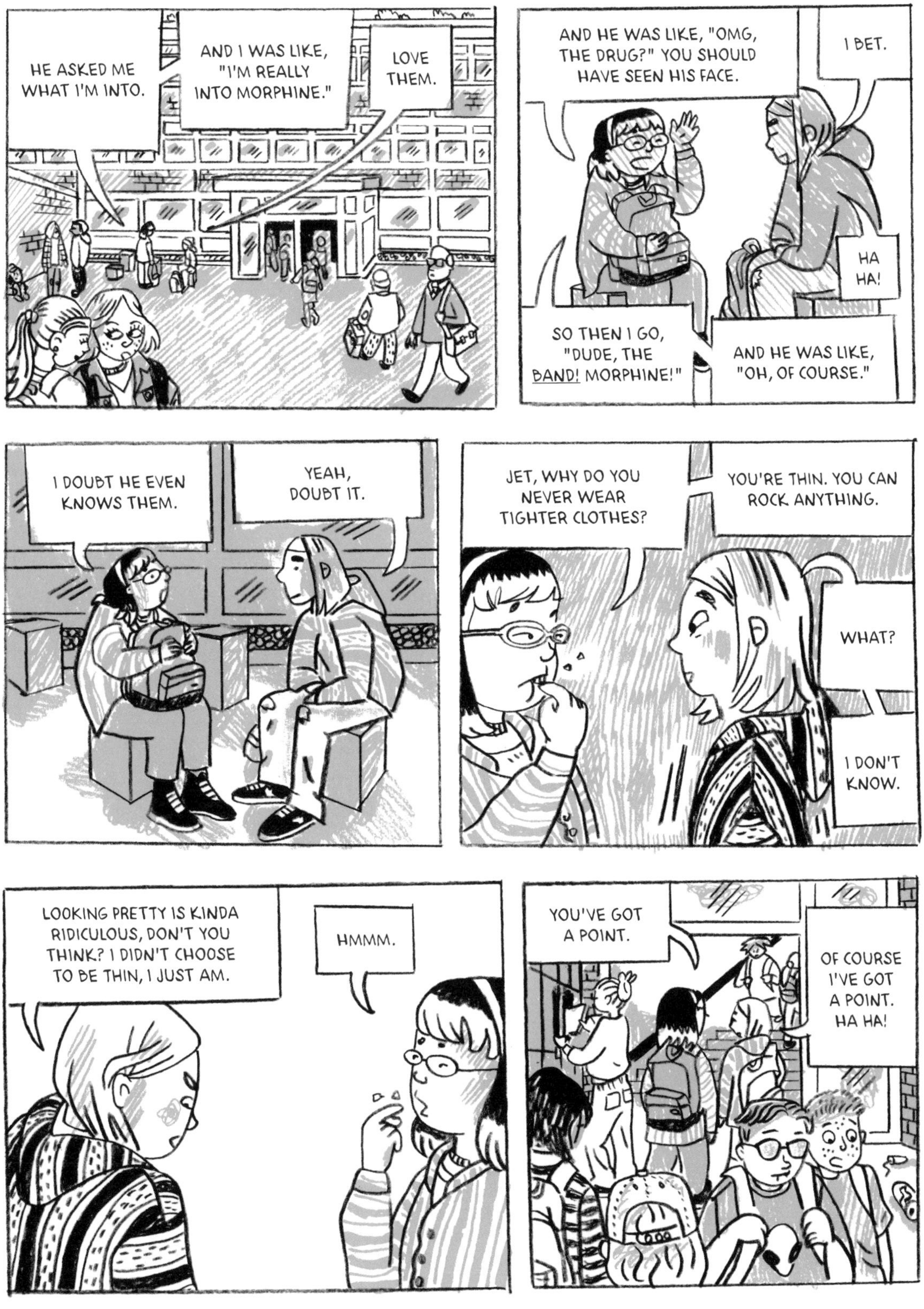

HE ASKED ME WHAT I'M INTO.
AND I WAS LIKE, "I'M REALLY INTO MORPHINE."
LOVE THEM.
AND HE WAS LIKE, "OMG, THE DRUG?" YOU SHOULD HAVE SEEN HIS FACE.
I BET.
HA HA!
SO THEN I GO, "DUDE, THE BAND! MORPHINE!"
AND HE WAS LIKE, "OH, OF COURSE."
I DOUBT HE EVEN KNOWS THEM.
YEAH, DOUBT IT.
JET, WHY DO YOU NEVER WEAR TIGHTER CLOTHES?
YOU'RE THIN. YOU CAN ROCK ANYTHING.
WHAT?
I DON'T KNOW.
LOOKING PRETTY IS KINDA RIDICULOUS, DON'T YOU THINK? I DIDN'T CHOOSE TO BE THIN, I JUST AM.
HMMM.
YOU'VE GOT A POINT.
OF COURSE I'VE GOT A POINT. HA HA!

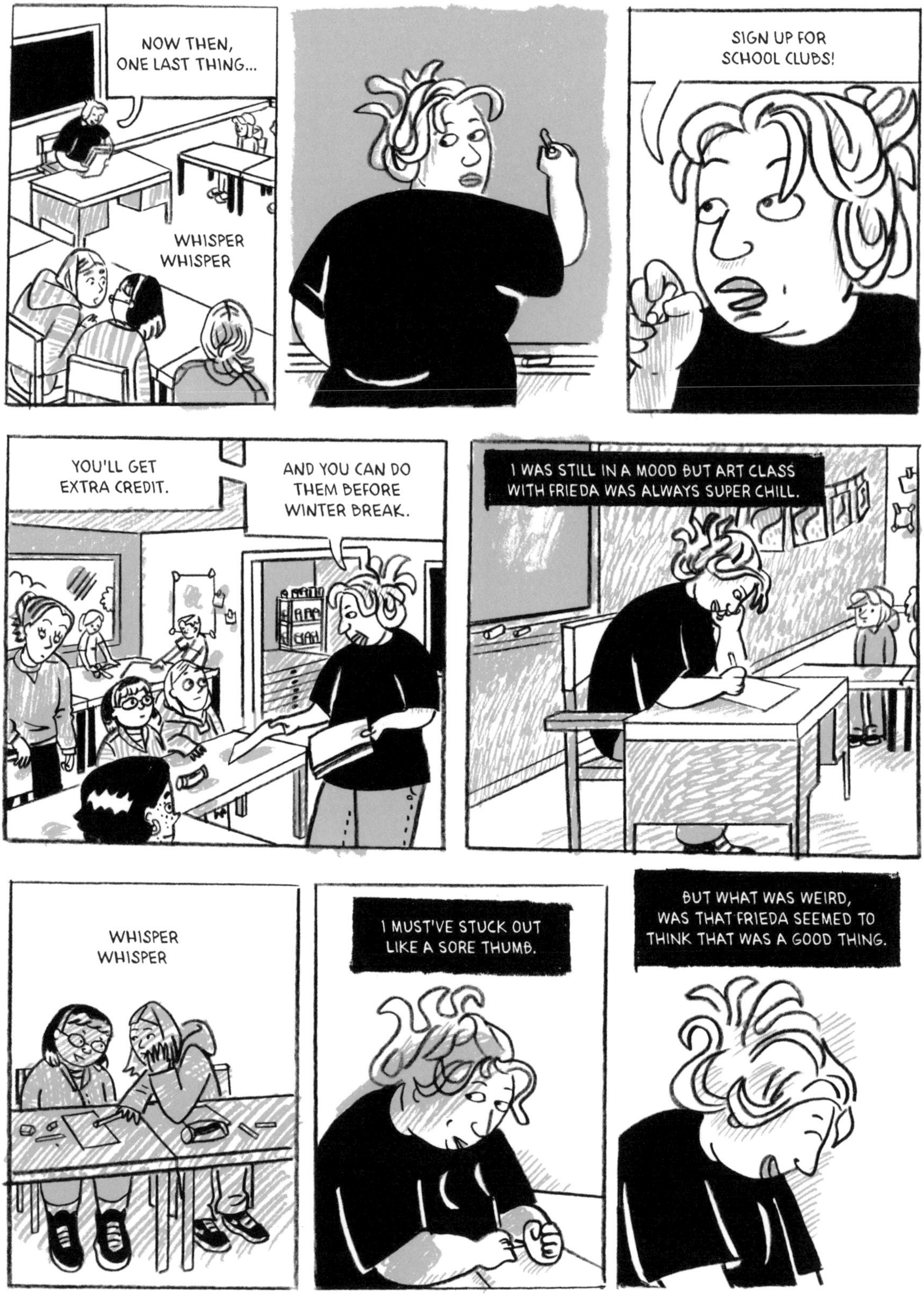

NOW THEN, ONE LAST THING...
WHISPER WHISPER
SIGN UP FOR SCHOOL CLUBS!
YOU'LL GET EXTRA CREDIT.
AND YOU CAN DO THEM BEFORE WINTER BREAK.
I WAS STILL IN A MOOD BUT ART CLASS WITH FRIEDA WAS ALWAYS SUPER CHILL.
WHISPER WHISPER
I MUST'VE STUCK OUT LIKE A SORE THUMB.
BUT WHAT WAS WEIRD, WAS THAT FRIEDA SEEMED TO THINK THAT WAS A GOOD THING.

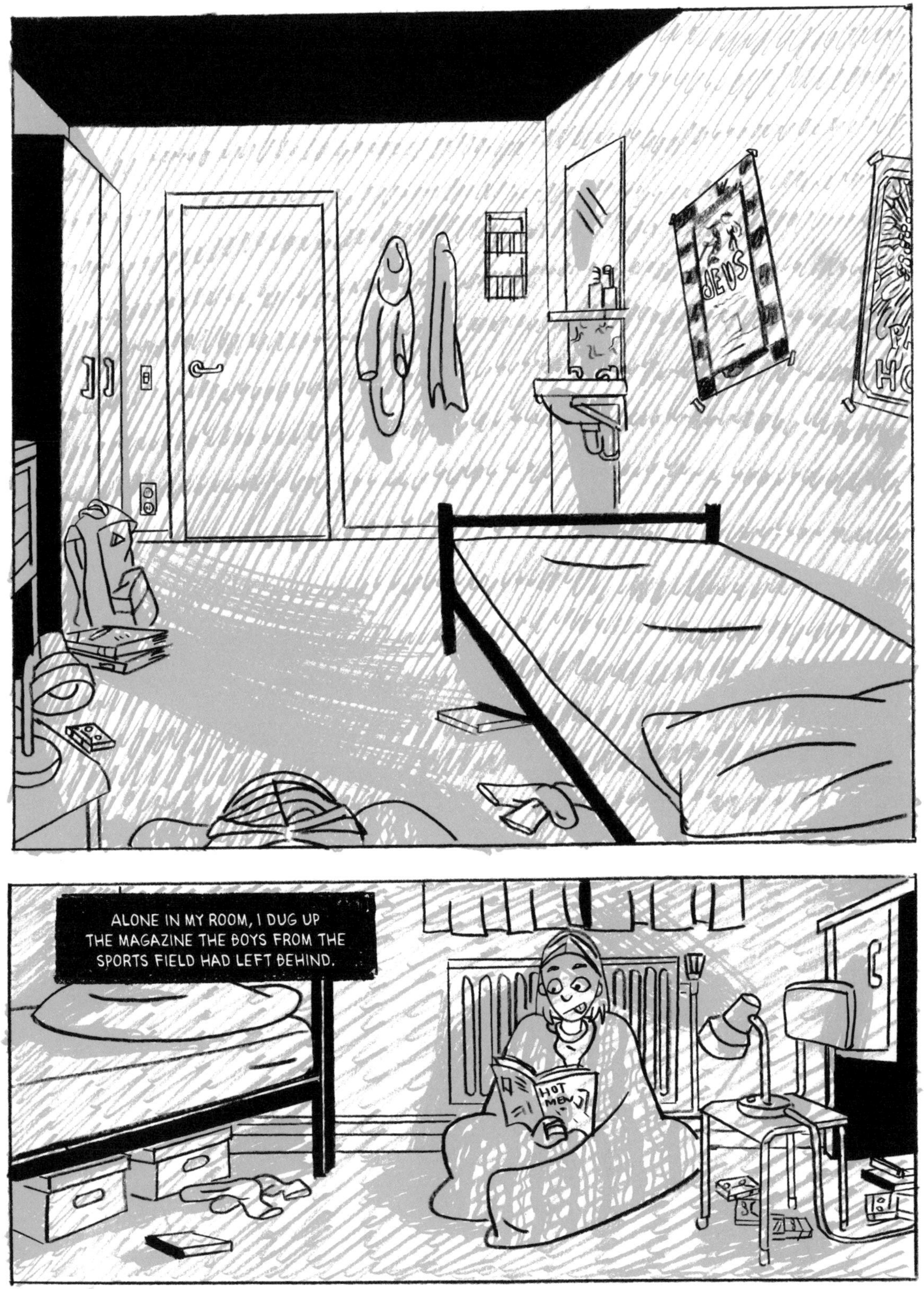
ALONE IN MY ROOM, I DUG UP THE MAGAZINE THE BOYS FROM THE SPORTS FIELD HAD LEFT BEHIND.

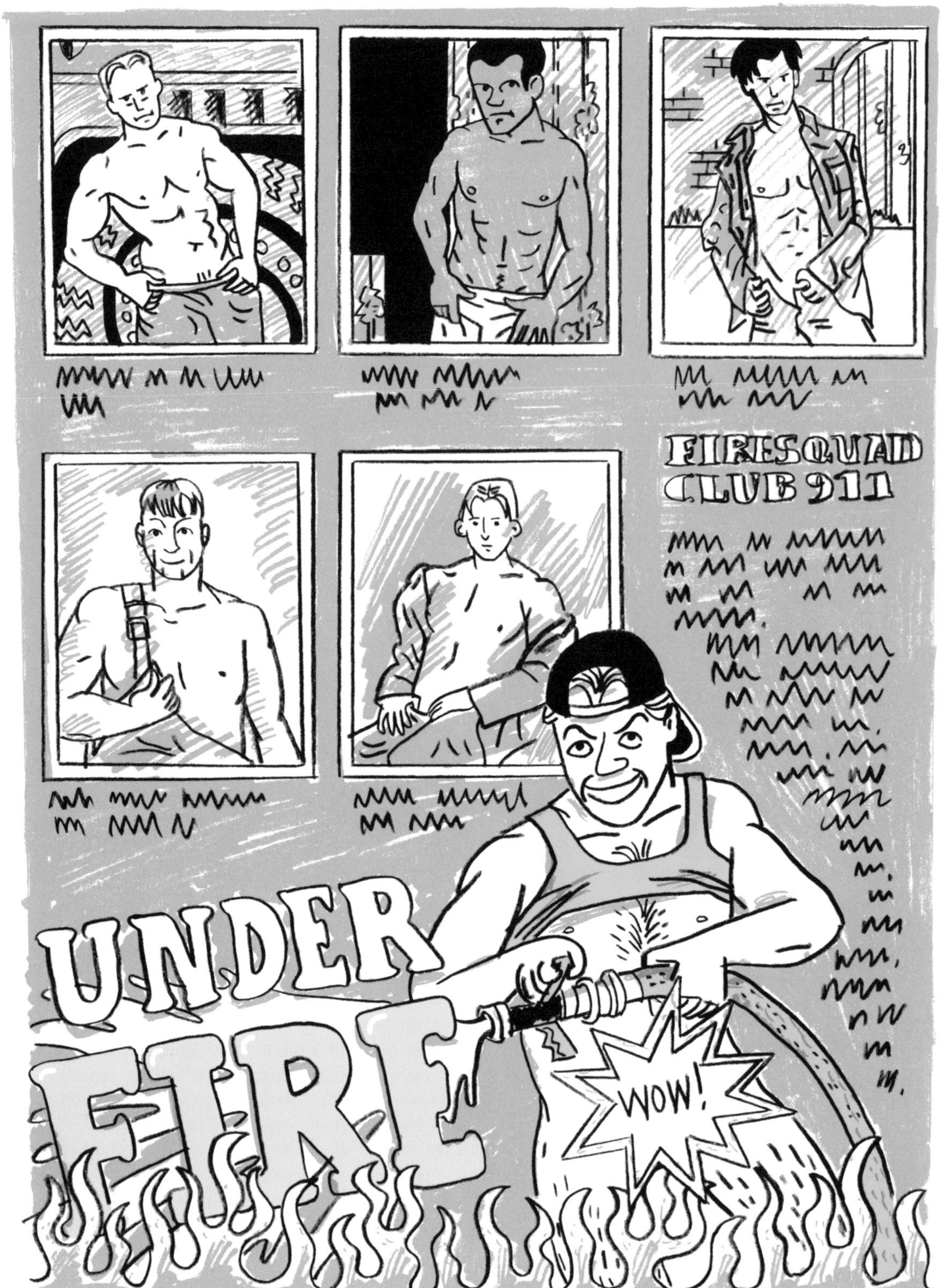
FIRESQUAD
CLUB 911
UNDER
FIRE
WOW!

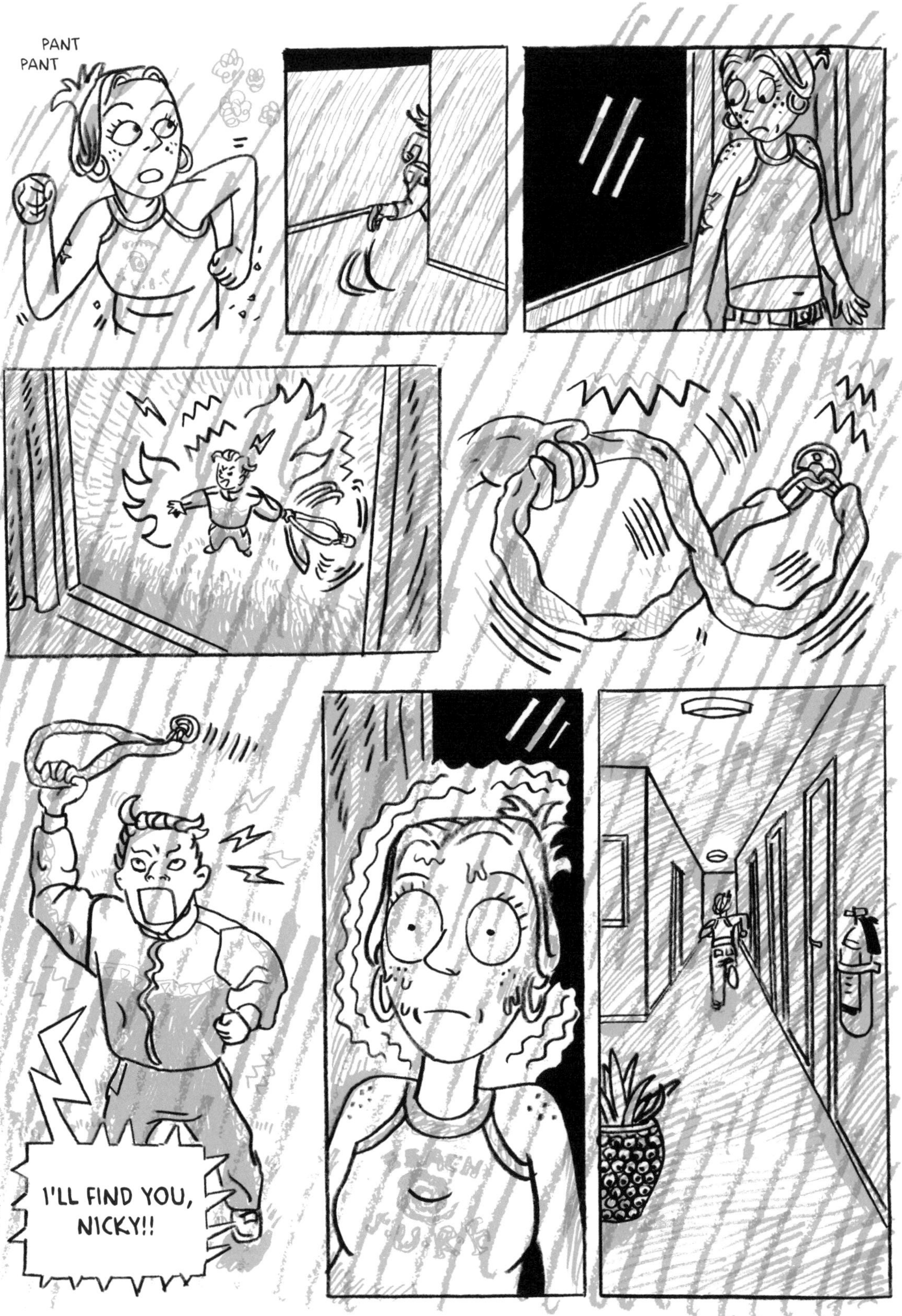
PANT
PANT
I'LL FIND YOU, NICKY!!

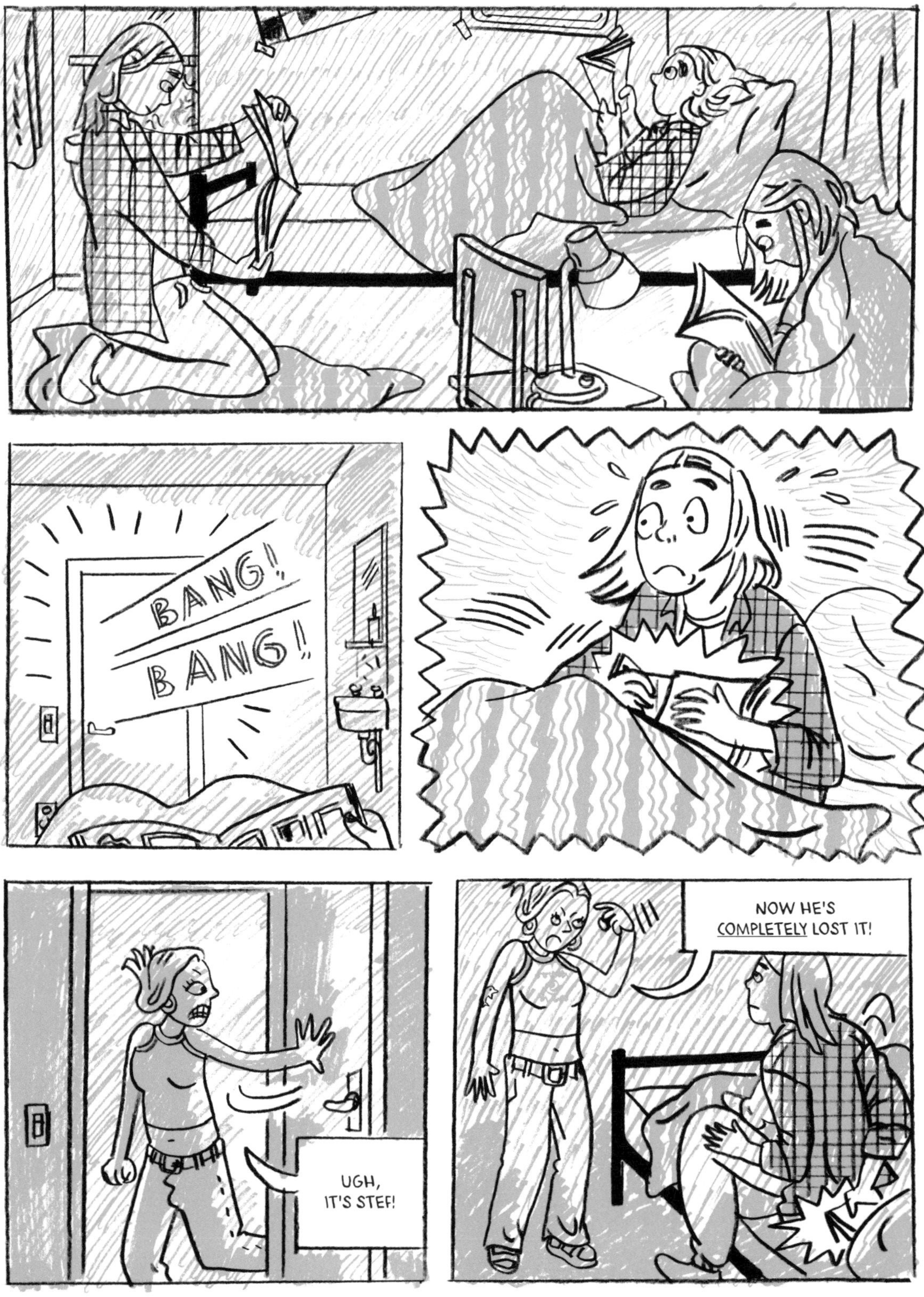
BANG!
BANG!
UGH, IT'S STEF!
NOW HE'S COMPLETELY LOST IT!

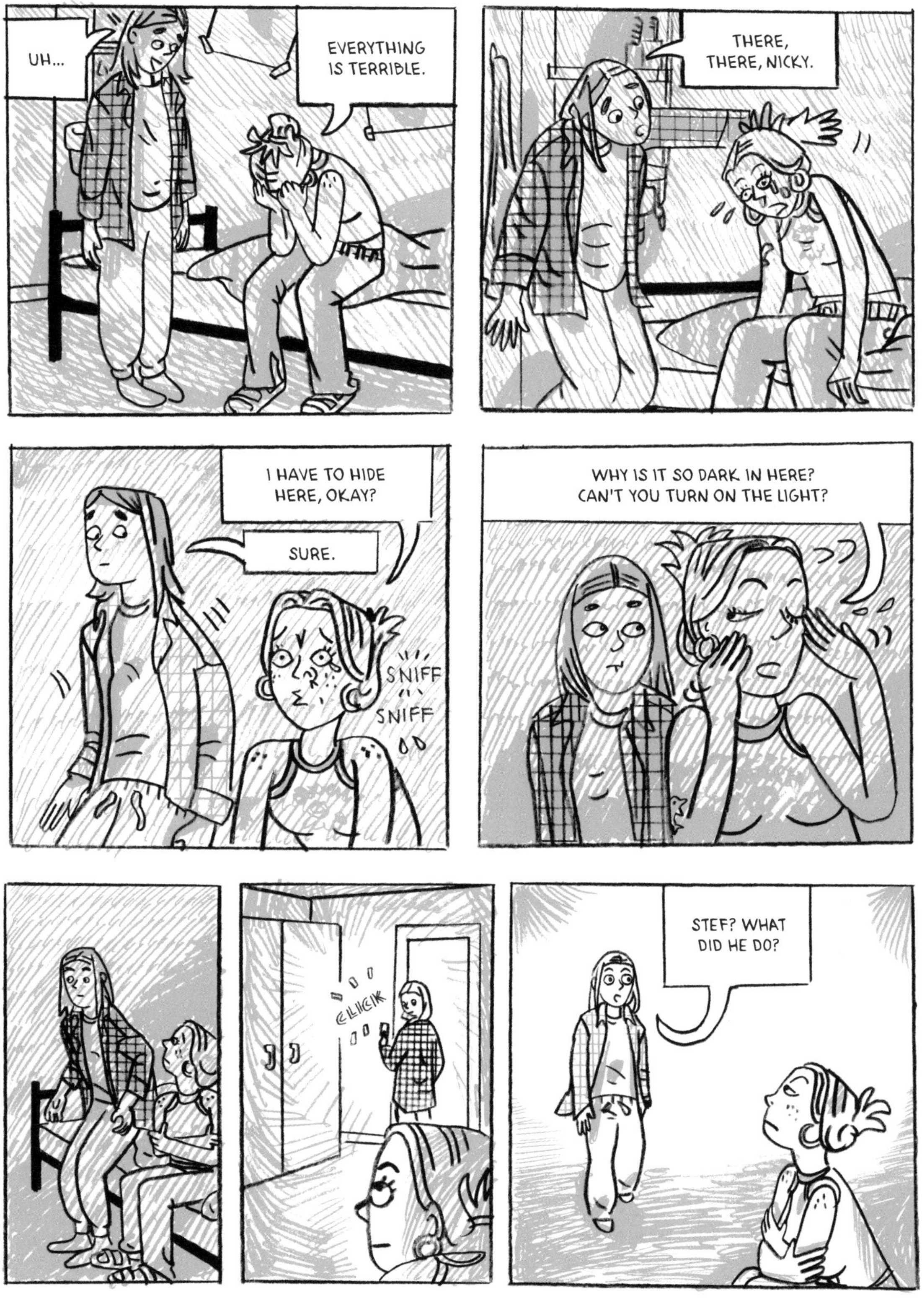
UH...
EVERYTHING IS TERRIBLE.
THERE, THERE, NICKY.
I HAVE TO HIDE HERE, OKAY?
SURE.
SNIFF
SNIFF
WHY IS IT SO DARK IN HERE? CAN'T YOU TURN ON THE LIGHT?
CLICK
STEF? WHAT DID HE DO?

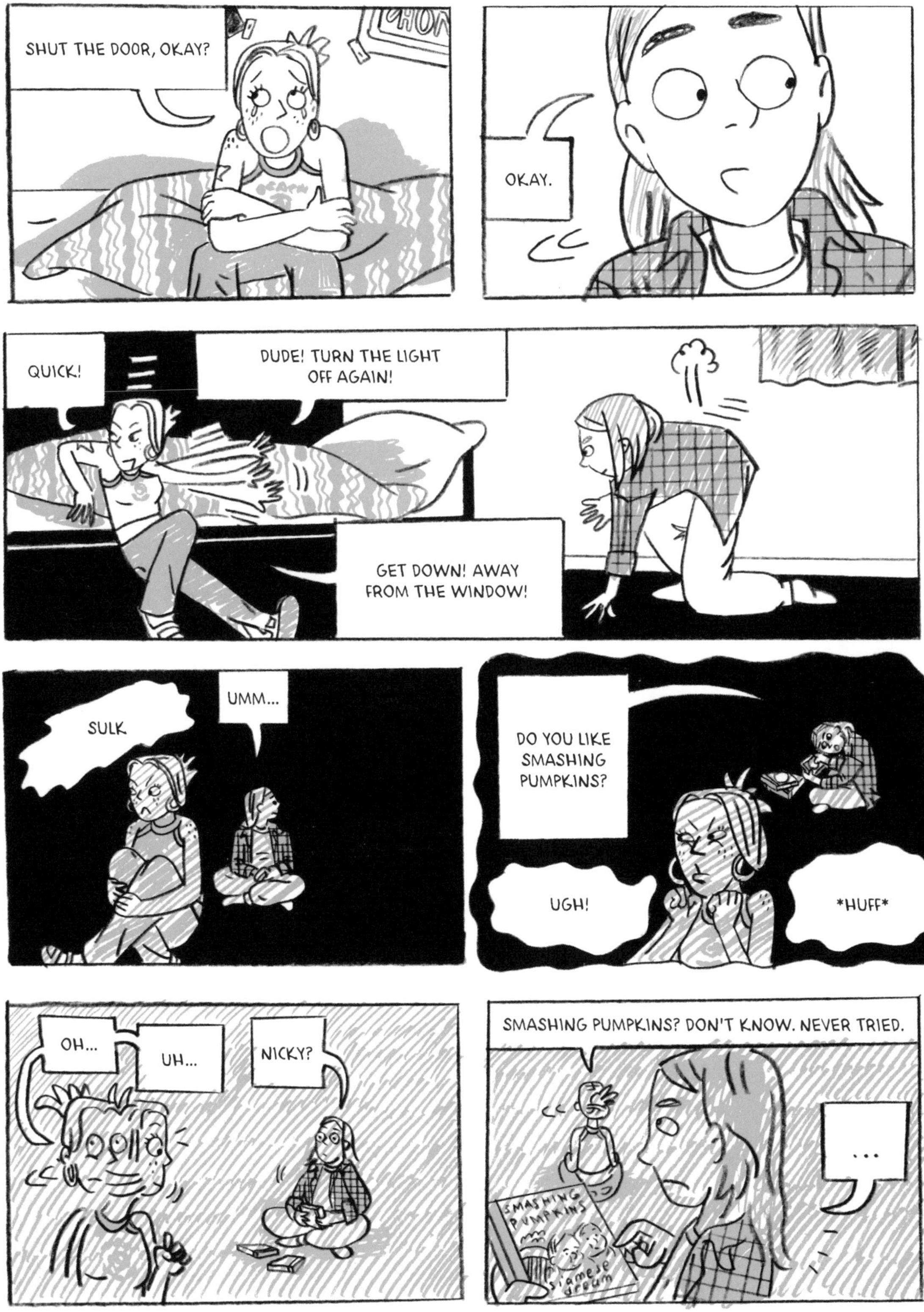
SHUT THE DOOR, OKAY?
OKAY.
QUICK!
DUDE! TURN THE LIGHT OFF AGAIN!
GET DOWN! AWAY FROM THE WINDOW!
SULK.
UMM...
DO YOU LIKE SMASHING PUMPKINS?
UGH!
HUFF
OH...
UH...
NICKY?
SMASHING PUMPKINS? DON'T KNOW. NEVER TRIED.
...
SMASHING PUMPKINS
siamese dream

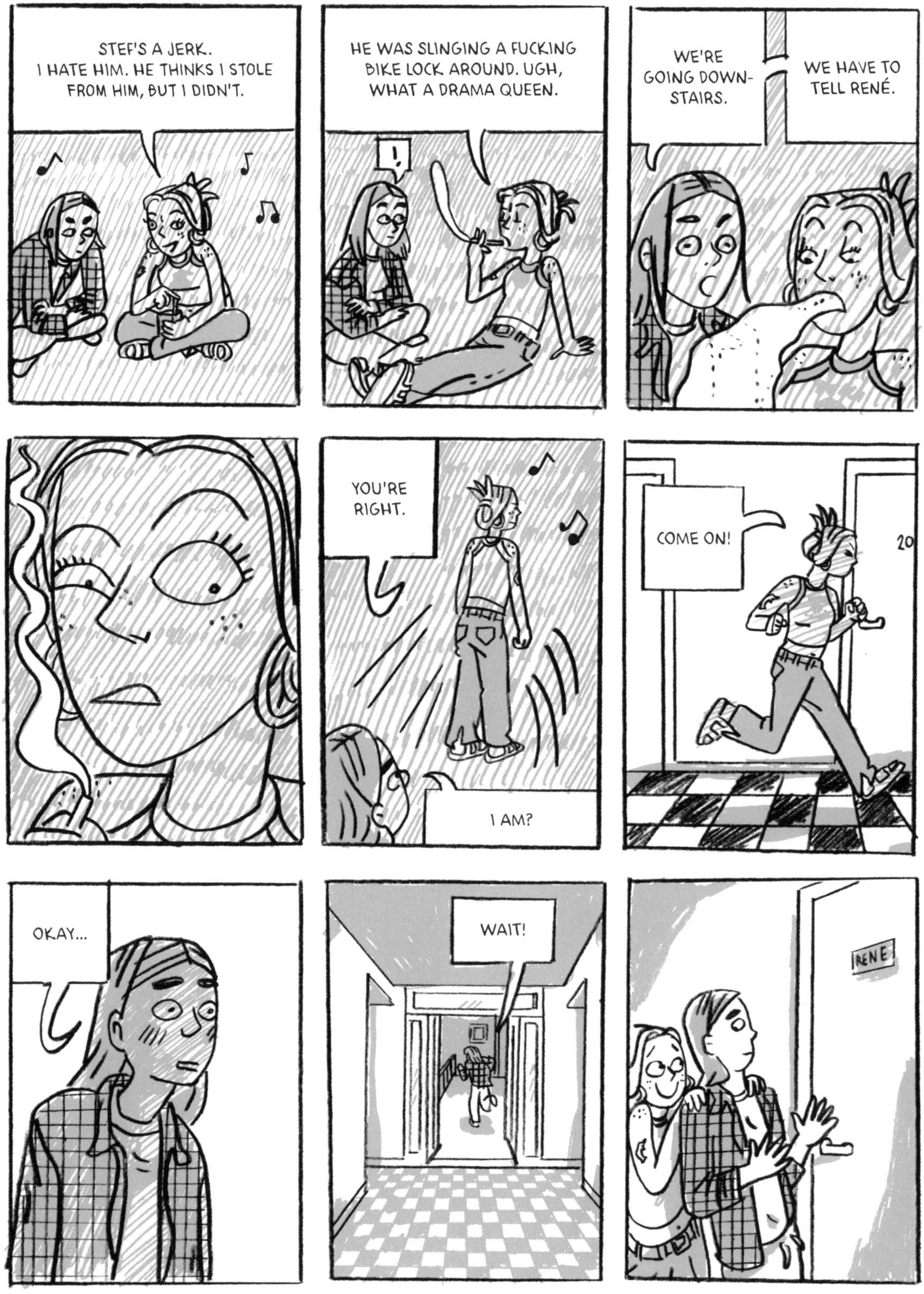
STEF'S A JERK. I HATE HIM. HE THINKS I STOLE FROM HIM, BUT I DIDN'T.
!
HE WAS SLINGING A FUCKING BIKE LOCK AROUND. UGH, WHAT A DRAMA QUEEN.
WE'RE GOING DOWN-STAIRS.
WE HAVE TO TELL RENÉ.
YOU'RE RIGHT.
I AM?
COME ON!
20
OKAY...
WAIT!
RENE

*"TODAY" BY SMASHING PUMPKINS

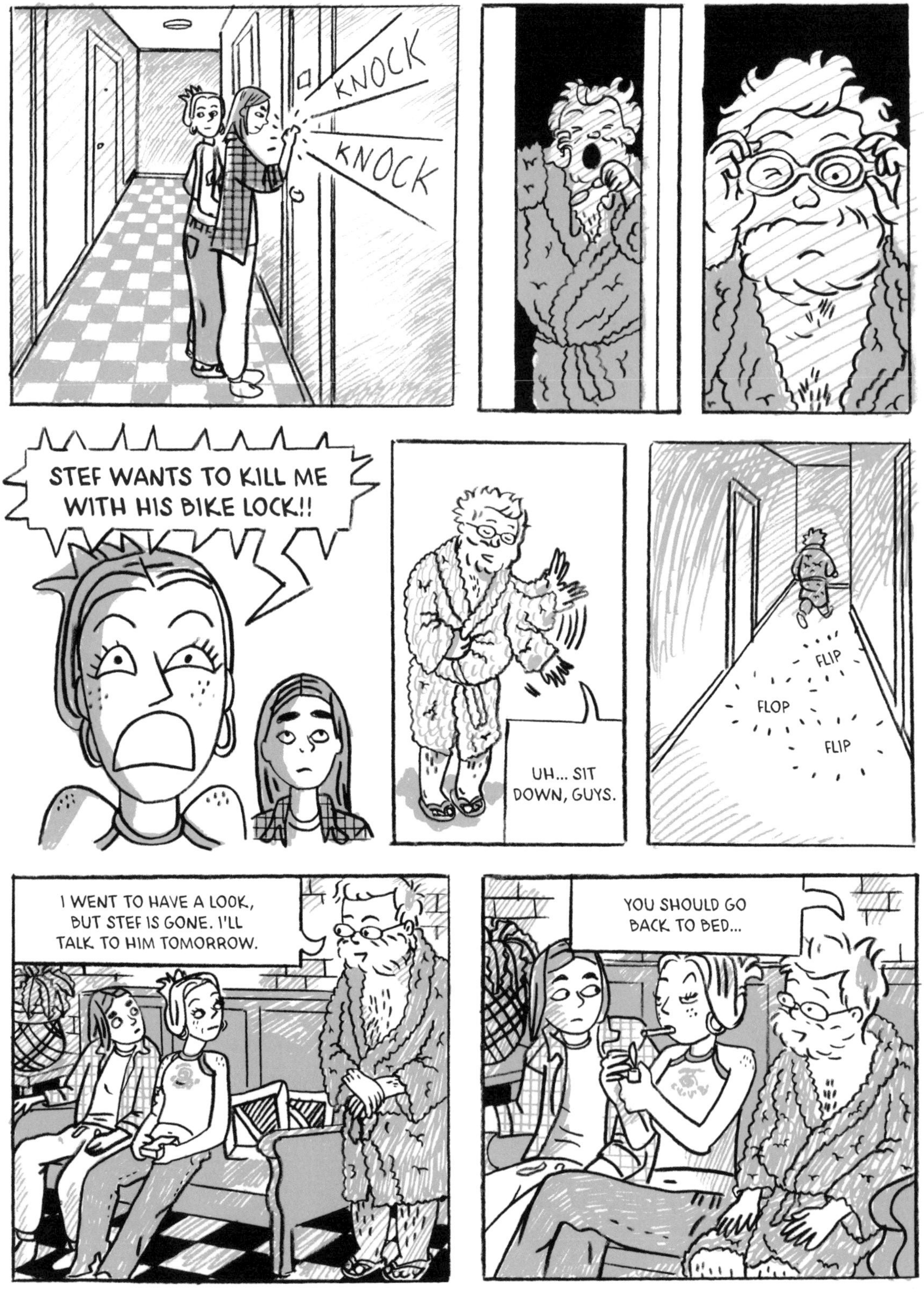
KNOCK
KNOCK
STEF WANTS TO KILL ME WITH HIS BIKE LOCK!!
UH... SIT DOWN, GUYS.
FLIP
FLOP
FLIP
I WENT TO HAVE A LOOK, BUT STEF IS GONE. I'LL TALK TO HIM TOMORROW.
YOU SHOULD GO BACK TO BED...

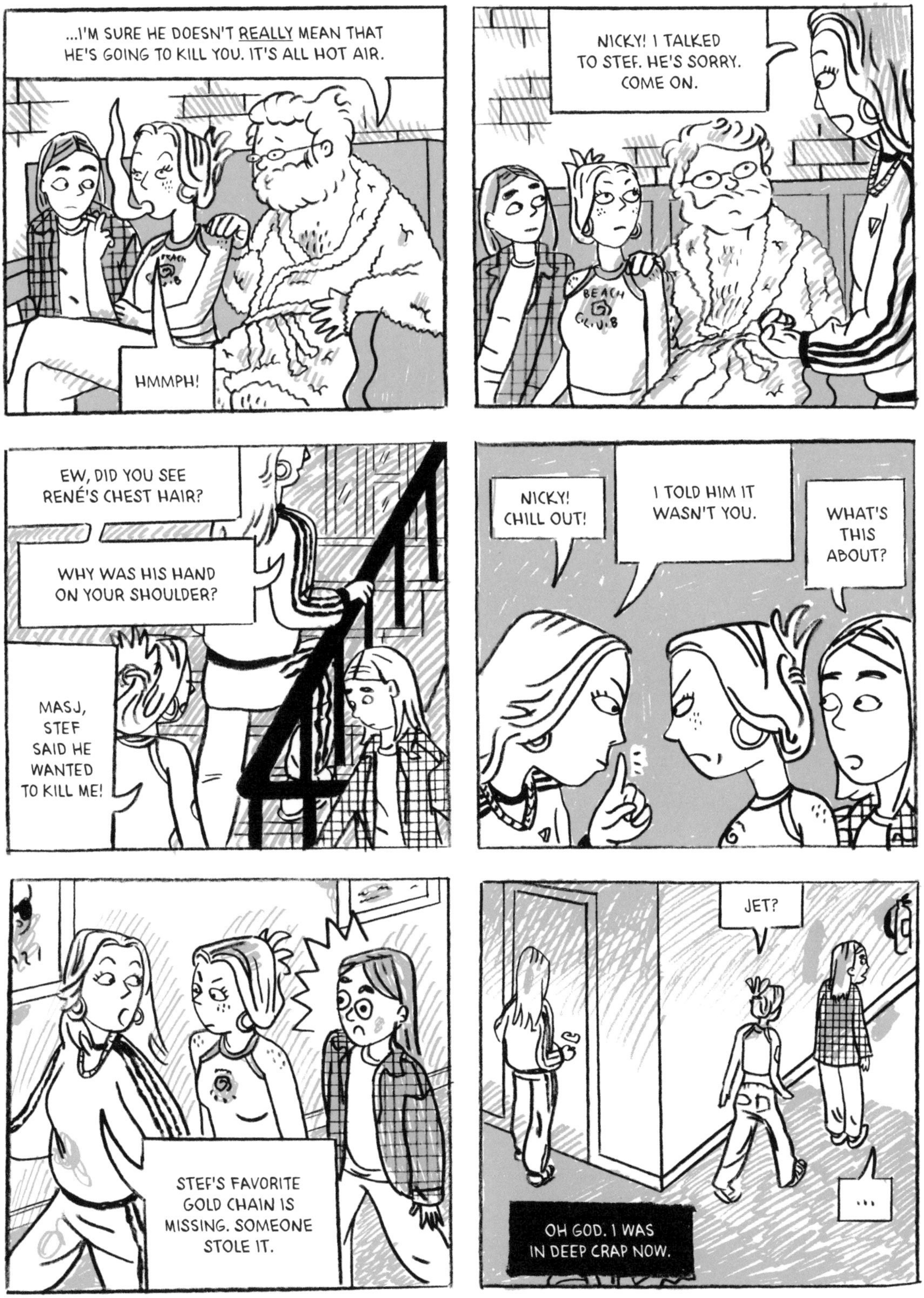

...I'M SURE HE DOESN'T REALLY MEAN THAT HE'S GOING TO KILL YOU. IT'S ALL HOT AIR.
HMMPH!
NICKY! I TALKED TO STEF. HE'S SORRY. COME ON.
EW, DID YOU SEE RENÉ'S CHEST HAIR?
WHY WAS HIS HAND ON YOUR SHOULDER?
MASJ, STEF SAID HE WANTED TO KILL ME!
NICKY! CHILL OUT!
I TOLD HIM IT WASN'T YOU.
WHAT'S THIS ABOUT?
STEF'S FAVORITE GOLD CHAIN IS MISSING. SOMEONE STOLE IT.
JET?
...
OH GOD. I WAS IN DEEP CRAP NOW.

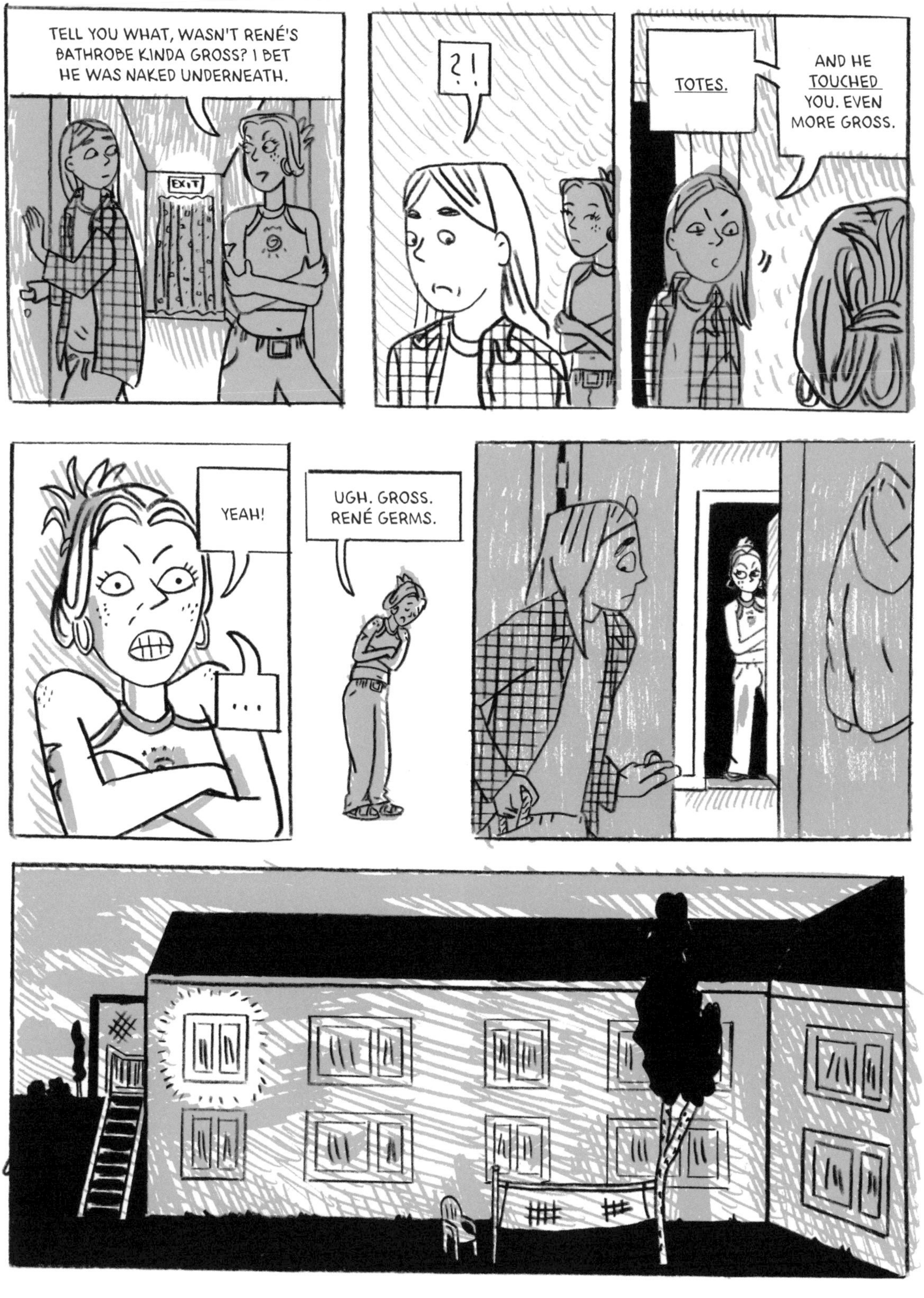
TELL YOU WHAT, WASN'T RENÉ'S BATHROBE KINDA GROSS? I BET HE WAS NAKED UNDERNEATH.
EXIT
?!
TOTES.
AND HE TOUCHED YOU. EVEN MORE GROSS.
YEAH!
...
UGH. GROSS. RENÉ GERMS.

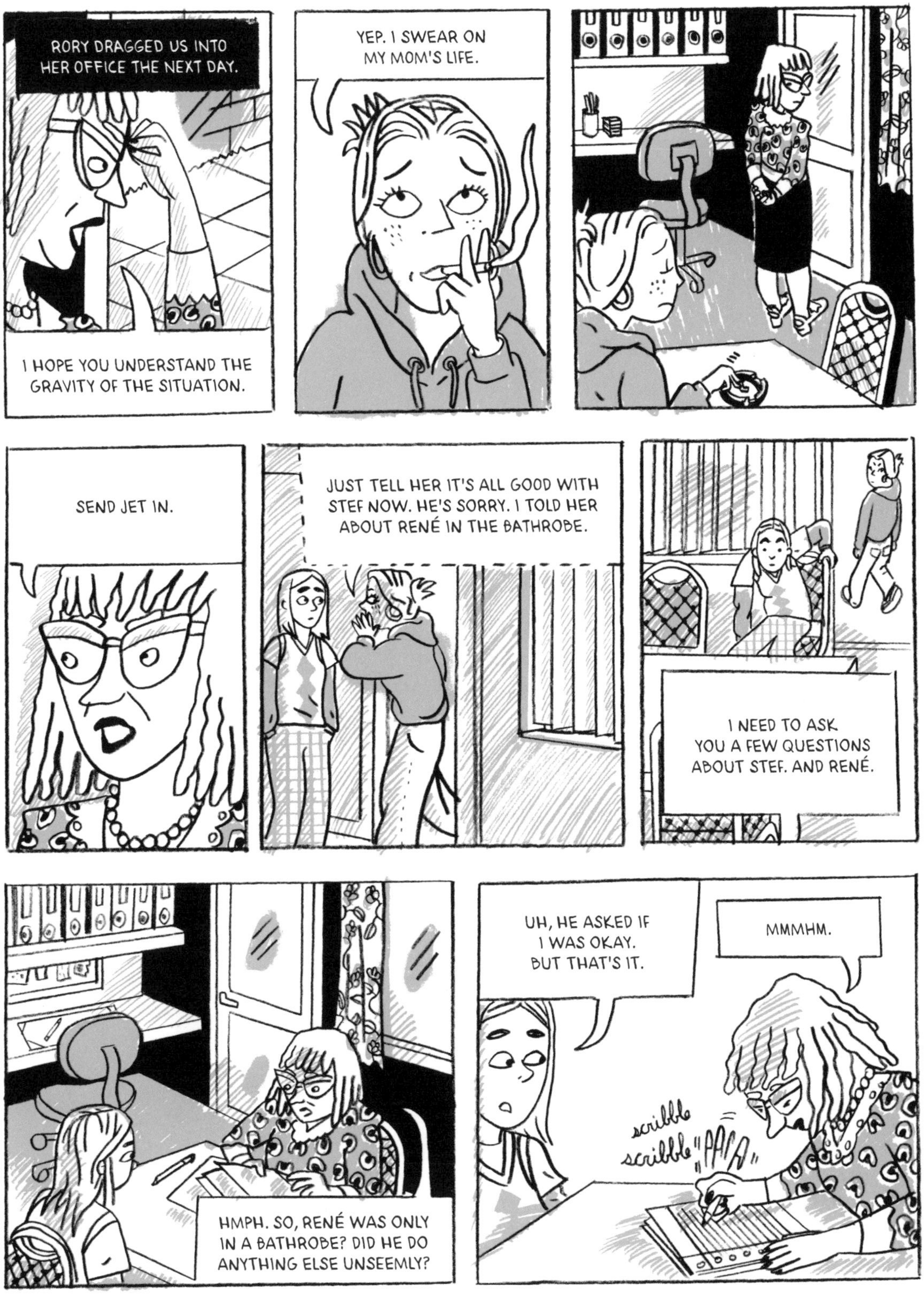
RORY DRAGGED US INTO HER OFFICE THE NEXT DAY.
I HOPE YOU UNDERSTAND THE GRAVITY OF THE SITUATION.
YEP. I SWEAR ON MY MOM'S LIFE.
SEND JET IN.
JUST TELL HER IT'S ALL GOOD WITH STEF NOW. HE'S SORRY. I TOLD HER ABOUT RENÉ IN THE BATHROBE.
I NEED TO ASK YOU A FEW QUESTIONS ABOUT STEF. AND RENÉ.
HMPH. SO, RENÉ WAS ONLY IN A BATHROBE? DID HE DO ANYTHING ELSE UNSEEMLY?
UH, HE ASKED IF I WAS OKAY. BUT THAT'S IT.
MMMHM.
scribble
scribble "PAPA"

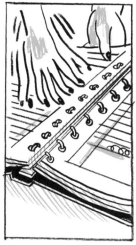

I FEEL BAD FOR COMPLAINING ABOUT RENÉ.

FOR REAL? HE'S WEIRD.

AND WHAT ABOUT STEF?

RORY TOLD HIM TO APOLOGIZE. HE WAS JUST BEING AN IDIOT.

YOU DIDN'T REALLY THINK HE WAS GOING TO DO ANYTHING?

UH, YES. I DID THINK THAT.

WHY WERE THINGS ALWAYS SO OBVIOUS TO EVERYBODY BUT ME?!

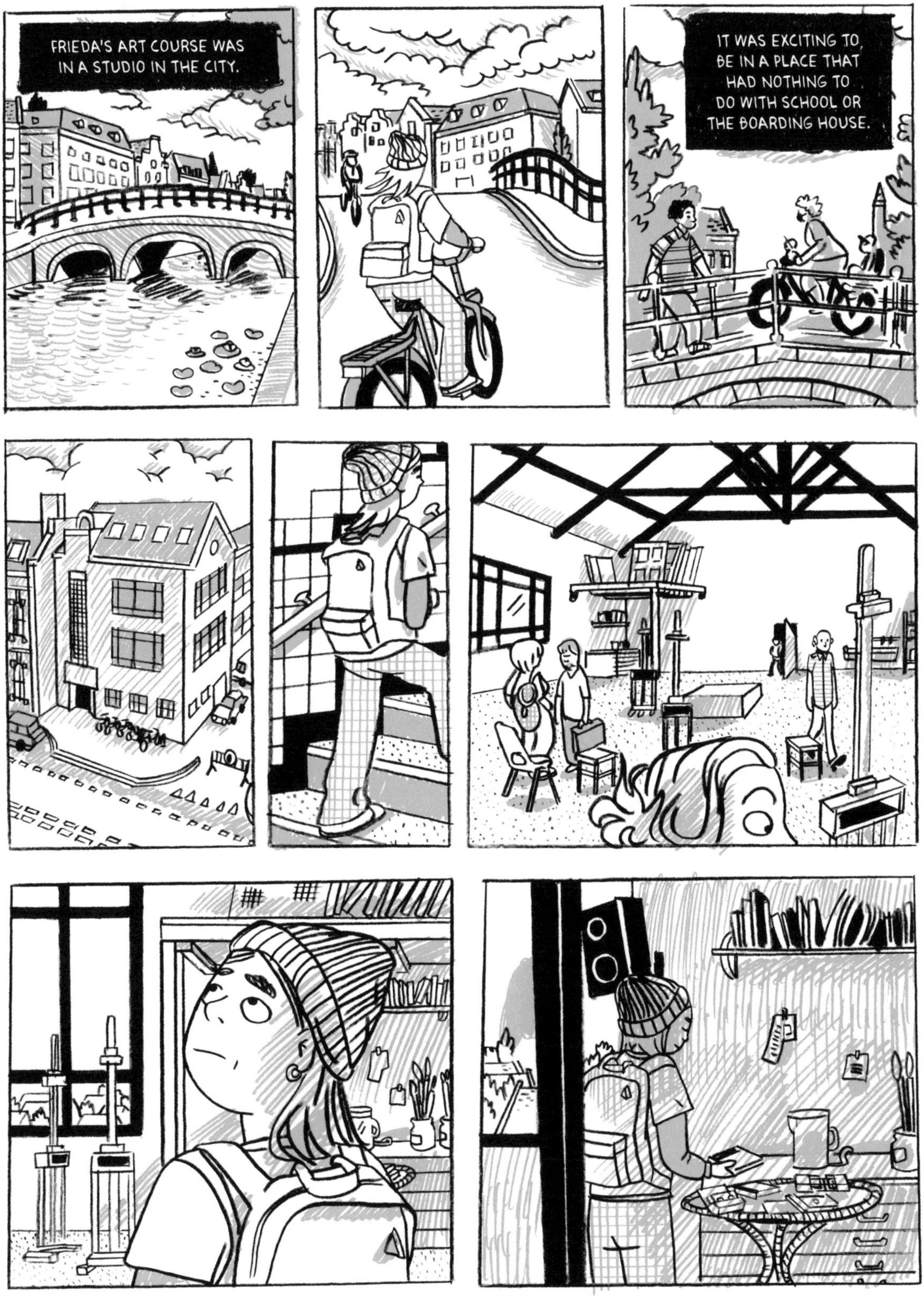
FRIEDA'S ART COURSE WAS IN A STUDIO IN THE CITY.
IT WAS EXCITING TO, BE IN A PLACE THAT HAD NOTHING TO DO WITH SCHOOL OR THE BOARDING HOUSE.

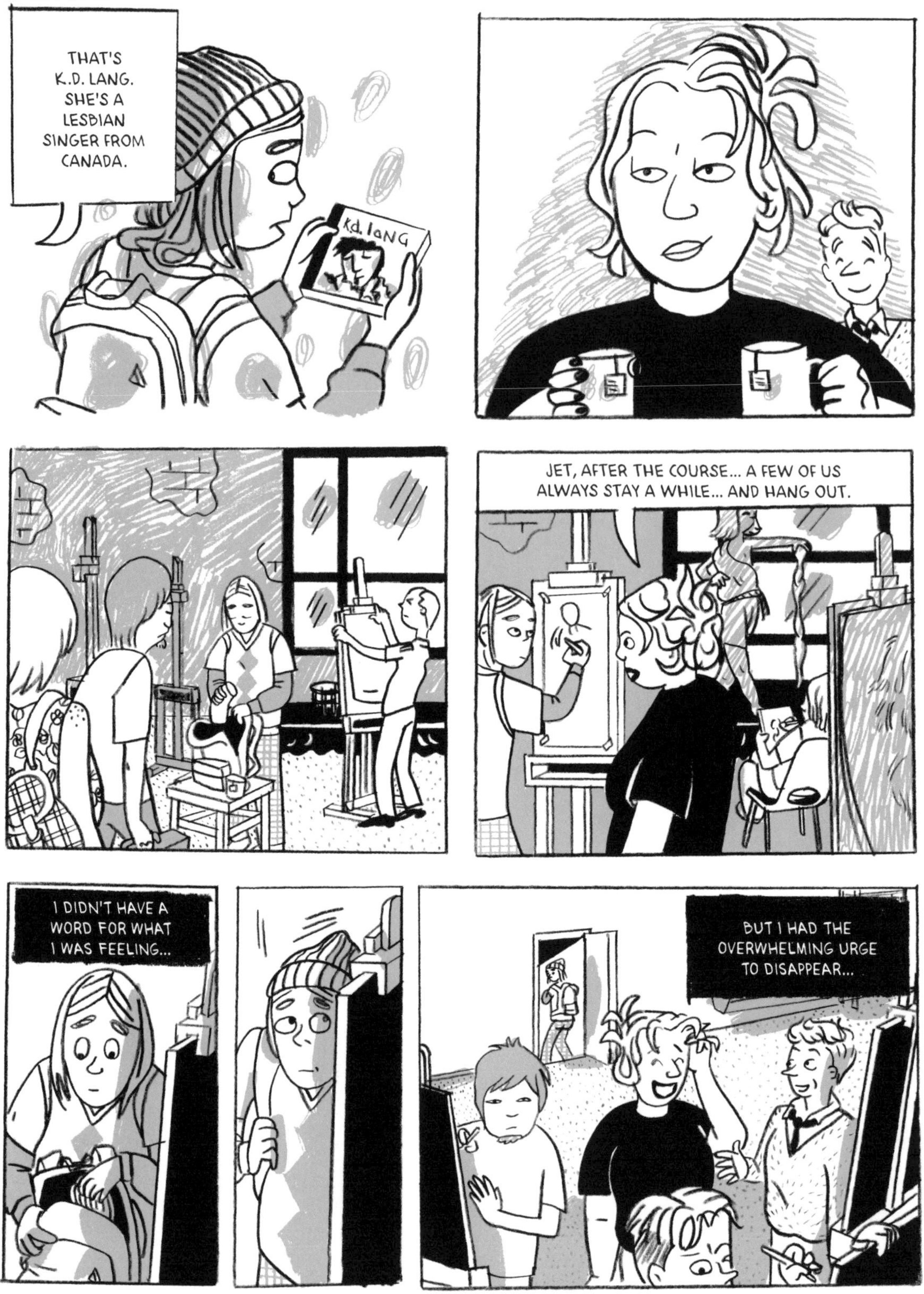
THAT'S K.D. LANG. SHE'S A LESBIAN SINGER FROM CANADA.
K.d. laNG
JET, AFTER THE COURSE... A FEW OF US ALWAYS STAY A WHILE... AND HANG OUT.
I DIDN'T HAVE A WORD FOR WHAT I WAS FEELING...
BUT I HAD THE OVERWHELMING URGE TO DISAPPEAR...

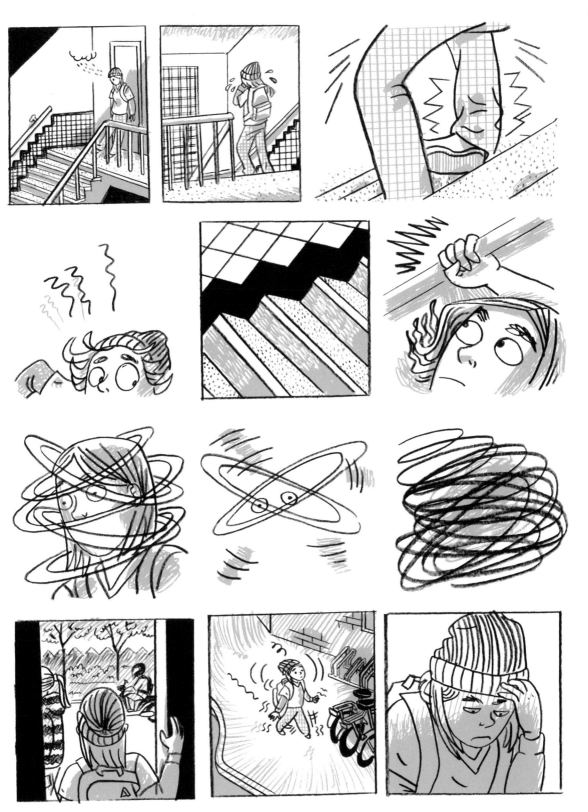

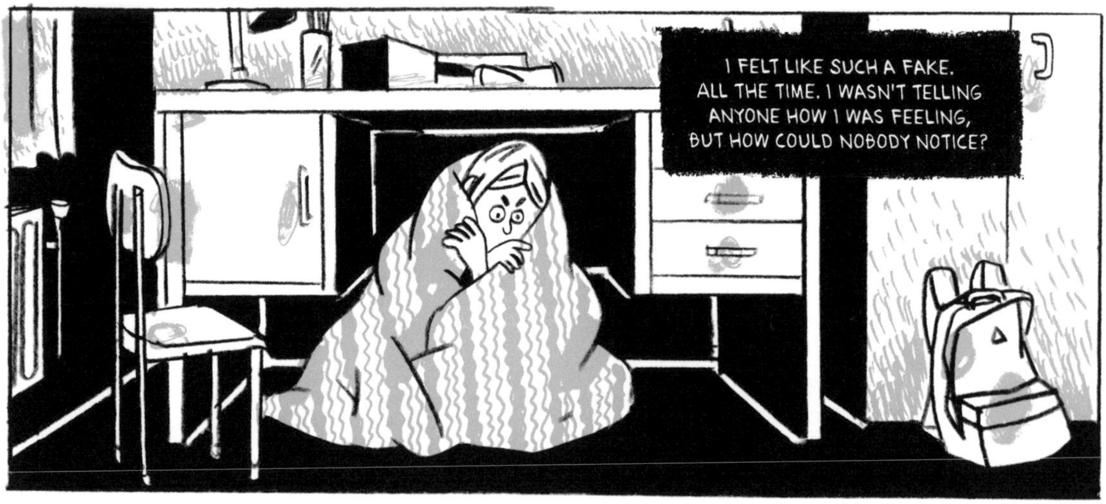
I FELT LIKE SUCH A FAKE. ALL THE TIME. I WASN'T TELLING ANYONE HOW I WAS FEELING, BUT HOW COULD NOBODY NOTICE?

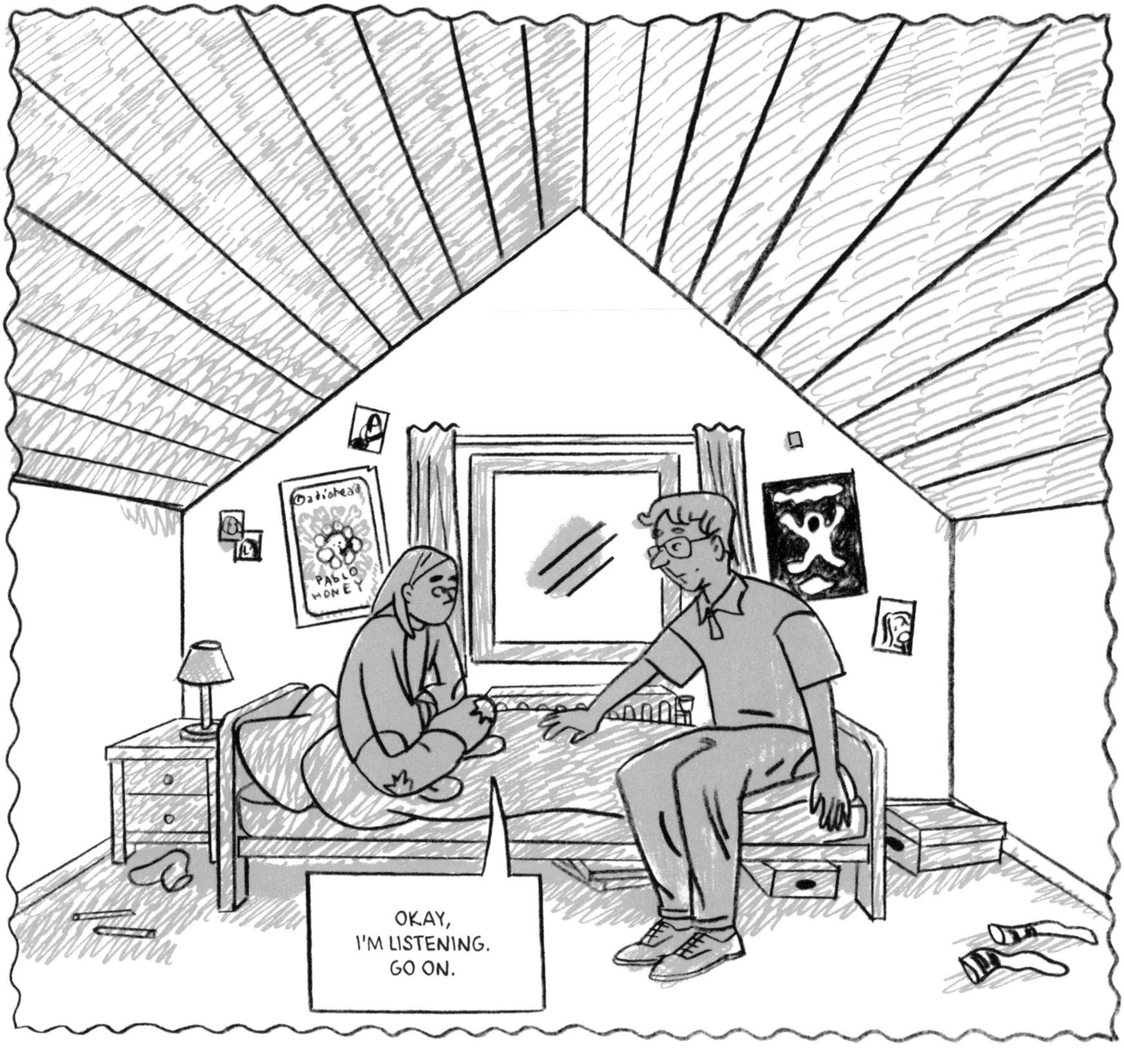
PABLO HONEY
OKAY, I'M LISTENING. GO ON.

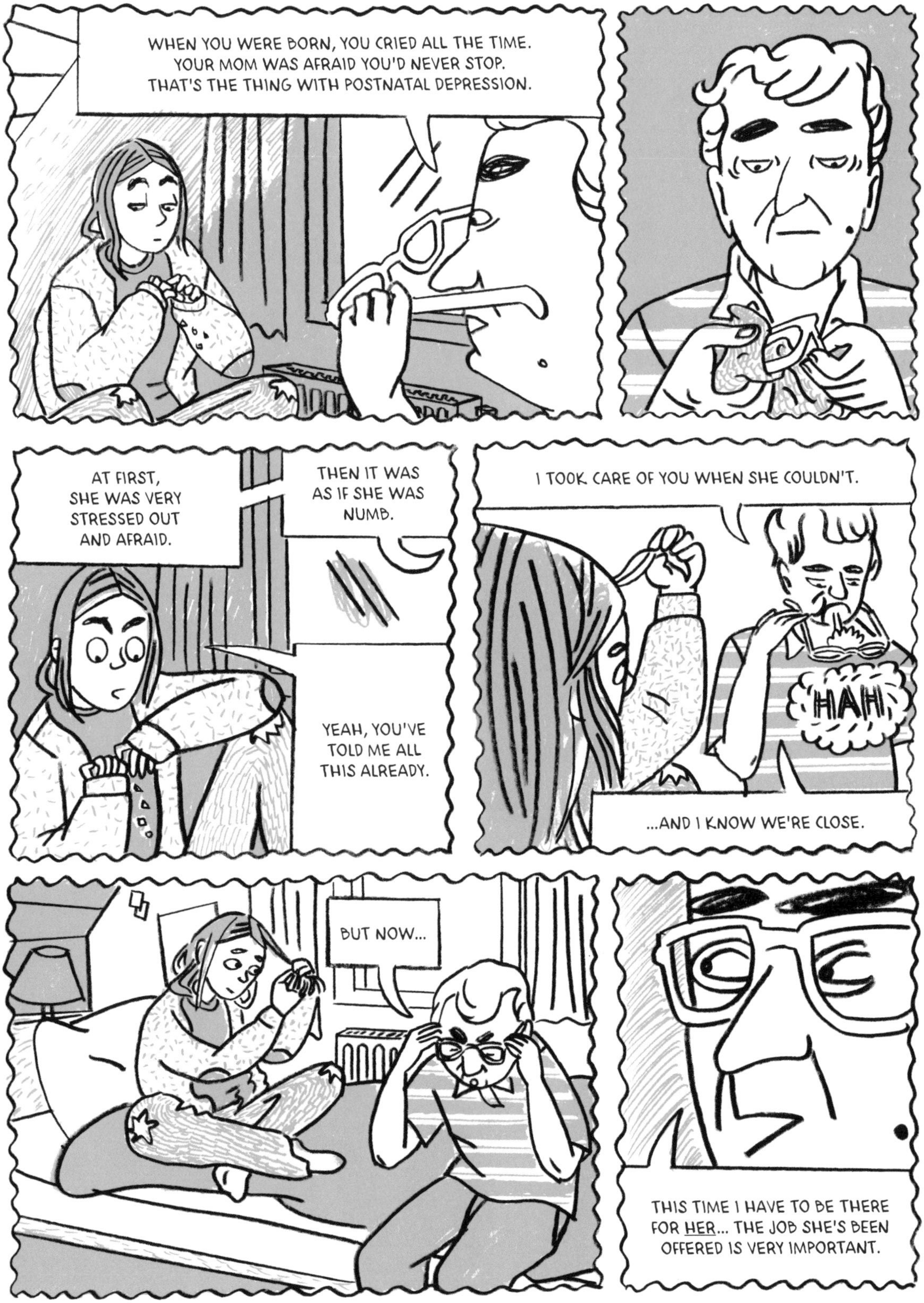
WHEN YOU WERE BORN, YOU CRIED ALL THE TIME. YOUR MOM WAS AFRAID YOU'D NEVER STOP. THAT'S THE THING WITH POSTNATAL DEPRESSION.
AT FIRST, SHE WAS VERY STRESSED OUT AND AFRAID.
THEN IT WAS AS IF SHE WAS NUMB.
YEAH, YOU'VE TOLD ME ALL THIS ALREADY.
I TOOK CARE OF YOU WHEN SHE COULDN'T.
HAH
...AND I KNOW WE'RE CLOSE.
BUT NOW...
THIS TIME I HAVE TO BE THERE FOR HER... THE JOB SHE'S BEEN OFFERED IS VERY IMPORTANT.

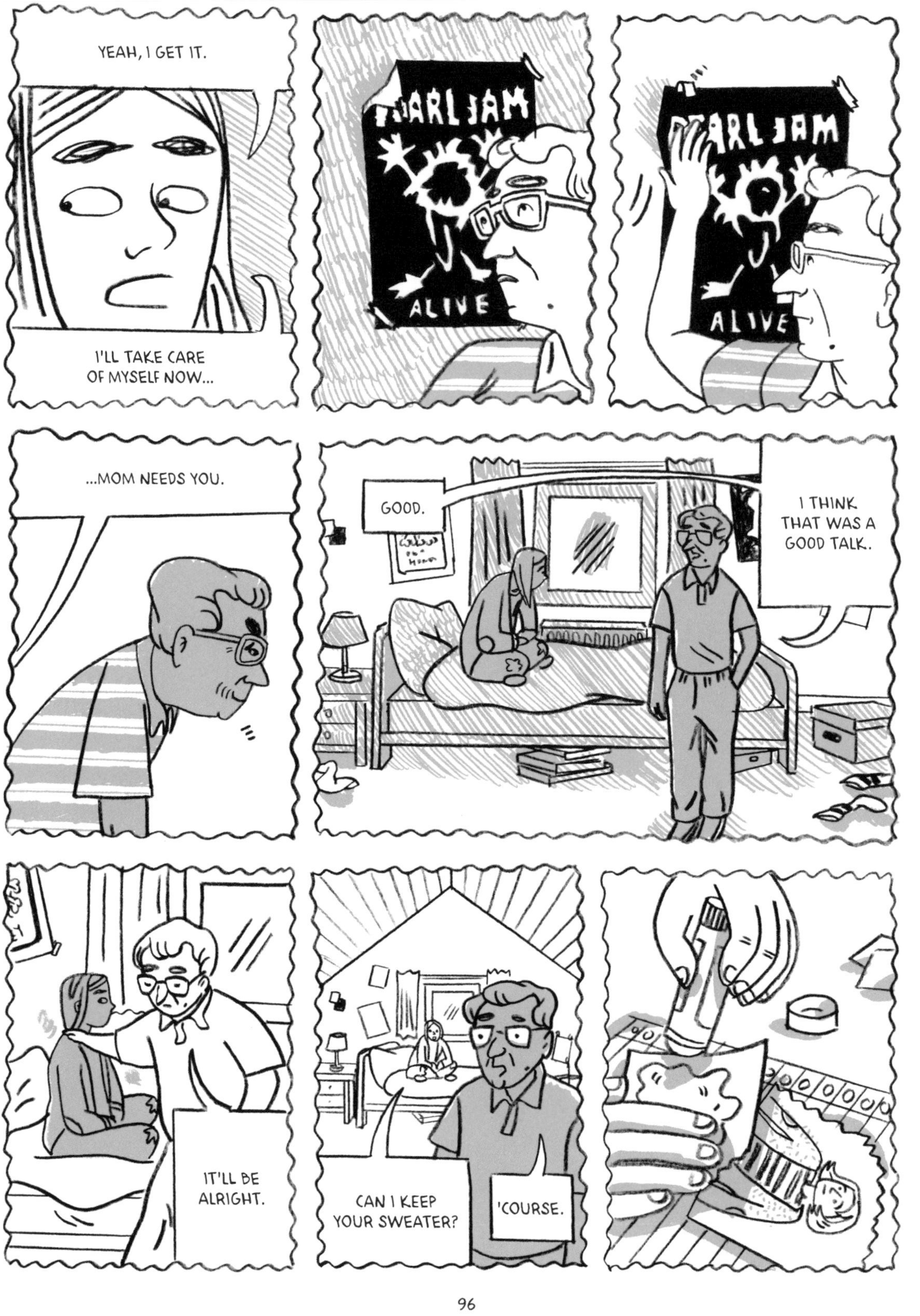
YEAH, I GET IT.
I'LL TAKE CARE OF MYSELF NOW...
ALIVE
ALIVE
...MOM NEEDS YOU.
I THINK THAT WAS A GOOD TALK.
GOOD.
IT'LL BE ALRIGHT.
CAN I KEEP YOUR SWEATER?
'COURSE.

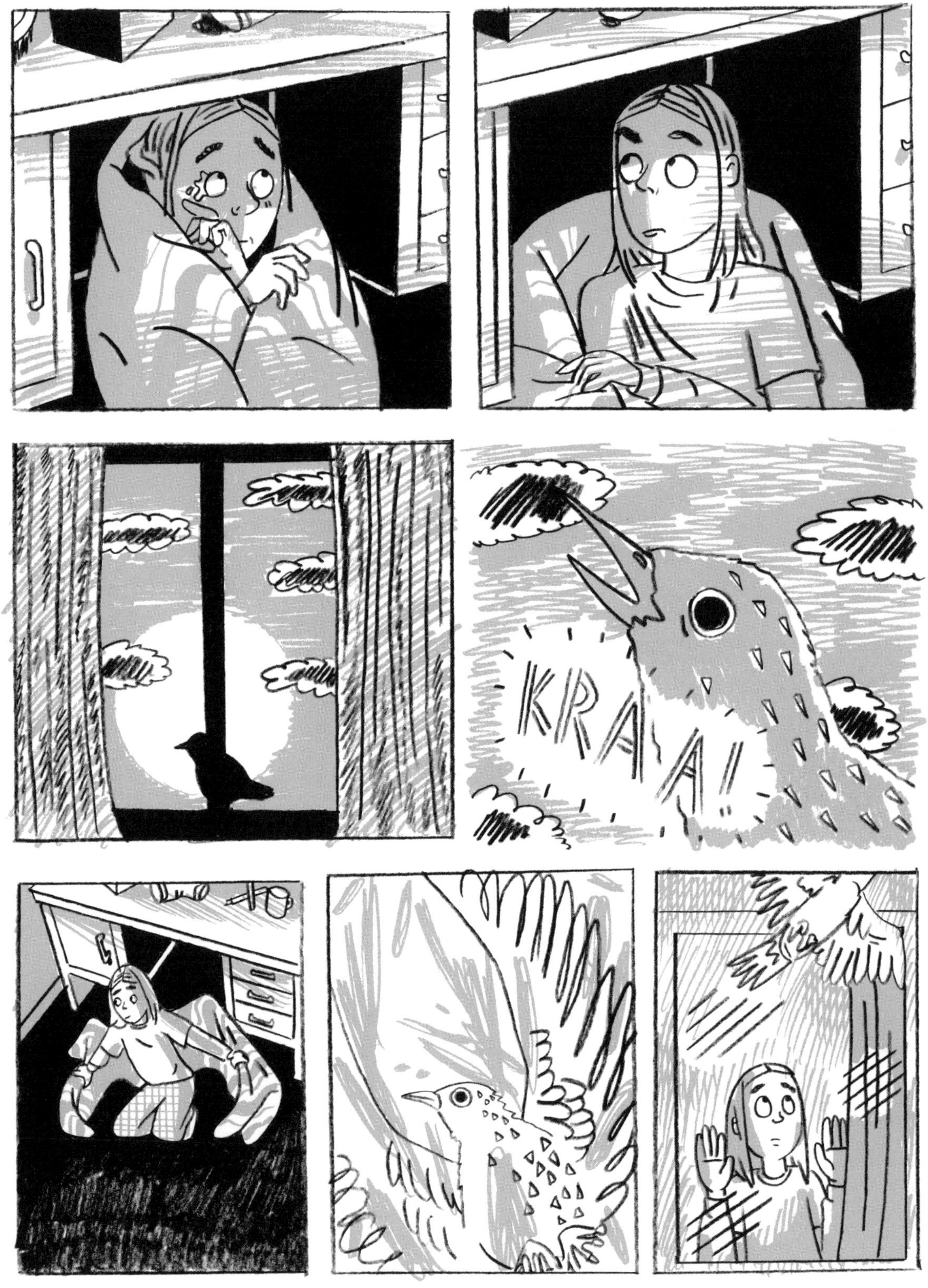
KRAA!

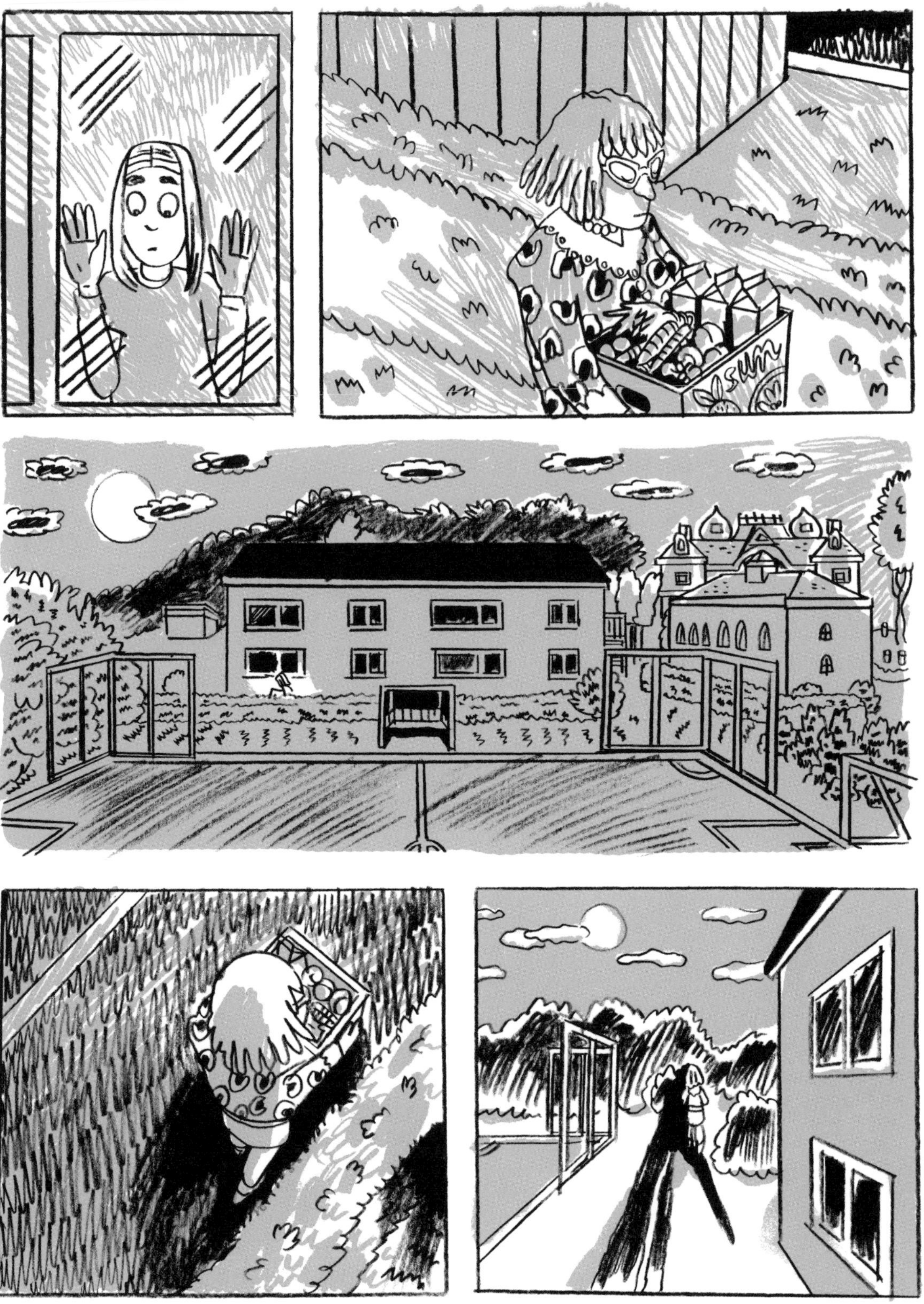

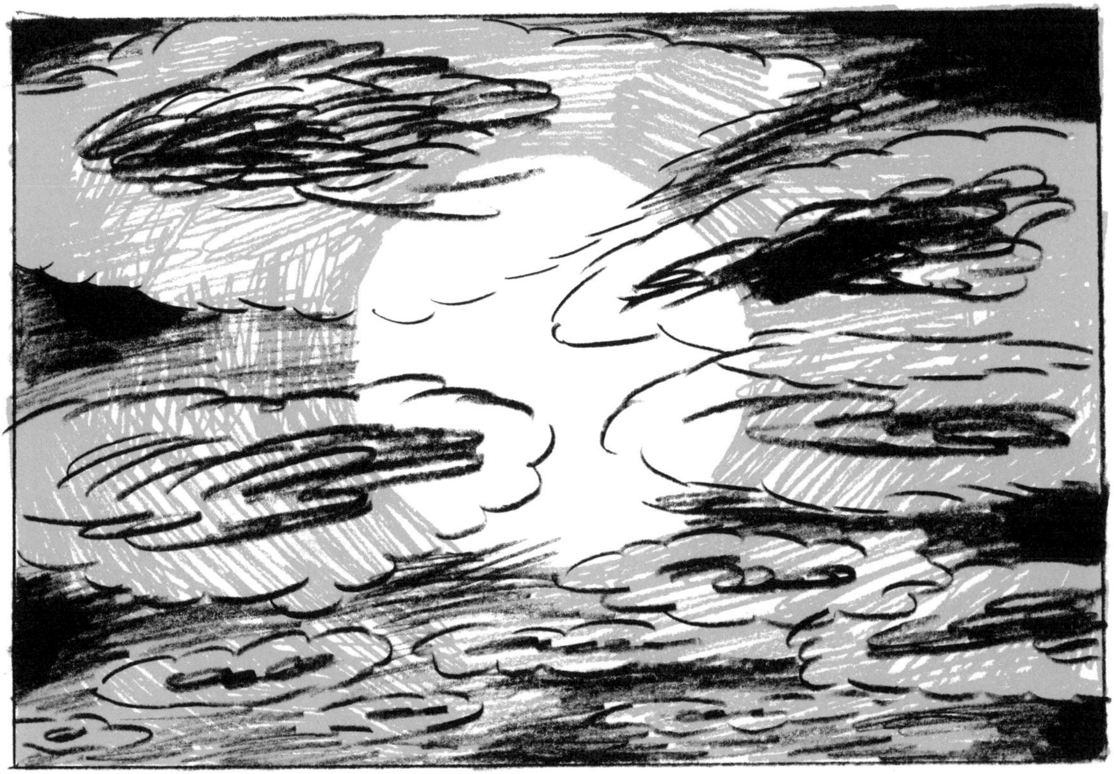

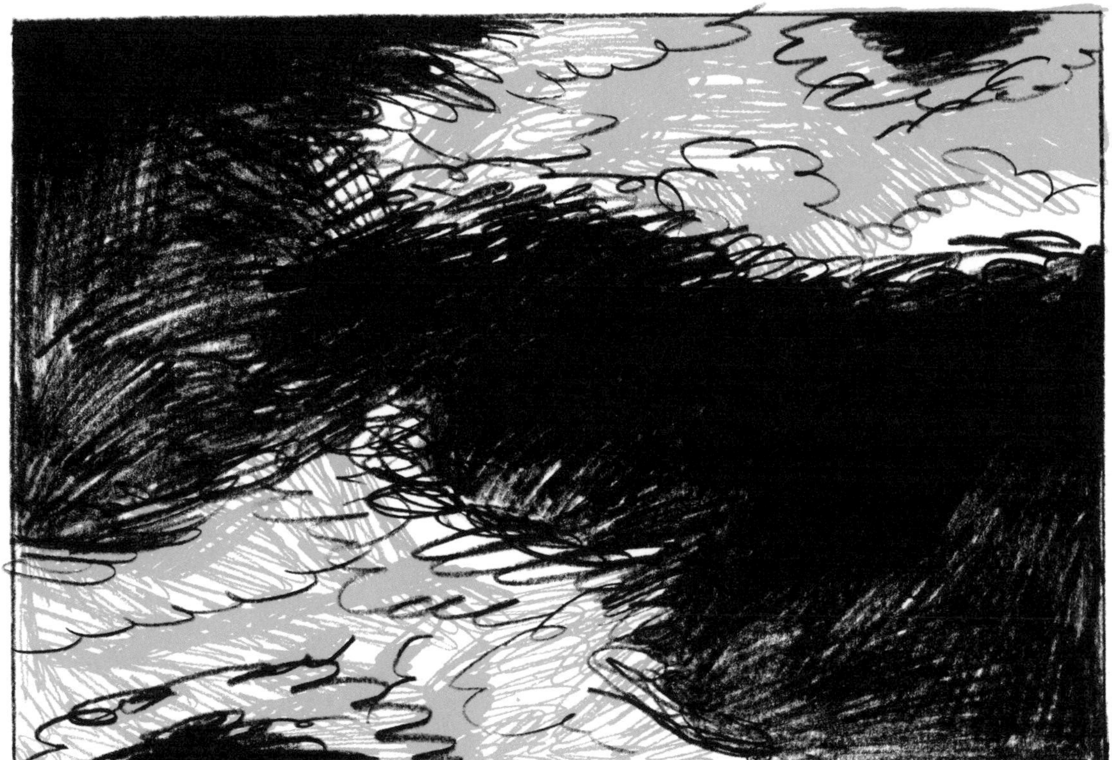

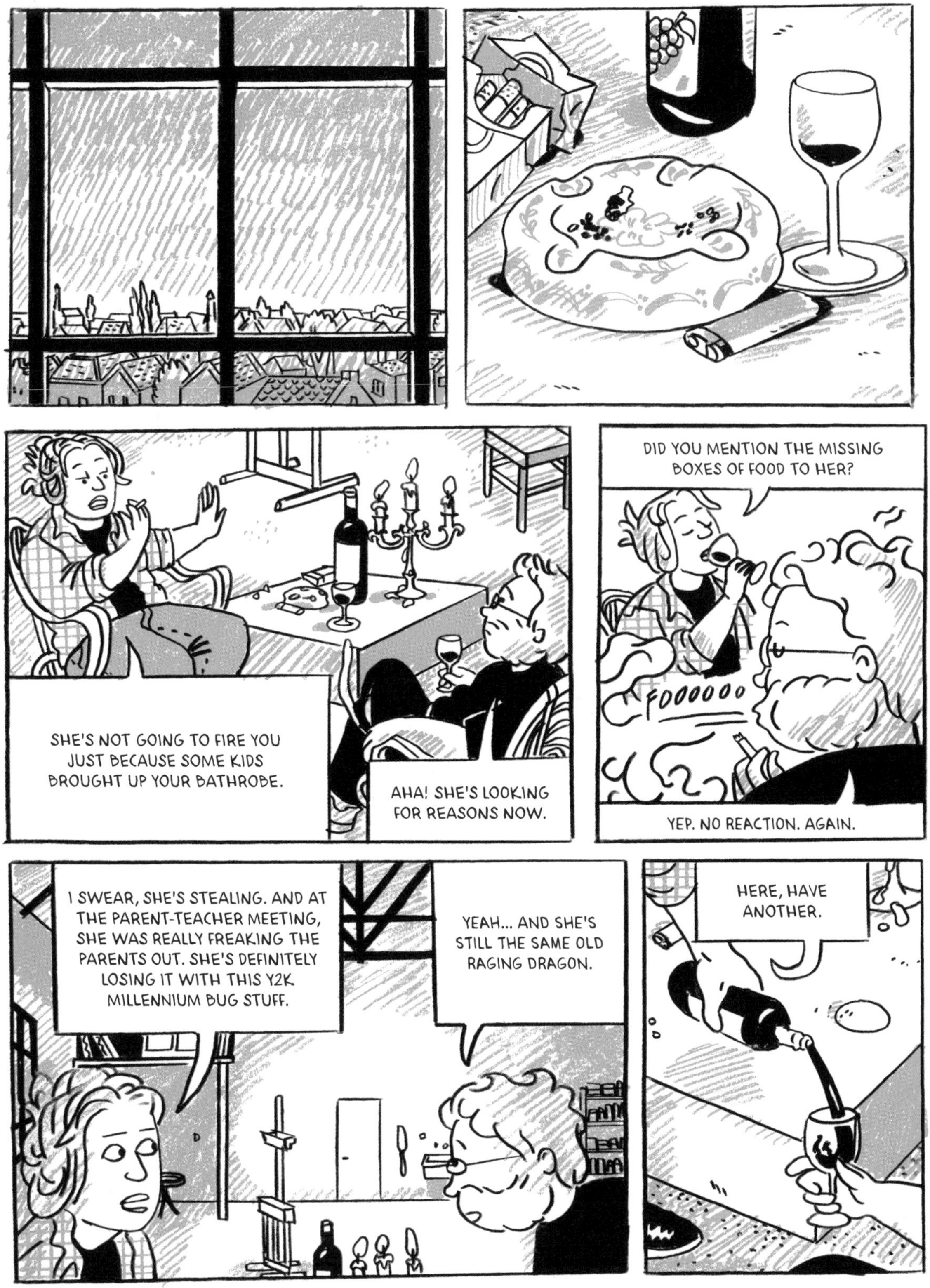
SHE'S NOT GOING TO FIRE YOU JUST BECAUSE SOME KIDS BROUGHT UP YOUR BATHROBE.
AHA! SHE'S LOOKING FOR REASONS NOW.
DID YOU MENTION THE MISSING BOXES OF FOOD TO HER?
FOOOOOO
YEP. NO REACTION. AGAIN.
I SWEAR, SHE'S STEALING. AND AT THE PARENT-TEACHER MEETING, SHE WAS REALLY FREAKING THE PARENTS OUT. SHE'S DEFINITELY LOSING IT WITH THIS Y2K MILLENNIUM BUG STUFF.
YEAH... AND SHE'S STILL THE SAME OLD RAGING DRAGON.
HERE, HAVE ANOTHER.

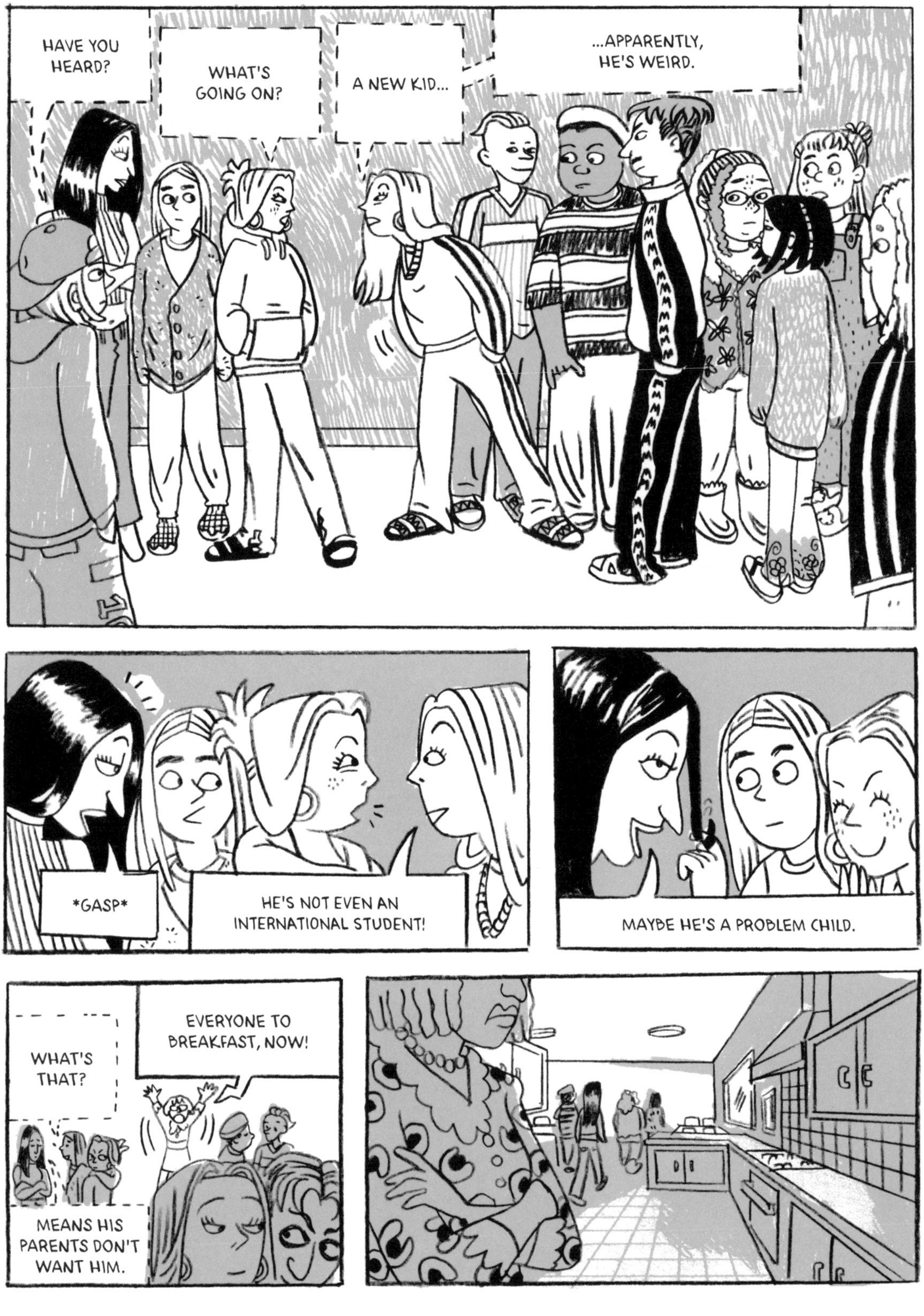
HAVE YOU HEARD?
WHAT'S GOING ON?
A NEW KID...
...APPARENTLY, HE'S WEIRD.
GASP
HE'S NOT EVEN AN INTERNATIONAL STUDENT!
MAYBE HE'S A PROBLEM CHILD.
WHAT'S THAT?
MEANS HIS PARENTS DON'T WANT HIM.
EVERYONE TO BREAKFAST, NOW!

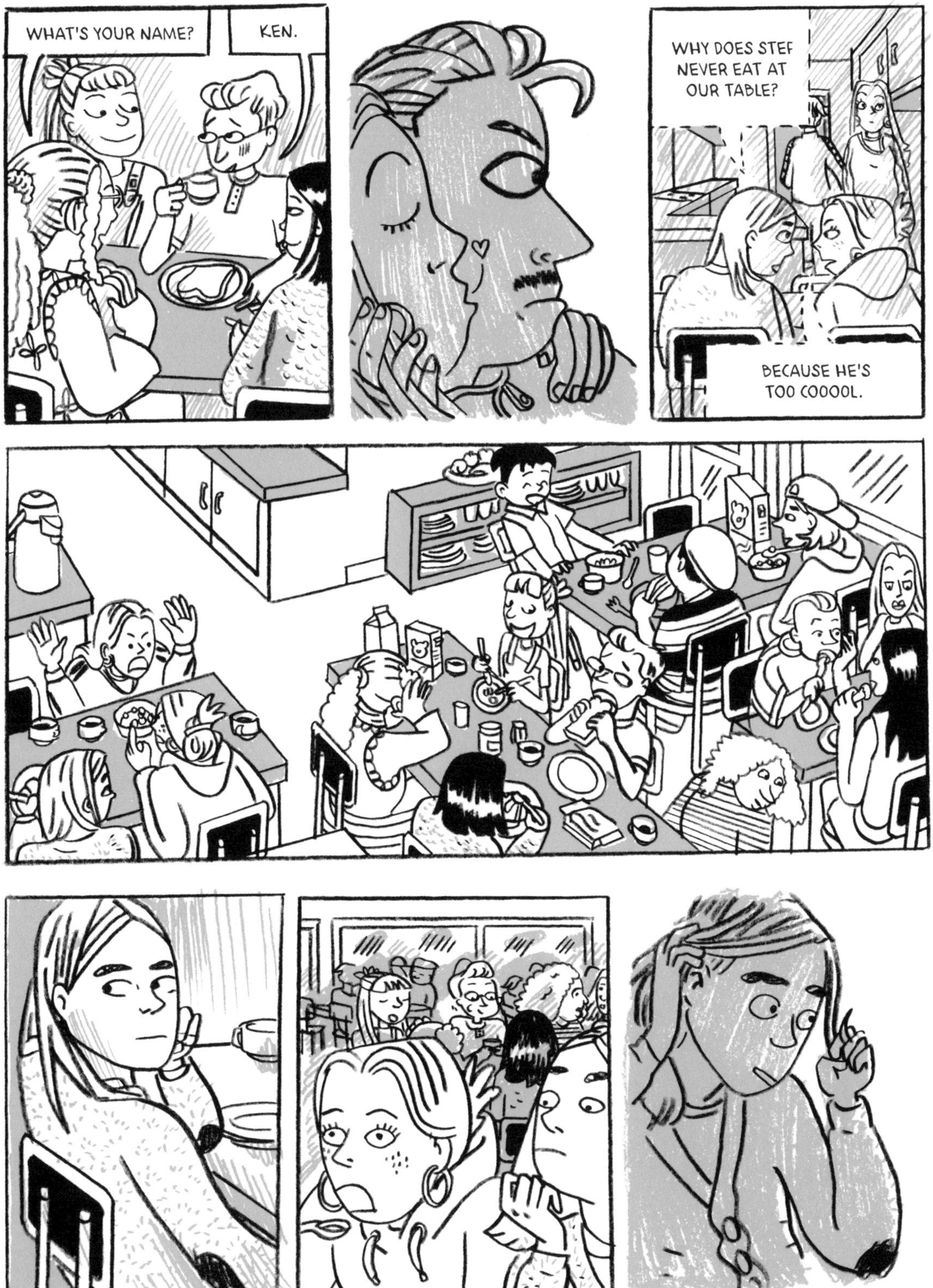
WHAT'S YOUR NAME?
KEN.
WHY DOES STEF NEVER EAT AT OUR TABLE?
BECAUSE HE'S TOO COOOOL.

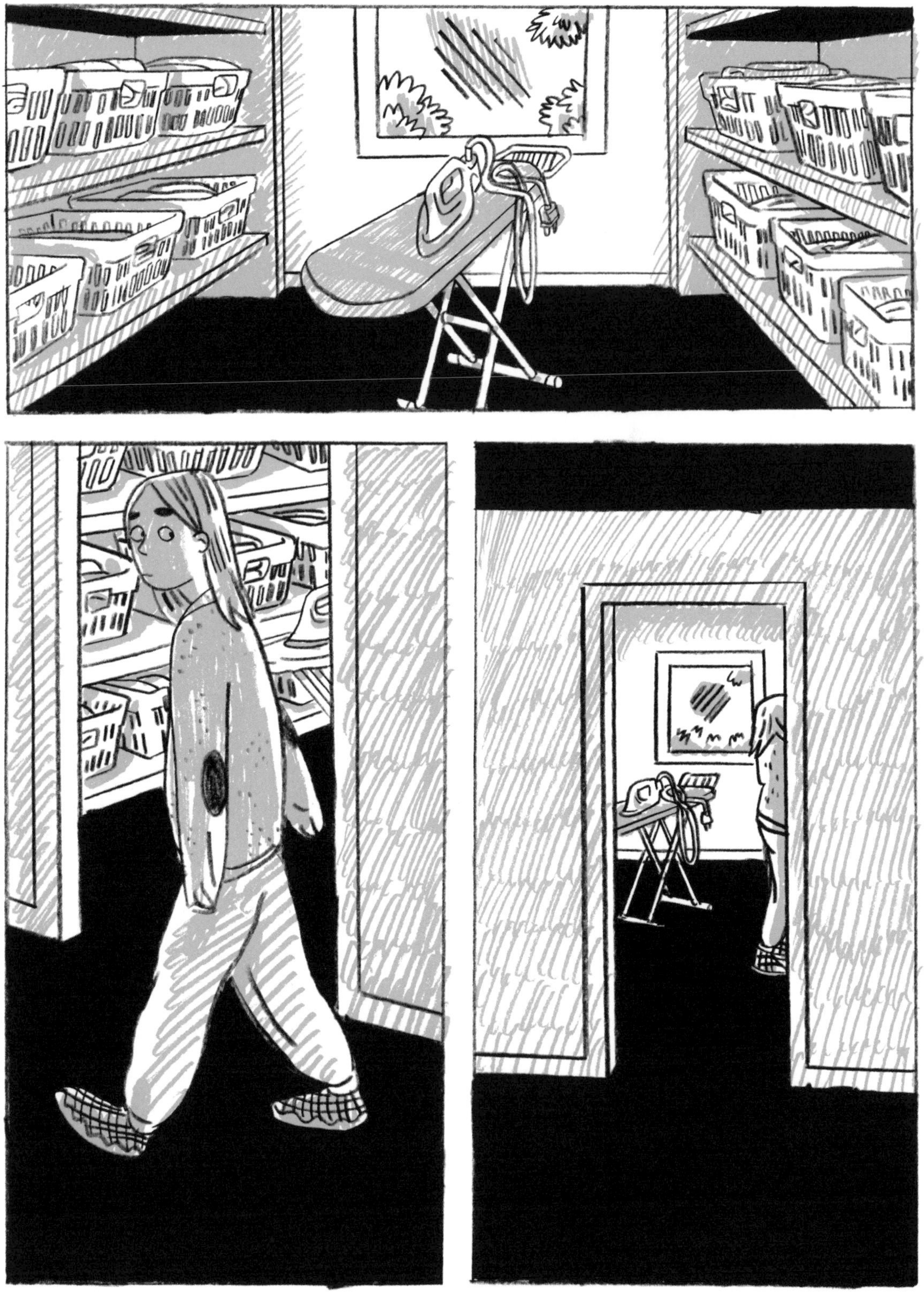

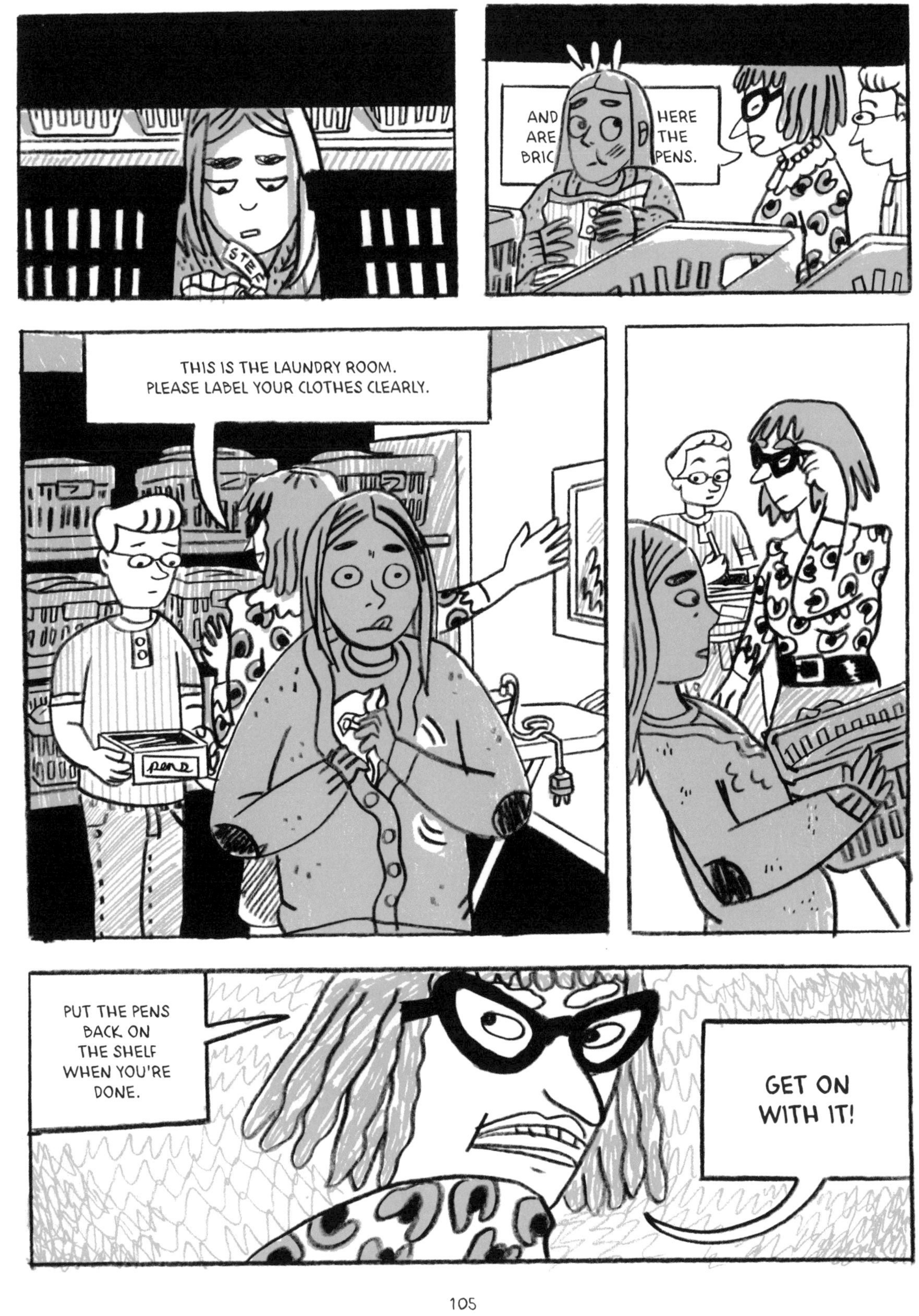
STEF
AND ARE BRIC
HERE THE PENS.
THIS IS THE LAUNDRY ROOM. PLEASE LABEL YOUR CLOTHES CLEARLY.
pens
PUT THE PENS BACK ON THE SHELF WHEN YOU'RE DONE.
GET ON WITH IT!

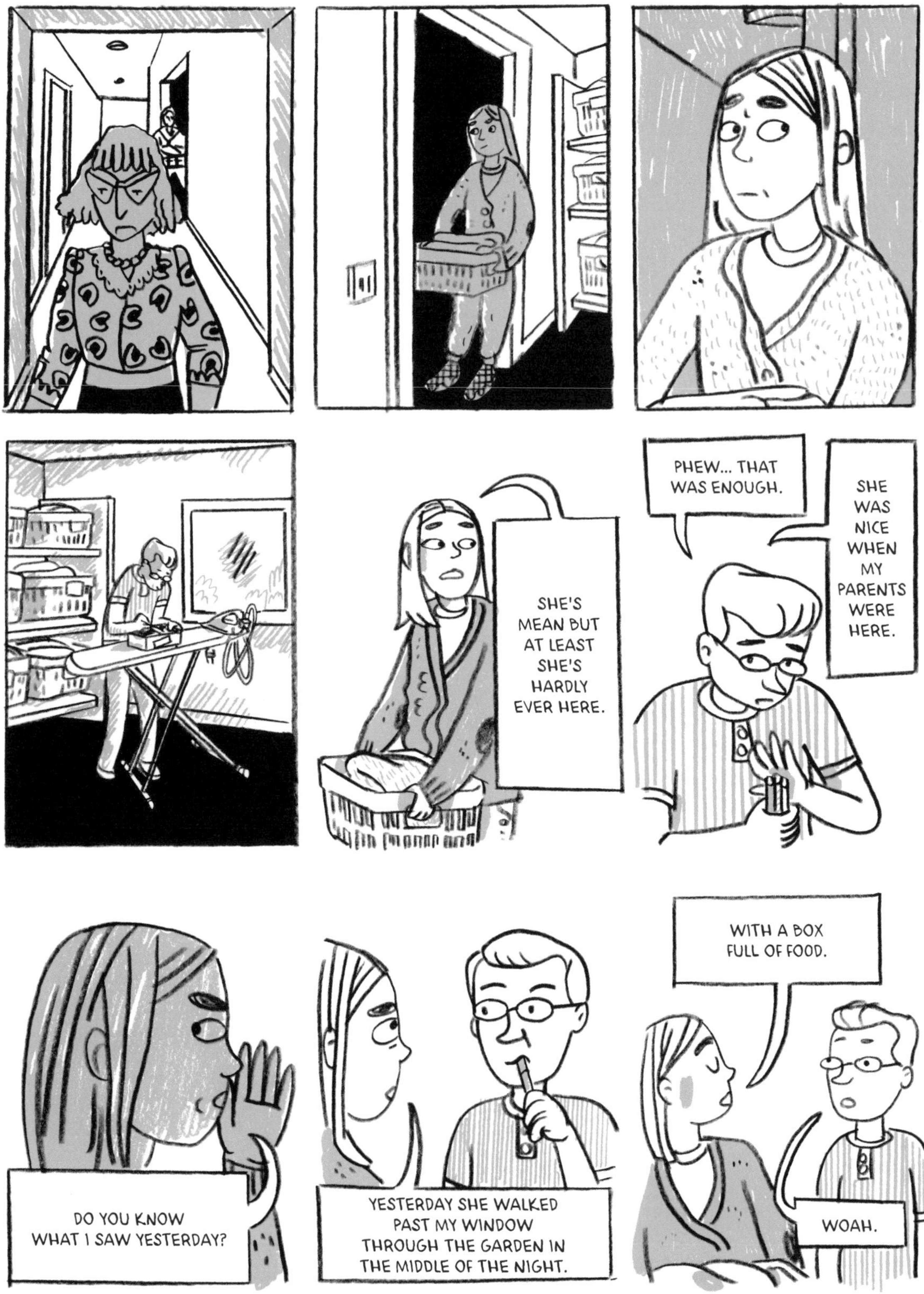
SHE'S MEAN BUT AT LEAST SHE'S HARDLY EVER HERE.
PHEW... THAT WAS ENOUGH.
SHE WAS NICE WHEN MY PARENTS WERE HERE.
DO YOU KNOW WHAT I SAW YESTERDAY?
YESTERDAY SHE WALKED PAST MY WINDOW THROUGH THE GARDEN IN THE MIDDLE OF THE NIGHT.
WITH A BOX FULL OF FOOD.
WOAH.

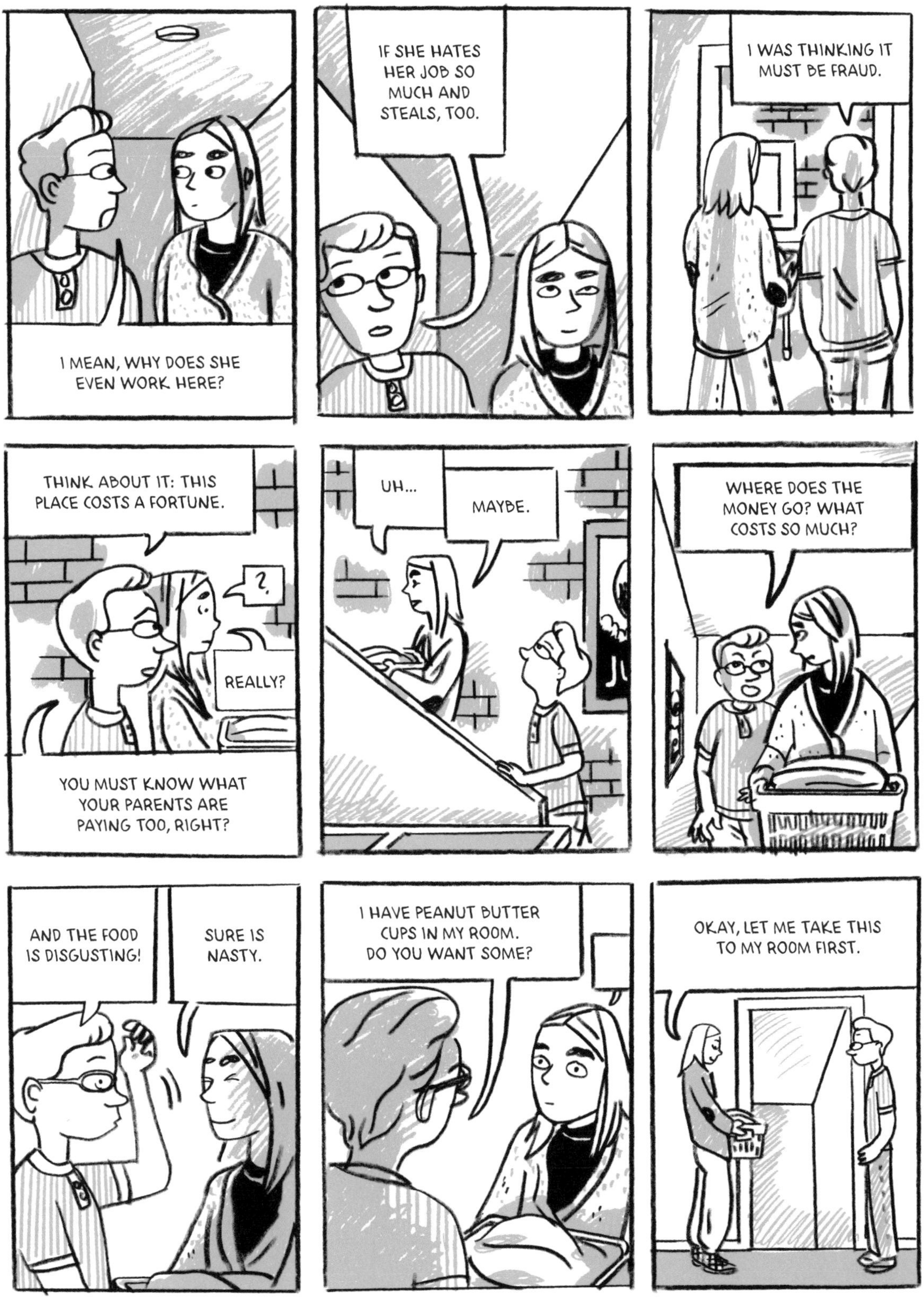
I MEAN, WHY DOES SHE EVEN WORK HERE?
IF SHE HATES HER JOB SO MUCH AND STEALS, TOO.
I WAS THINKING IT MUST BE FRAUD.
THINK ABOUT IT: THIS PLACE COSTS A FORTUNE.
?
REALLY?
YOU MUST KNOW WHAT YOUR PARENTS ARE PAYING TOO, RIGHT?
UH...
MAYBE.
WHERE DOES THE MONEY GO? WHAT COSTS SO MUCH?
AND THE FOOD IS DISGUSTING!
SURE IS NASTY.
I HAVE PEANUT BUTTER CUPS IN MY ROOM. DO YOU WANT SOME?
OKAY, LET ME TAKE THIS TO MY ROOM FIRST.

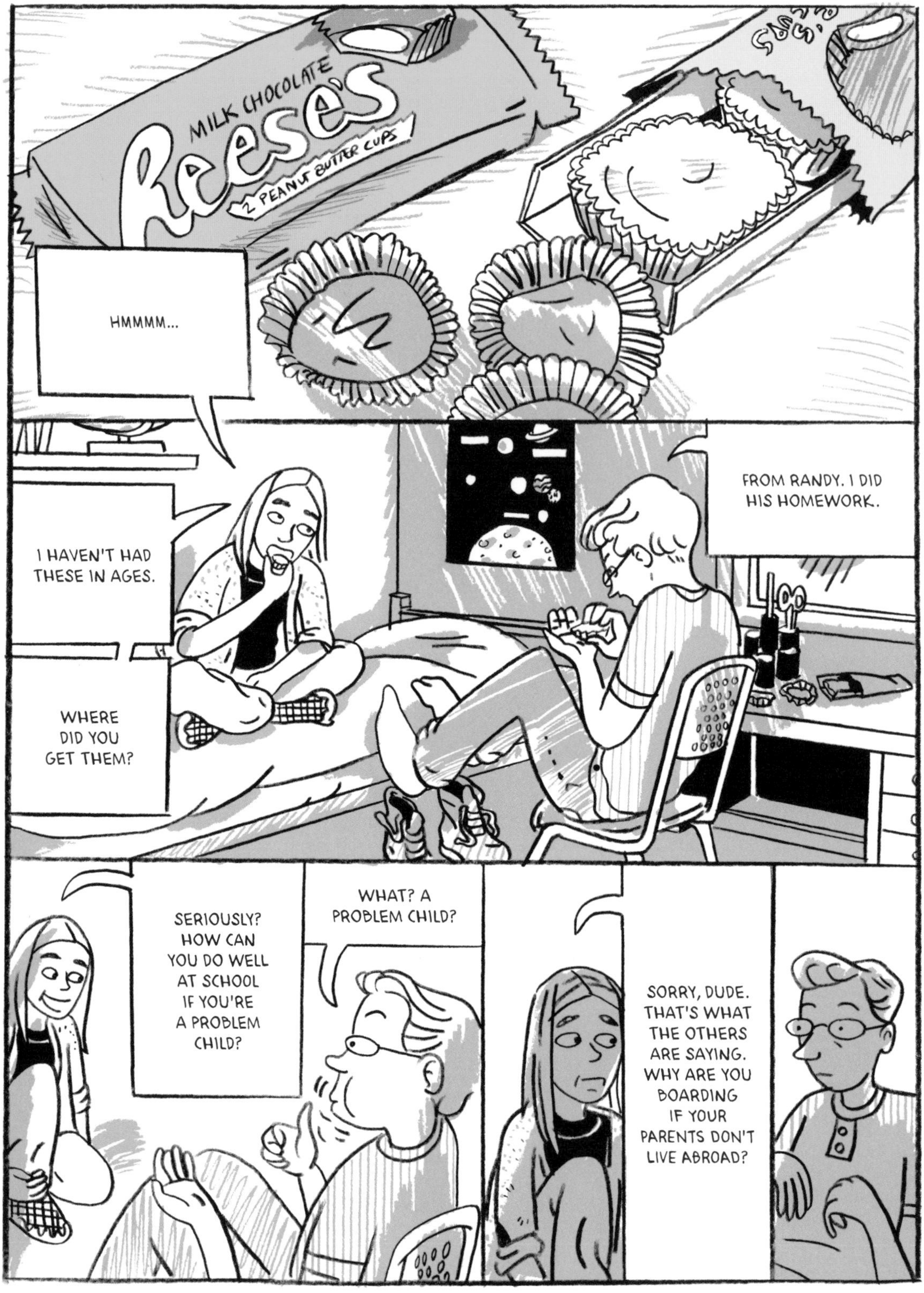
MILK CHOCOLATE
Reese's
2 PEANUT BUTTER CUPS
HMMMM...
I HAVEN'T HAD THESE IN AGES.
WHERE DID YOU GET THEM?
FROM RANDY. I DID HIS HOMEWORK.
SERIOUSLY? HOW CAN YOU DO WELL AT SCHOOL IF YOU'RE A PROBLEM CHILD?
WHAT? A PROBLEM CHILD?
SORRY, DUDE. THAT'S WHAT THE OTHERS ARE SAYING. WHY ARE YOU BOARDING IF YOUR PARENTS DON'T LIVE ABROAD?

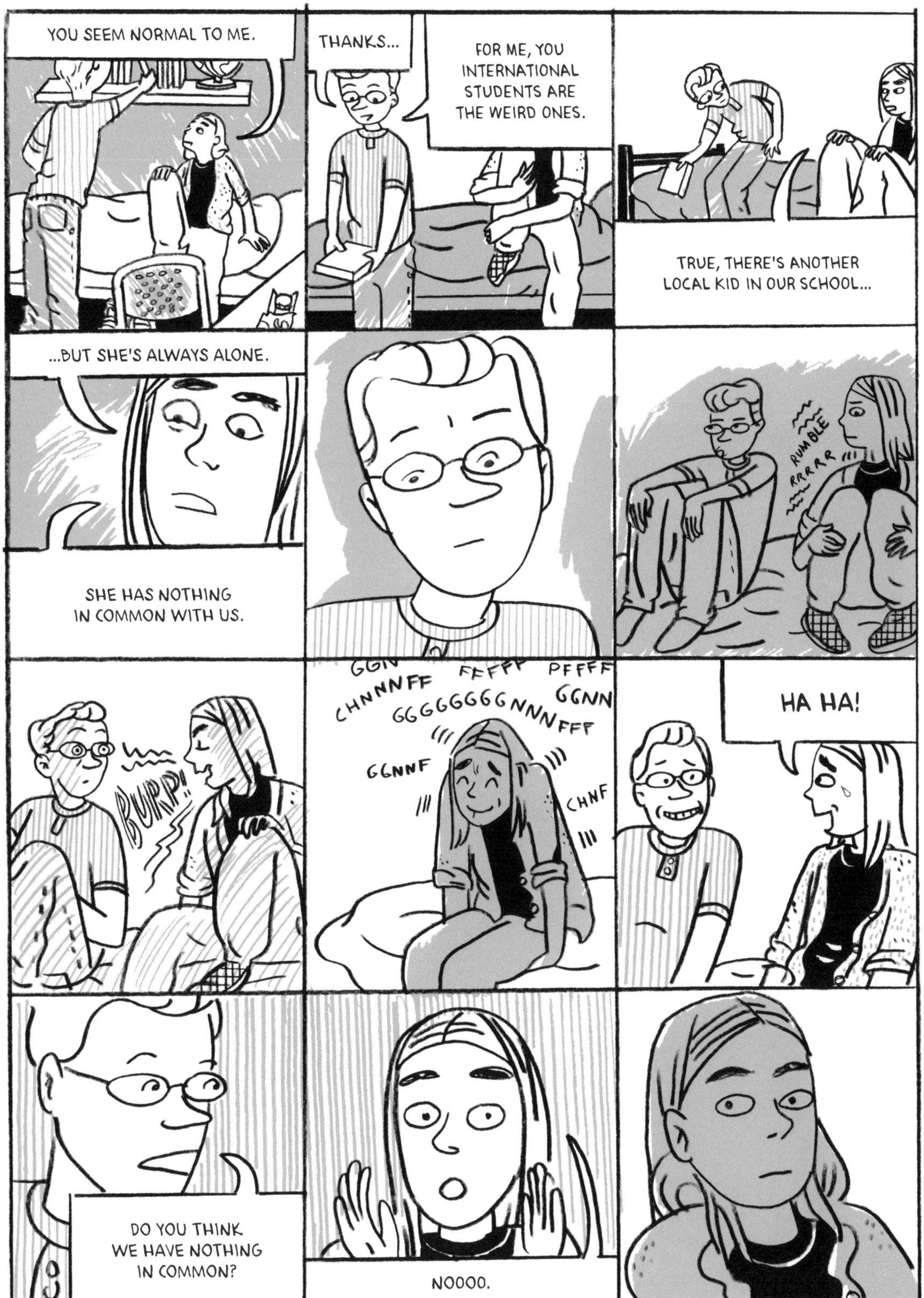
YOU SEEM NORMAL TO ME.
THANKS...
FOR ME, YOU INTERNATIONAL STUDENTS ARE THE WEIRD ONES.
TRUE, THERE'S ANOTHER LOCAL KID IN OUR SCHOOL...
...BUT SHE'S ALWAYS ALONE.
SHE HAS NOTHING IN COMMON WITH US.
RUMBLE
RRRRRR
BURP!
GGN
FFFFF
PFFFF
CHNNNFF
GGNN
GGGGGGGGNNNFFF
GGNNF
CHNF
HA HA!
DO YOU THINK WE HAVE NOTHING IN COMMON?
NOOOO.

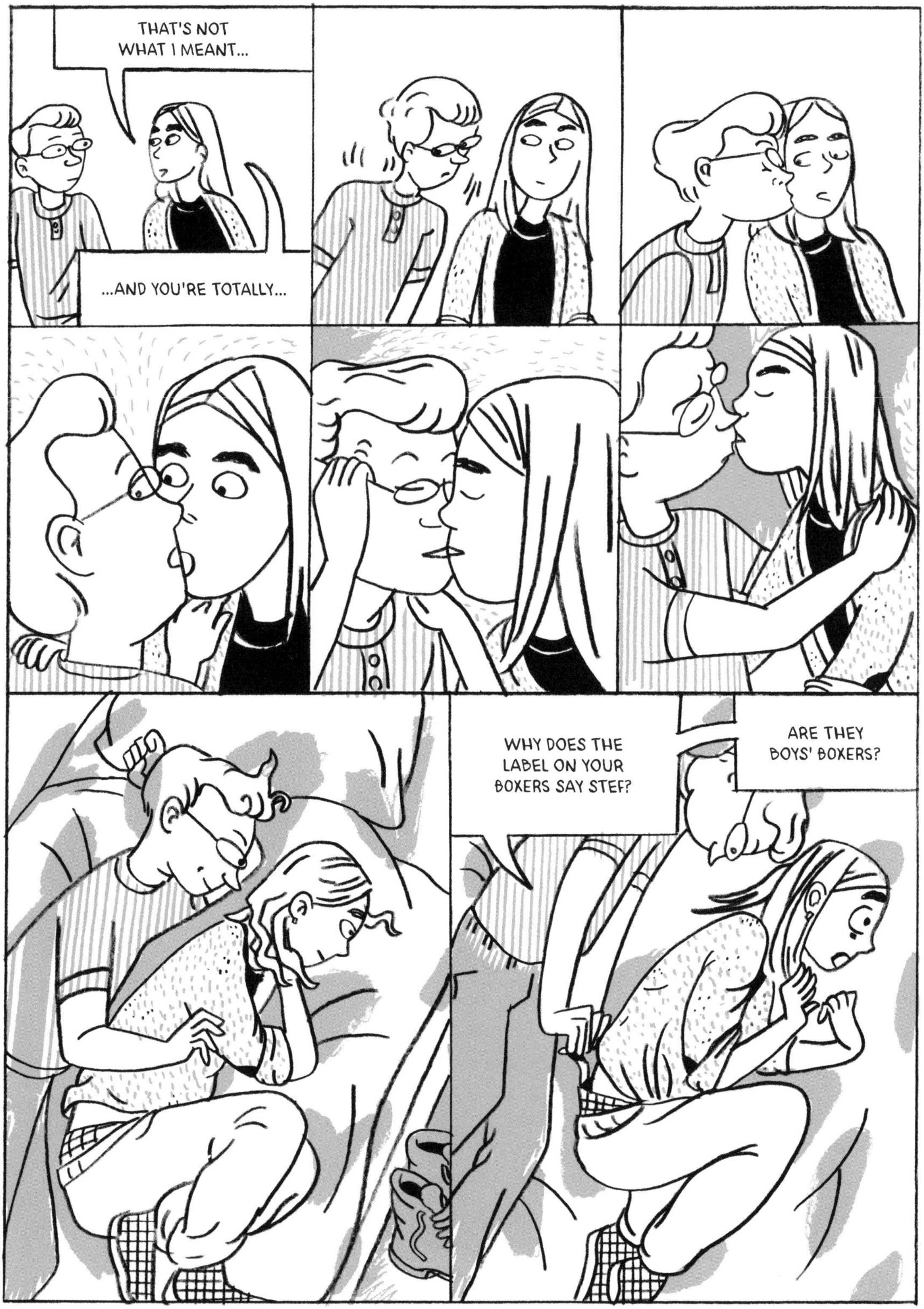
THAT'S NOT WHAT I MEANT...
...AND YOU'RE TOTALLY...
WHY DOES THE LABEL ON YOUR BOXERS SAY STEF?
ARE THEY BOYS' BOXERS?

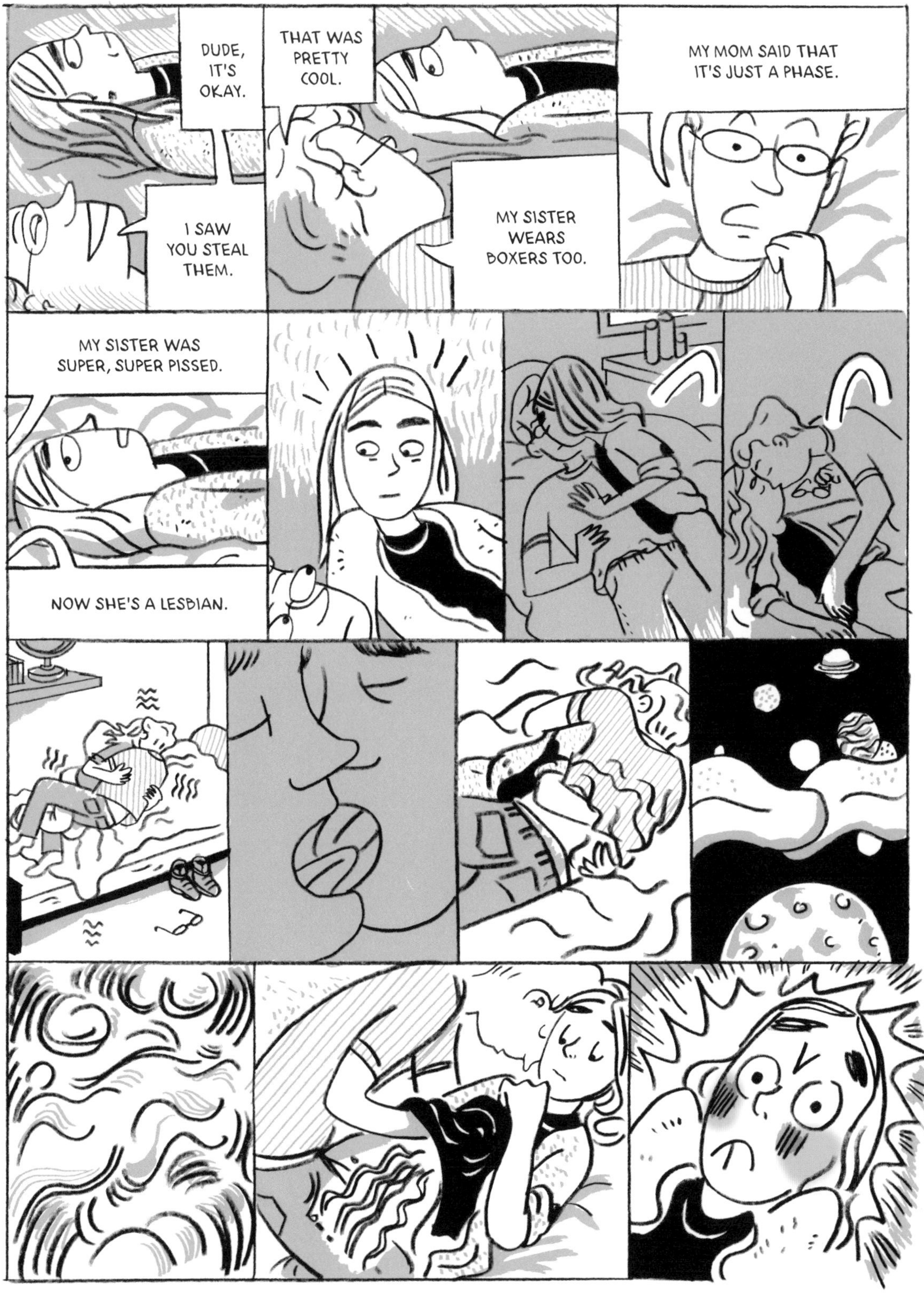
DUDE, IT'S OKAY.
I SAW YOU STEAL THEM.
THAT WAS PRETTY COOL.
MY SISTER WEARS BOXERS TOO.
MY MOM SAID THAT IT'S JUST A PHASE.
MY SISTER WAS SUPER, SUPER PISSED.
NOW SHE'S A LESBIAN.

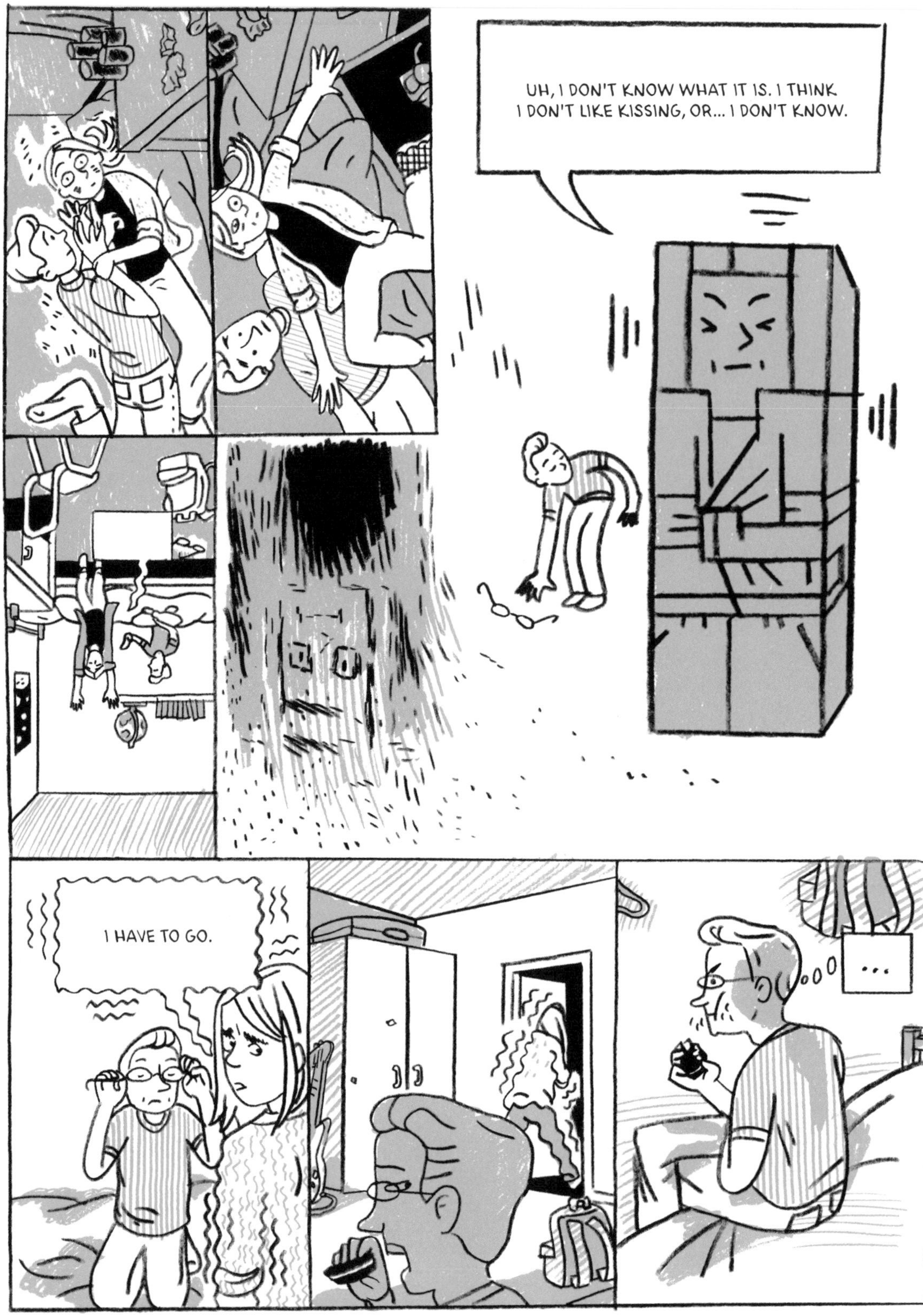
UH, I DON'T KNOW WHAT IT IS. I THINK I DON'T LIKE KISSING, OR... I DON'T KNOW.
I HAVE TO GO.
...

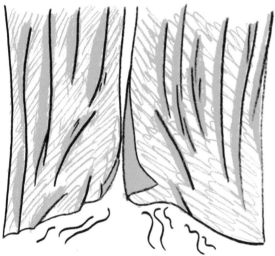
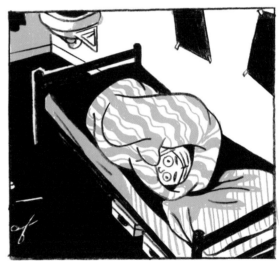

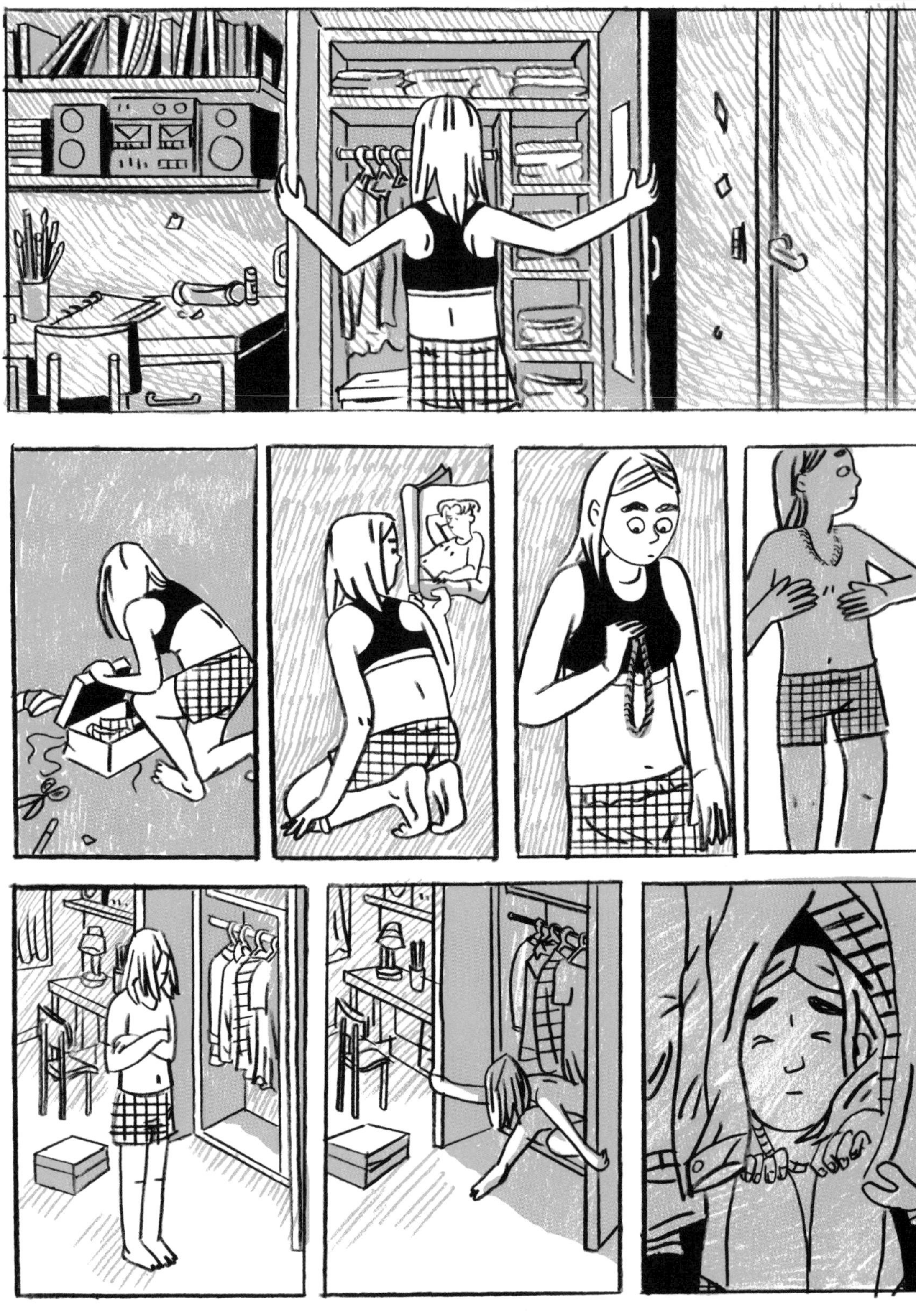

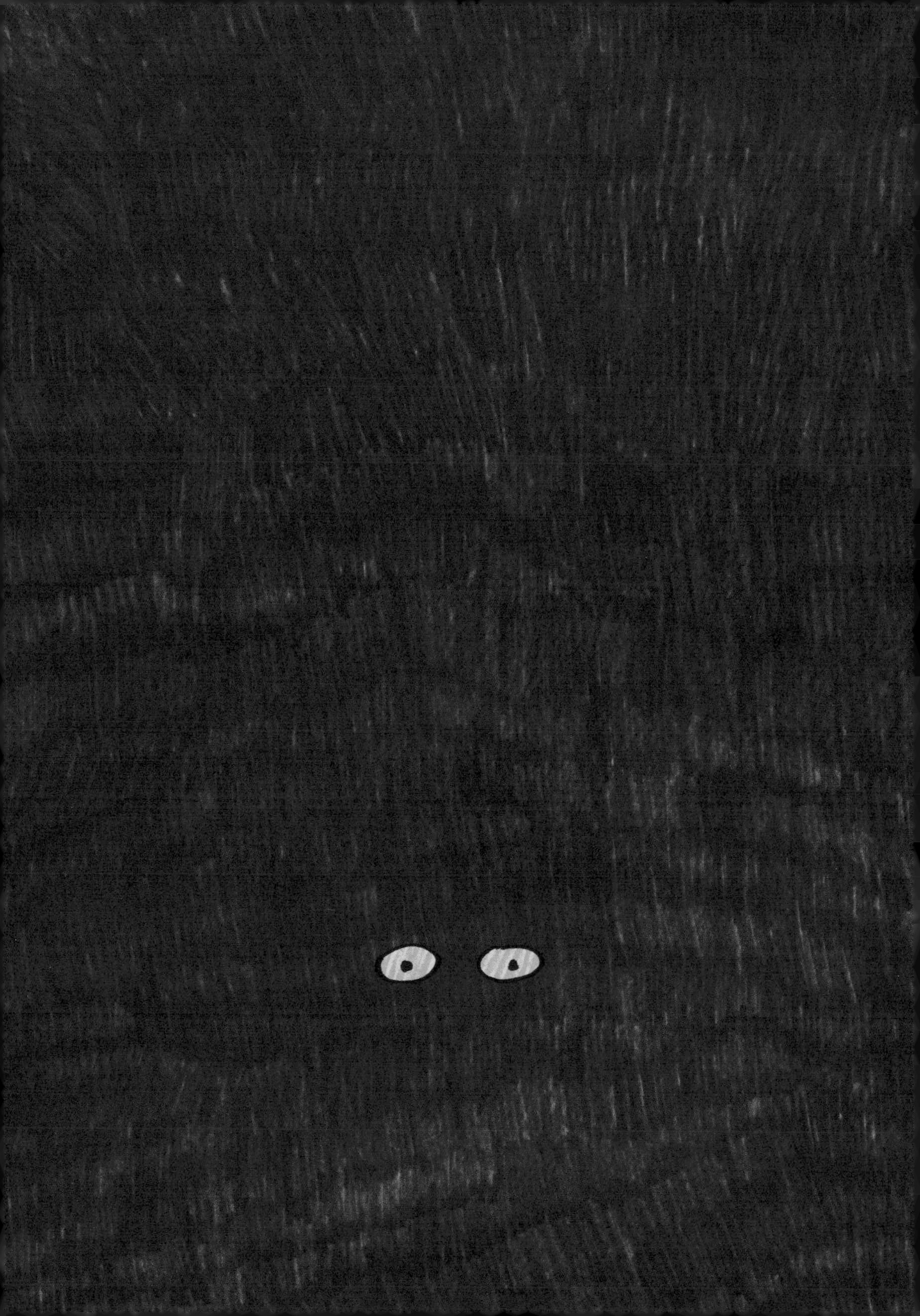

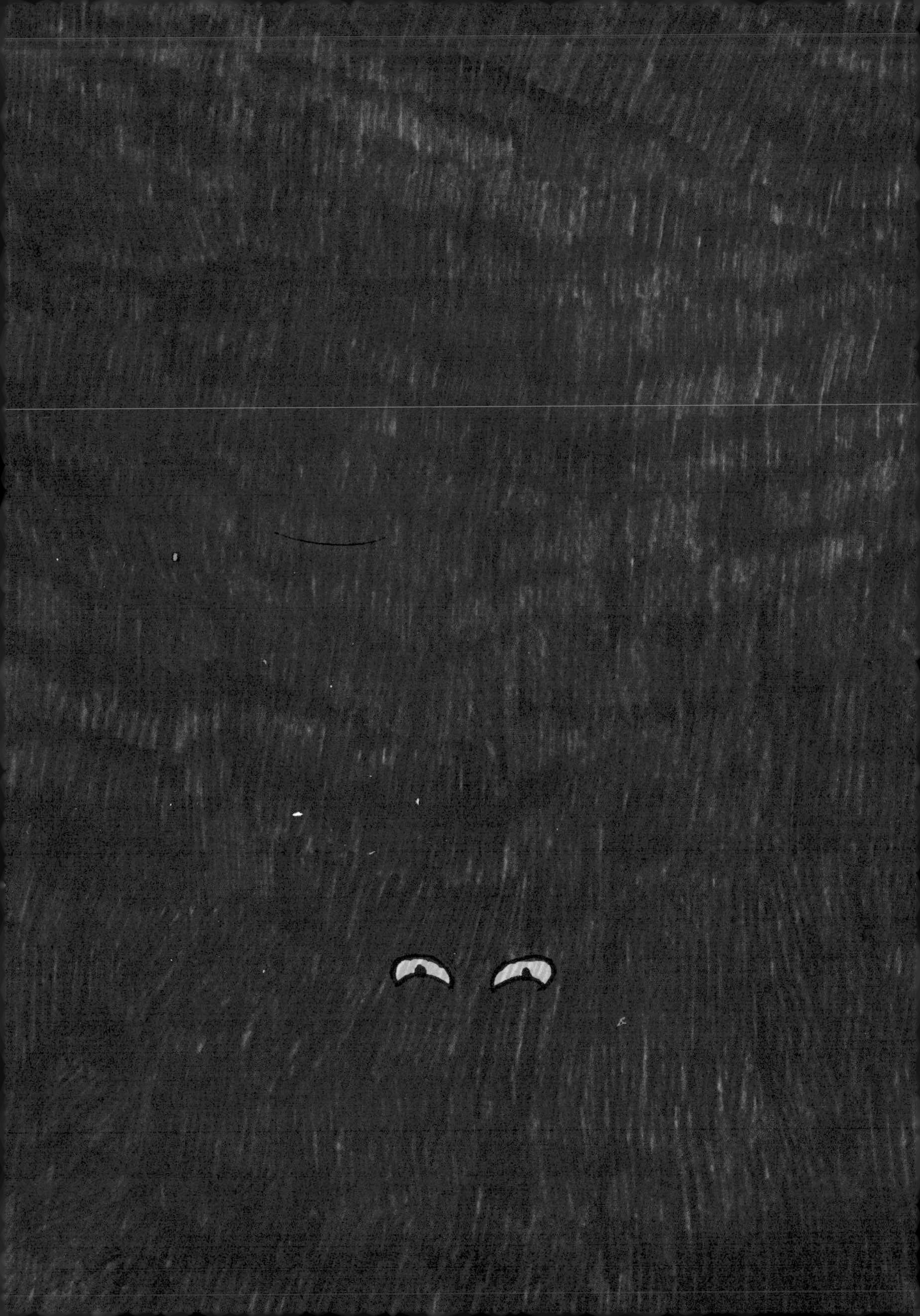

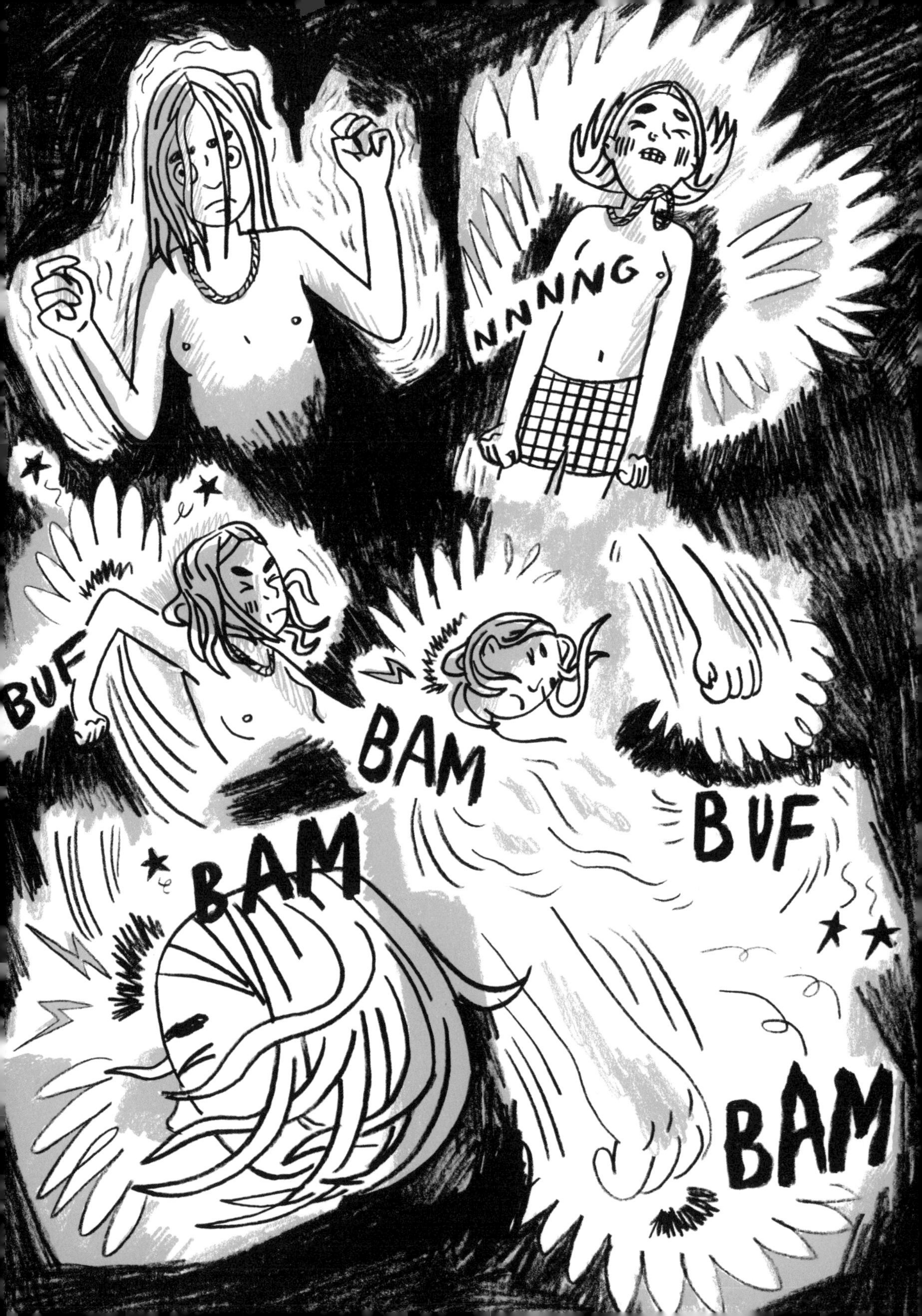
NNNNG
BUF
BAM
BUF
BAM
BAM

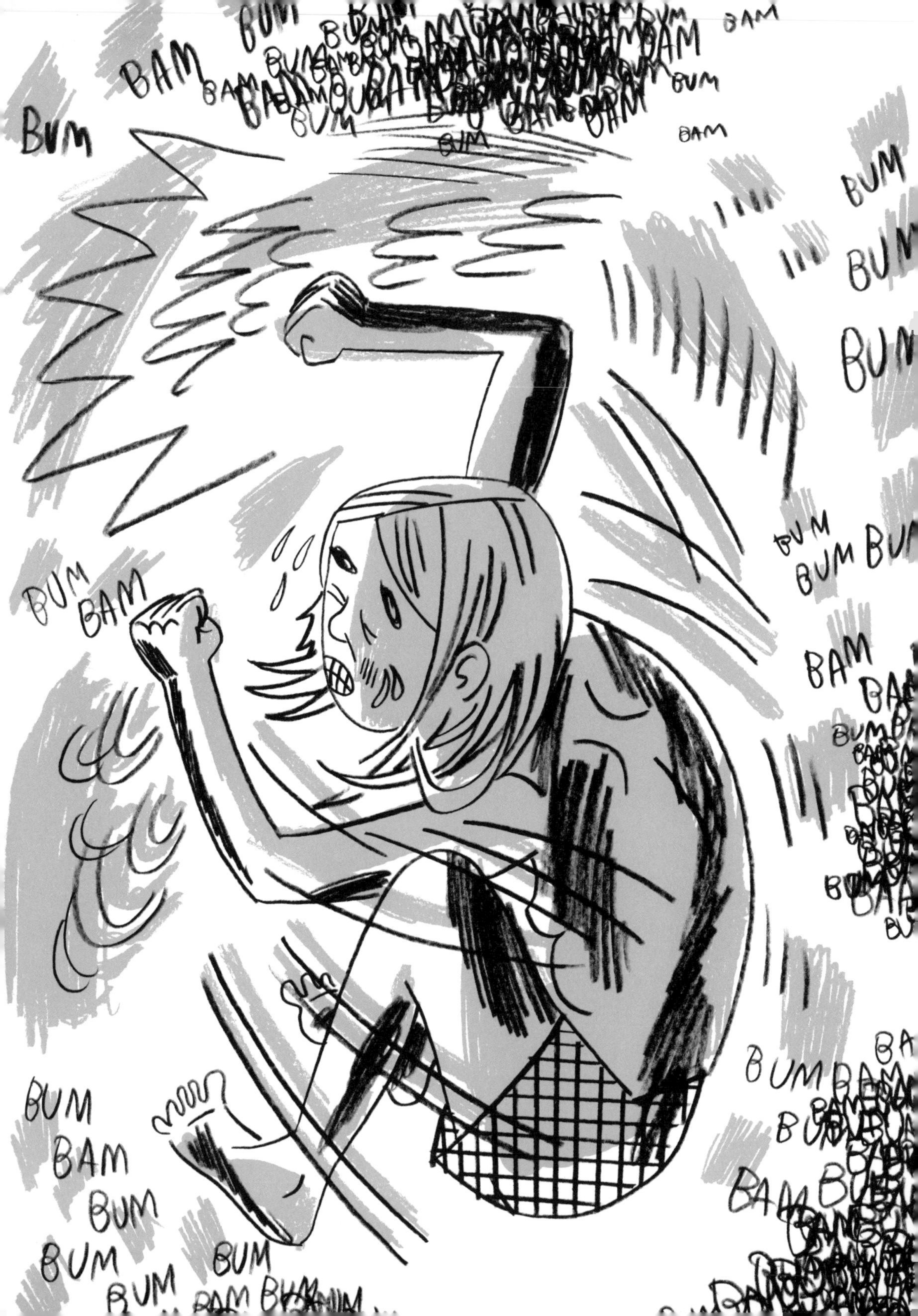
BUM
BAM
BAM
BAM
BUM
BAM
BUM
BUM
BUM
BUM
BAM
BUM
BUM BUM
BAM
BUM BAM
BUM
BAM
BUM
BUM
BUM
BUM
BUM
BUM

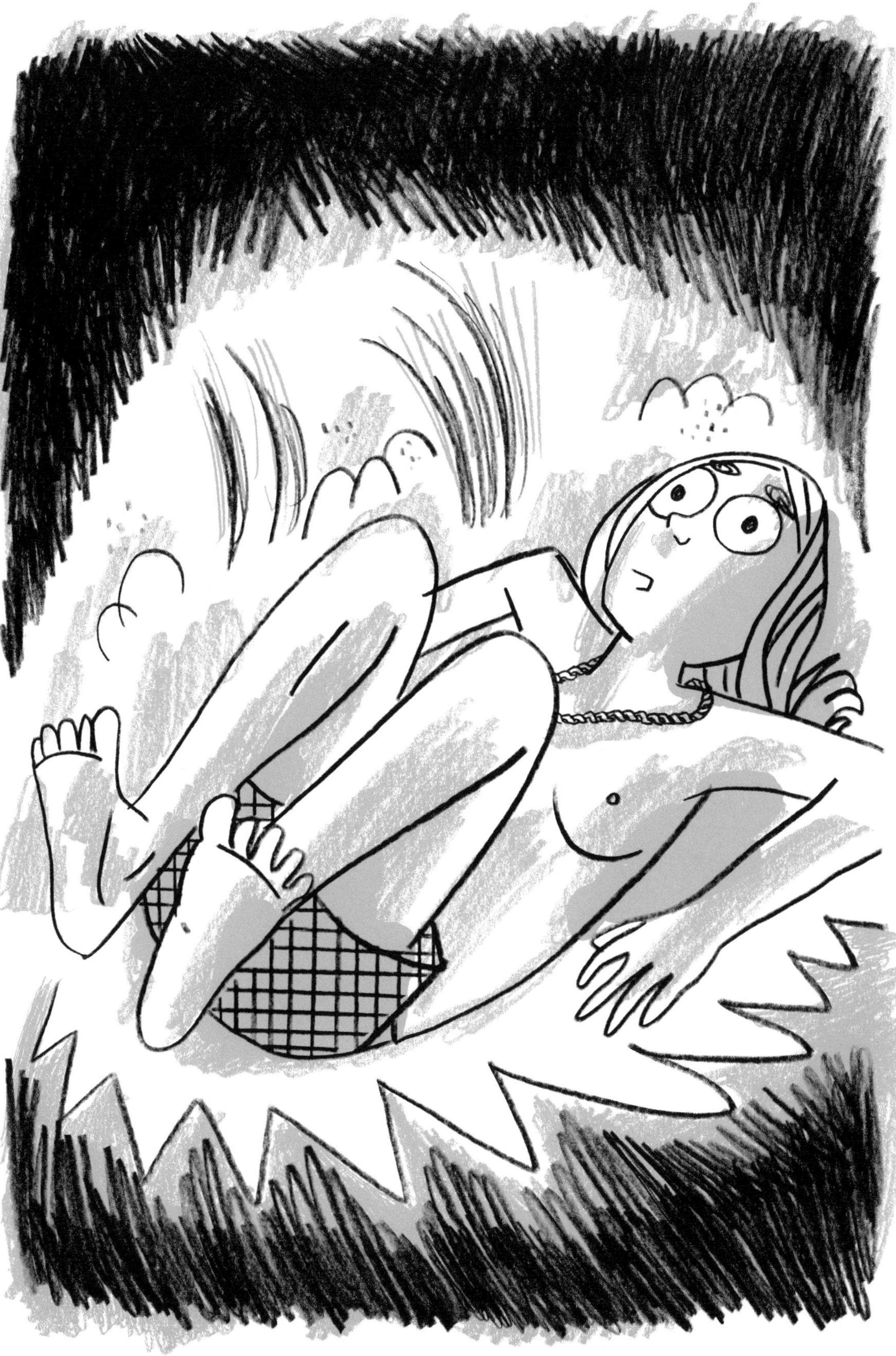

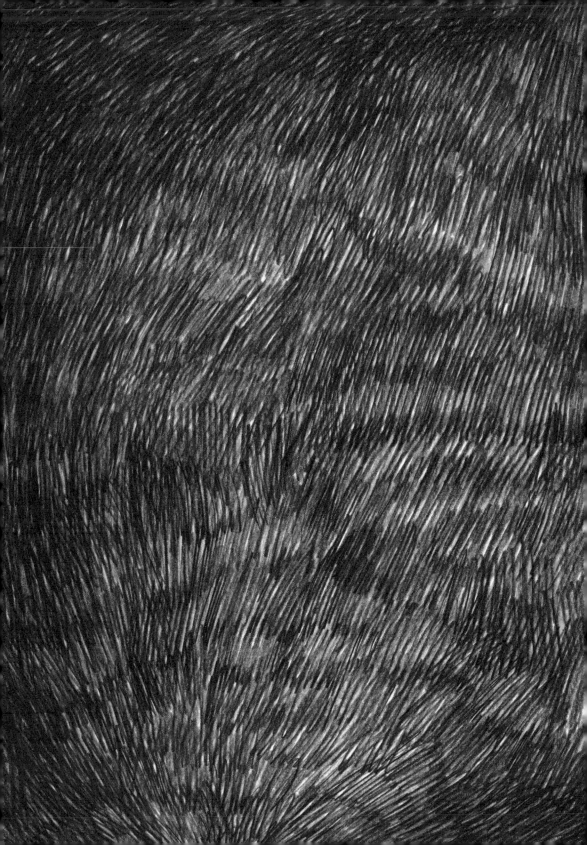

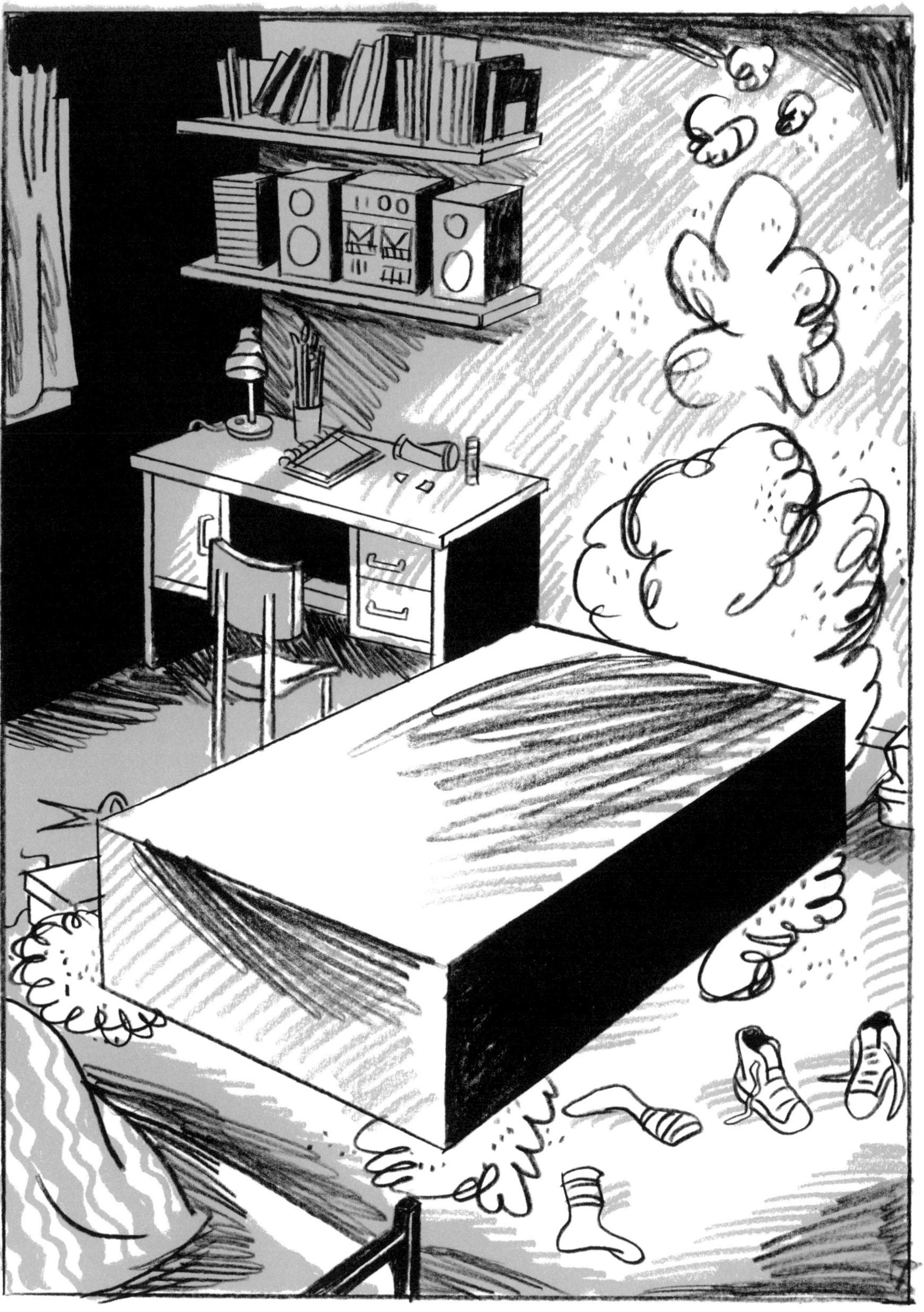

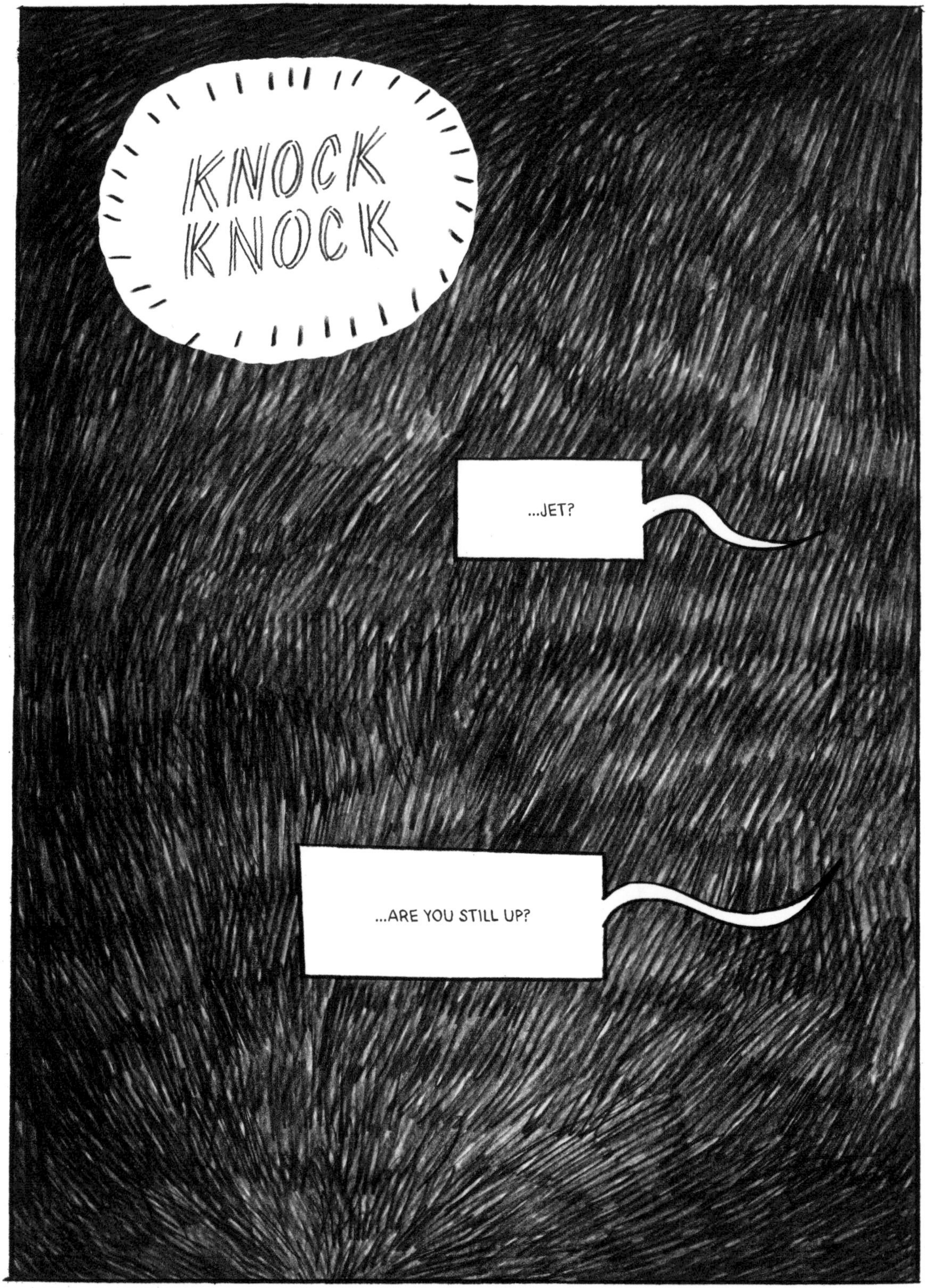
KNOCK KNOCK
...JET?
...ARE YOU STILL UP?

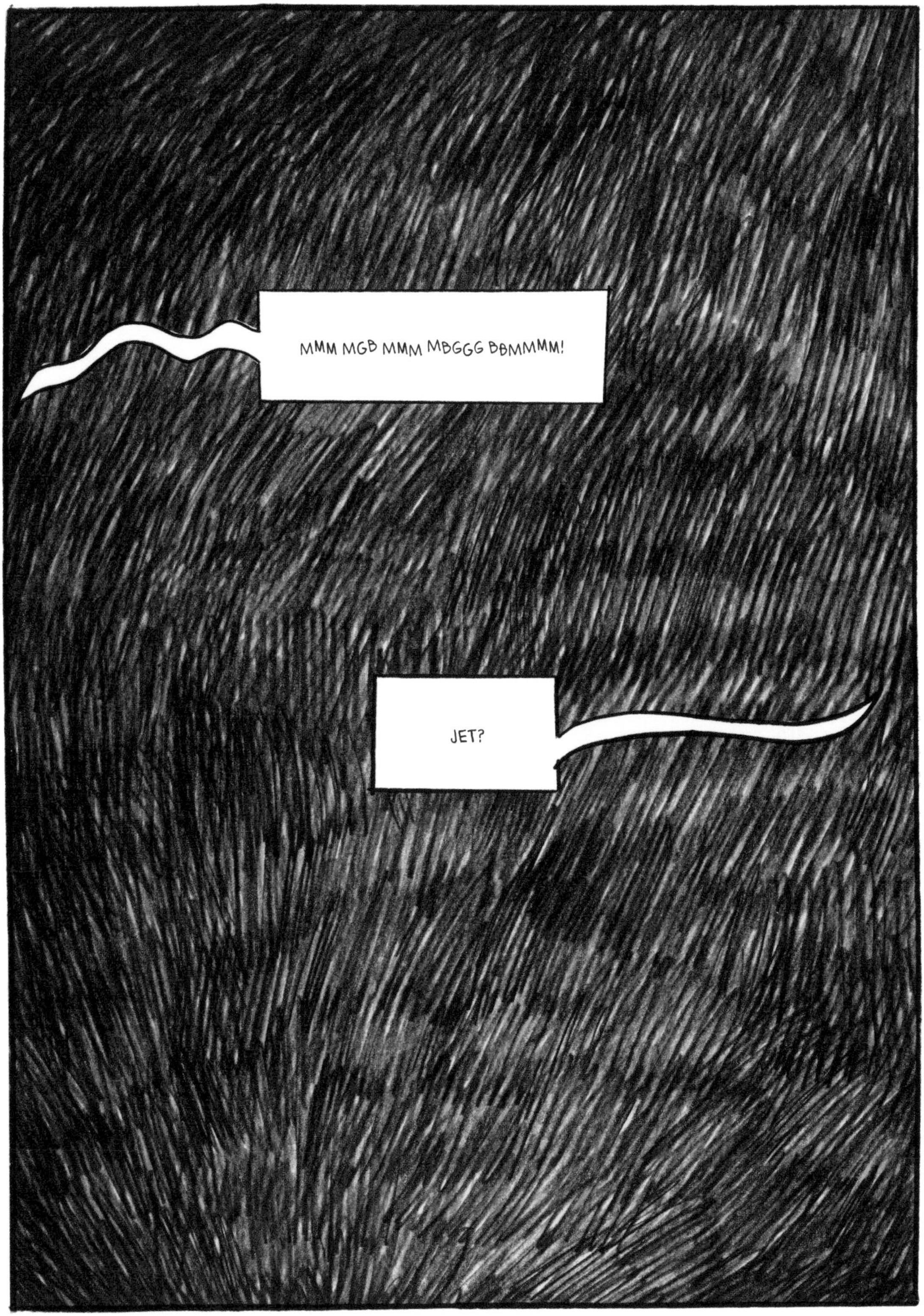
MMM MGB MMM MBGGG BBMMMM!
JET?

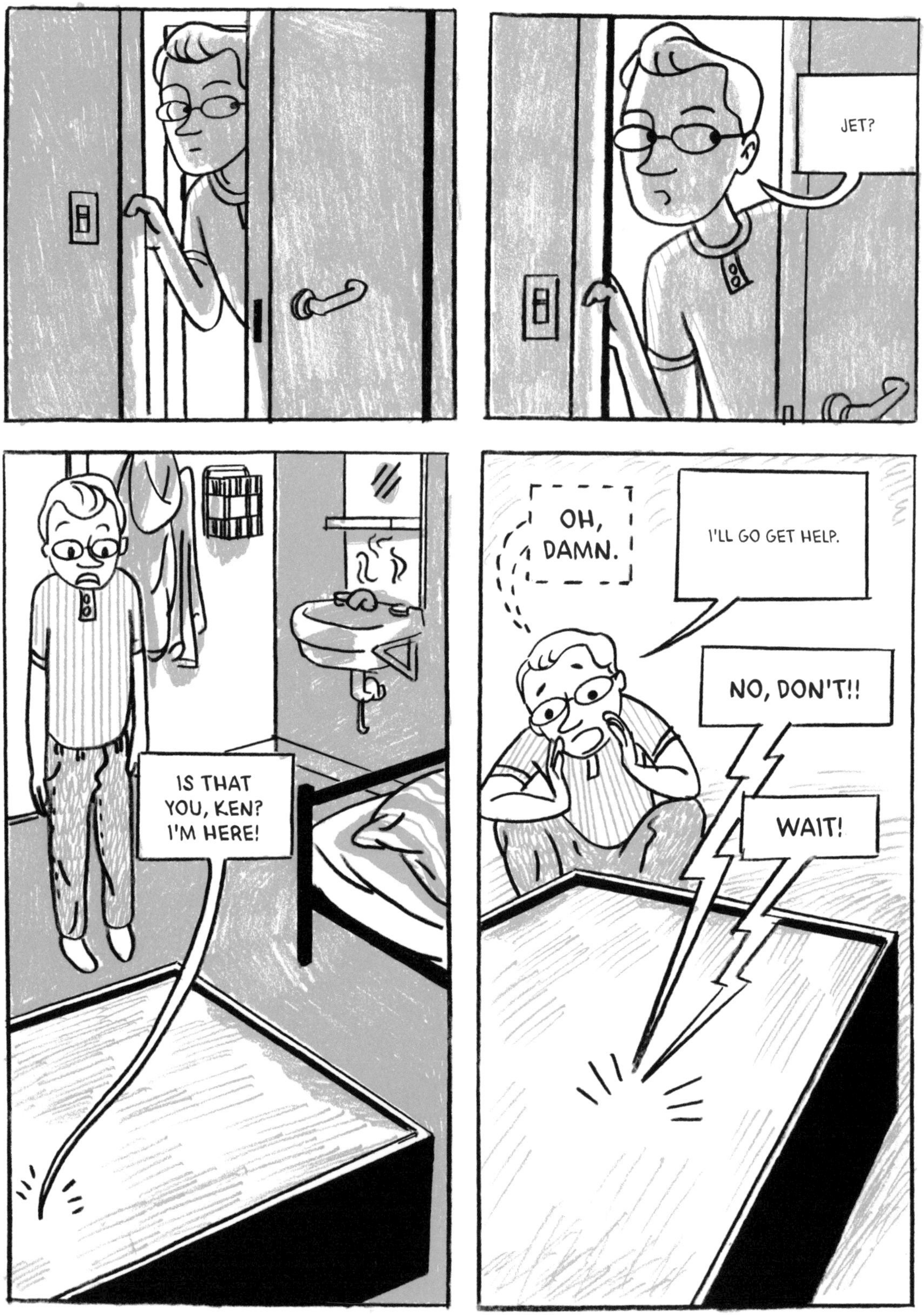
JET?
IS THAT YOU, KEN? I'M HERE!
OH, DAMN.
I'LL GO GET HELP.
NO, DON'T!!
WAIT!

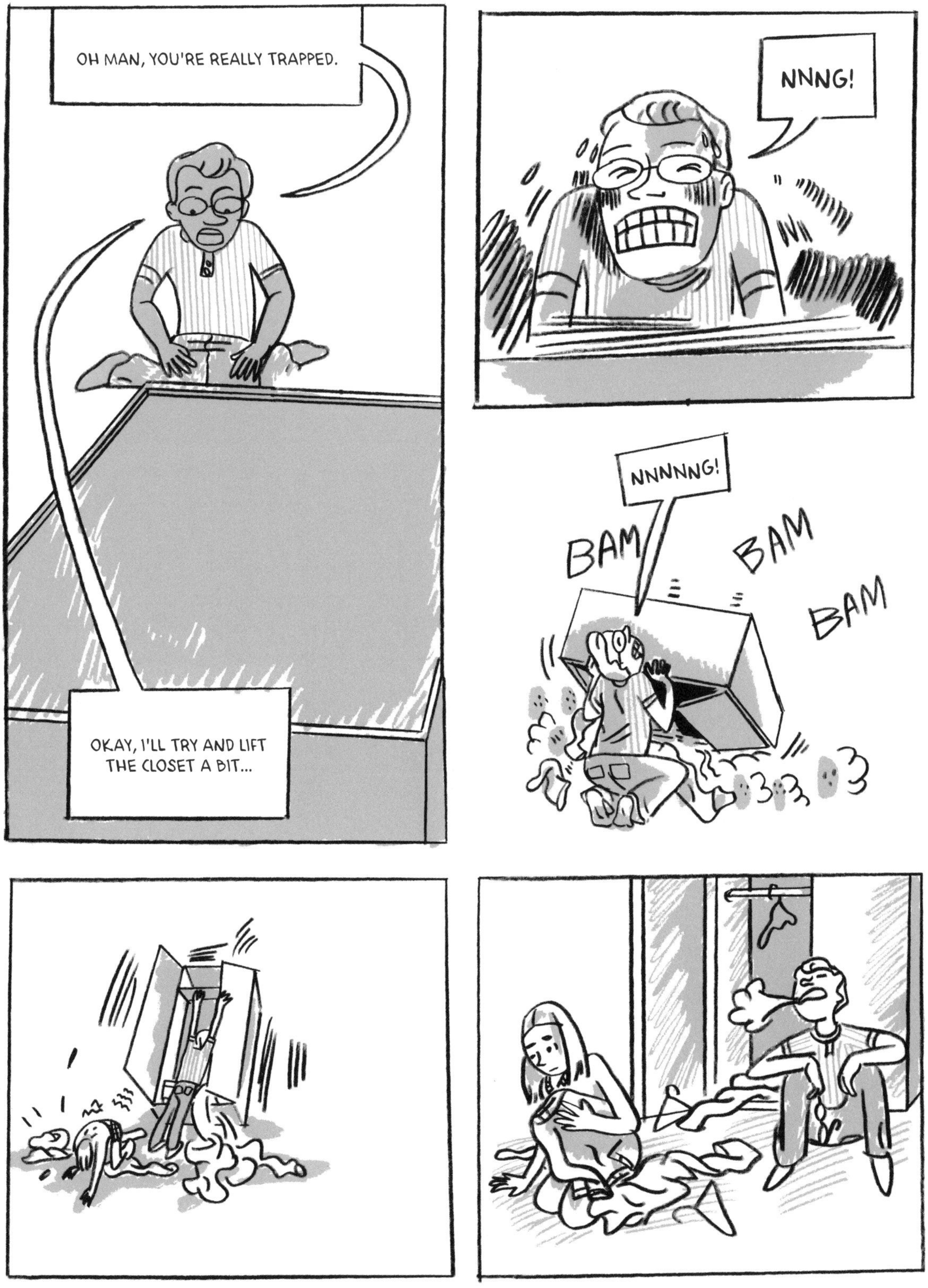
OH MAN, YOU'RE REALLY TRAPPED.
OKAY, I'LL TRY AND LIFT THE CLOSET A BIT...
NNNG!
NNNNNG!
BAM
BAM
BAM

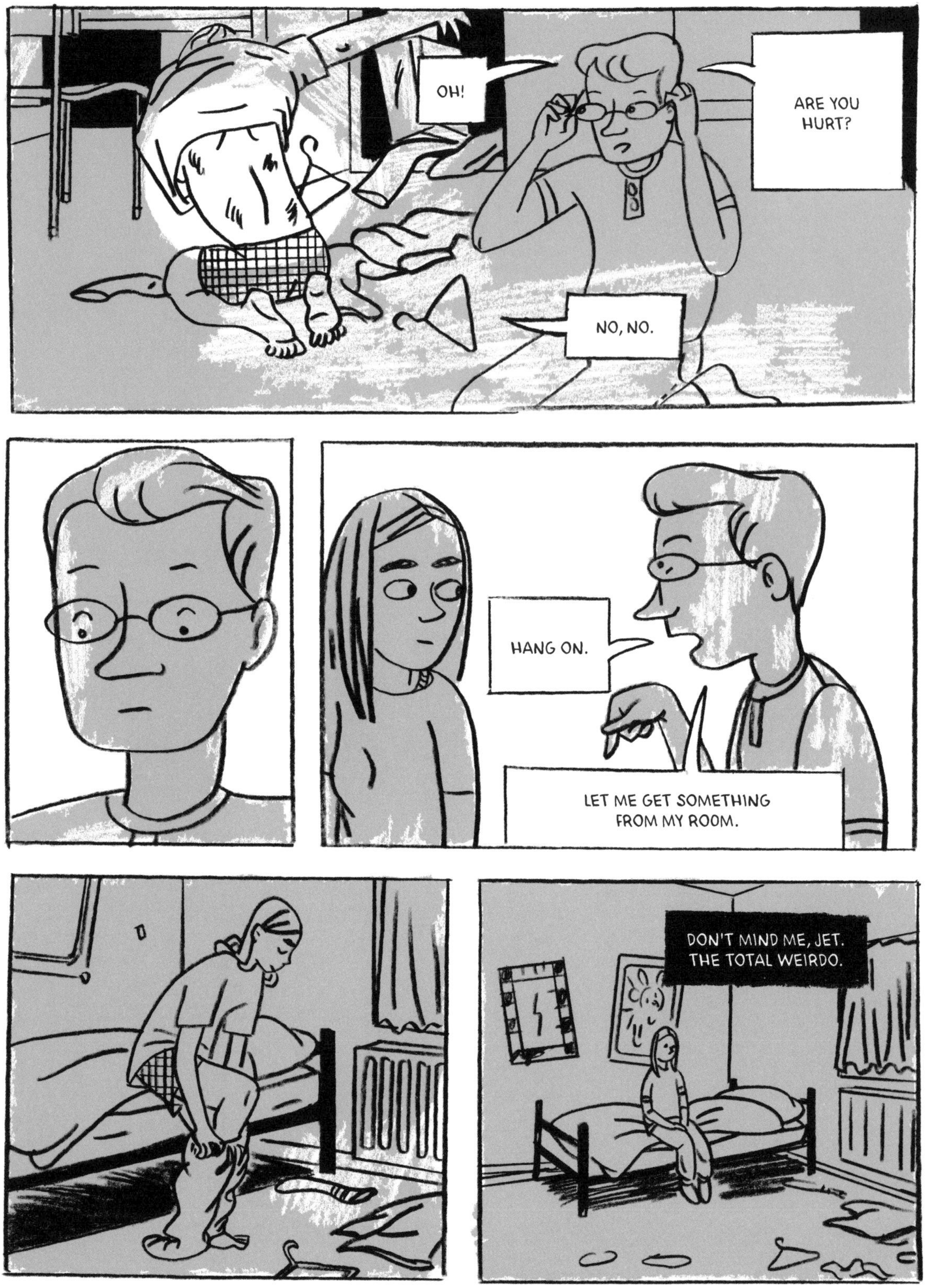
OH!
ARE YOU HURT?
NO, NO.
HANG ON.
LET ME GET SOMETHING FROM MY ROOM.
DON'T MIND ME, JET. THE TOTAL WEIRDO.

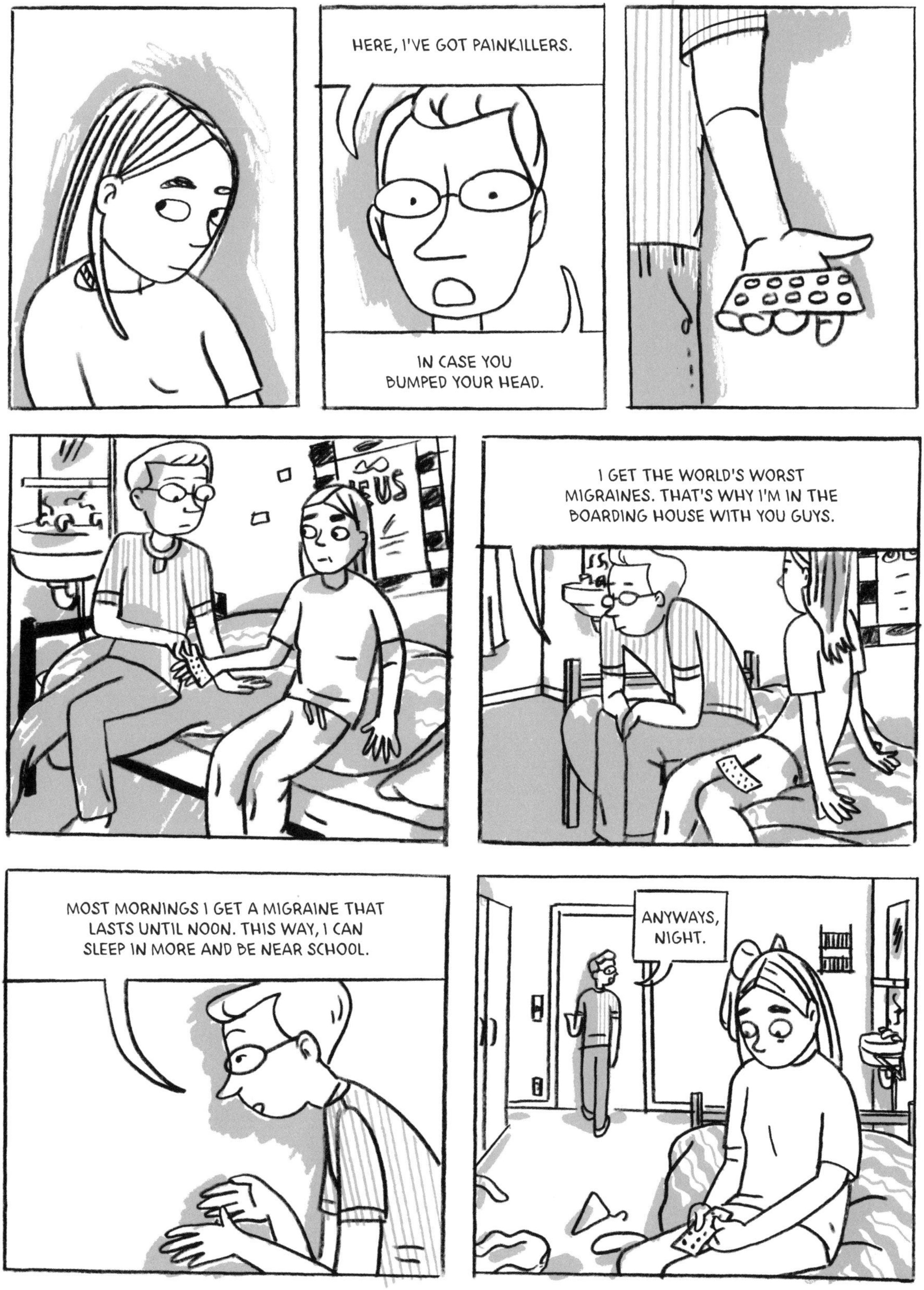
HERE, I'VE GOT PAINKILLERS.
IN CASE YOU BUMPED YOUR HEAD.
I GET THE WORLD'S WORST MIGRAINES. THAT'S WHY I'M IN THE BOARDING HOUSE WITH YOU GUYS.
MOST MORNINGS I GET A MIGRAINE THAT LASTS UNTIL NOON. THIS WAY, I CAN SLEEP IN MORE AND BE NEAR SCHOOL.
ANYWAYS, NIGHT.

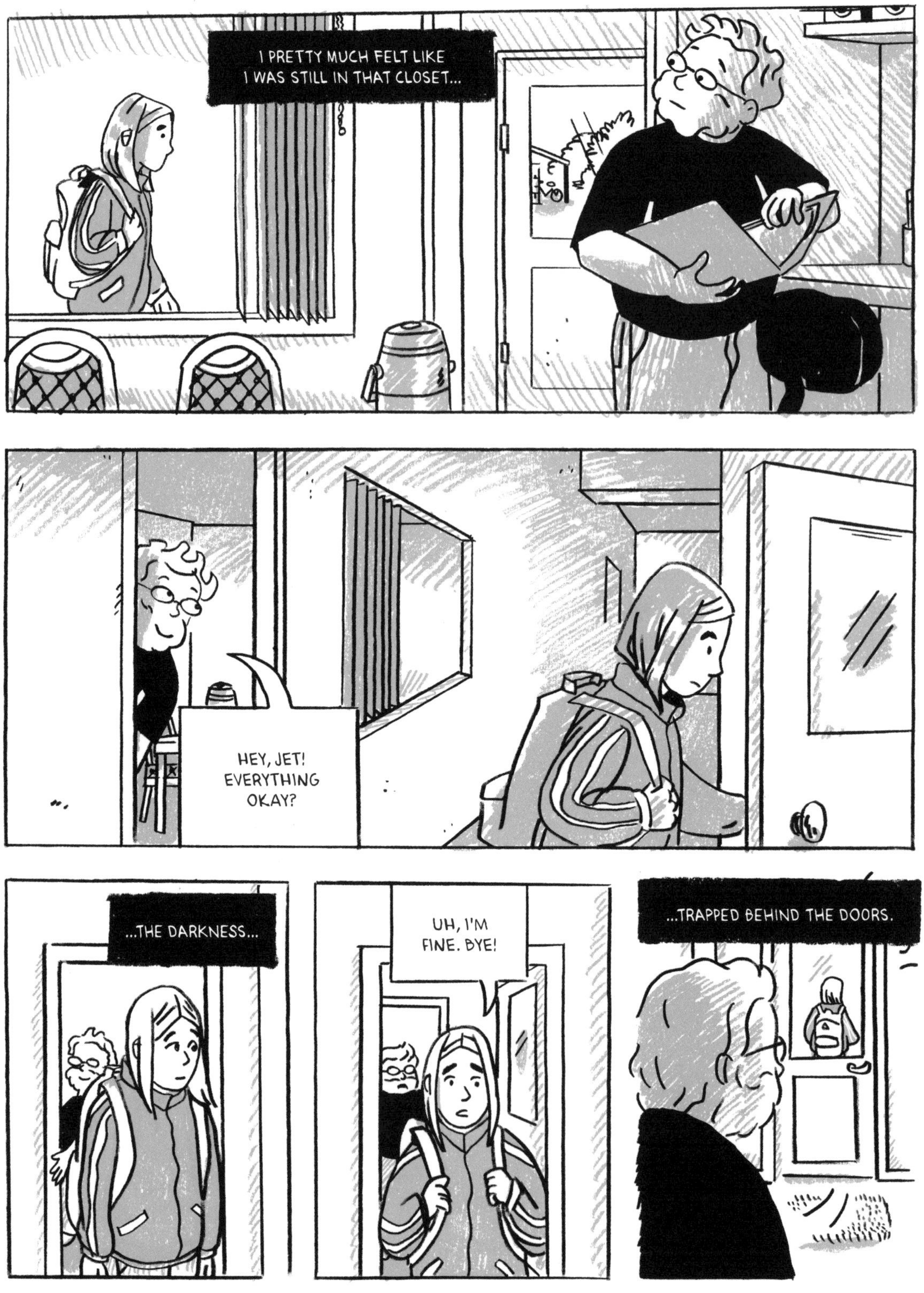
I PRETTY MUCH FELT LIKE I WAS STILL IN THAT CLOSET...
HEY, JET! EVERYTHING OKAY?
...THE DARKNESS...
UH, I'M FINE. BYE!
...TRAPPED BEHIND THE DOORS.

*"SO REAL" BY JEFF BUCKLEY

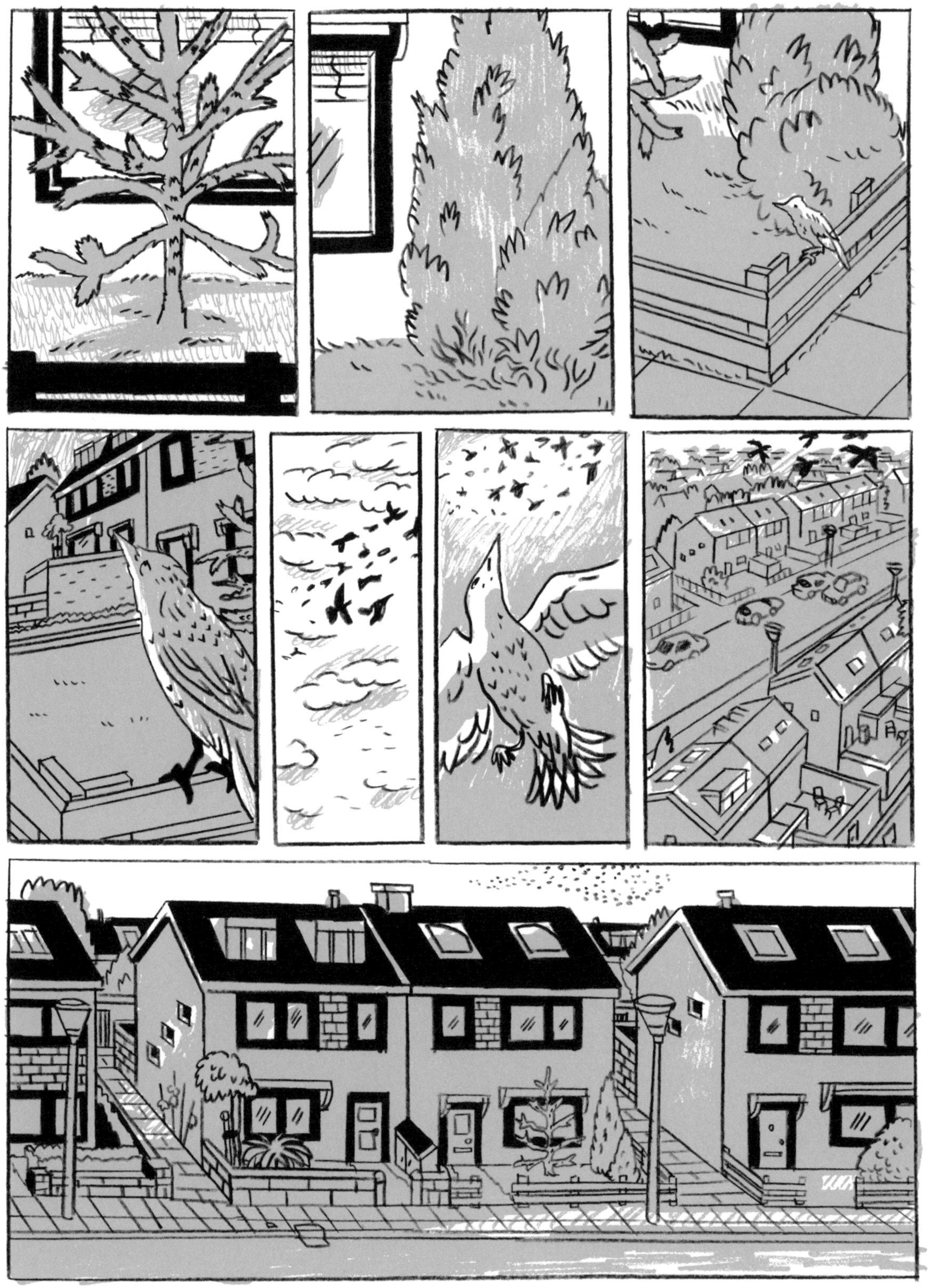

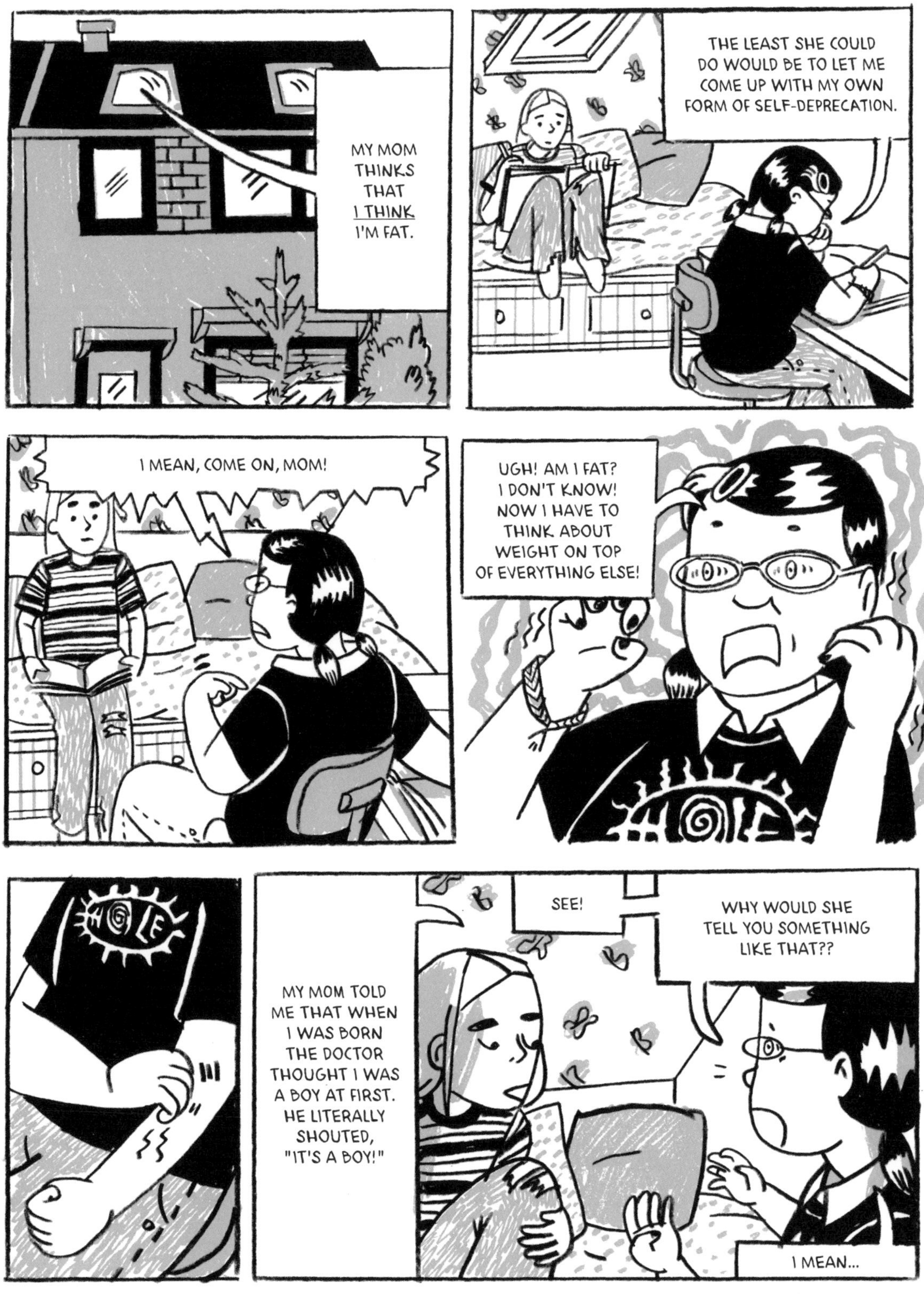
MY MOM THINKS THAT I THINK I'M FAT.
THE LEAST SHE COULD DO WOULD BE TO LET ME COME UP WITH MY OWN FORM OF SELF-DEPRECATION.
I MEAN, COME ON, MOM!
UGH! AM I FAT? I DON'T KNOW! NOW I HAVE TO THINK ABOUT WEIGHT ON TOP OF EVERYTHING ELSE!
HOLE
MY MOM TOLD ME THAT WHEN I WAS BORN THE DOCTOR THOUGHT I WAS A BOY AT FIRST. HE LITERALLY SHOUTED, "IT'S A BOY!"
SEE!
WHY WOULD SHE TELL YOU SOMETHING LIKE THAT??
I MEAN...

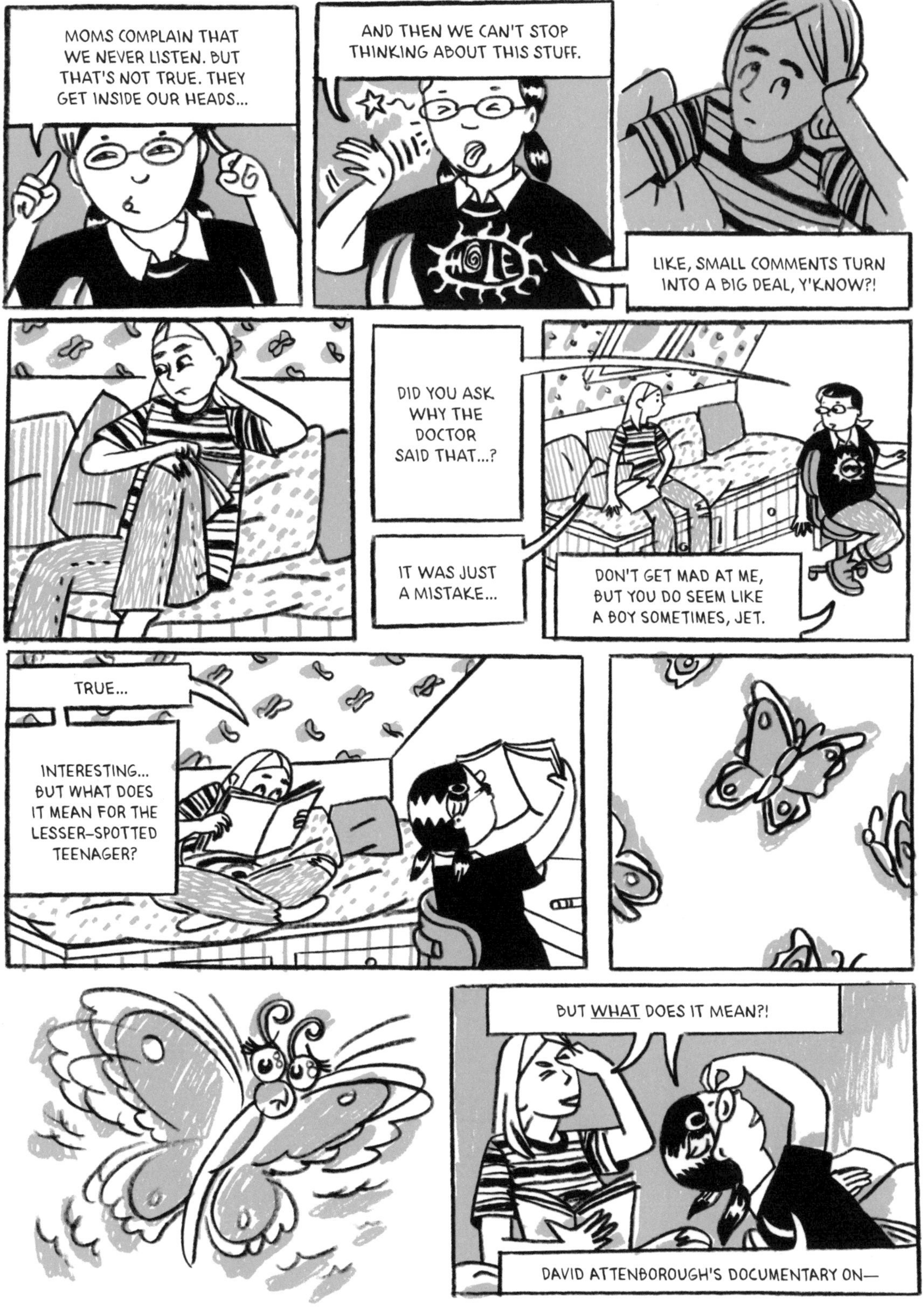
MOMS COMPLAIN THAT WE NEVER LISTEN. BUT THAT'S NOT TRUE. THEY GET INSIDE OUR HEADS...
AND THEN WE CAN'T STOP THINKING ABOUT THIS STUFF.
LIKE, SMALL COMMENTS TURN INTO A BIG DEAL, Y'KNOW?!
DID YOU ASK WHY THE DOCTOR SAID THAT...?
IT WAS JUST A MISTAKE...
DON'T GET MAD AT ME, BUT YOU DO SEEM LIKE A BOY SOMETIMES, JET.
TRUE...
INTERESTING... BUT WHAT DOES IT MEAN FOR THE LESSER-SPOTTED TEENAGER?
BUT WHAT DOES IT MEAN?!
DAVID ATTENBOROUGH'S DOCUMENTARY ON—

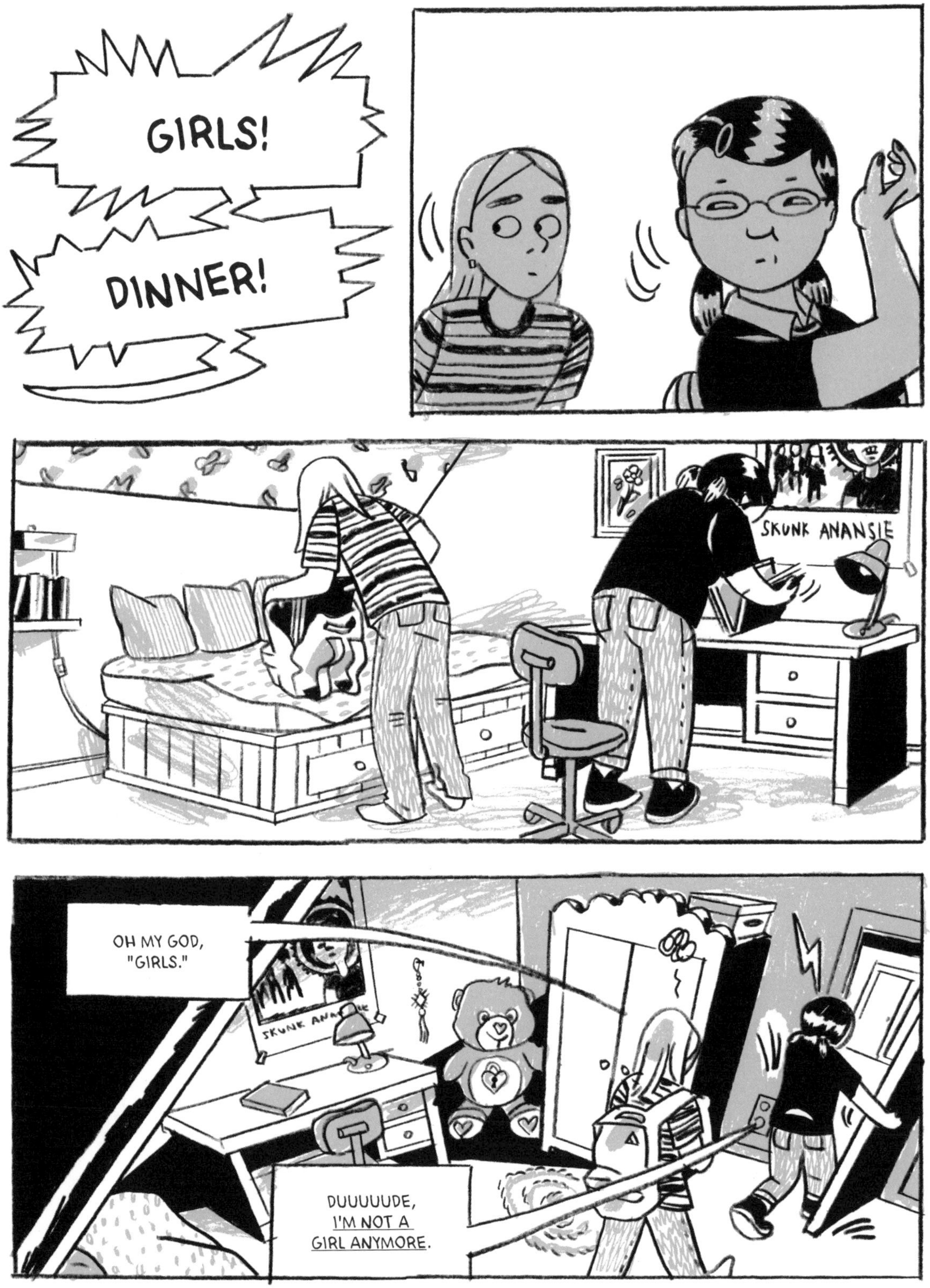
GIRLS!
DINNER!
SKUNK ANANSIE
OH MY GOD, "GIRLS."
DUUUUUDE, I'M NOT A GIRL ANYMORE.

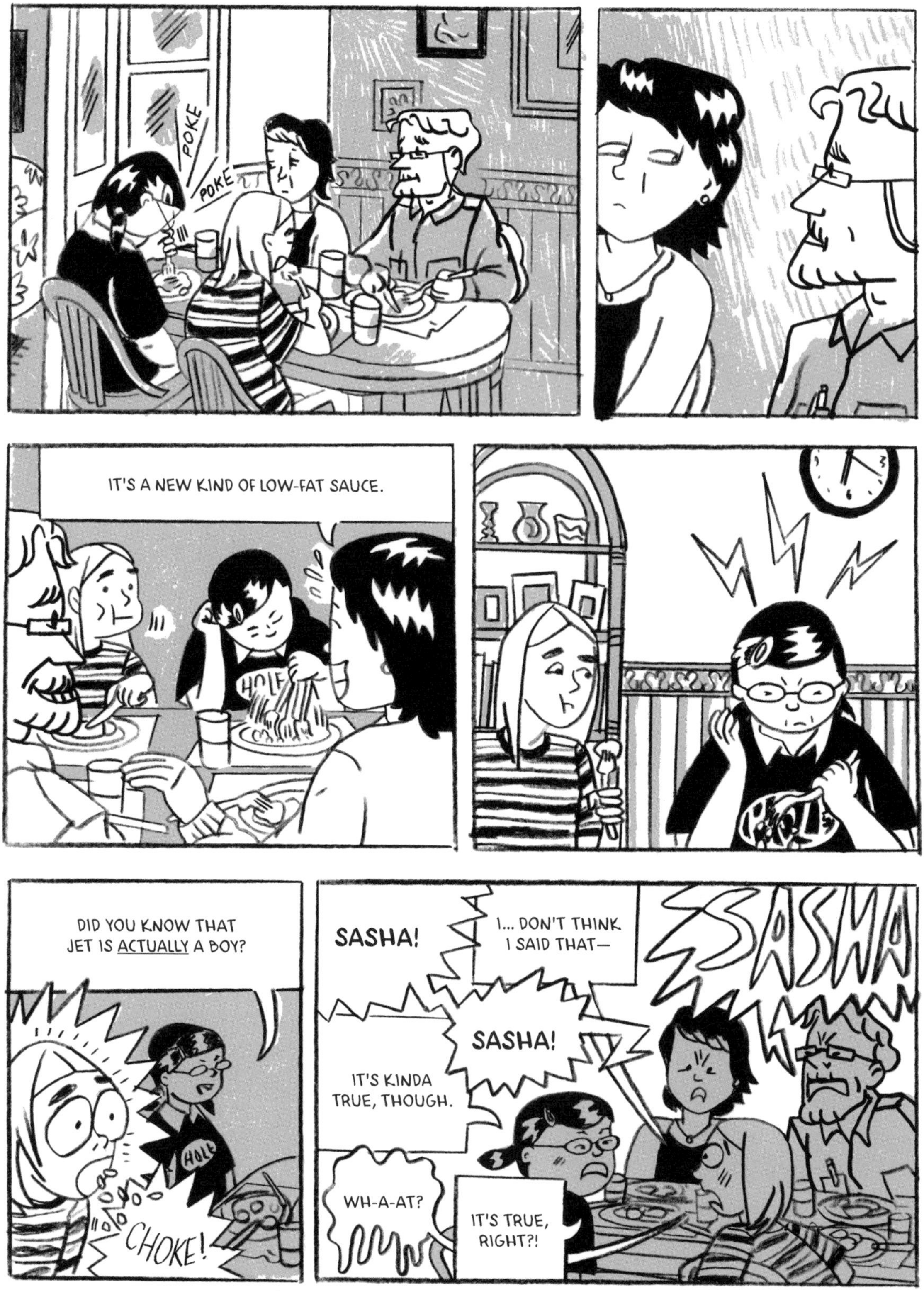
POKE
POKE
IT'S A NEW KIND OF LOW-FAT SAUCE.
DID YOU KNOW THAT JET IS ACTUALLY A BOY?
CHOKE!
SASHA!
I... DON'T THINK I SAID THAT—
SASHA
SASHA!
IT'S KINDA TRUE, THOUGH.
WH-A-AT?
IT'S TRUE, RIGHT?!

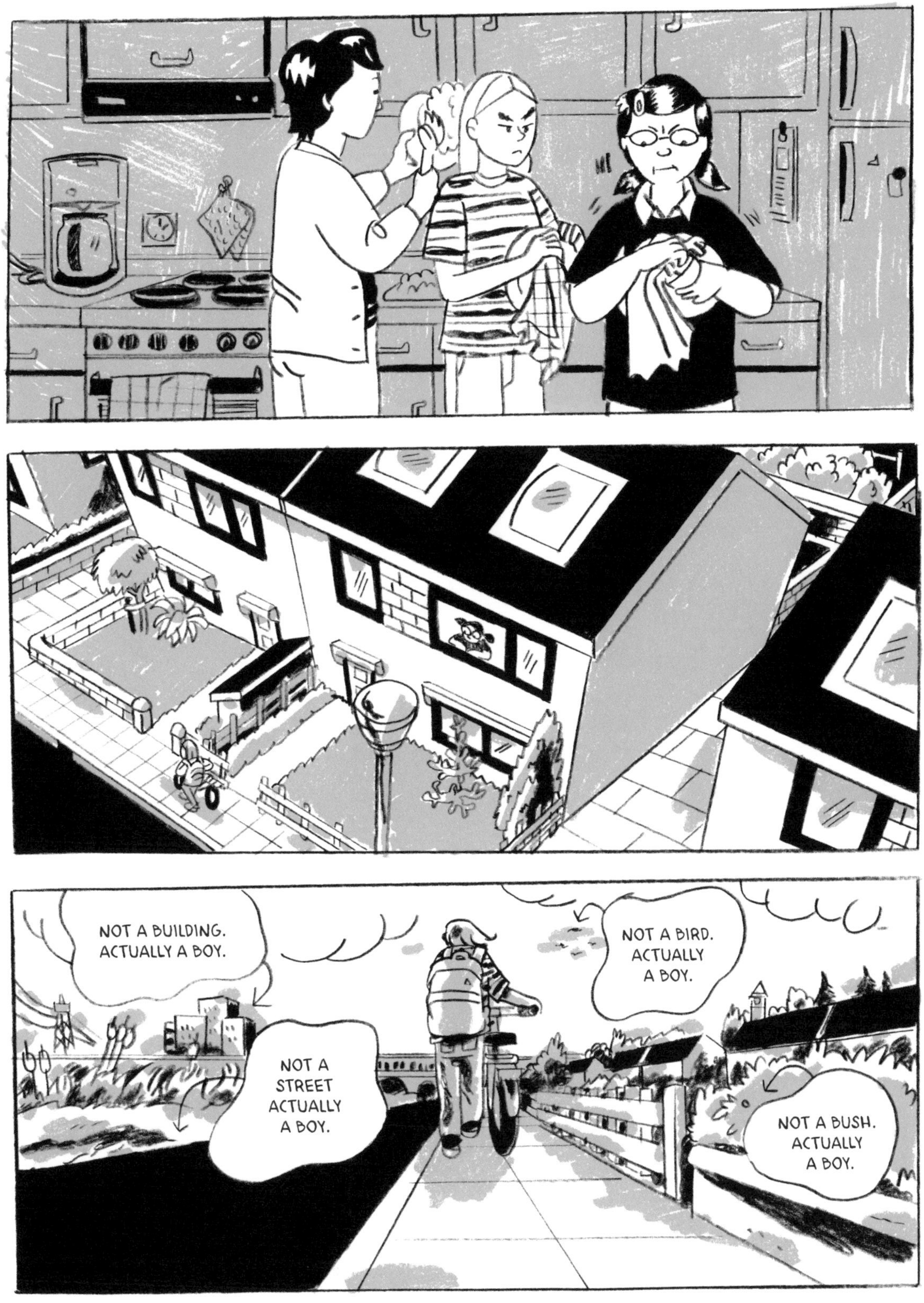
NOT A BUILDING.
ACTUALLY A BOY.
NOT A STREET ACTUALLY A BOY.
NOT A BIRD. ACTUALLY A BOY.
NOT A BUSH. ACTUALLY A BOY.

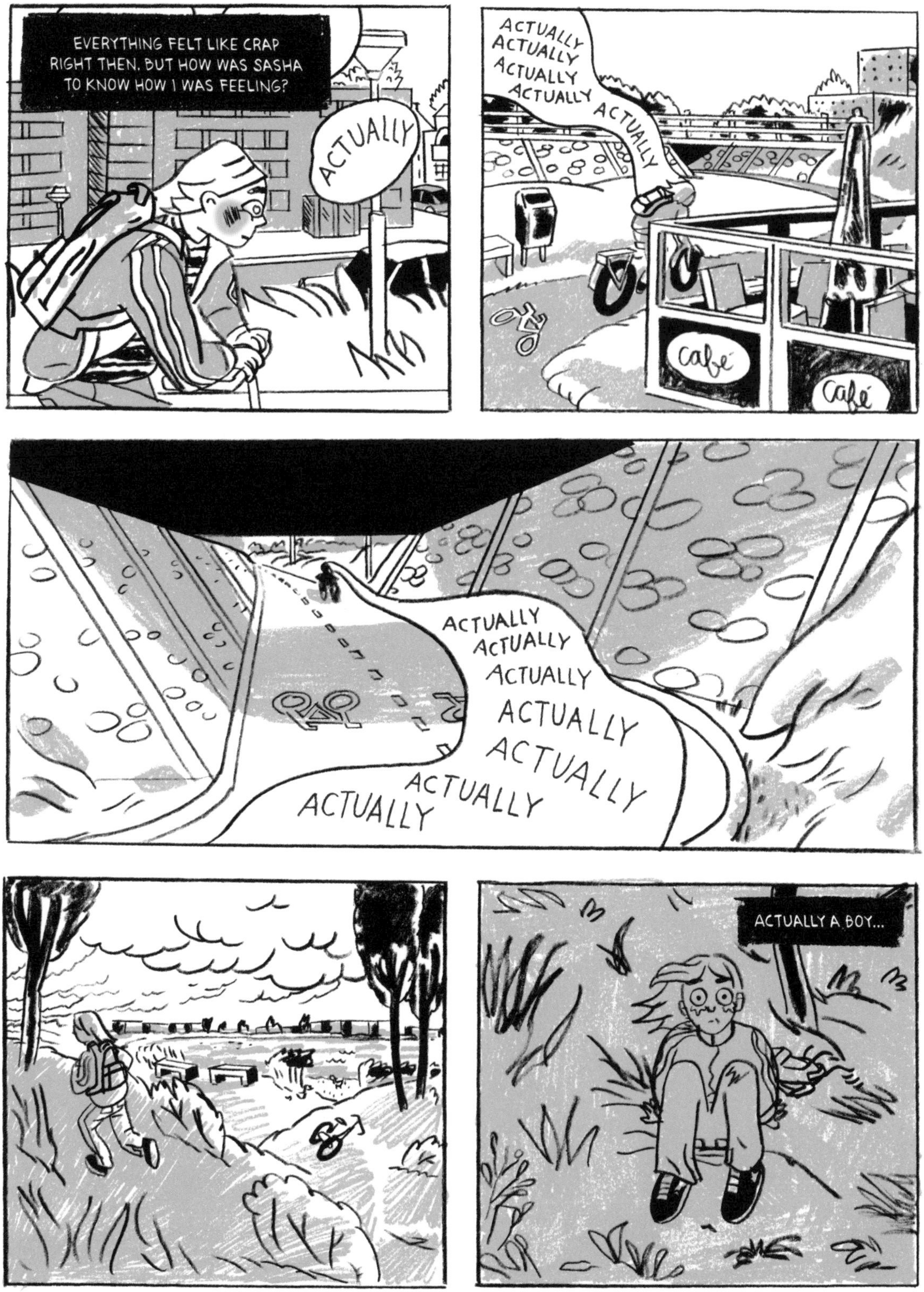
EVERYTHING FELT LIKE CRAP RIGHT THEN. BUT HOW WAS SASHA TO KNOW HOW I WAS FEELING?
ACTUALLY
ACTUALLY
ACTUALLY
ACTUALLY
ACTUALLY
ACTUALLY
café
café
ACTUALLY
ACTUALLY
ACTUALLY
ACTUALLY
ACTUALLY
ACTUALLY
ACTUALLY
ACTUALLY A BOY...

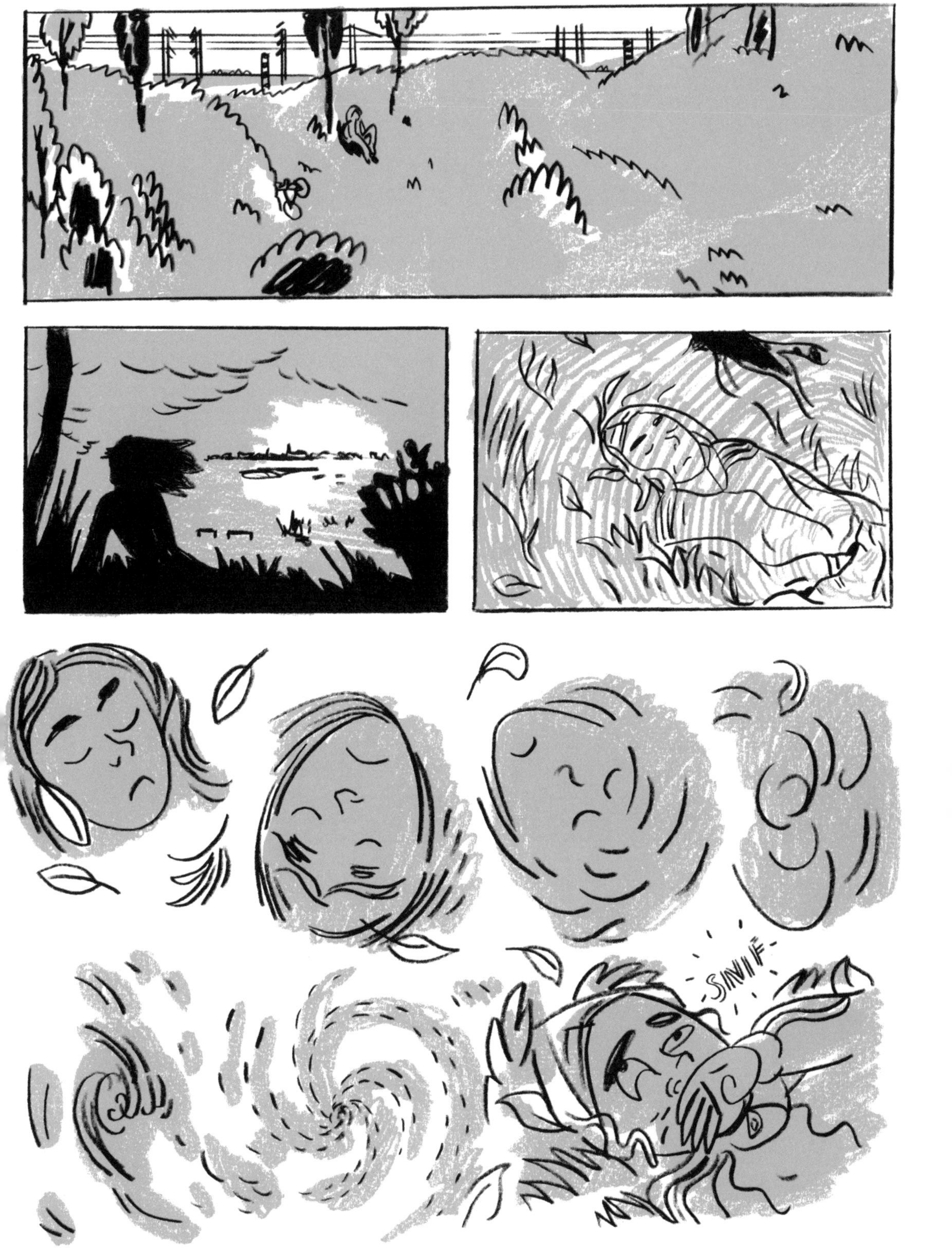
SNIF

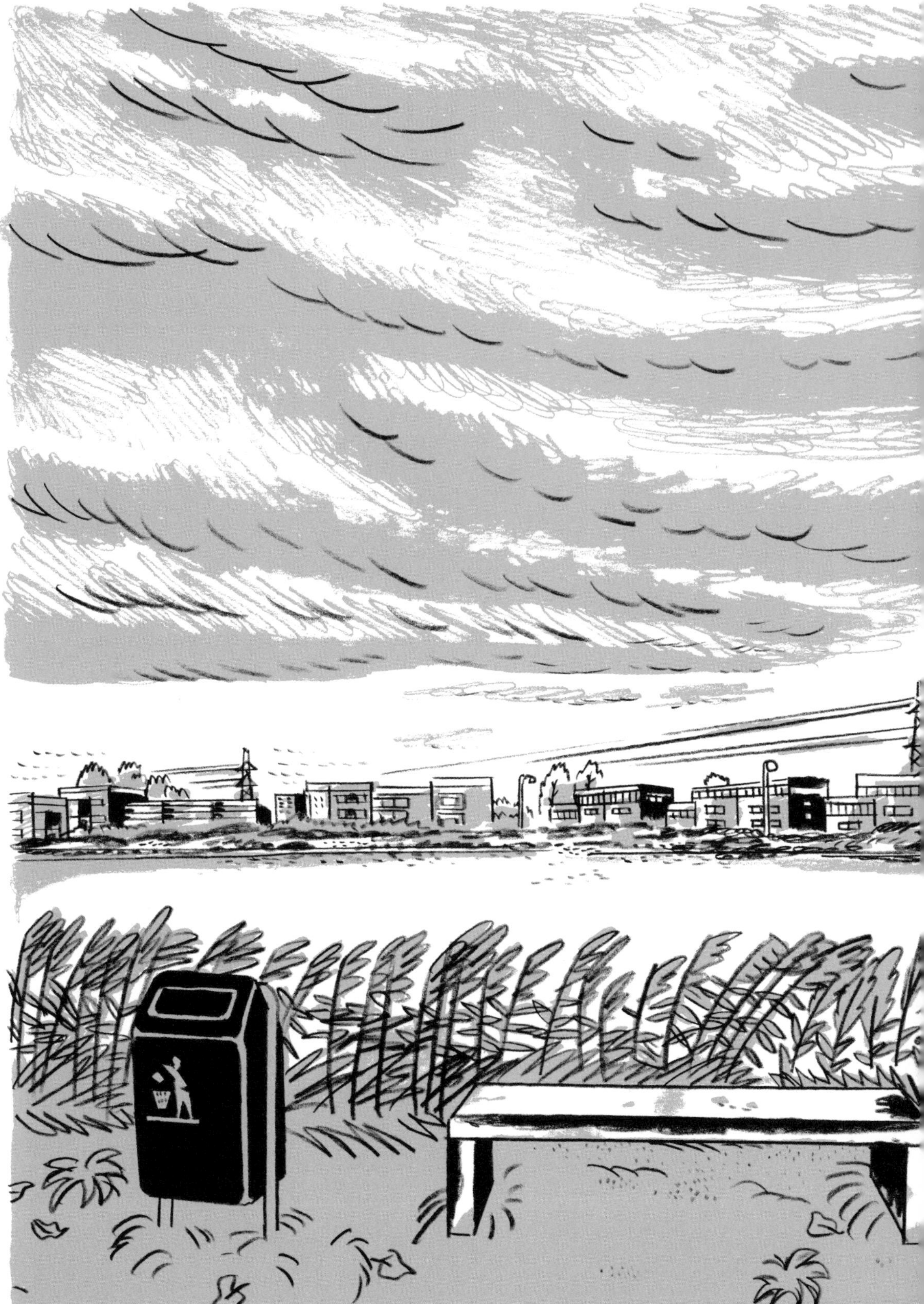

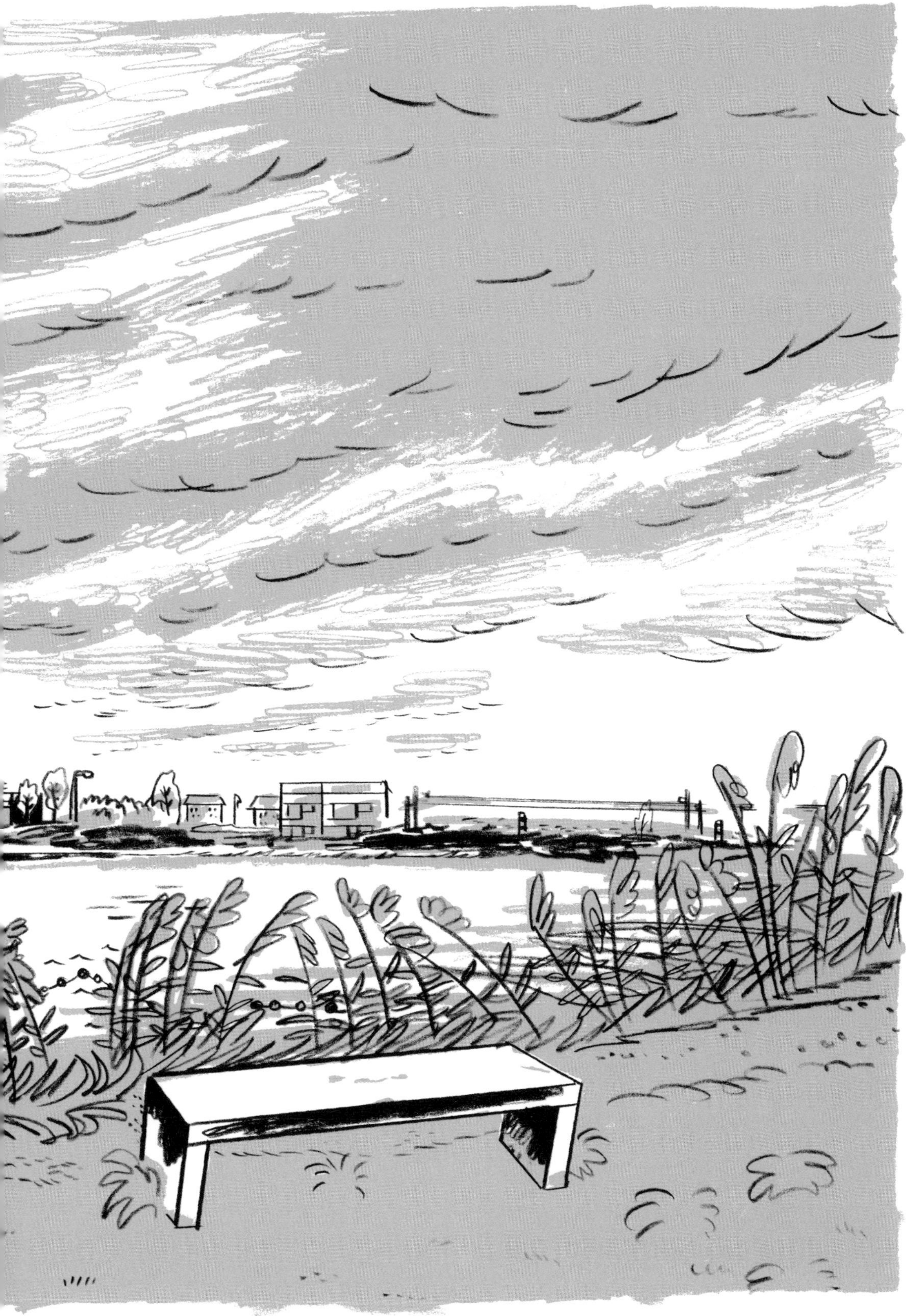

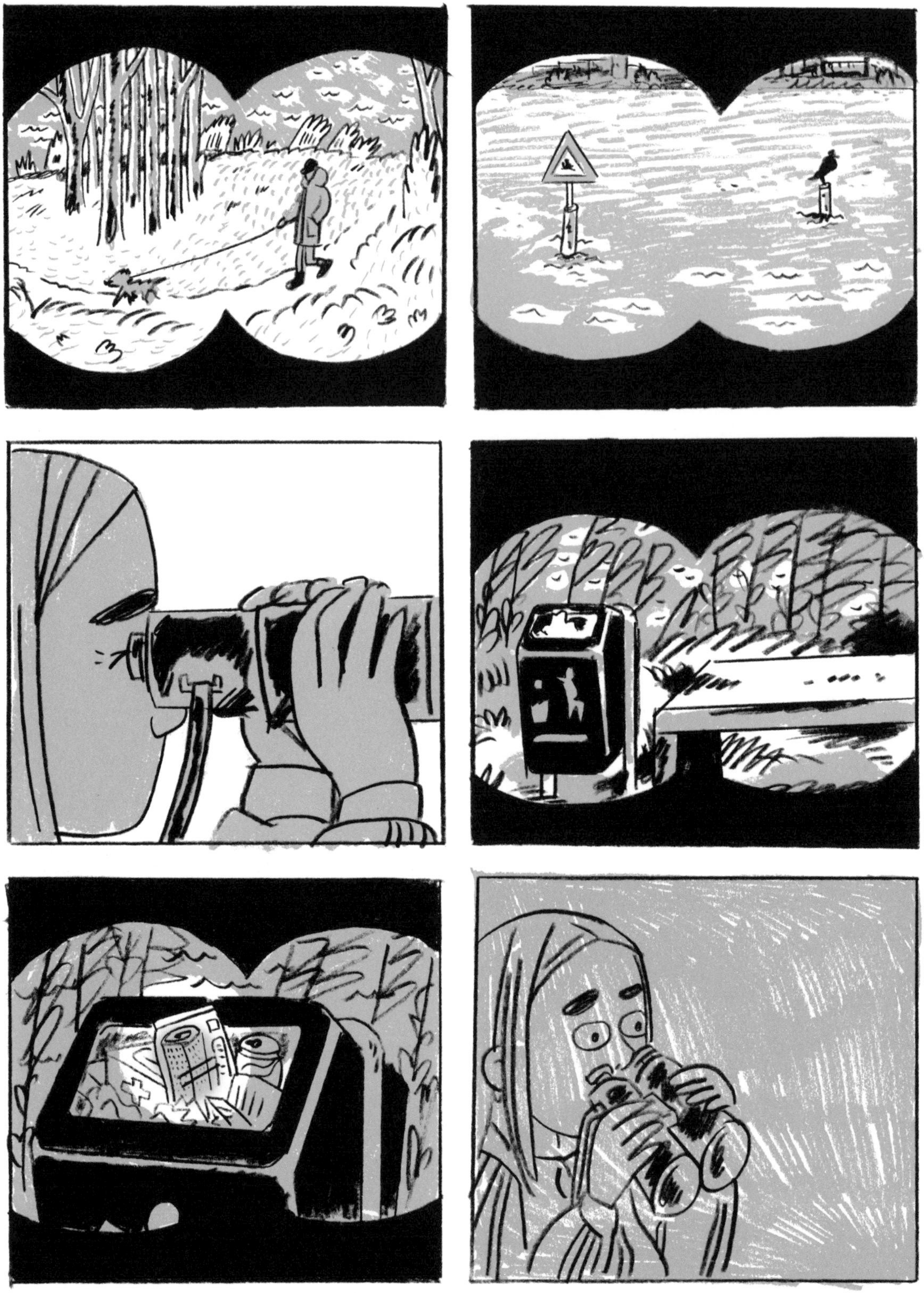

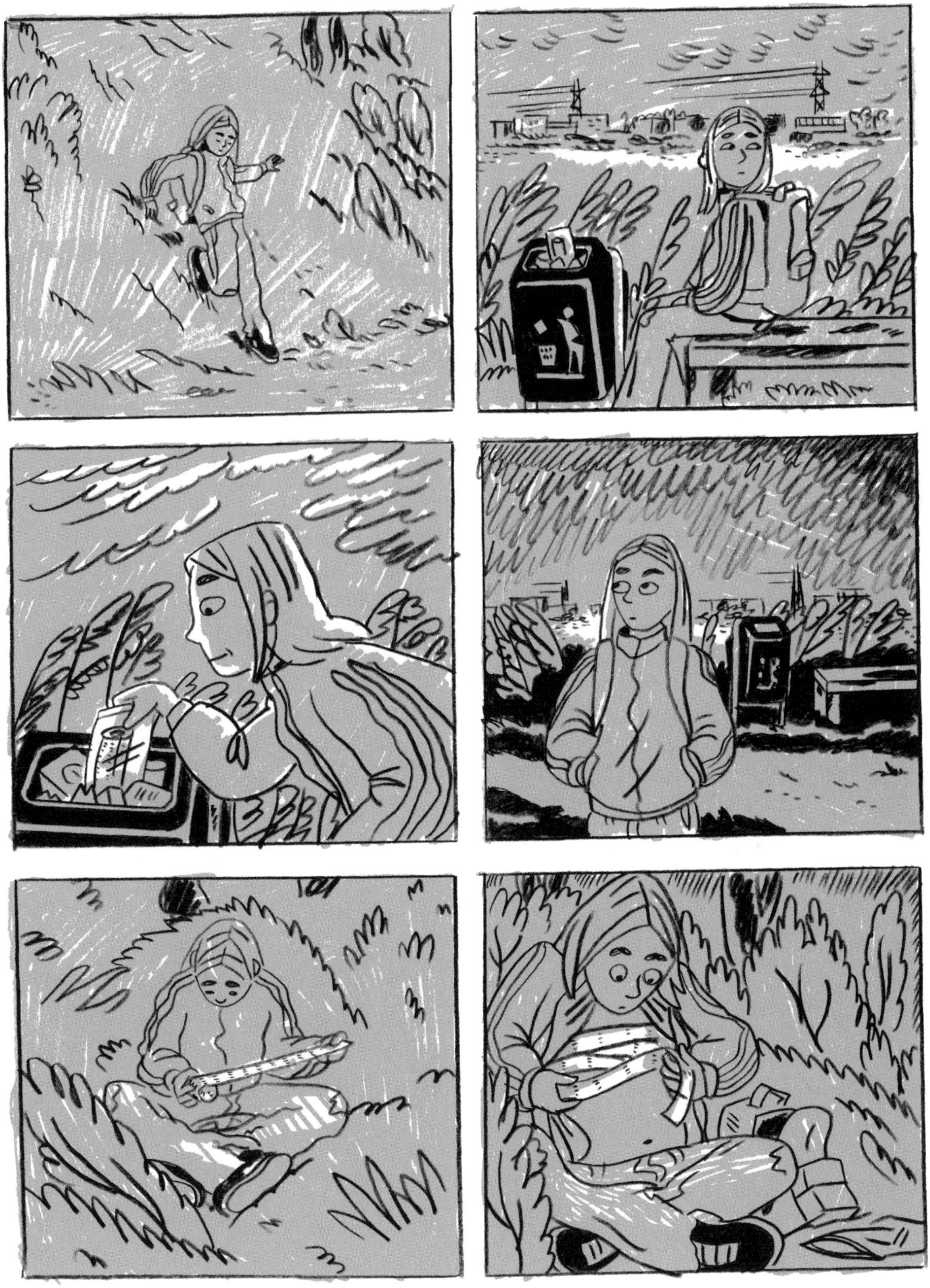

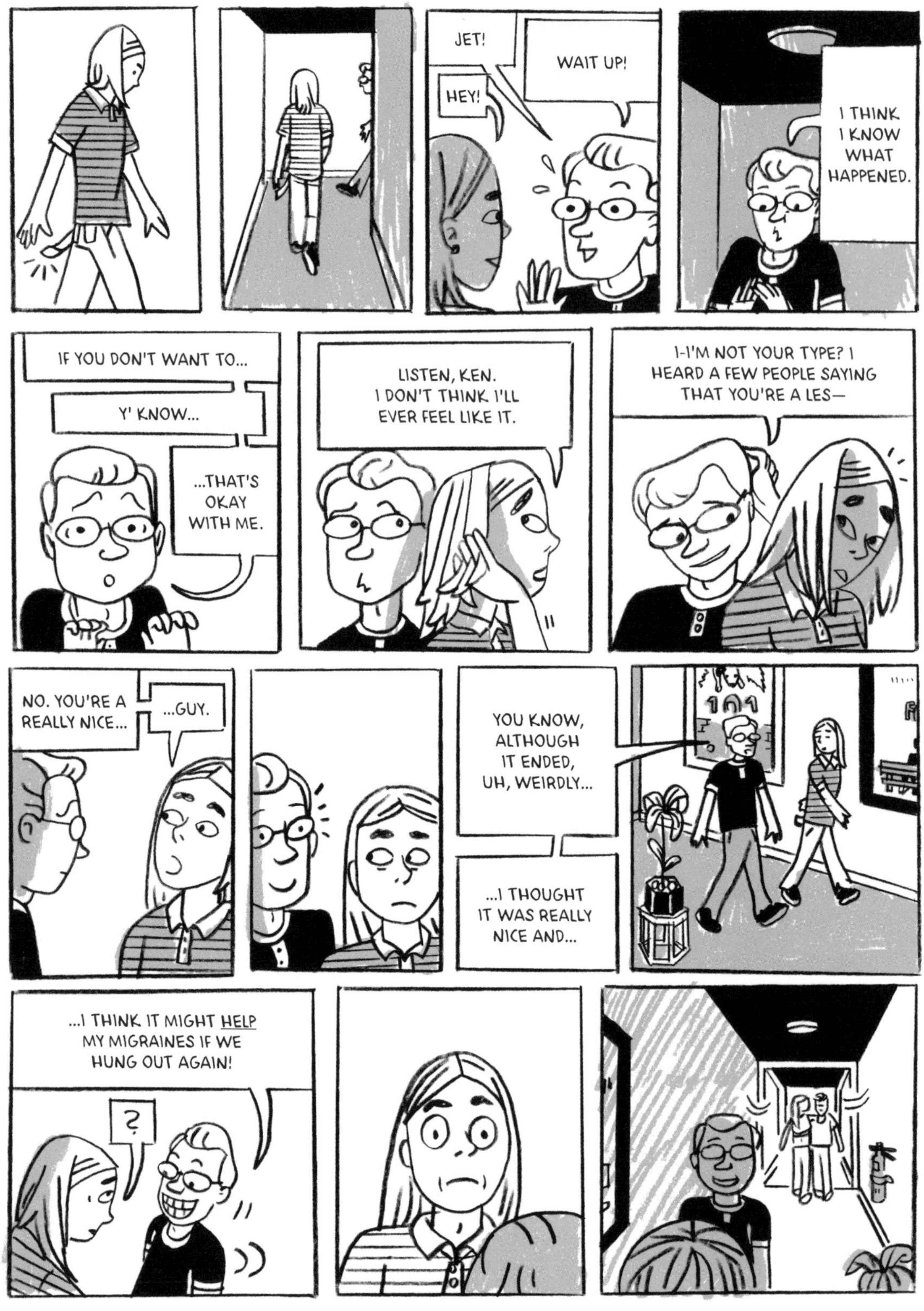

JET!
HEY!
WAIT UP!
I THINK I KNOW WHAT HAPPENED.
IF YOU DON'T WANT TO...
Y' KNOW...
...THAT'S OKAY WITH ME.
LISTEN, KEN. I DON'T THINK I'LL EVER FEEL LIKE IT.
I-I'M NOT YOUR TYPE? I HEARD A FEW PEOPLE SAYING THAT YOU'RE A LES—
NO. YOU'RE A REALLY NICE...
...GUY.
YOU KNOW, ALTHOUGH IT ENDED, UH, WEIRDLY...
...I THOUGHT IT WAS REALLY NICE AND...
101
...I THINK IT MIGHT HELP MY MIGRAINES IF WE HUNG OUT AGAIN!
?

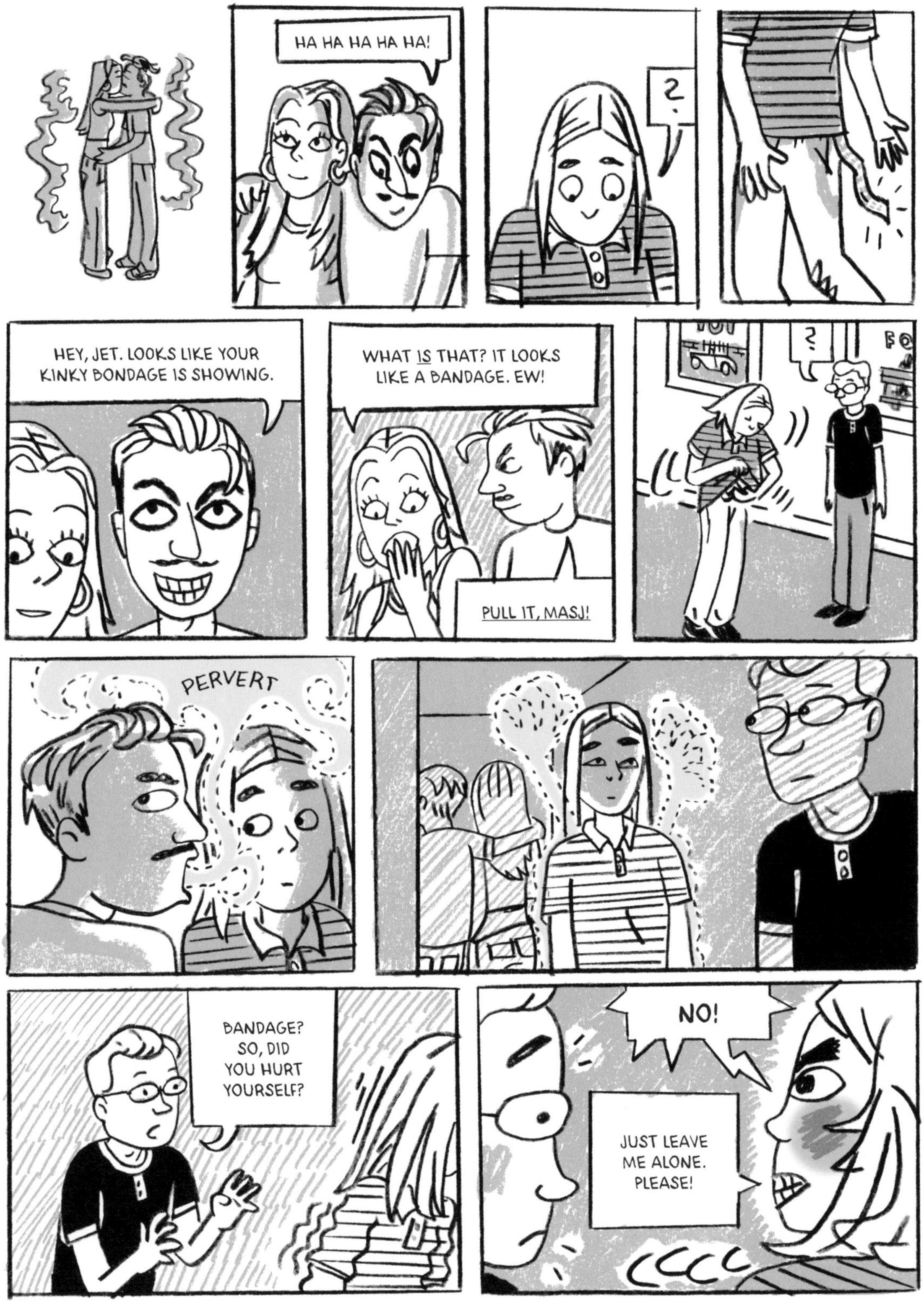
HA HA HA HA HA!
?
HEY, JET. LOOKS LIKE YOUR KINKY BONDAGE IS SHOWING.
WHAT IS THAT? IT LOOKS LIKE A BANDAGE. EW!
PULL IT, MASJ!
?
PERVERT
BANDAGE? SO, DID YOU HURT YOURSELF?
NO!
JUST LEAVE ME ALONE. PLEASE!

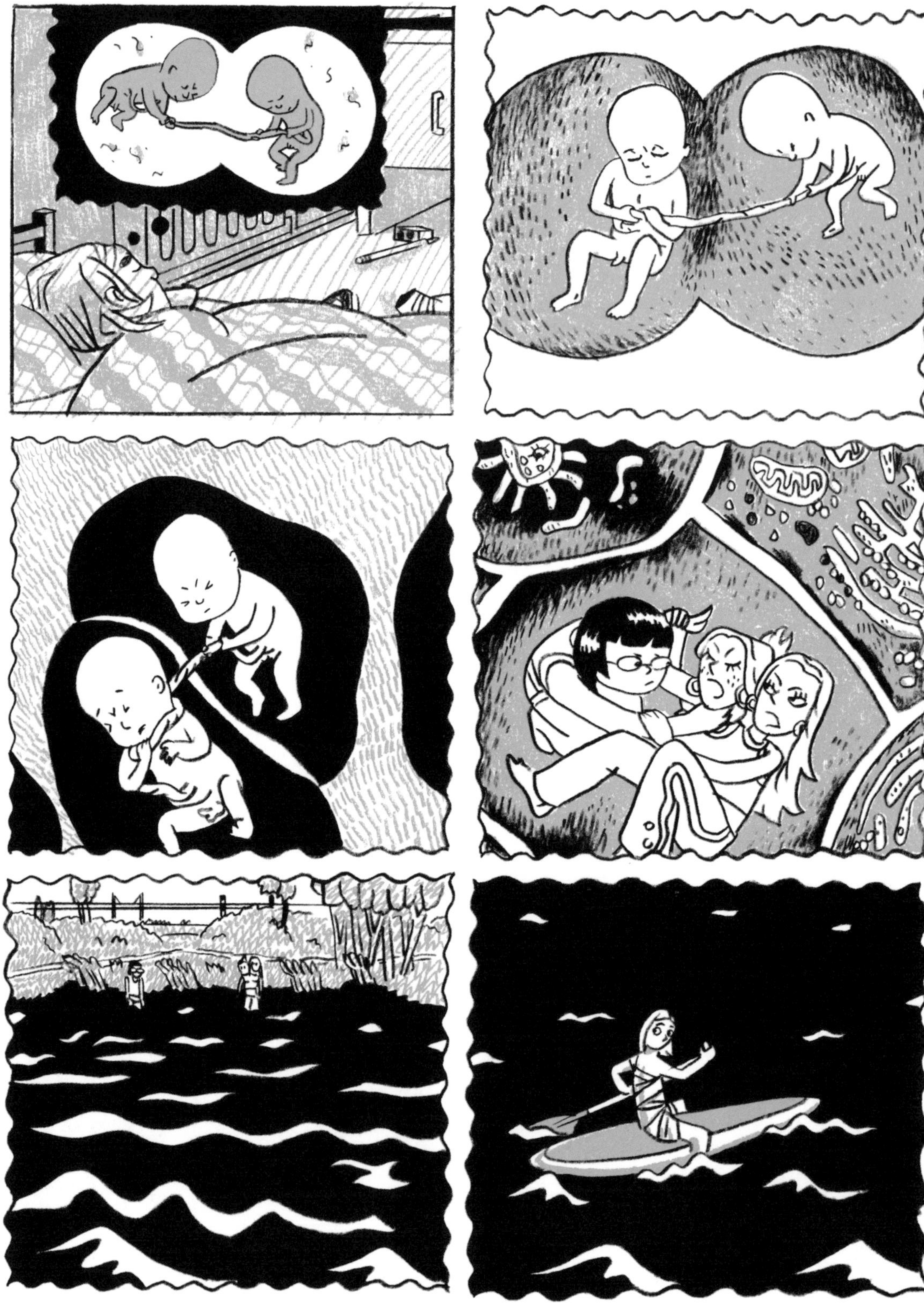

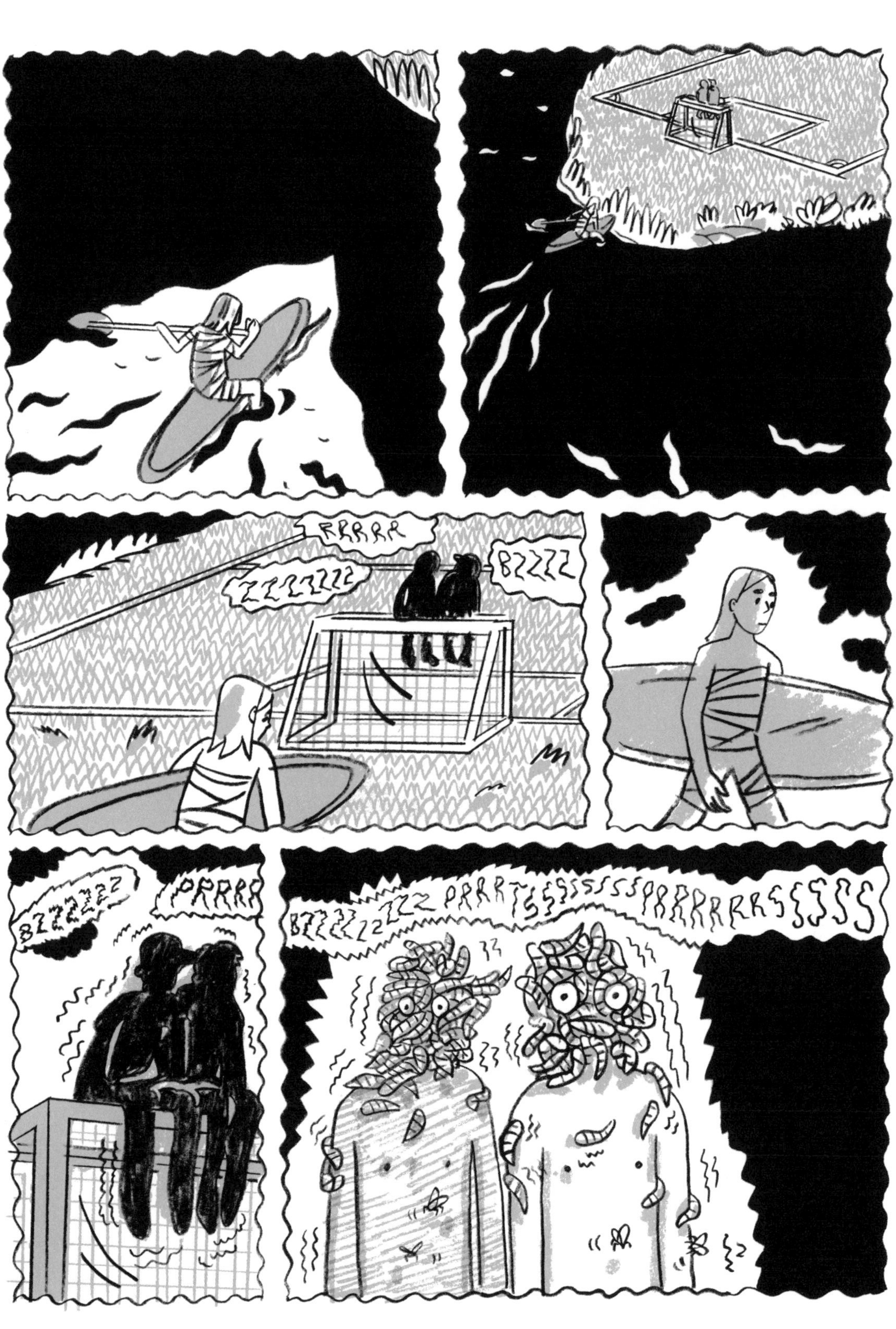
RRRRR
ZZZZZZZ
BZZZZ
BZZZZZZZ
PRRRR
BZZZZZZZZZZ PRRRTSSSSSSSSSSPRRRRRRRRSSSSSS

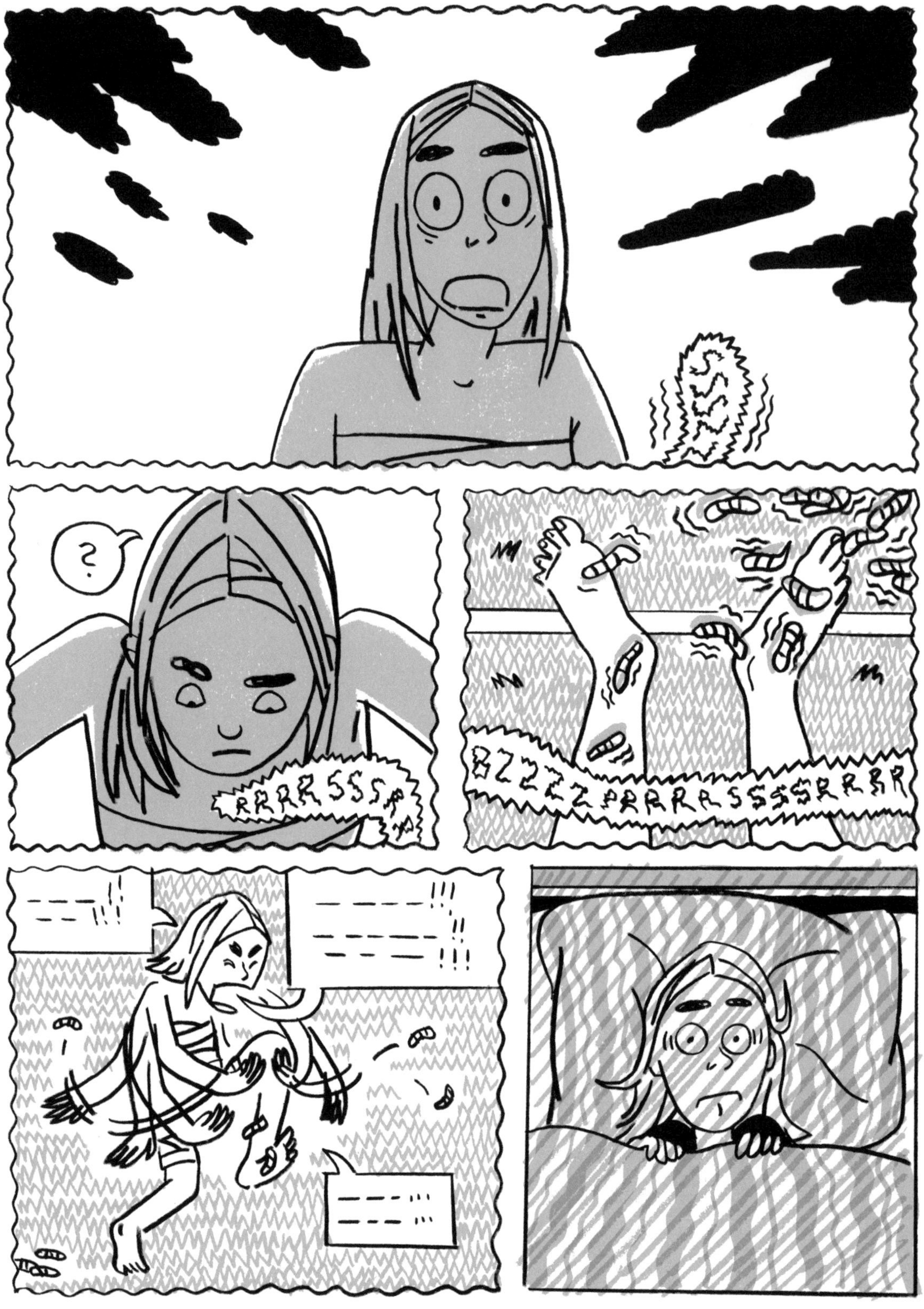
?

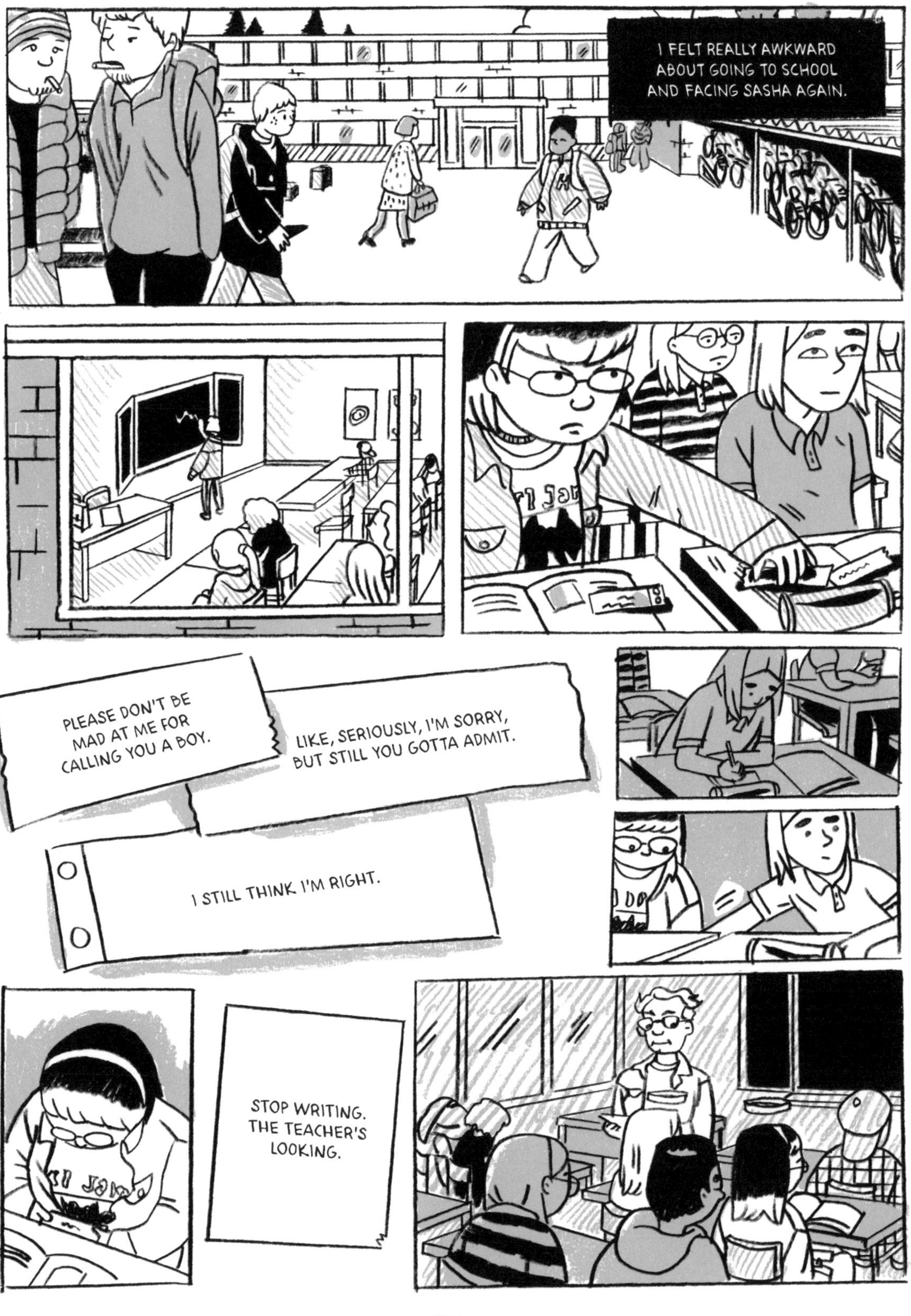
I FELT REALLY AWKWARD ABOUT GOING TO SCHOOL AND FACING SASHA AGAIN.
PLEASE DON'T BE MAD AT ME FOR CALLING YOU A BOY.
LIKE, SERIOUSLY, I'M SORRY, BUT STILL YOU GOTTA ADMIT.
I STILL THINK I'M RIGHT.
STOP WRITING. THE TEACHER'S LOOKING.

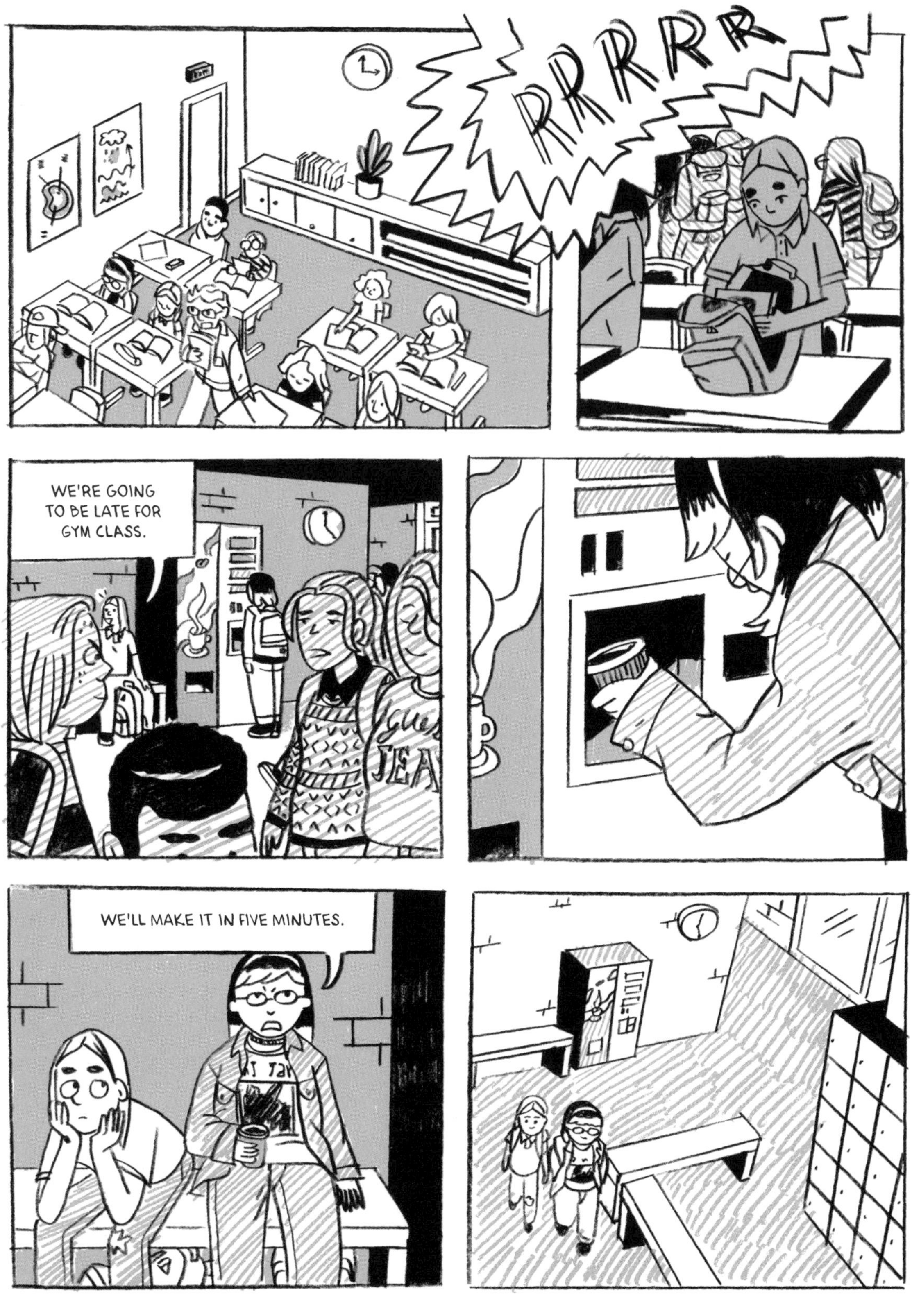
RRRRRR
WE'RE GOING TO BE LATE FOR GYM CLASS.
WE'LL MAKE IT IN FIVE MINUTES.

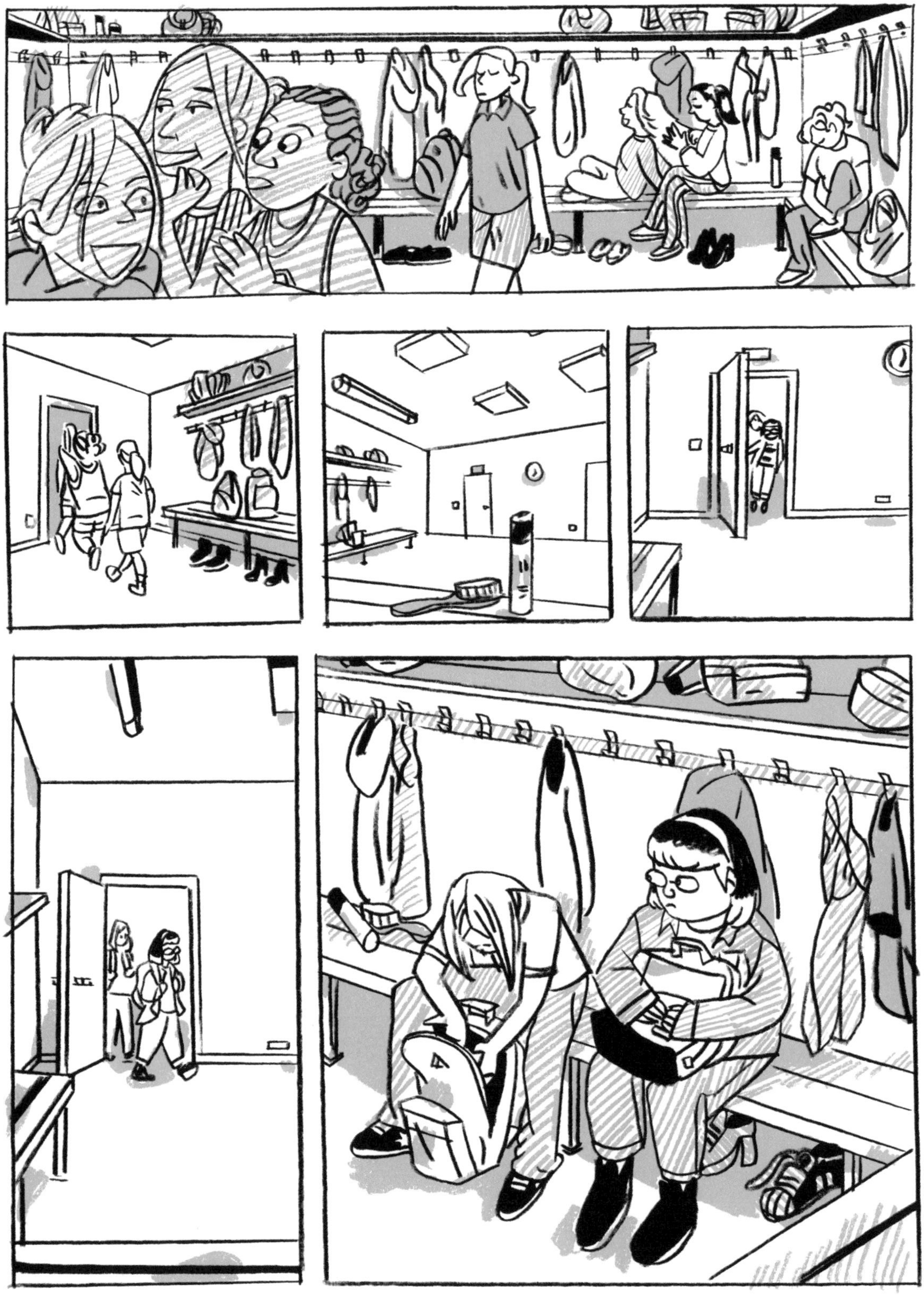

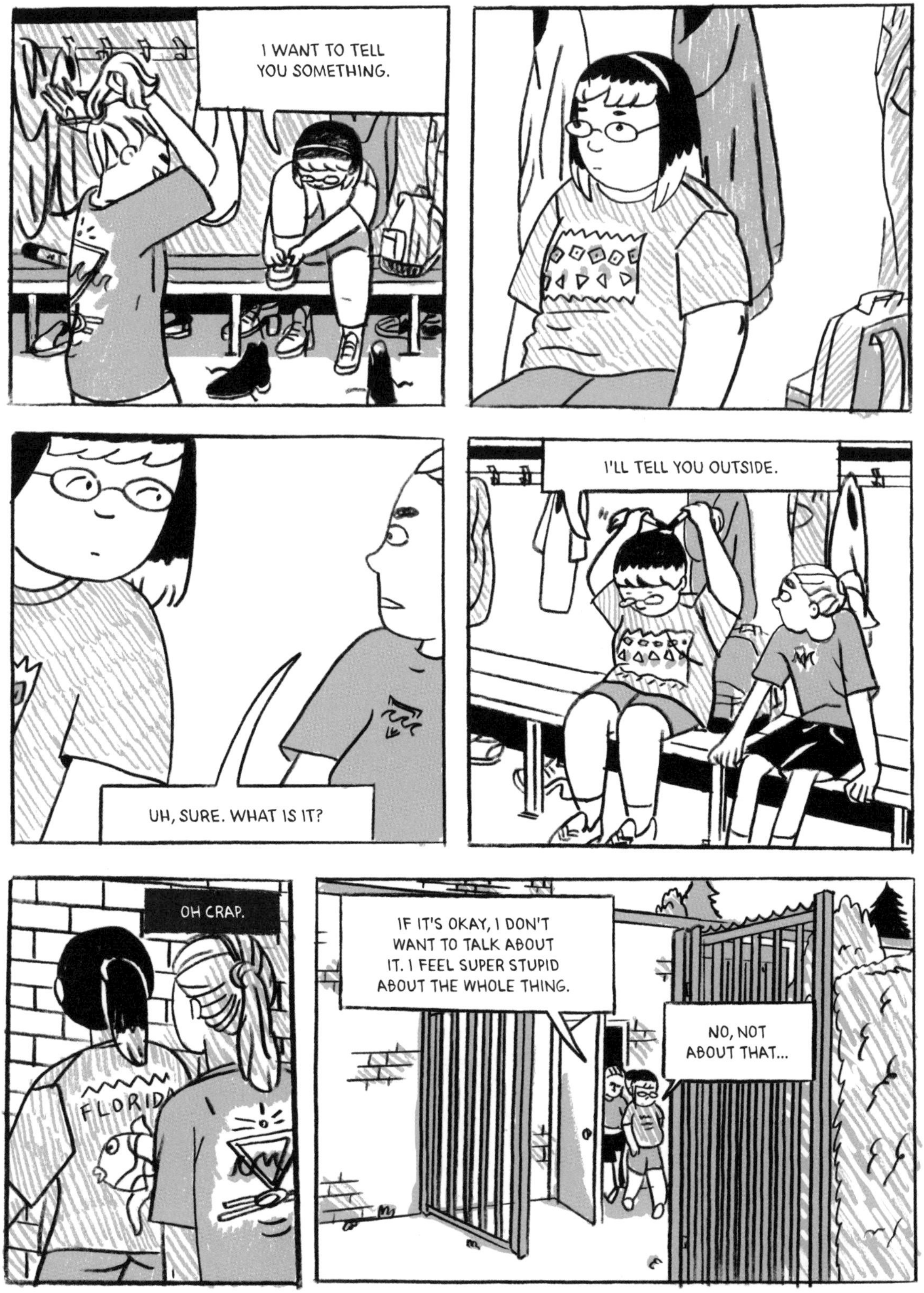
I WANT TO TELL YOU SOMETHING.
UH, SURE. WHAT IS IT?
I'LL TELL YOU OUTSIDE.
OH CRAP.
FLORIDA
IF IT'S OKAY, I DON'T WANT TO TALK ABOUT IT. I FEEL SUPER STUPID ABOUT THE WHOLE THING.
NO, NOT ABOUT THAT...

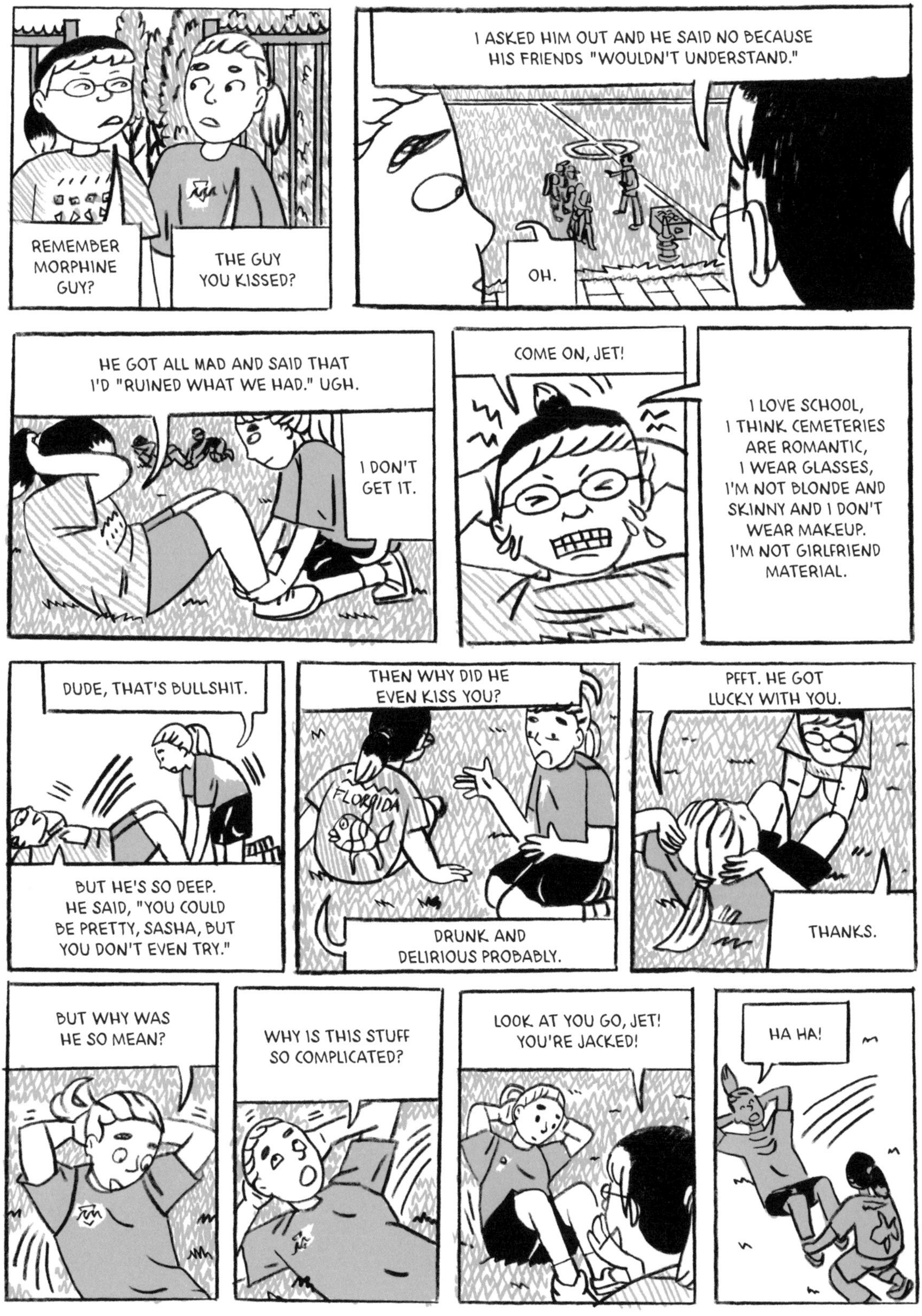
REMEMBER MORPHINE GUY?
THE GUY YOU KISSED?
I ASKED HIM OUT AND HE SAID NO BECAUSE HIS FRIENDS "WOULDN'T UNDERSTAND."
OH.
HE GOT ALL MAD AND SAID THAT I'D "RUINED WHAT WE HAD." UGH.
I DON'T GET IT.
COME ON, JET!
I LOVE SCHOOL, I THINK CEMETERIES ARE ROMANTIC, I WEAR GLASSES, I'M NOT BLONDE AND SKINNY AND I DON'T WEAR MAKEUP. I'M NOT GIRLFRIEND MATERIAL.
DUDE, THAT'S BULLSHIT.
BUT HE'S SO DEEP. HE SAID, "YOU COULD BE PRETTY, SASHA, BUT YOU DON'T EVEN TRY."
THEN WHY DID HE EVEN KISS YOU?
FLORIDA
DRUNK AND DELIRIOUS PROBABLY.
PFFT. HE GOT LUCKY WITH YOU.
THANKS.
BUT WHY WAS HE SO MEAN?
WHY IS THIS STUFF SO COMPLICATED?
LOOK AT YOU GO, JET! YOU'RE JACKED!
HA HA!

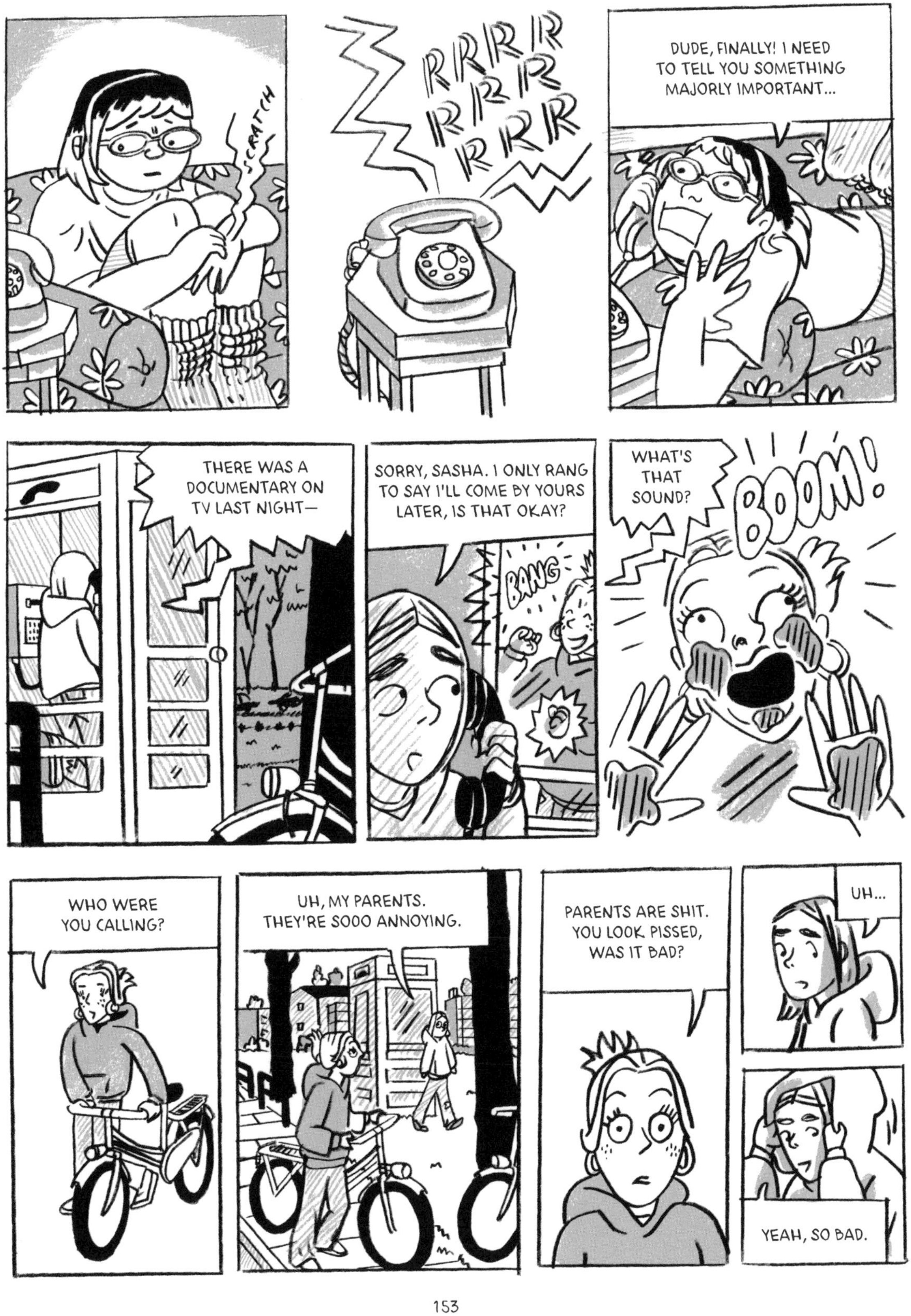
SCRATCH
RRRR RRR RRR
DUDE, FINALLY! I NEED TO TELL YOU SOMETHING MAJORLY IMPORTANT...
THERE WAS A DOCUMENTARY ON TV LAST NIGHT—
SORRY, SASHA. I ONLY RANG TO SAY I'LL COME BY YOURS LATER, IS THAT OKAY?
BANG
WHAT'S THAT SOUND?
BOOM!
WHO WERE YOU CALLING?
UH, MY PARENTS. THEY'RE SOOO ANNOYING.
PARENTS ARE SHIT. YOU LOOK PISSED, WAS IT BAD?
UH...
YEAH, SO BAD.

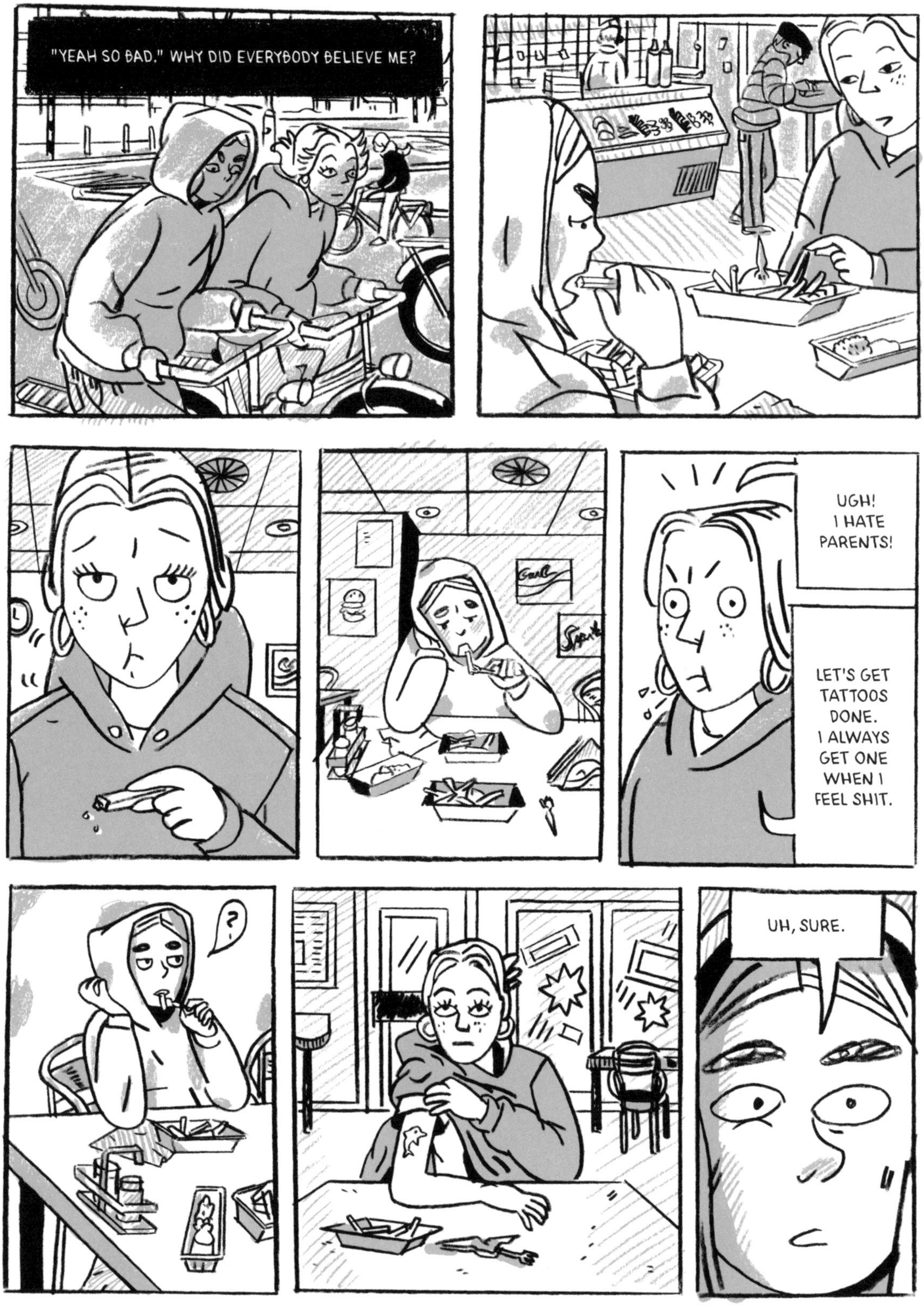
"YEAH SO BAD." WHY DID EVERYBODY BELIEVE ME?
UGH! I HATE PARENTS!
LET'S GET TATTOOS DONE. I ALWAYS GET ONE WHEN I FEEL SHIT.
?
UH, SURE.

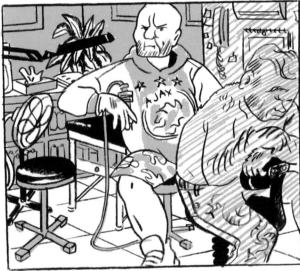

SO, YOU GIRLS WANT TATTOOS.

YOU'LL HAVE TO MAKE AN APPOINTMENT.

WE'VE GOT A SLOT ON THE 20TH.

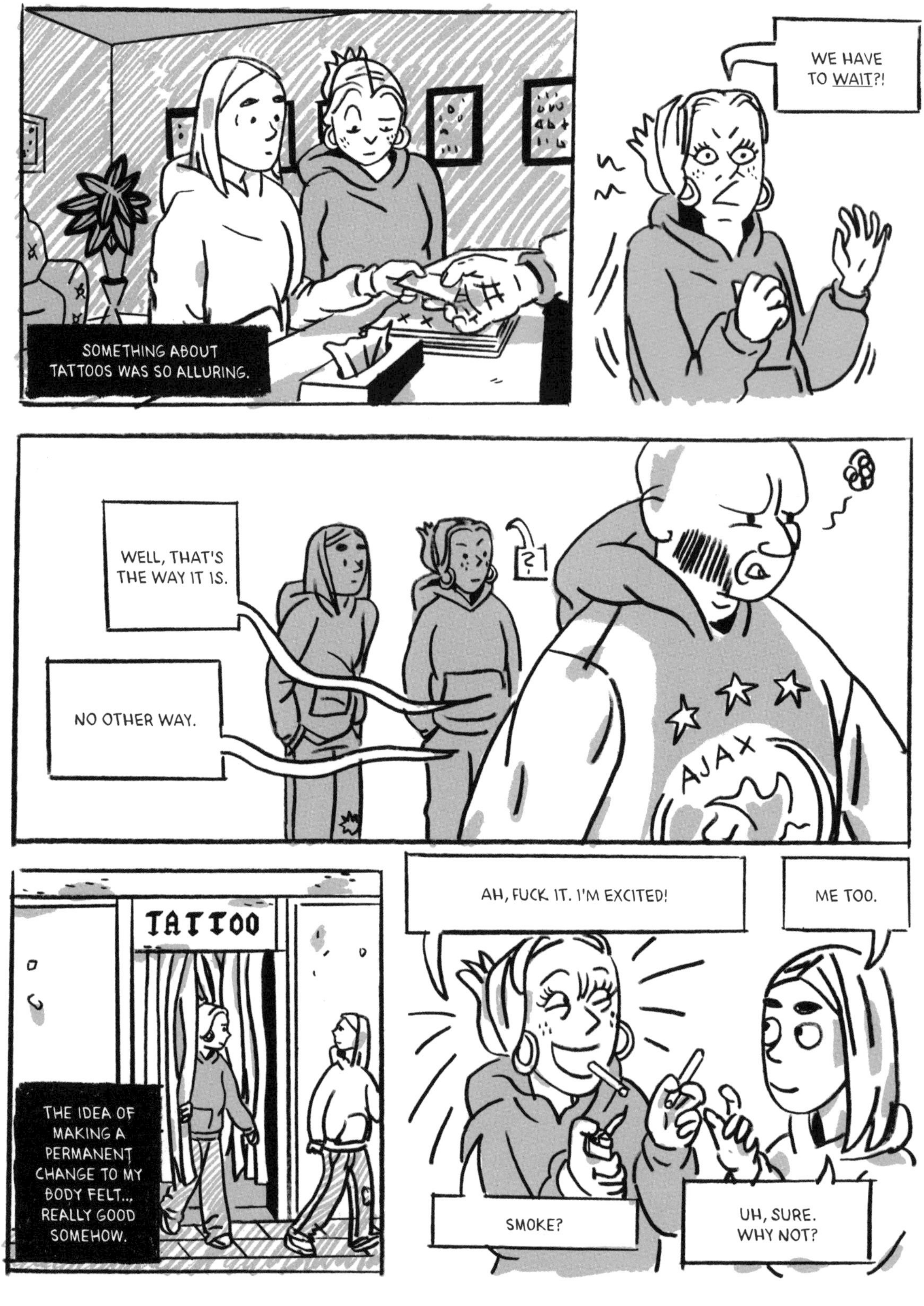
SOMETHING ABOUT TATTOOS WAS SO ALLURING.
WE HAVE TO WAIT?!
WELL, THAT'S THE WAY IT IS.
NO OTHER WAY.
AJAX
TATTOO
THE IDEA OF MAKING A PERMANENT CHANGE TO MY BODY FELT... REALLY GOOD SOMEHOW.
AH, FUCK IT. I'M EXCITED!
ME TOO.
SMOKE?
UH, SURE. WHY NOT?

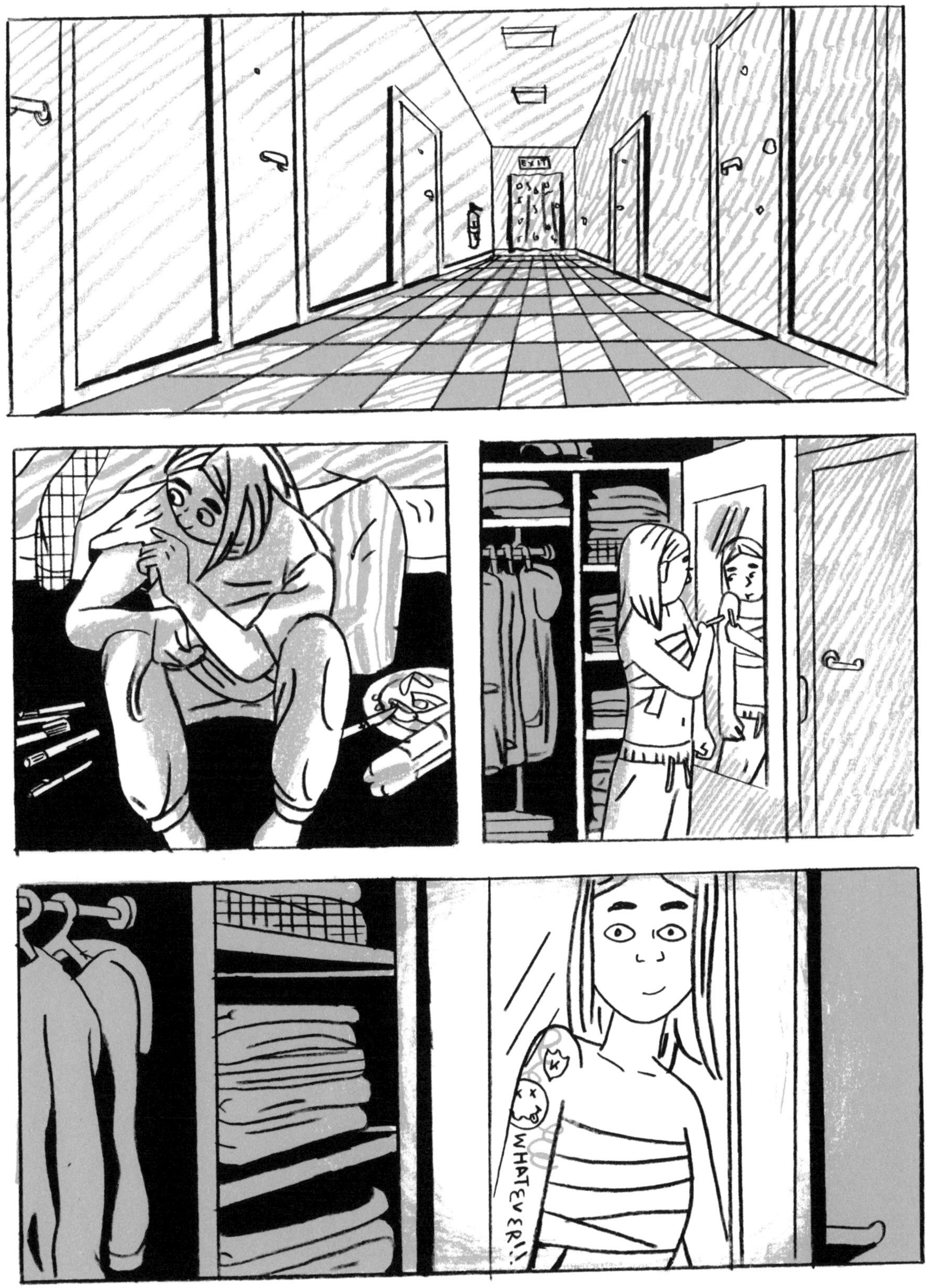
EXIT
WHATEVER!!

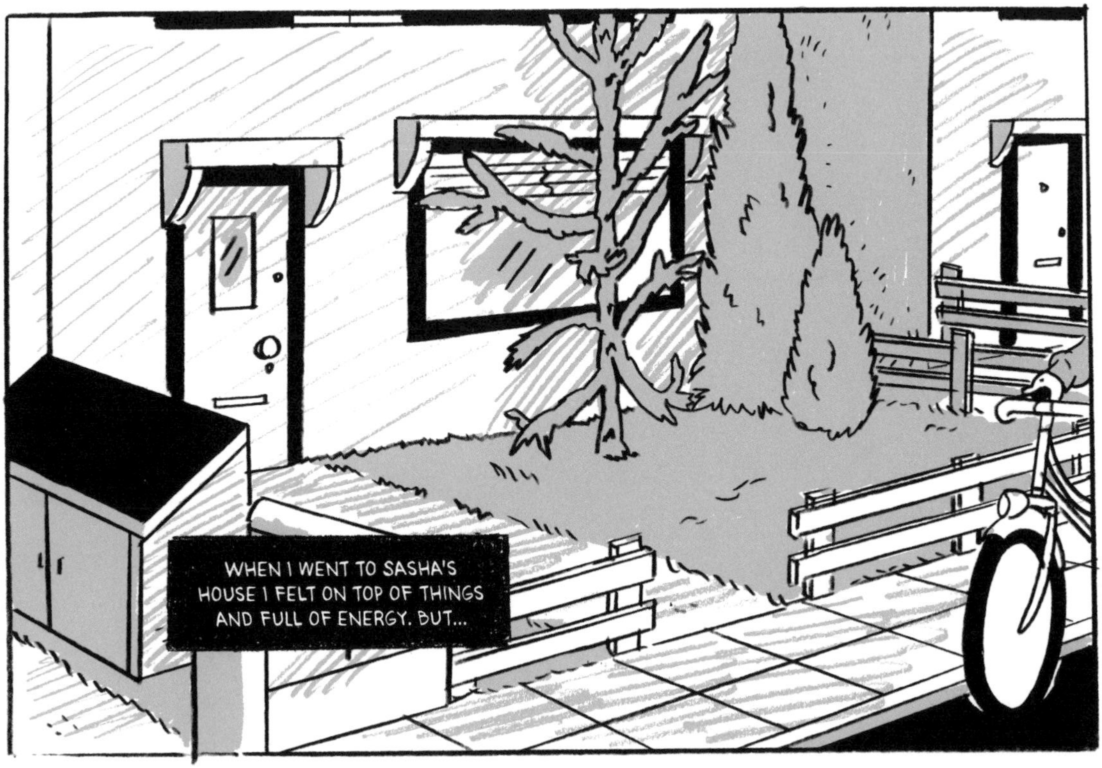
WHEN I WENT TO SASHA'S HOUSE I FELT ON TOP OF THINGS AND FULL OF ENERGY. BUT...

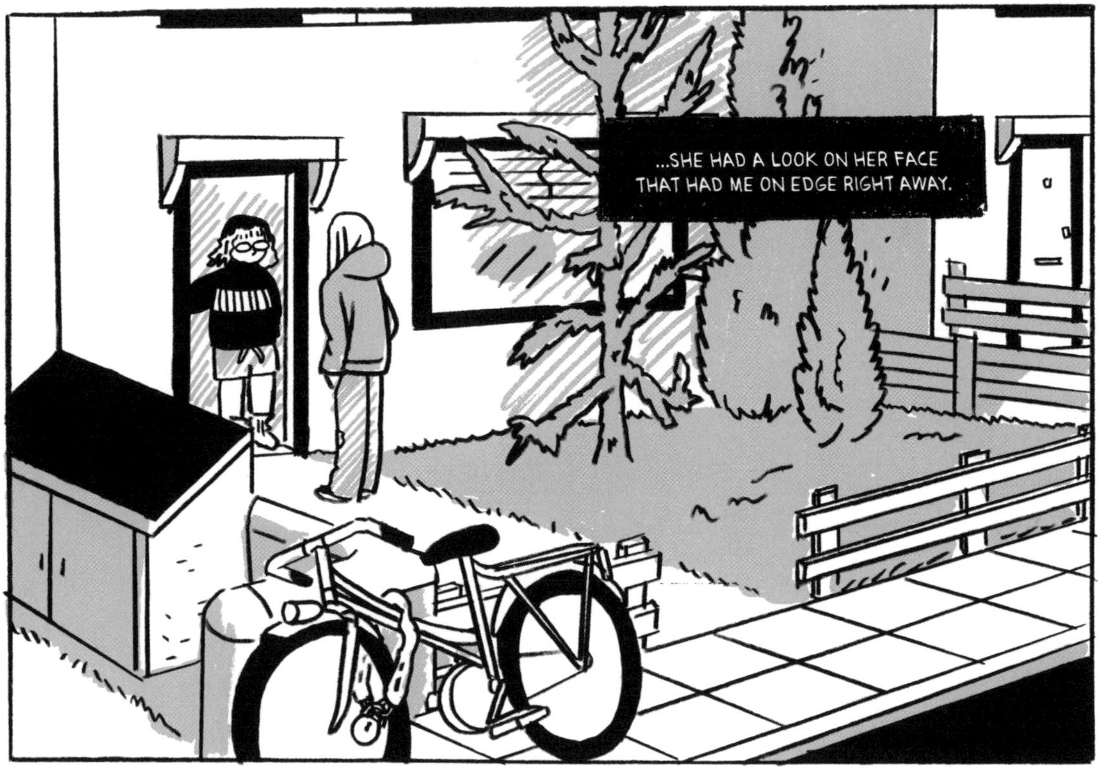
...SHE HAD A LOOK ON HER FACE THAT HAD ME ON EDGE RIGHT AWAY.

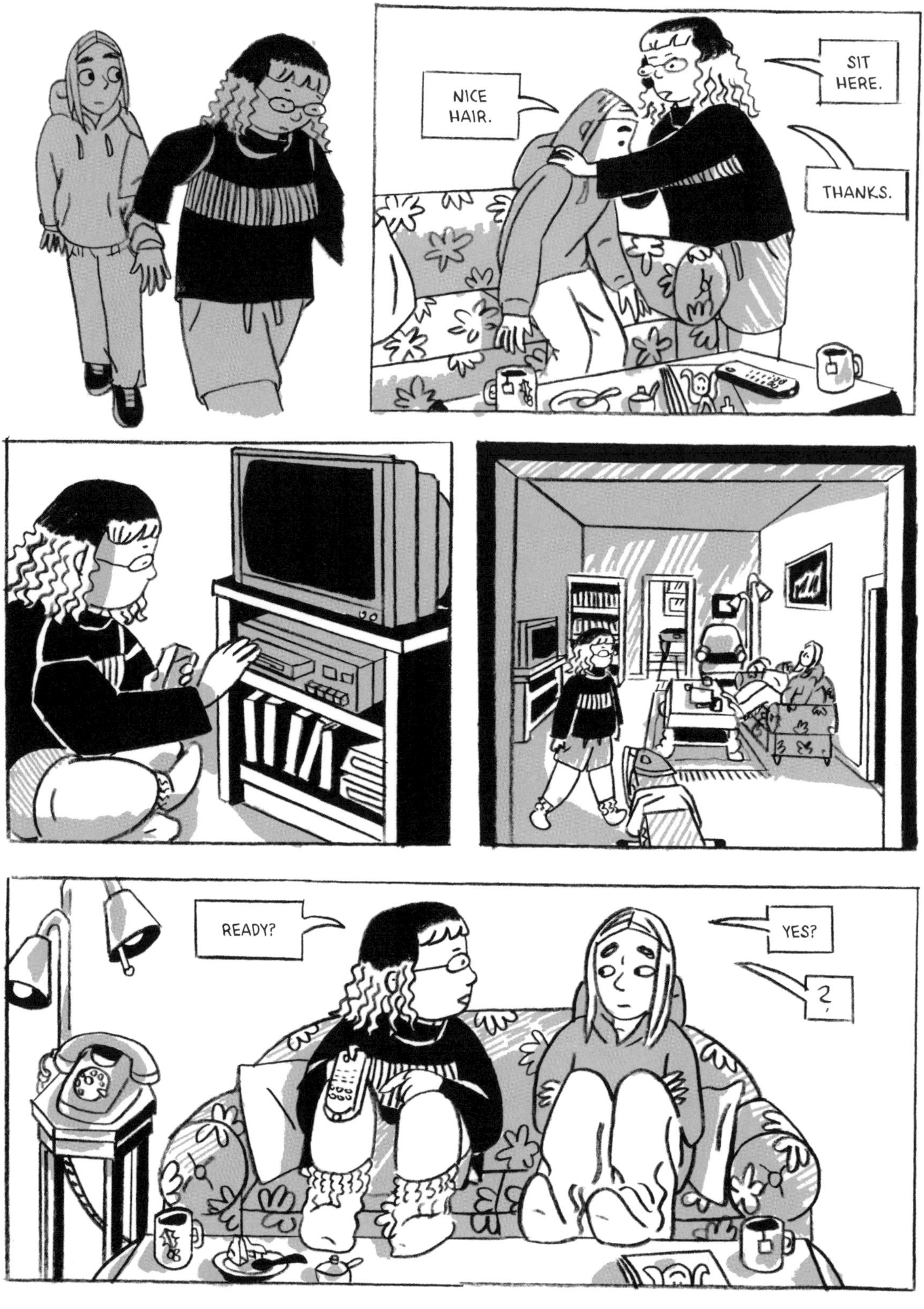
NICE HAIR.
SIT HERE.
THANKS.
READY?
YES?
?

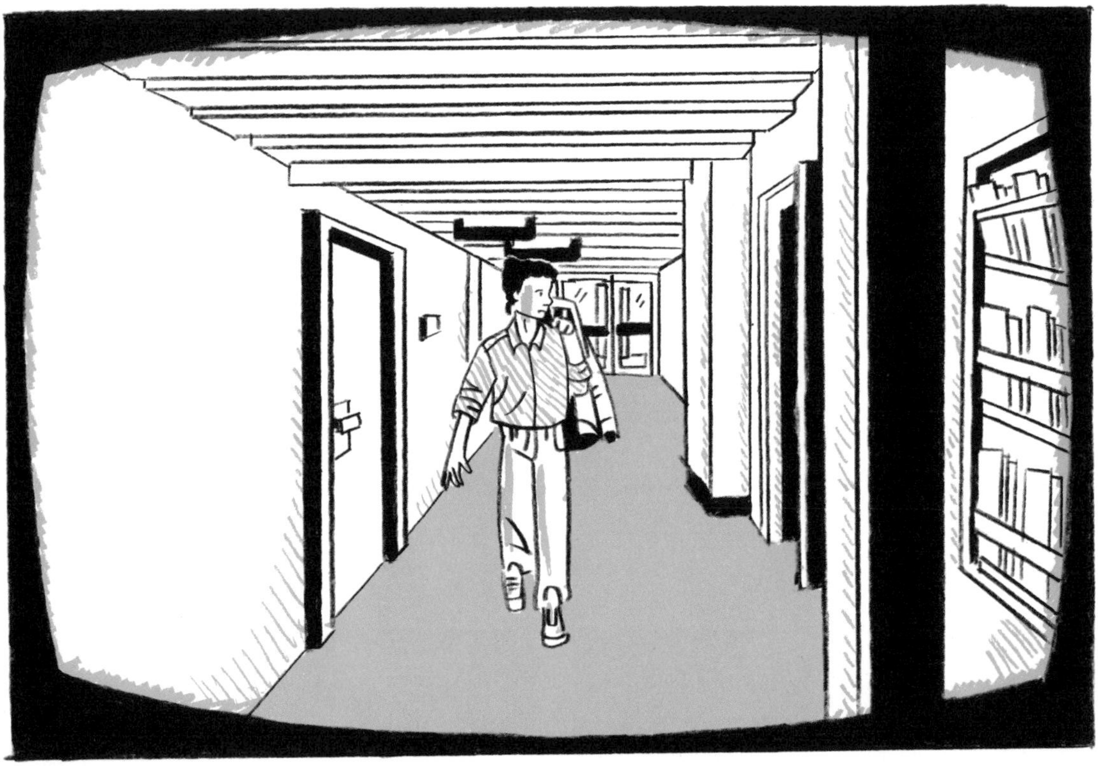

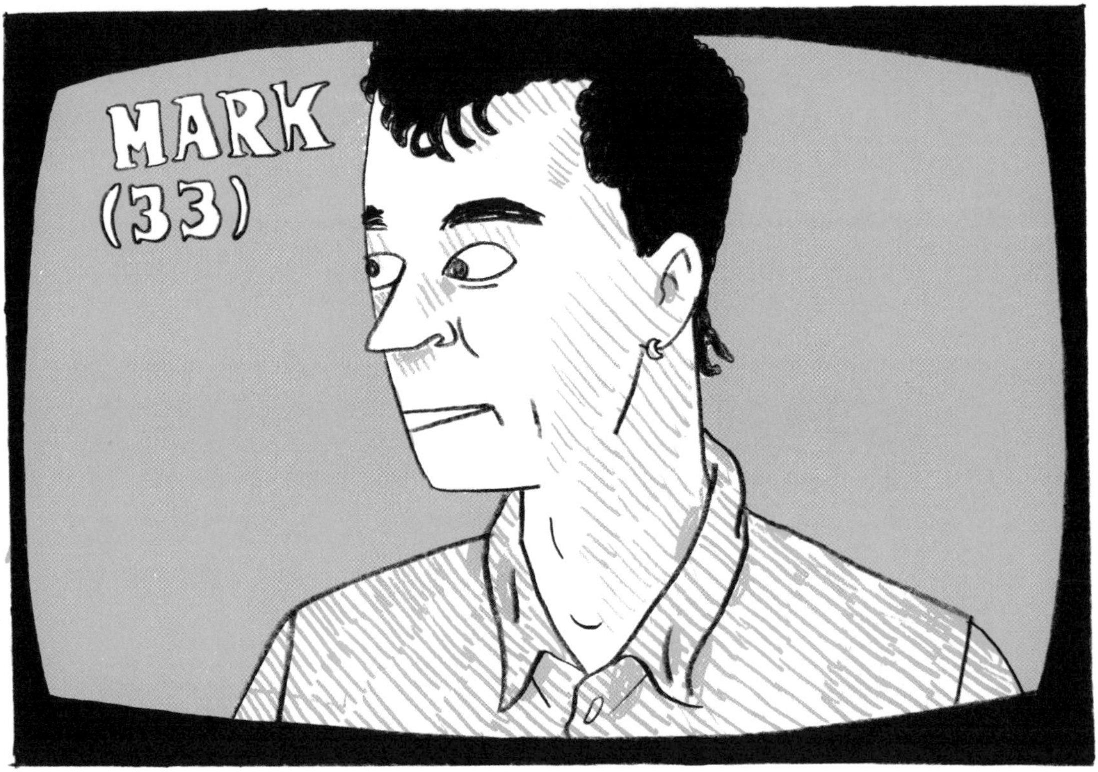
MARK
(33)

SO, YOU THOUGHT,
"ACTUALLY, I FEEL LIKE A MAN..."

YES.

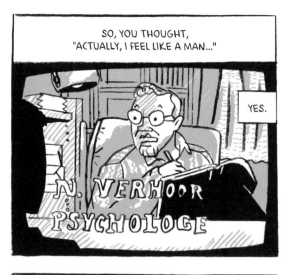

BUT WHAT STOPPED YOU WAS
THAT YOU DIDN'T DARE TO...?

I DIDN'T DARE BE MYSELF. SO I...

...ALWAYS TRIED IN SOME CLUMSY
WAY TO BE A WOMAN...

...BUT THEN I FAILED AT THAT,
WHICH IN TURN MADE ME UNHAPPY.

REALLY? UH-HUH, INTERESTING.

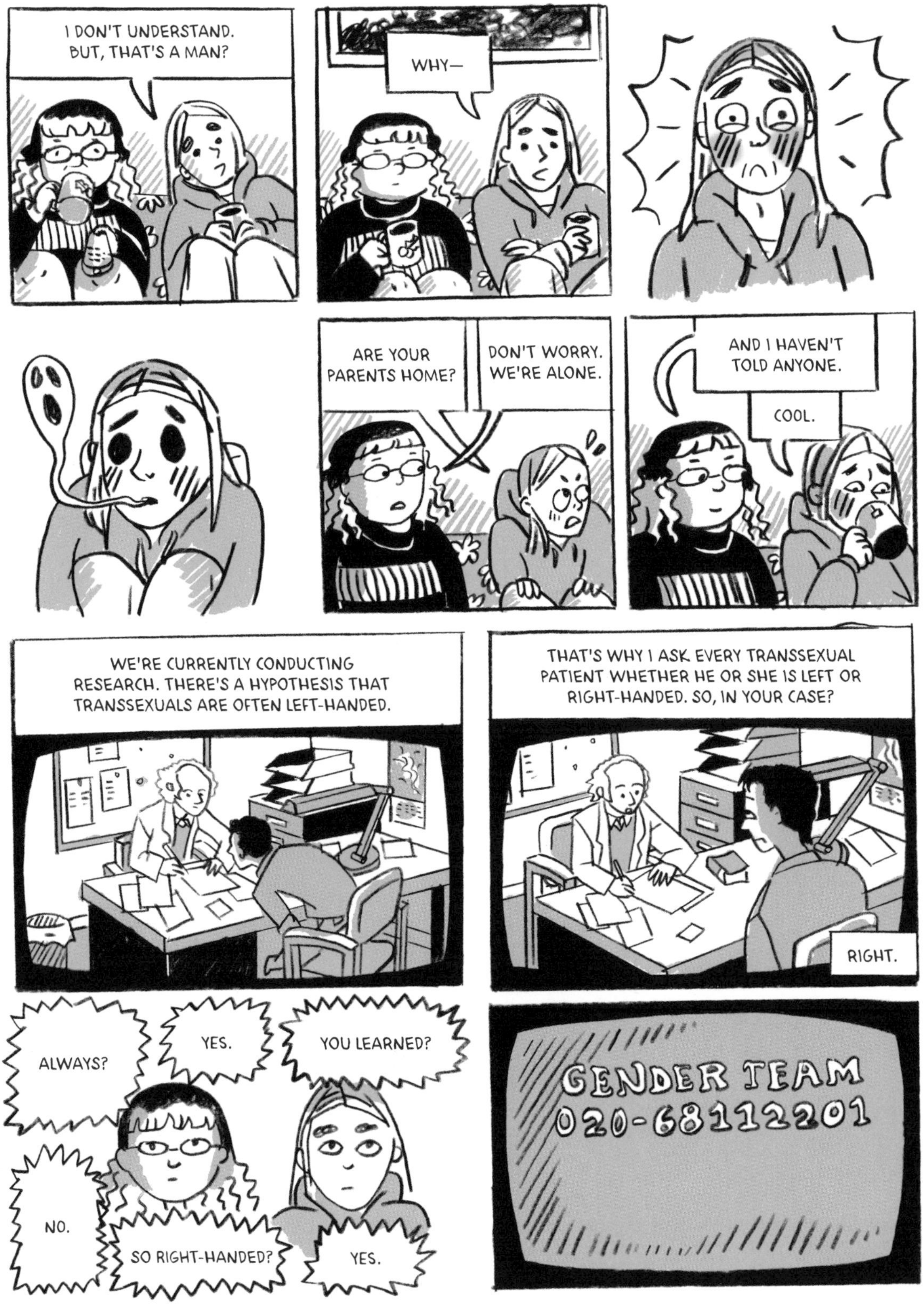
I DON'T UNDERSTAND. BUT, THAT'S A MAN?
WHY—
ARE YOUR PARENTS HOME?
DON'T WORRY. WE'RE ALONE.
AND I HAVEN'T TOLD ANYONE.
COOL.
WE'RE CURRENTLY CONDUCTING RESEARCH. THERE'S A HYPOTHESIS THAT TRANSSEXUALS ARE OFTEN LEFT-HANDED.
THAT'S WHY I ASK EVERY TRANSSEXUAL PATIENT WHETHER HE OR SHE IS LEFT OR RIGHT-HANDED. SO, IN YOUR CASE?
RIGHT.
ALWAYS?
YES.
YOU LEARNED?
NO.
SO RIGHT-HANDED?
YES.
GENDER TEAM
020-68112201

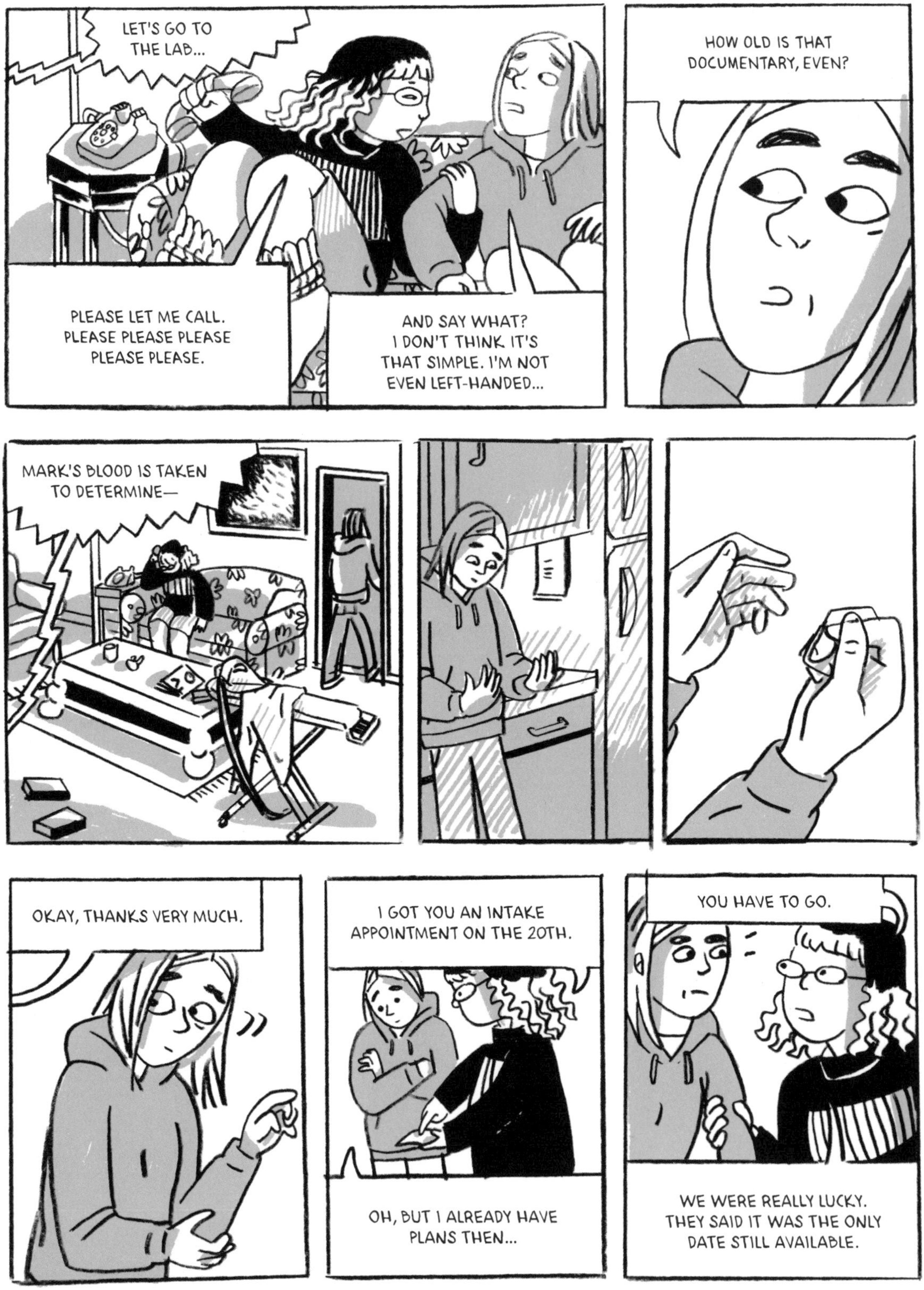
LET'S GO TO THE LAB...
PLEASE LET ME CALL. PLEASE PLEASE PLEASE PLEASE PLEASE.
AND SAY WHAT? I DON'T THINK IT'S THAT SIMPLE. I'M NOT EVEN LEFT-HANDED...
HOW OLD IS THAT DOCUMENTARY, EVEN?
MARK'S BLOOD IS TAKEN TO DETERMINE—
OKAY, THANKS VERY MUCH.
I GOT YOU AN INTAKE APPOINTMENT ON THE 20TH.
OH, BUT I ALREADY HAVE PLANS THEN...
YOU HAVE TO GO.
WE WERE REALLY LUCKY. THEY SAID IT WAS THE ONLY DATE STILL AVAILABLE.

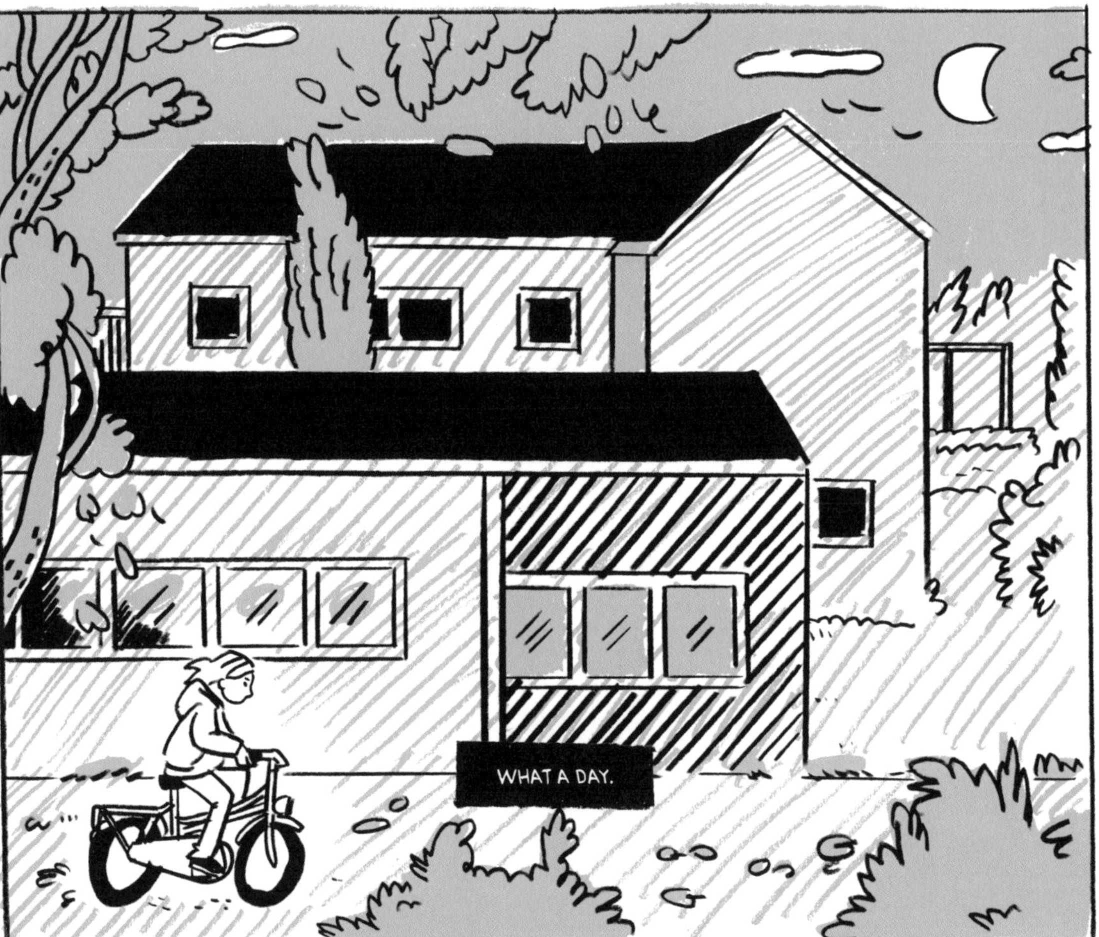
WHAT A DAY.

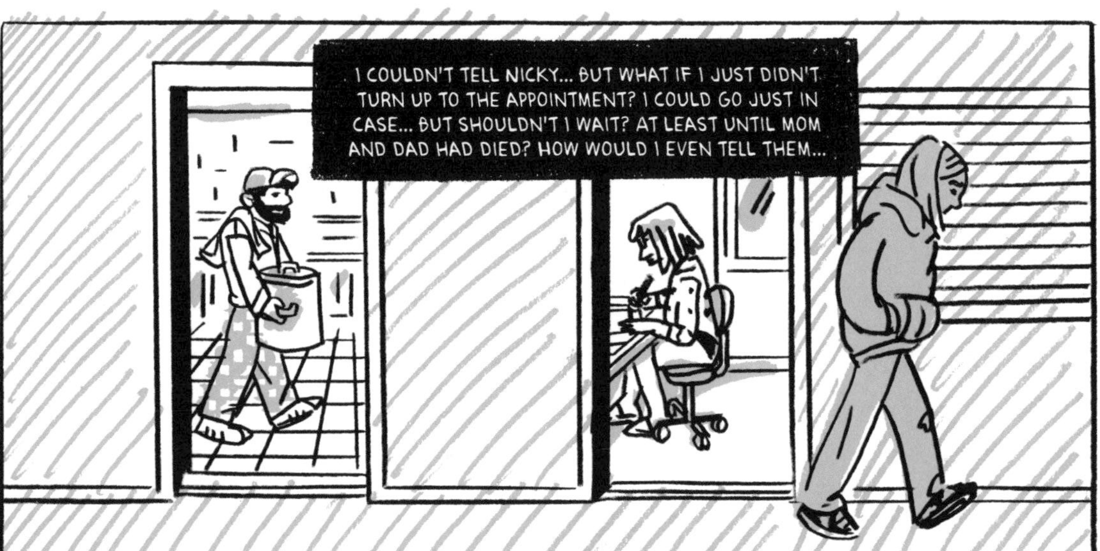
I COULDN'T TELL NICKY... BUT WHAT IF I JUST DIDN'T TURN UP TO THE APPOINTMENT? I COULD GO JUST IN CASE... BUT SHOULDN'T I WAIT? AT LEAST UNTIL MOM AND DAD HAD DIED? HOW WOULD I EVEN TELL THEM...

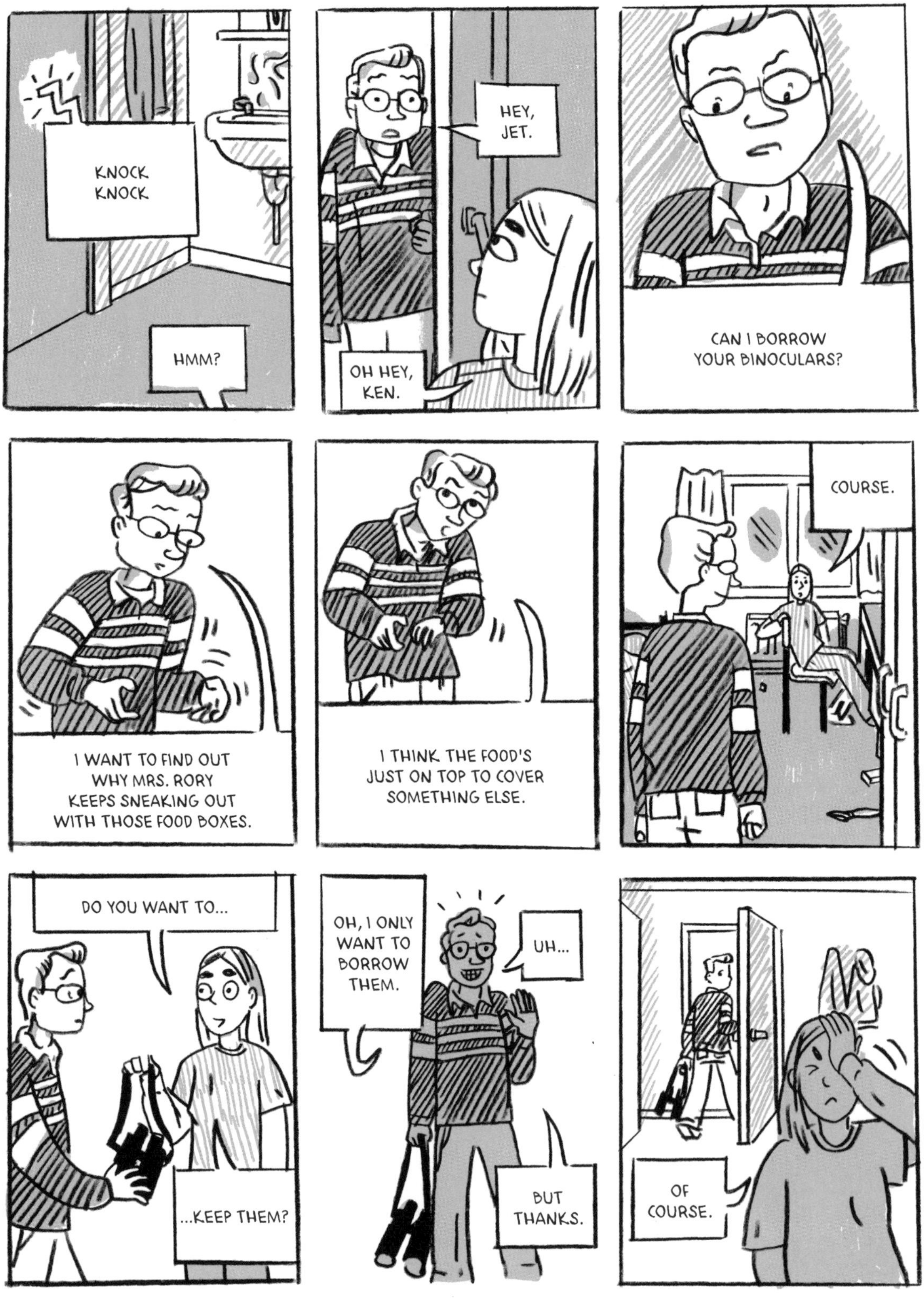
KNOCK KNOCK
HMM?
HEY, JET.
OH HEY, KEN.
CAN I BORROW YOUR BINOCULARS?
I WANT TO FIND OUT WHY MRS. RORY KEEPS SNEAKING OUT WITH THOSE FOOD BOXES.
I THINK THE FOOD'S JUST ON TOP TO COVER SOMETHING ELSE.
COURSE.
DO YOU WANT TO...
...KEEP THEM?
OH, I ONLY WANT TO BORROW THEM.
UH...
BUT THANKS.
OF COURSE.

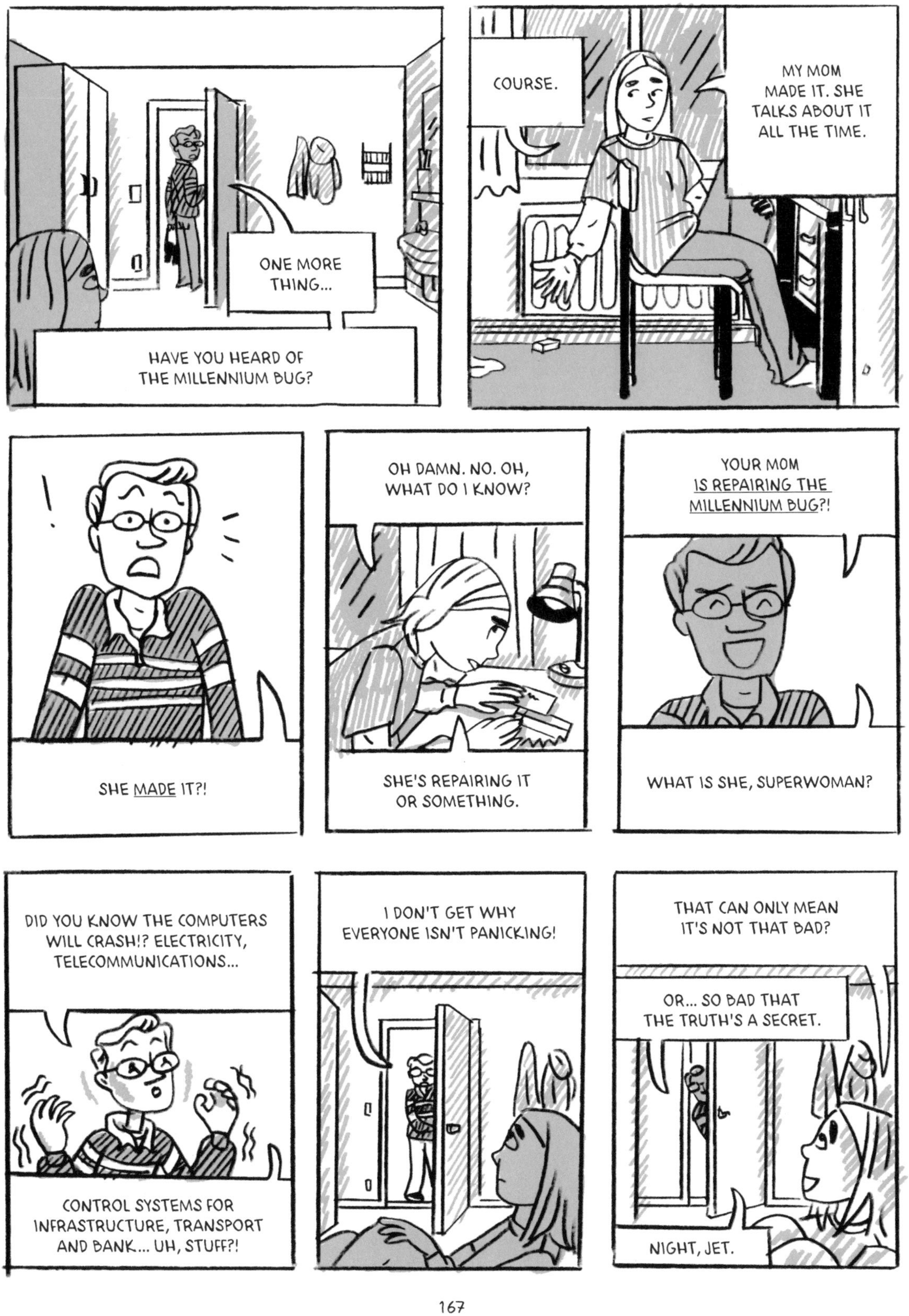
ONE MORE THING...
HAVE YOU HEARD OF THE MILLENNIUM BUG?
COURSE.
MY MOM MADE IT. SHE TALKS ABOUT IT ALL THE TIME.
!
SHE MADE IT?!
OH DAMN. NO. OH, WHAT DO I KNOW?
SHE'S REPAIRING IT OR SOMETHING.
YOUR MOM IS REPAIRING THE MILLENNIUM BUG?!
WHAT IS SHE, SUPERWOMAN?
DID YOU KNOW THE COMPUTERS WILL CRASH!? ELECTRICITY, TELECOMMUNICATIONS...
CONTROL SYSTEMS FOR INFRASTRUCTURE, TRANSPORT AND BANK... UH, STUFF?!
I DON'T GET WHY EVERYONE ISN'T PANICKING!
THAT CAN ONLY MEAN IT'S NOT THAT BAD?
OR... SO BAD THAT THE TRUTH'S A SECRET.
NIGHT, JET.

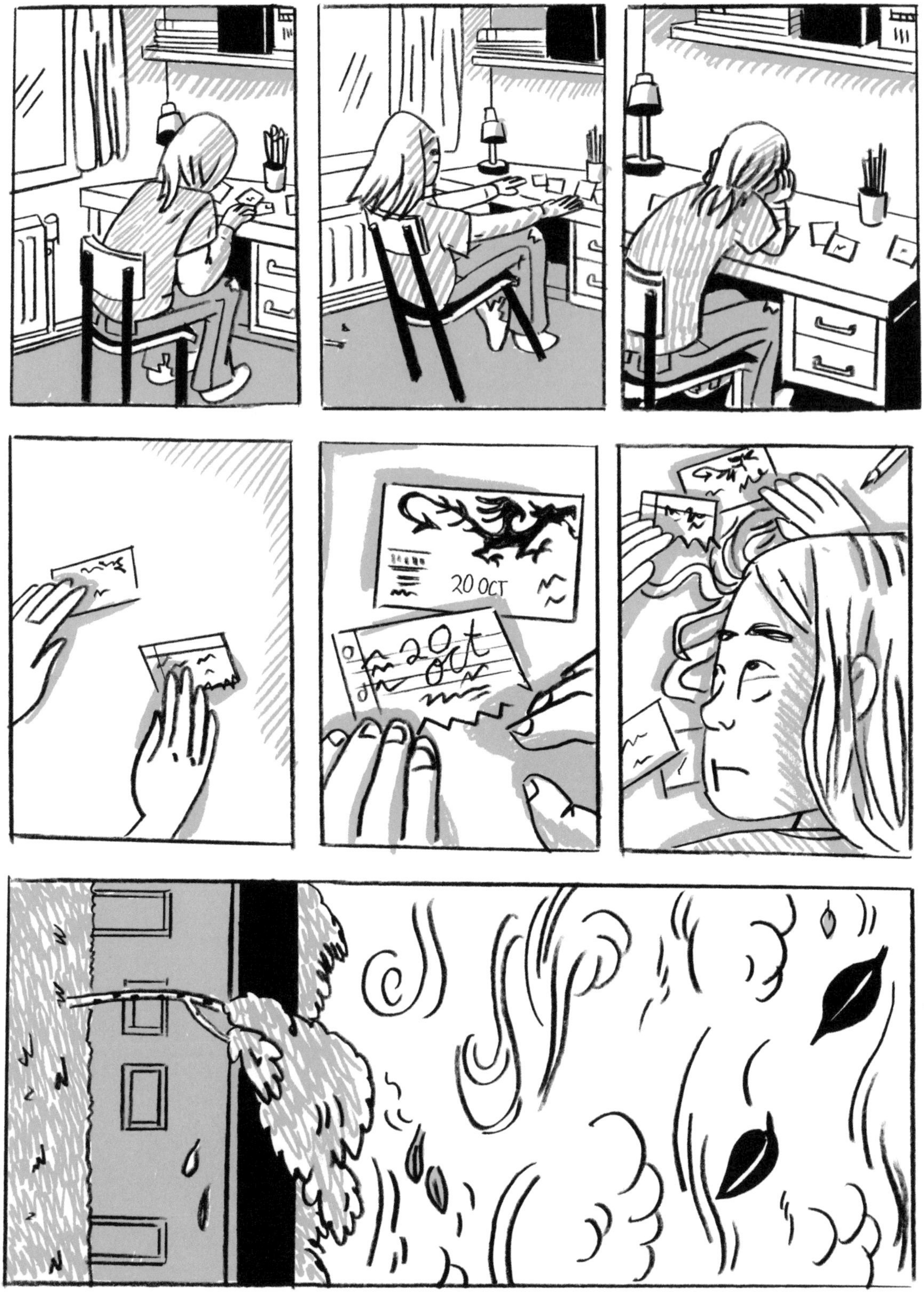
20 OCT
20 Oct

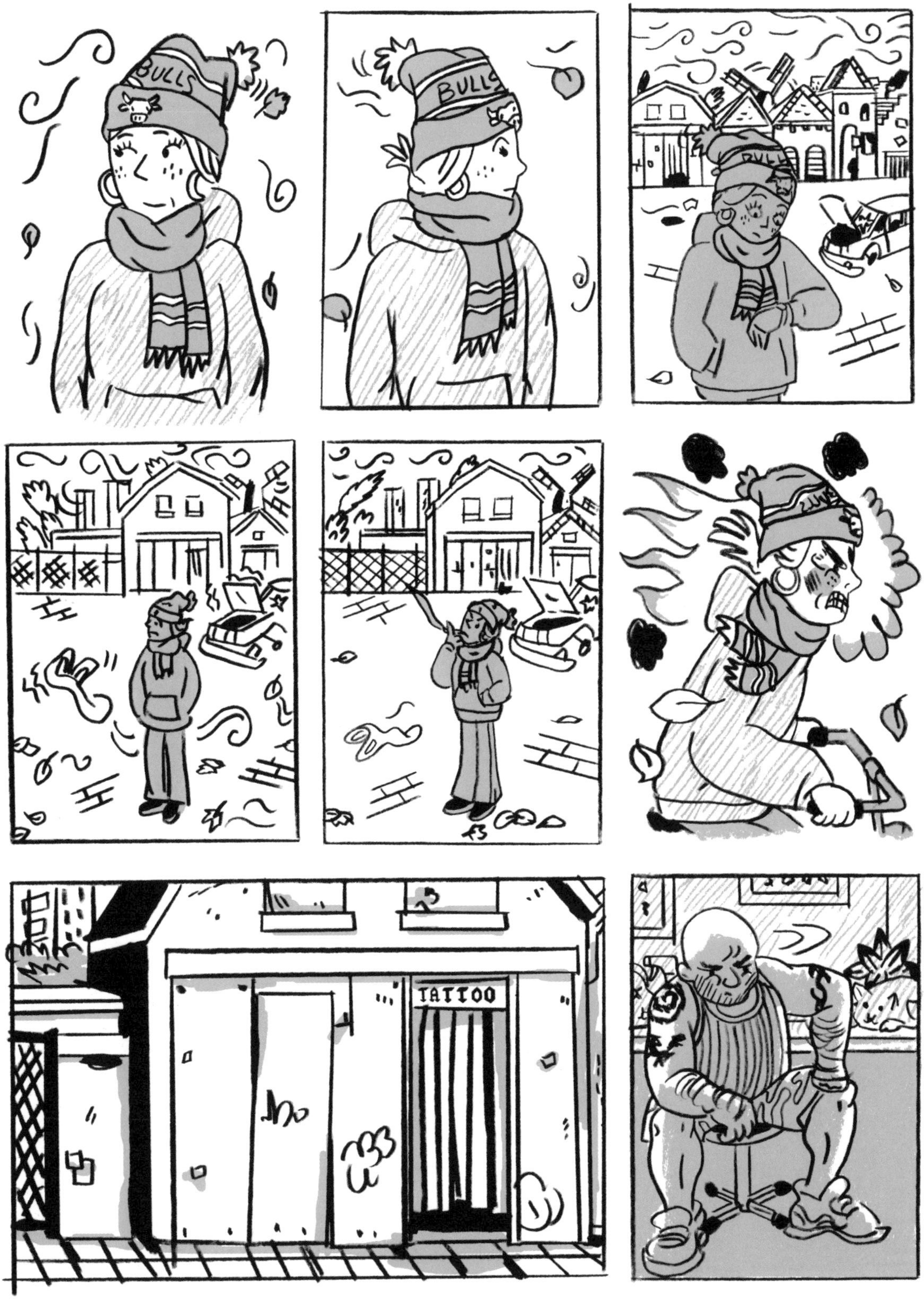
BULLS
BULLS
TATTOO

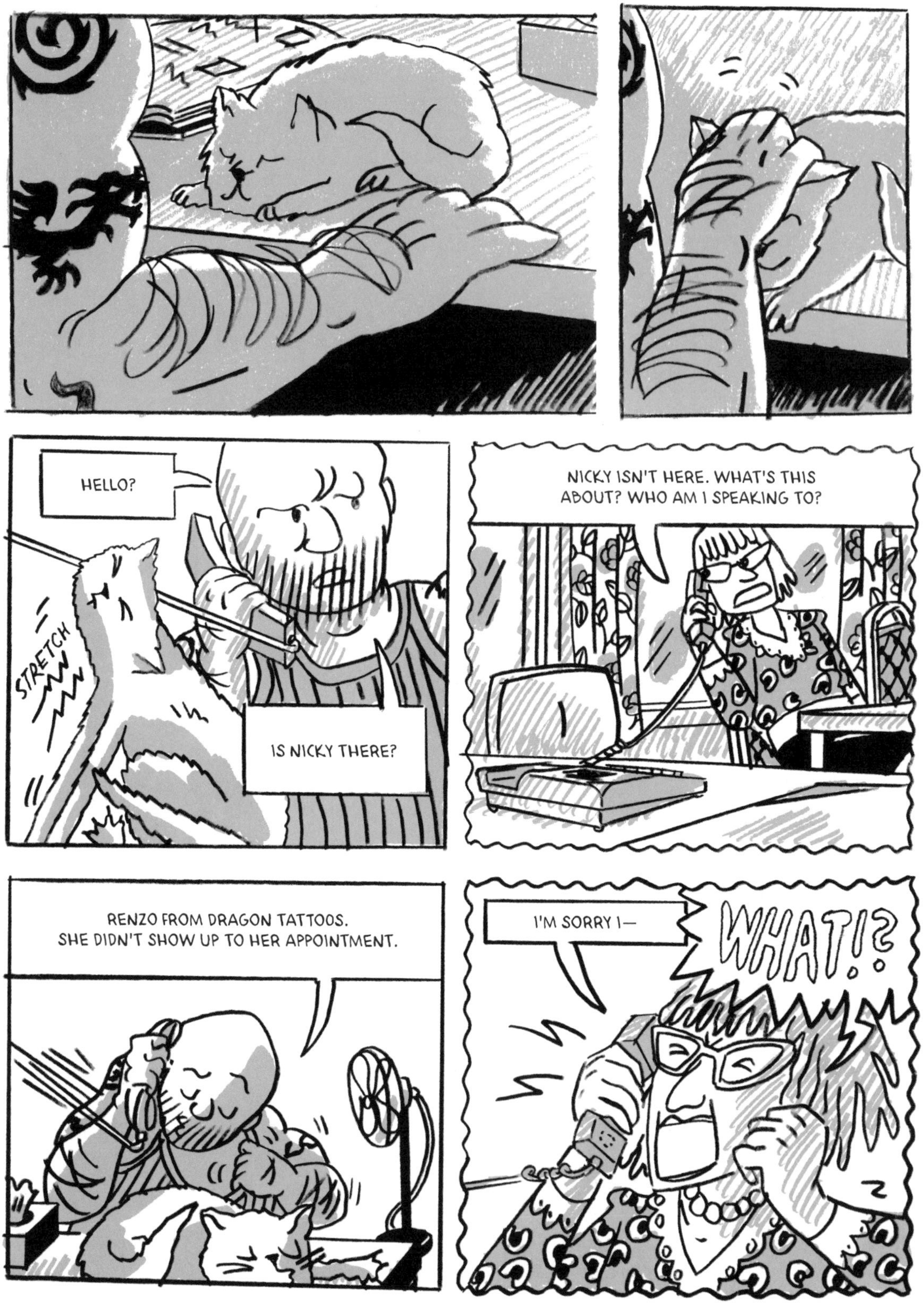
HELLO?
STRETCH
IS NICKY THERE?
NICKY ISN'T HERE. WHAT'S THIS ABOUT? WHO AM I SPEAKING TO?
RENZO FROM DRAGON TATTOOS.
SHE DIDN'T SHOW UP TO HER APPOINTMENT.
I'M SORRY I—
WHAT!?

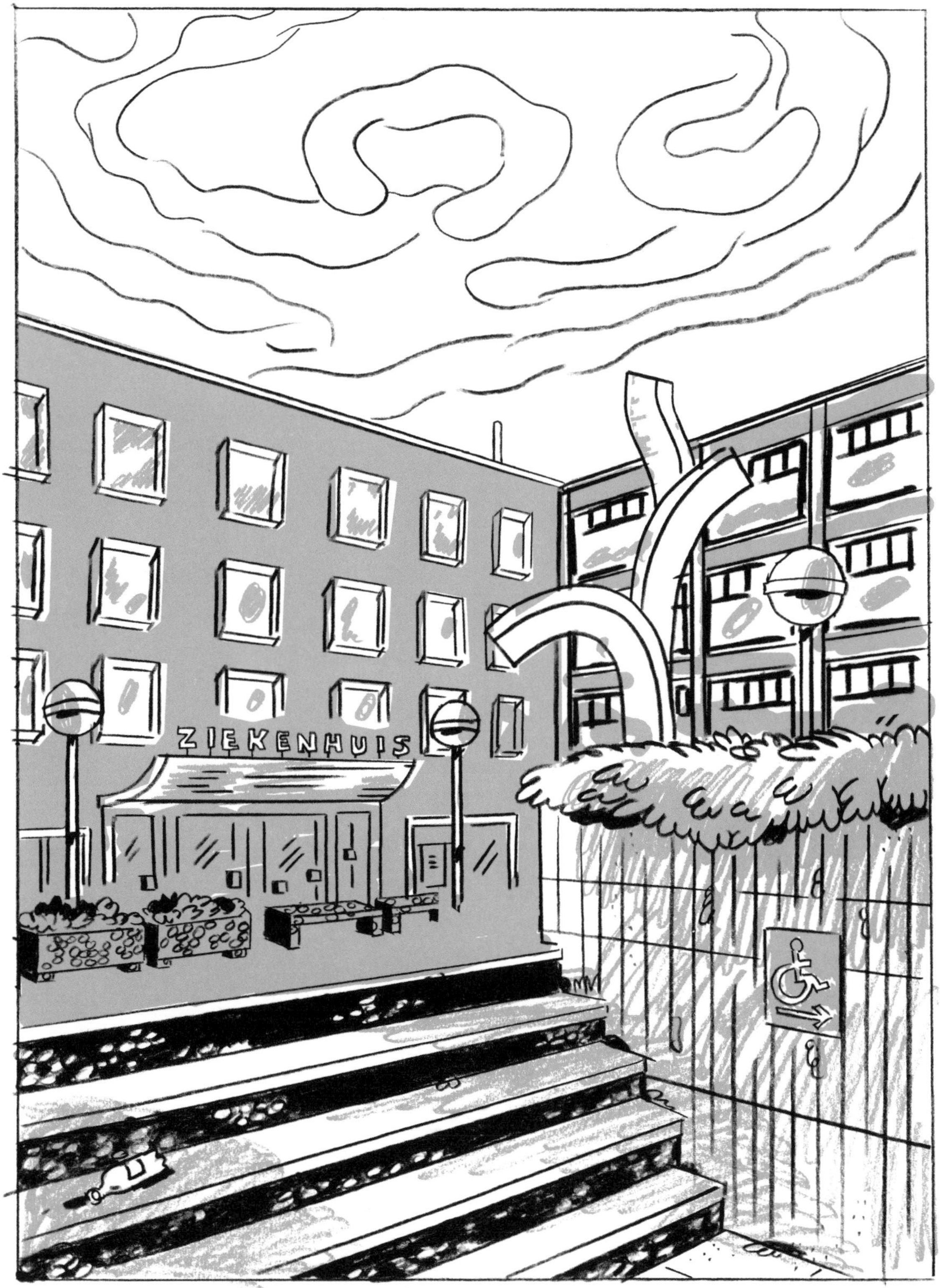
ZIEKENHUIS

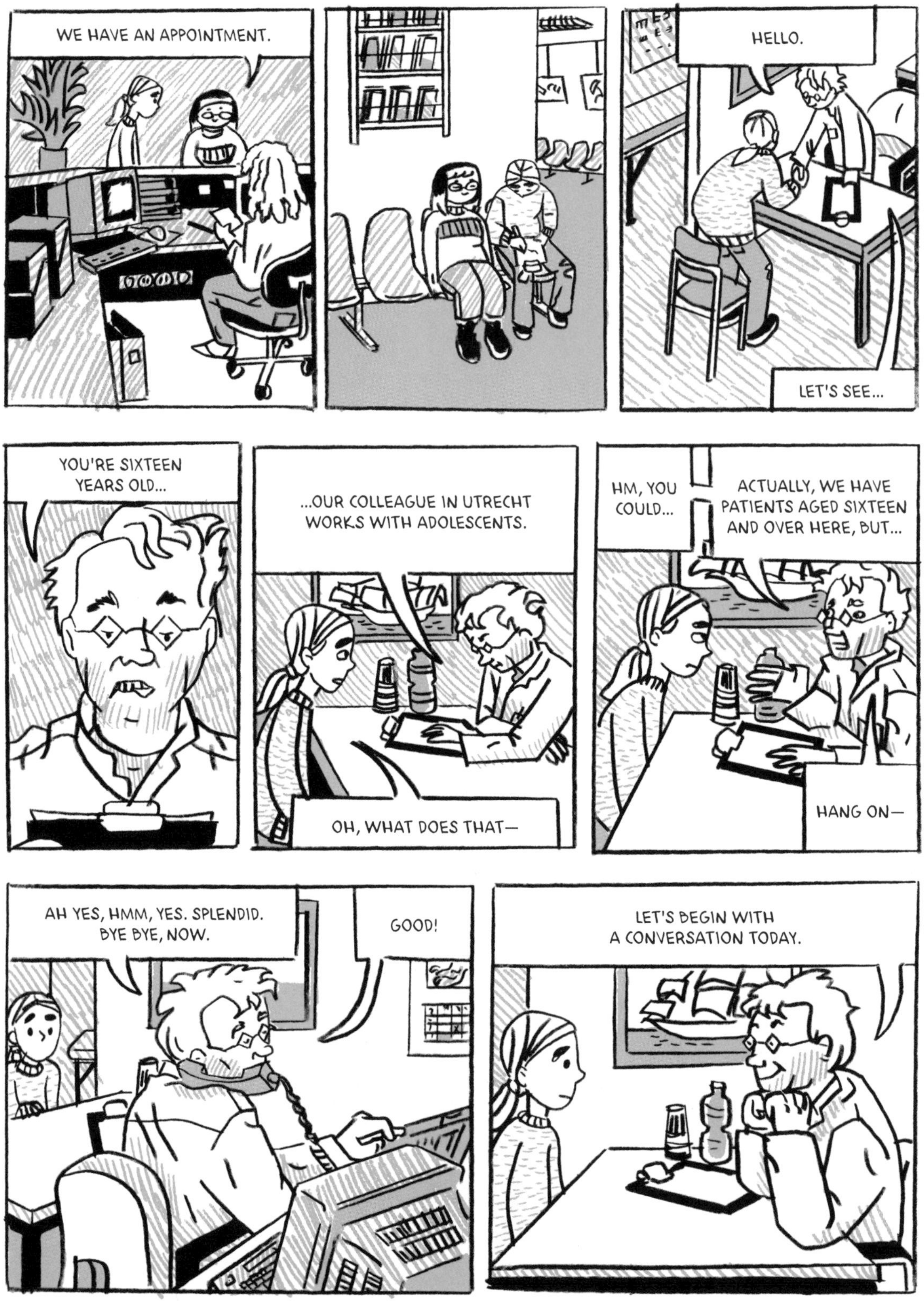
WE HAVE AN APPOINTMENT.
HELLO.
LET'S SEE...
YOU'RE SIXTEEN YEARS OLD...
...OUR COLLEAGUE IN UTRECHT WORKS WITH ADOLESCENTS.
OH, WHAT DOES THAT—
HM, YOU COULD...
ACTUALLY, WE HAVE PATIENTS AGED SIXTEEN AND OVER HERE, BUT...
HANG ON—
AH YES, HMM, YES. SPLENDID. BYE BYE, NOW.
GOOD!
LET'S BEGIN WITH A CONVERSATION TODAY.

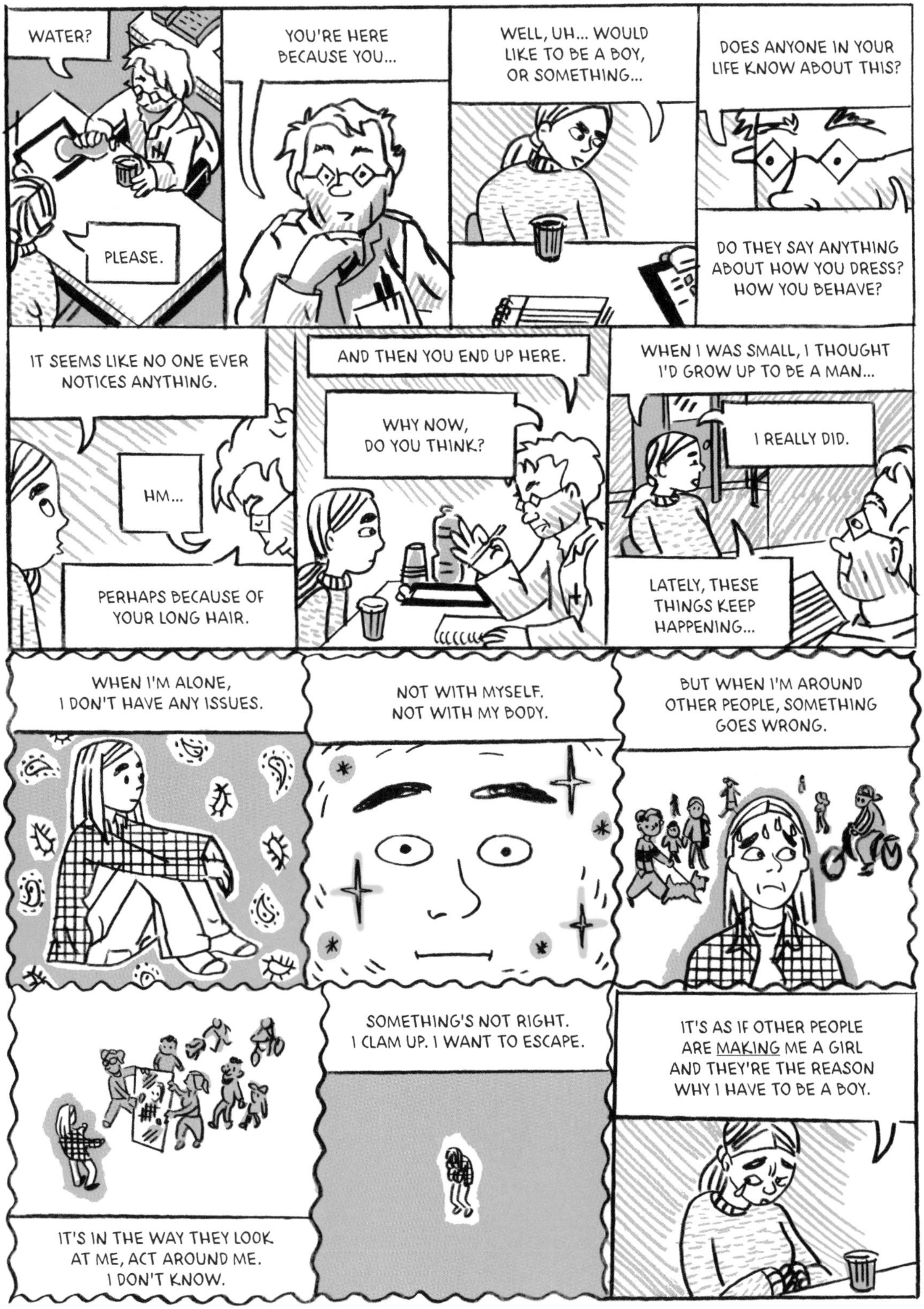
WATER?
PLEASE.
YOU'RE HERE BECAUSE YOU...
WELL, UH... WOULD LIKE TO BE A BOY, OR SOMETHING...
DOES ANYONE IN YOUR LIFE KNOW ABOUT THIS?
DO THEY SAY ANYTHING ABOUT HOW YOU DRESS? HOW YOU BEHAVE?
IT SEEMS LIKE NO ONE EVER NOTICES ANYTHING.
HM...
PERHAPS BECAUSE OF YOUR LONG HAIR.
AND THEN YOU END UP HERE.
WHY NOW, DO YOU THINK?
WHEN I WAS SMALL, I THOUGHT I'D GROW UP TO BE A MAN...
I REALLY DID.
LATELY, THESE THINGS KEEP HAPPENING...
WHEN I'M ALONE, I DON'T HAVE ANY ISSUES.
NOT WITH MYSELF. NOT WITH MY BODY.
BUT WHEN I'M AROUND OTHER PEOPLE, SOMETHING GOES WRONG.
IT'S IN THE WAY THEY LOOK AT ME, ACT AROUND ME. I DON'T KNOW.
SOMETHING'S NOT RIGHT. I CLAM UP. I WANT TO ESCAPE.
IT'S AS IF OTHER PEOPLE ARE MAKING ME A GIRL AND THEY'RE THE REASON WHY I HAVE TO BE A BOY.

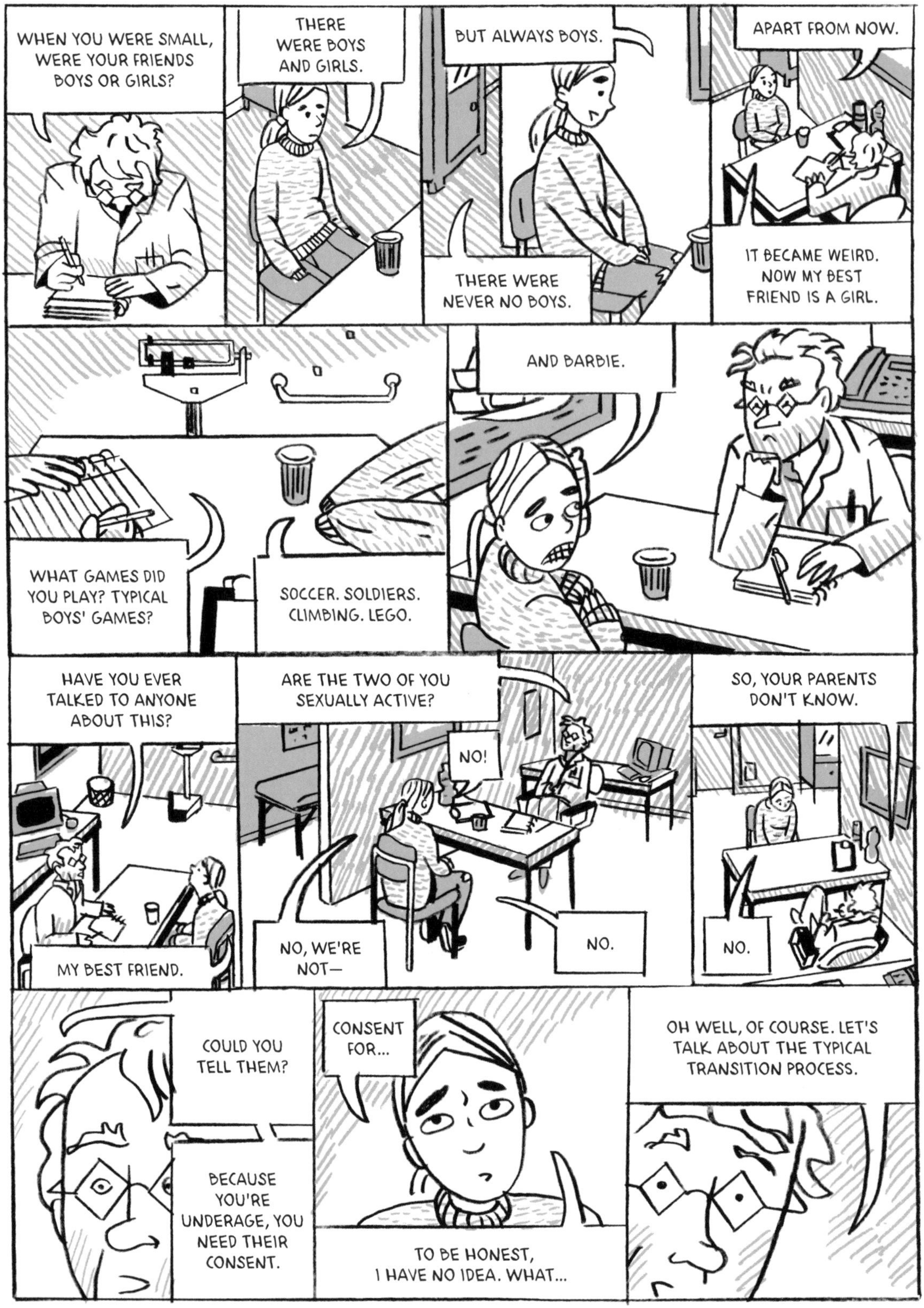
WHEN YOU WERE SMALL, WERE YOUR FRIENDS BOYS OR GIRLS?
THERE WERE BOYS AND GIRLS.
BUT ALWAYS BOYS.
THERE WERE NEVER NO BOYS.
APART FROM NOW.
IT BECAME WEIRD. NOW MY BEST FRIEND IS A GIRL.
WHAT GAMES DID YOU PLAY? TYPICAL BOYS' GAMES?
SOCCER. SOLDIERS. CLIMBING. LEGO.
AND BARBIE.
HAVE YOU EVER TALKED TO ANYONE ABOUT THIS?
MY BEST FRIEND.
ARE THE TWO OF YOU SEXUALLY ACTIVE?
NO!
NO, WE'RE NOT—
NO.
SO, YOUR PARENTS DON'T KNOW.
NO.
COULD YOU TELL THEM?
BECAUSE YOU'RE UNDERAGE, YOU NEED THEIR CONSENT.
CONSENT FOR...
TO BE HONEST, I HAVE NO IDEA. WHAT...
OH WELL, OF COURSE. LET'S TALK ABOUT THE TYPICAL TRANSITION PROCESS.

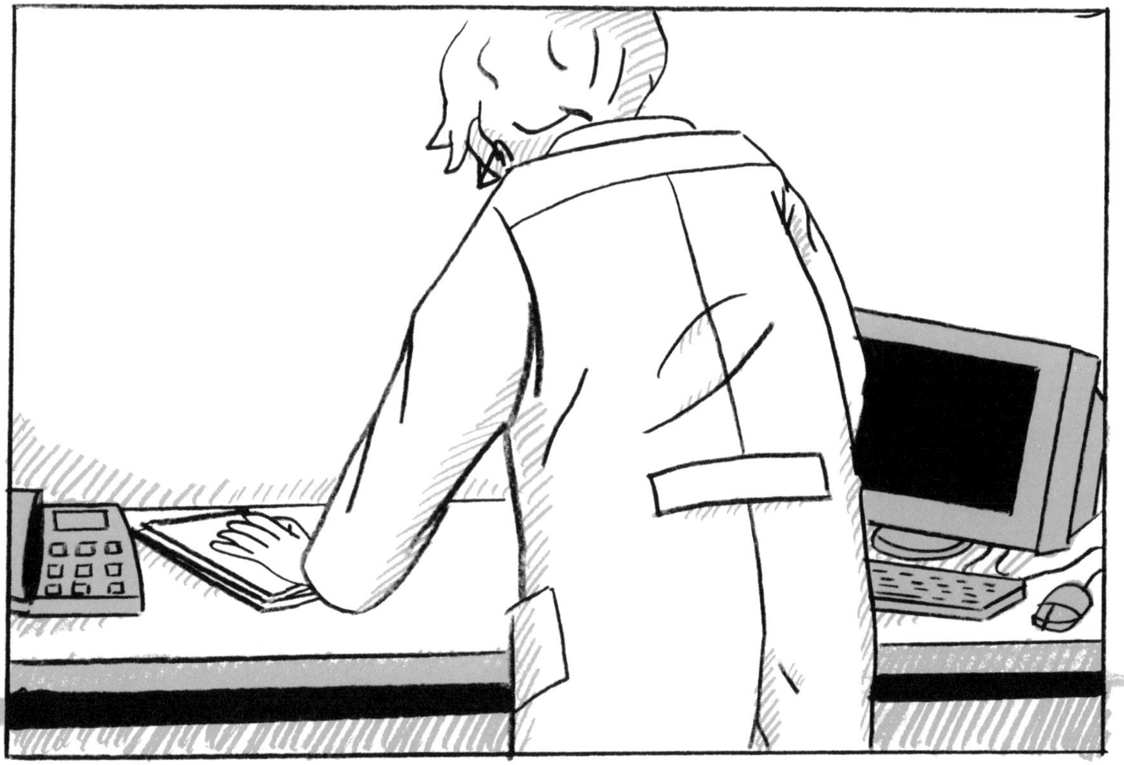

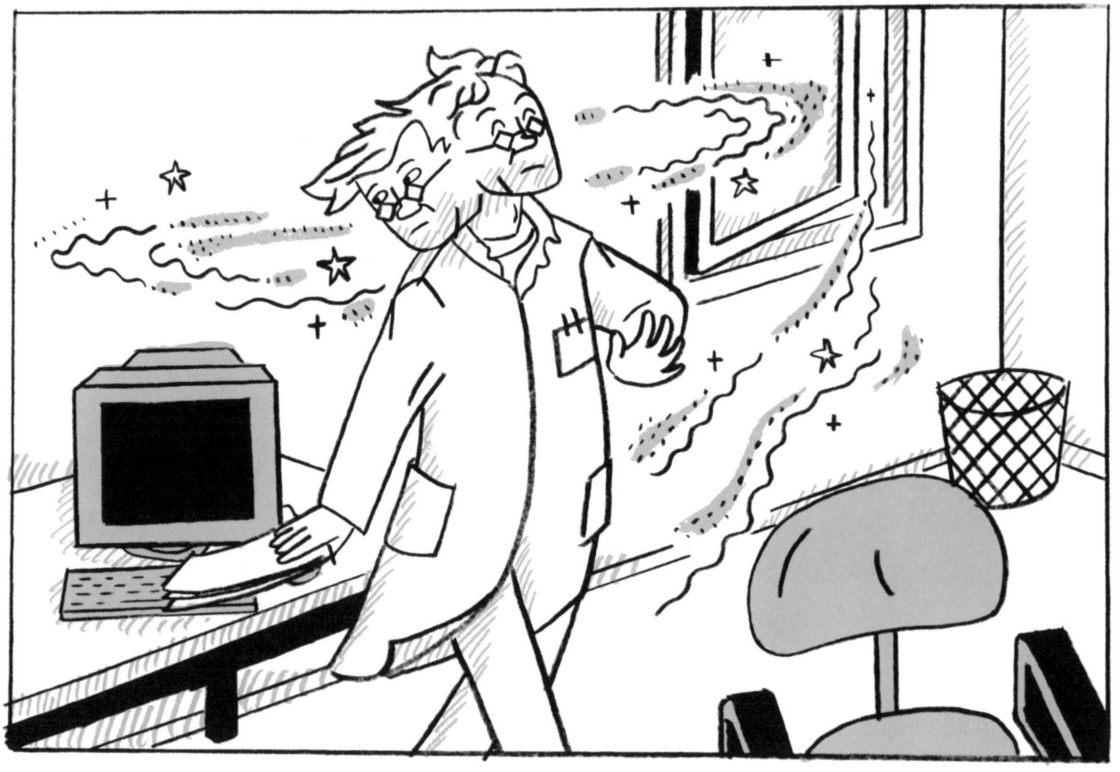

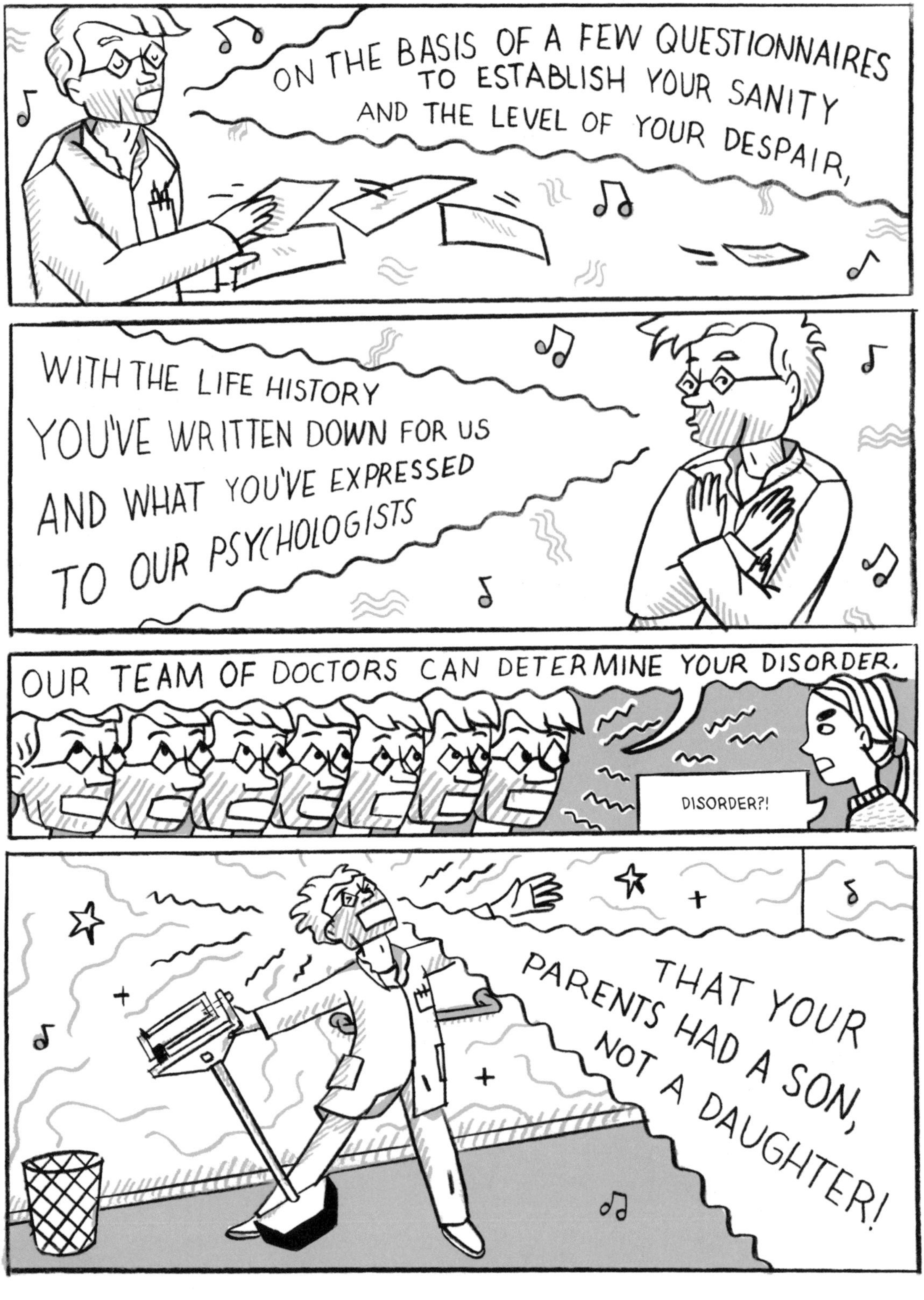
ON THE BASIS OF A FEW QUESTIONNAIRES TO ESTABLISH YOUR SANITY AND THE LEVEL OF YOUR DESPAIR,
WITH THE LIFE HISTORY YOU'VE WRITTEN DOWN FOR US AND WHAT YOU'VE EXPRESSED TO OUR PSYCHOLOGISTS
OUR TEAM OF DOCTORS CAN DETERMINE YOUR DISORDER.
DISORDER?!
THAT YOUR PARENTS HAD A SON, NOT A DAUGHTER!

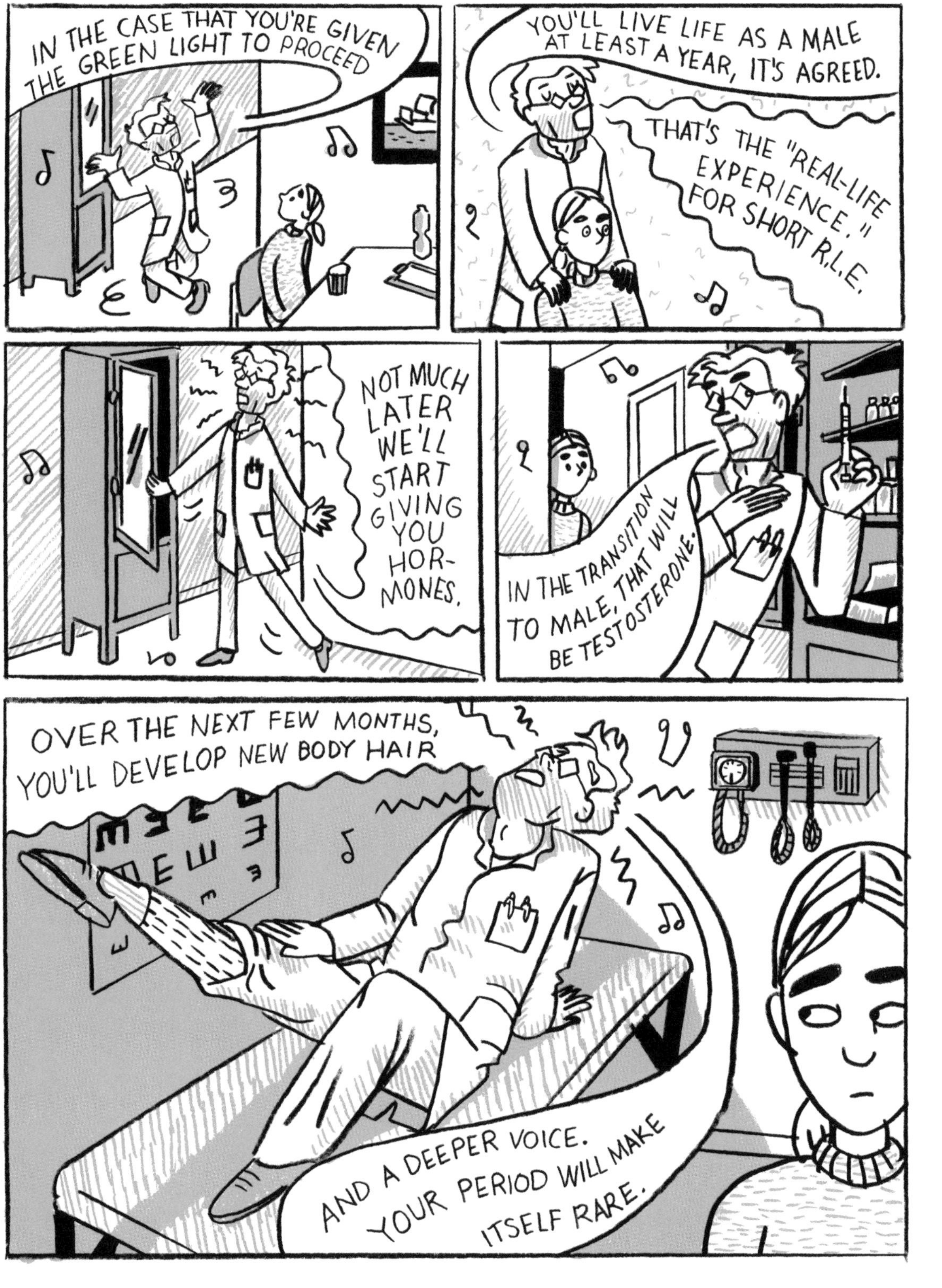
IN THE CASE THAT YOU'RE GIVEN THE GREEN LIGHT TO PROCEED
YOU'LL LIVE LIFE AS A MALE AT LEAST A YEAR, IT'S AGREED.
THAT'S THE "REAL-LIFE EXPERIENCE," FOR SHORT R.L.E.
NOT MUCH LATER WE'LL START GIVING YOU HOR-MONES.
IN THE TRANSITION TO MALE, THAT WILL BE TESTOSTERONE.
OVER THE NEXT FEW MONTHS, YOU'LL DEVELOP NEW BODY HAIR
AND A DEEPER VOICE. YOUR PERIOD WILL MAKE ITSELF RARE.

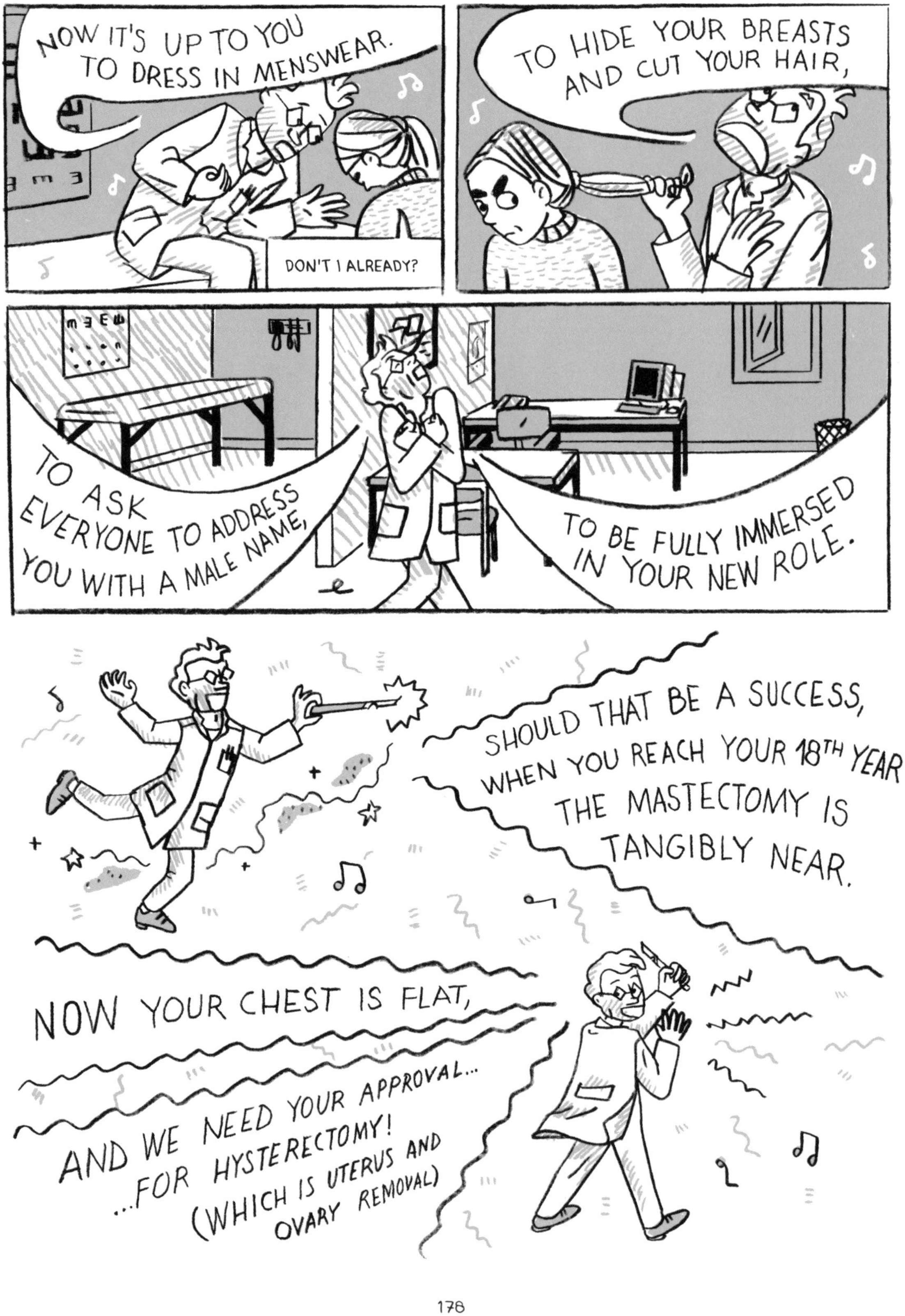
NOW IT'S UP TO YOU TO DRESS IN MENSWEAR.
DON'T I ALREADY?
TO HIDE YOUR BREASTS AND CUT YOUR HAIR,
TO ASK EVERYONE TO ADDRESS YOU WITH A MALE NAME,
TO BE FULLY IMMERSED IN YOUR NEW ROLE.
SHOULD THAT BE A SUCCESS, WHEN YOU REACH YOUR 18TH YEAR THE MASTECTOMY IS TANGIBLY NEAR.
NOW YOUR CHEST IS FLAT,
AND WE NEED YOUR APPROVAL...
...FOR HYSTERECTOMY!
(WHICH IS UTERUS AND OVARY REMOVAL)

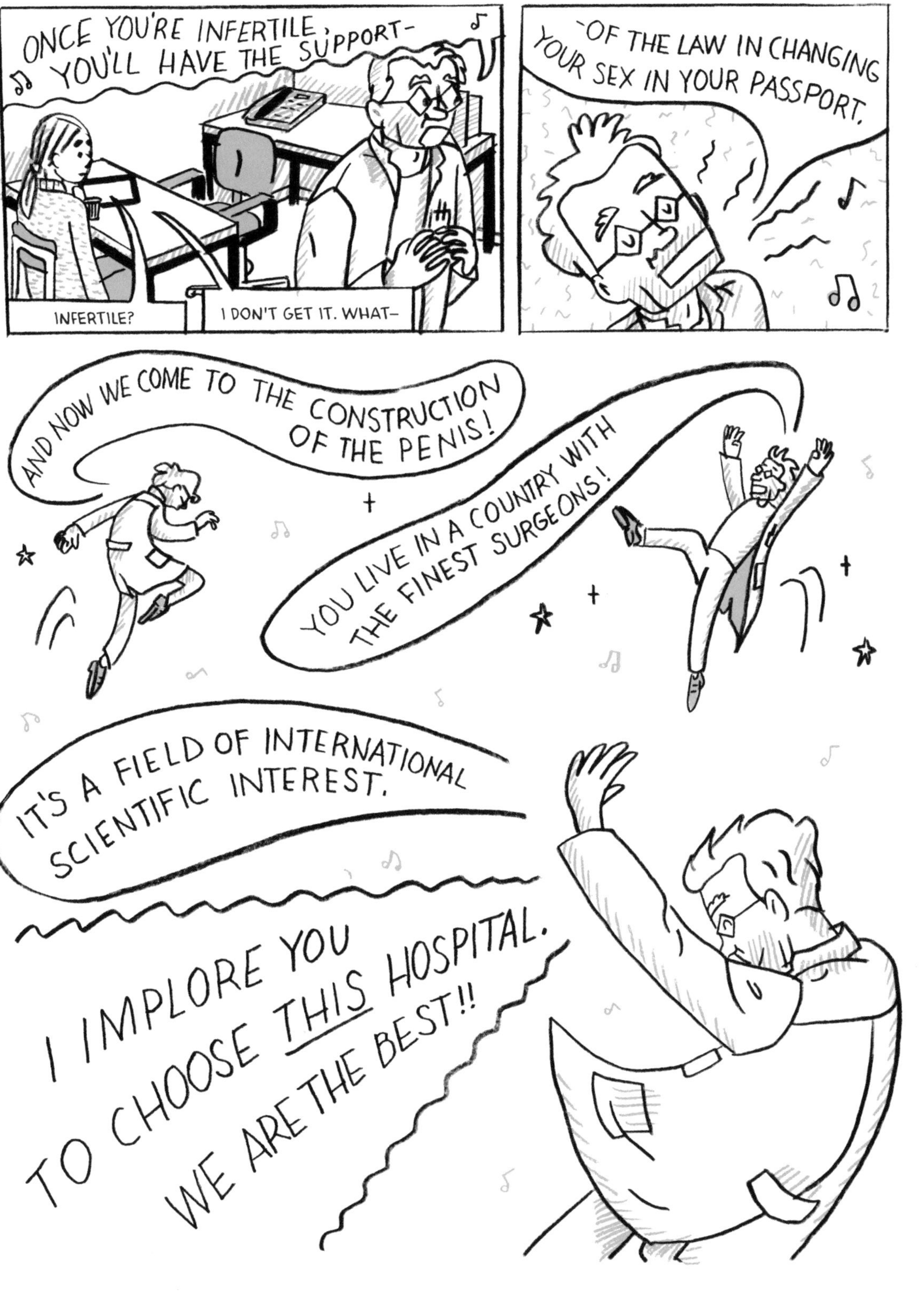
ONCE YOU'RE INFERTILE, YOU'LL HAVE THE SUPPORT-
INFERTILE?
I DON'T GET IT. WHAT-
-OF THE LAW IN CHANGING YOUR SEX IN YOUR PASSPORT.
AND NOW WE COME TO THE CONSTRUCTION OF THE PENIS!
YOU LIVE IN A COUNTRY WITH THE FINEST SURGEONS!
IT'S A FIELD OF INTERNATIONAL SCIENTIFIC INTEREST.
I IMPLORE YOU TO CHOOSE THIS HOSPITAL.
WE ARE THE BEST!!

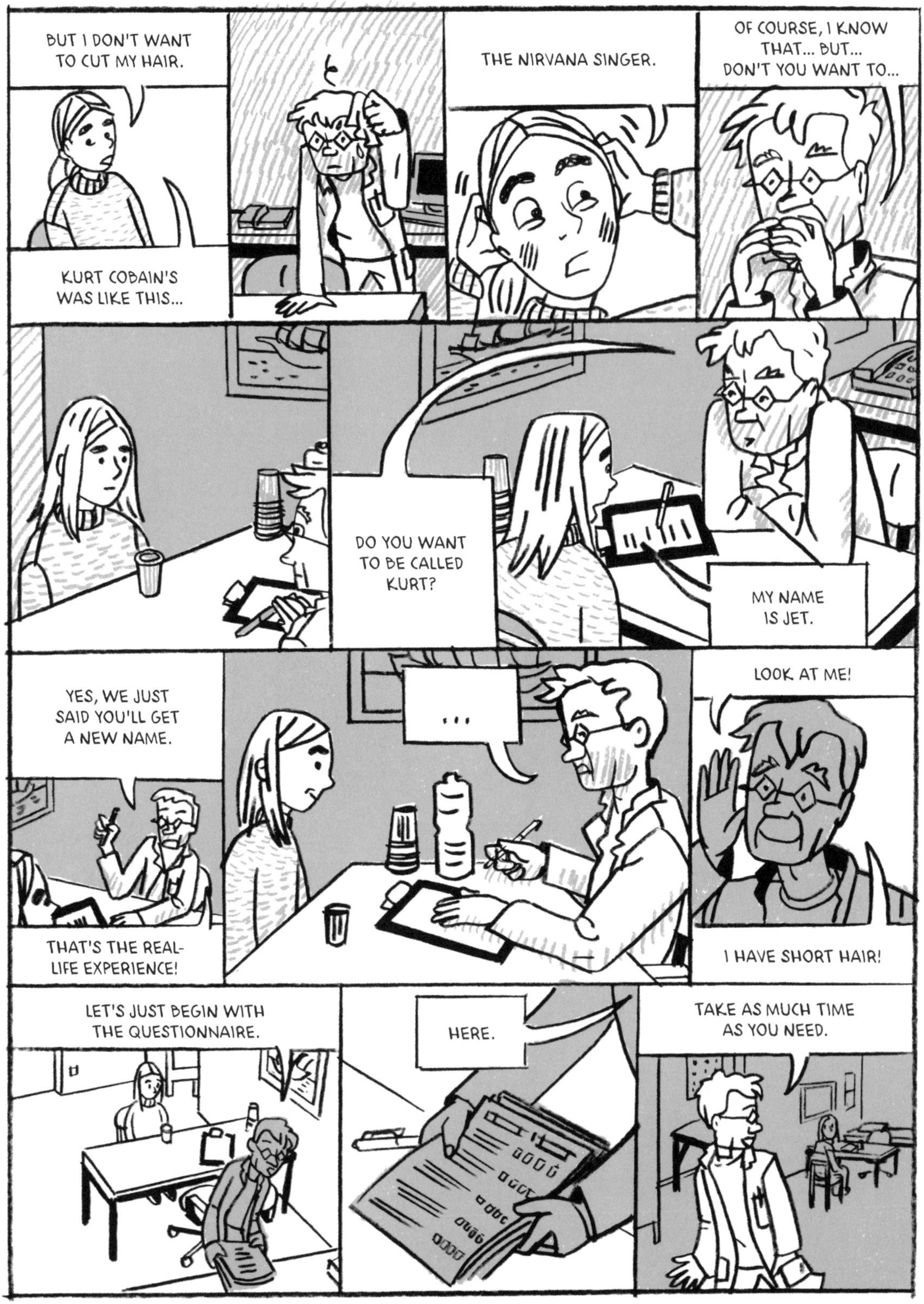
BUT I DON'T WANT TO CUT MY HAIR.
KURT COBAIN'S WAS LIKE THIS...
THE NIRVANA SINGER.
OF COURSE, I KNOW THAT... BUT... DON'T YOU WANT TO...
DO YOU WANT TO BE CALLED KURT?
MY NAME IS JET.
YES, WE JUST SAID YOU'LL GET A NEW NAME.
THAT'S THE REAL-LIFE EXPERIENCE!
...
LOOK AT ME!
I HAVE SHORT HAIR!
LET'S JUST BEGIN WITH THE QUESTIONNAIRE.
HERE.
TAKE AS MUCH TIME AS YOU NEED.

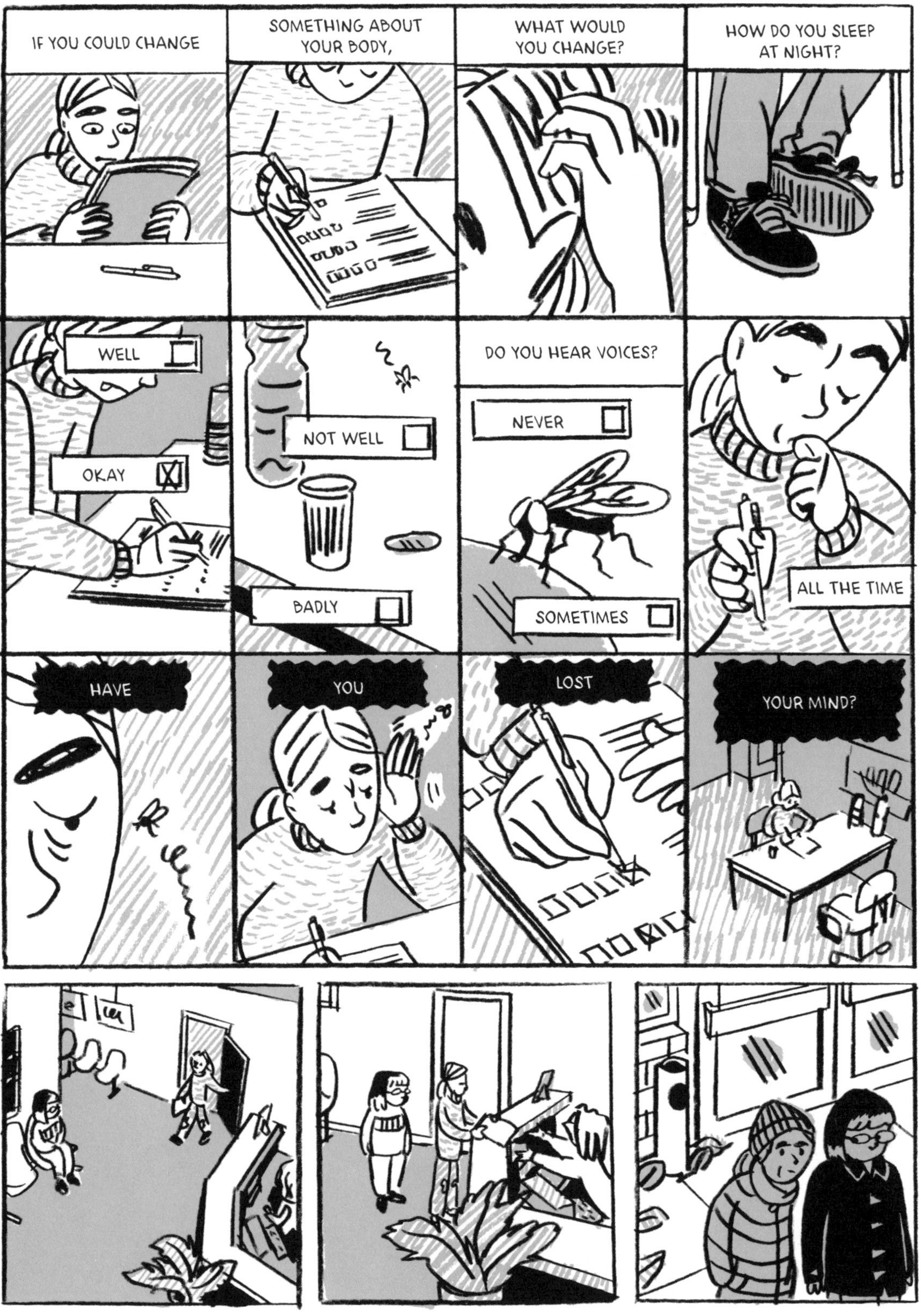
IF YOU COULD CHANGE
SOMETHING ABOUT YOUR BODY,
WHAT WOULD YOU CHANGE?
HOW DO YOU SLEEP AT NIGHT?
WELL
OKAY
NOT WELL
BADLY
DO YOU HEAR VOICES?
NEVER
SOMETIMES
ALL THE TIME
HAVE
YOU
LOST
YOUR MIND?

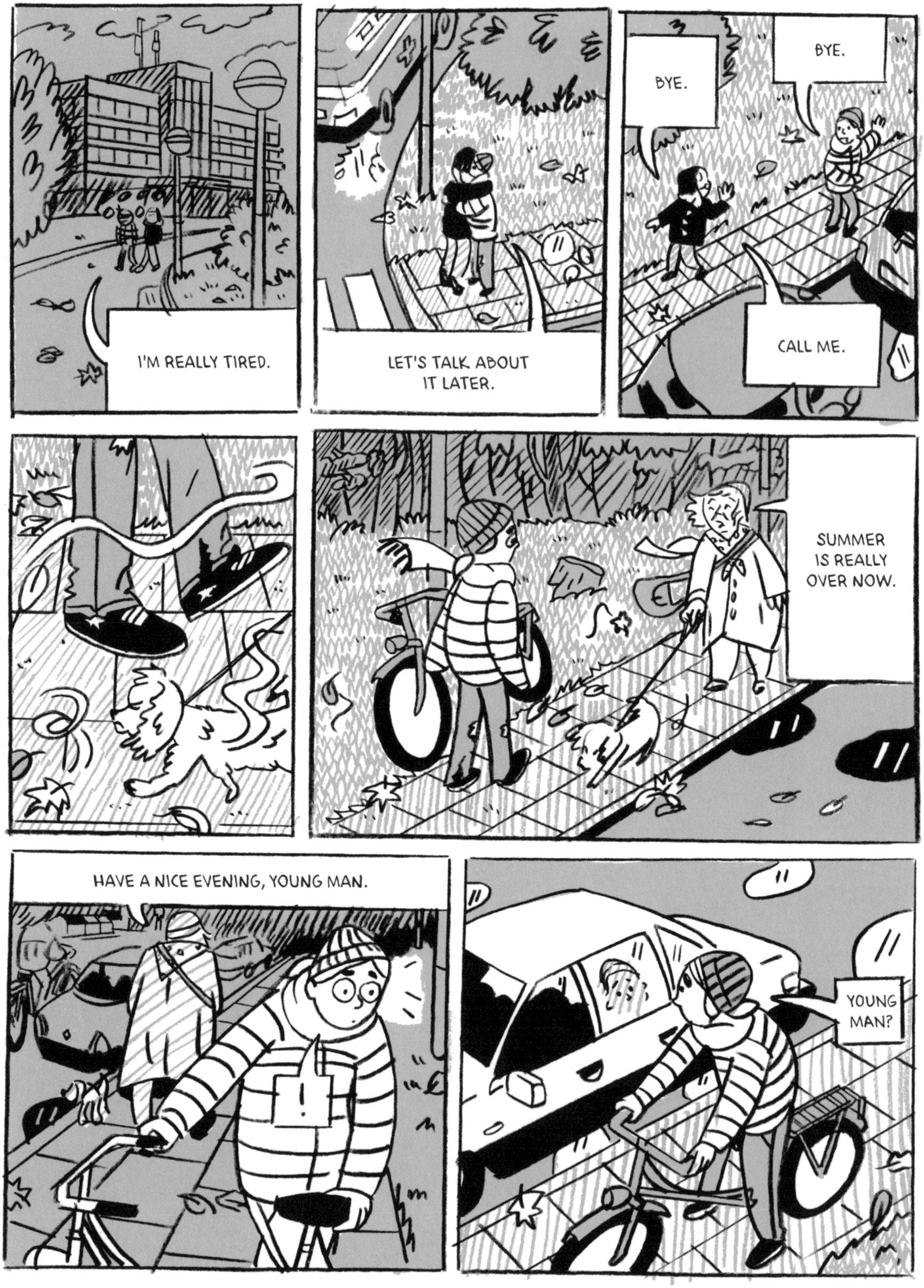
I'M REALLY TIRED.
LET'S TALK ABOUT IT LATER.
BYE.
BYE.
CALL ME.
SUMMER IS REALLY OVER NOW.
HAVE A NICE EVENING, YOUNG MAN.
!
YOUNG MAN?

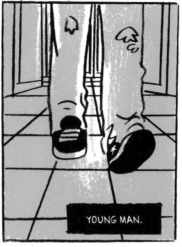

YOUNG MAN.

WHAT'S UP, JET!?
LIAR! OH YEAH,
STEF FOUND HIS
GOLD CHAIN IN YOUR
THINGS AND CALLED
THE POLICE. _NOT._
GOOD LUCK.

NICKY

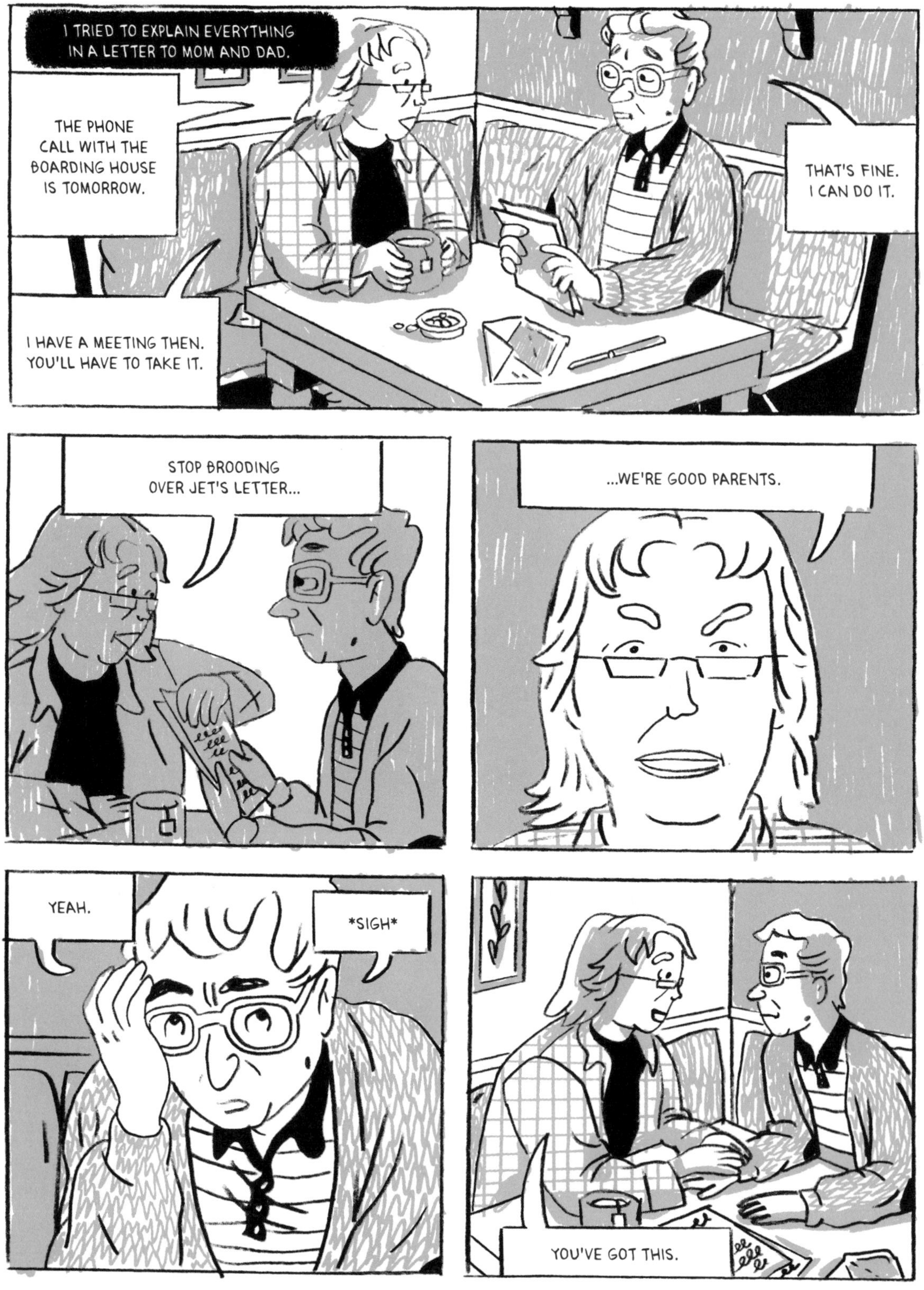
I TRIED TO EXPLAIN EVERYTHING IN A LETTER TO MOM AND DAD.
THE PHONE CALL WITH THE BOARDING HOUSE IS TOMORROW.
I HAVE A MEETING THEN. YOU'LL HAVE TO TAKE IT.
THAT'S FINE. I CAN DO IT.
STOP BROODING OVER JET'S LETTER...
...WE'RE GOOD PARENTS.
YEAH.
SIGH
YOU'VE GOT THIS.

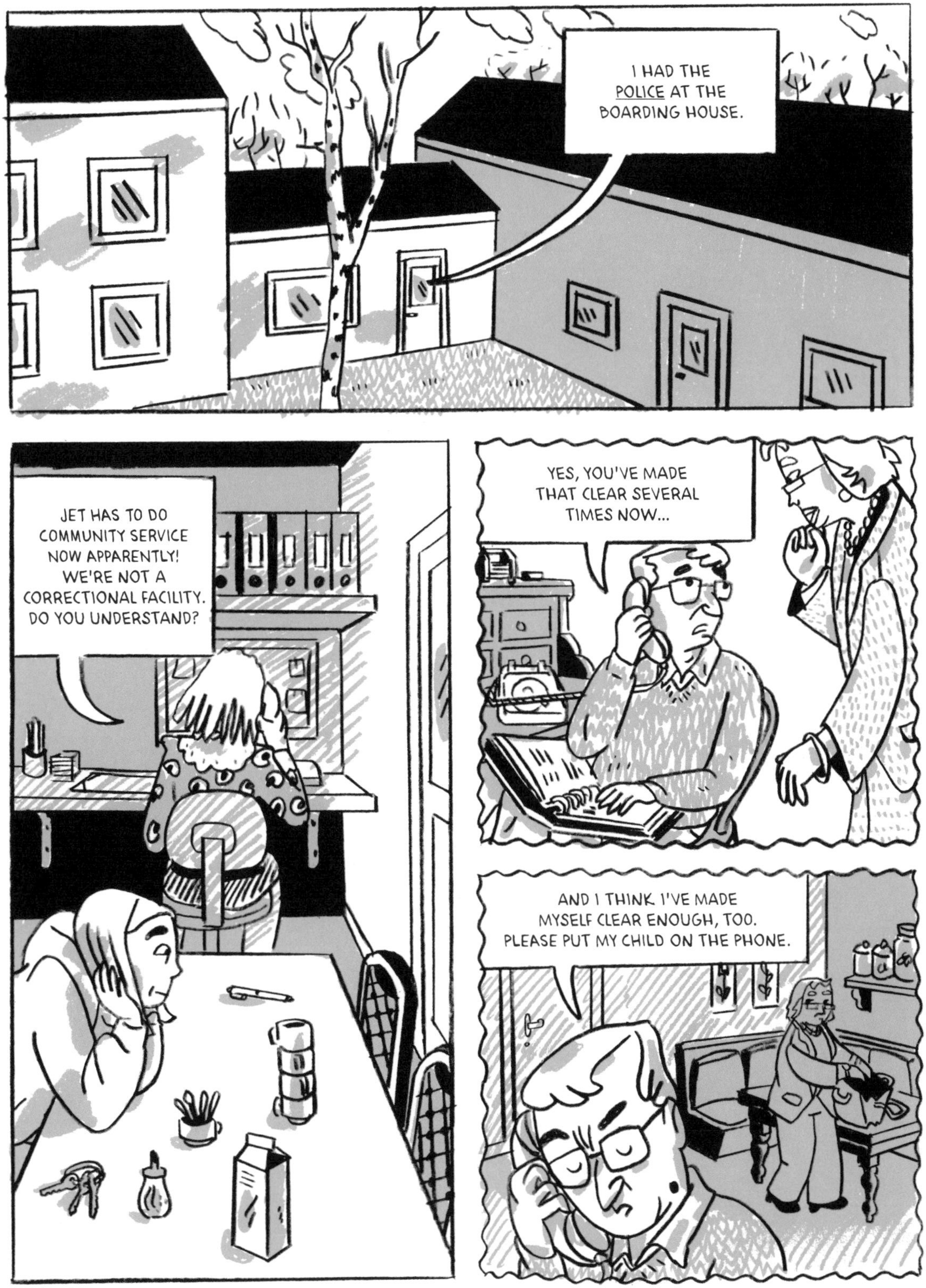

I HAD THE POLICE AT THE BOARDING HOUSE.
JET HAS TO DO COMMUNITY SERVICE NOW APPARENTLY! WE'RE NOT A CORRECTIONAL FACILITY. DO YOU UNDERSTAND?
YES, YOU'VE MADE THAT CLEAR SEVERAL TIMES NOW...
AND I THINK I'VE MADE MYSELF CLEAR ENOUGH, TOO. PLEASE PUT MY CHILD ON THE PHONE.

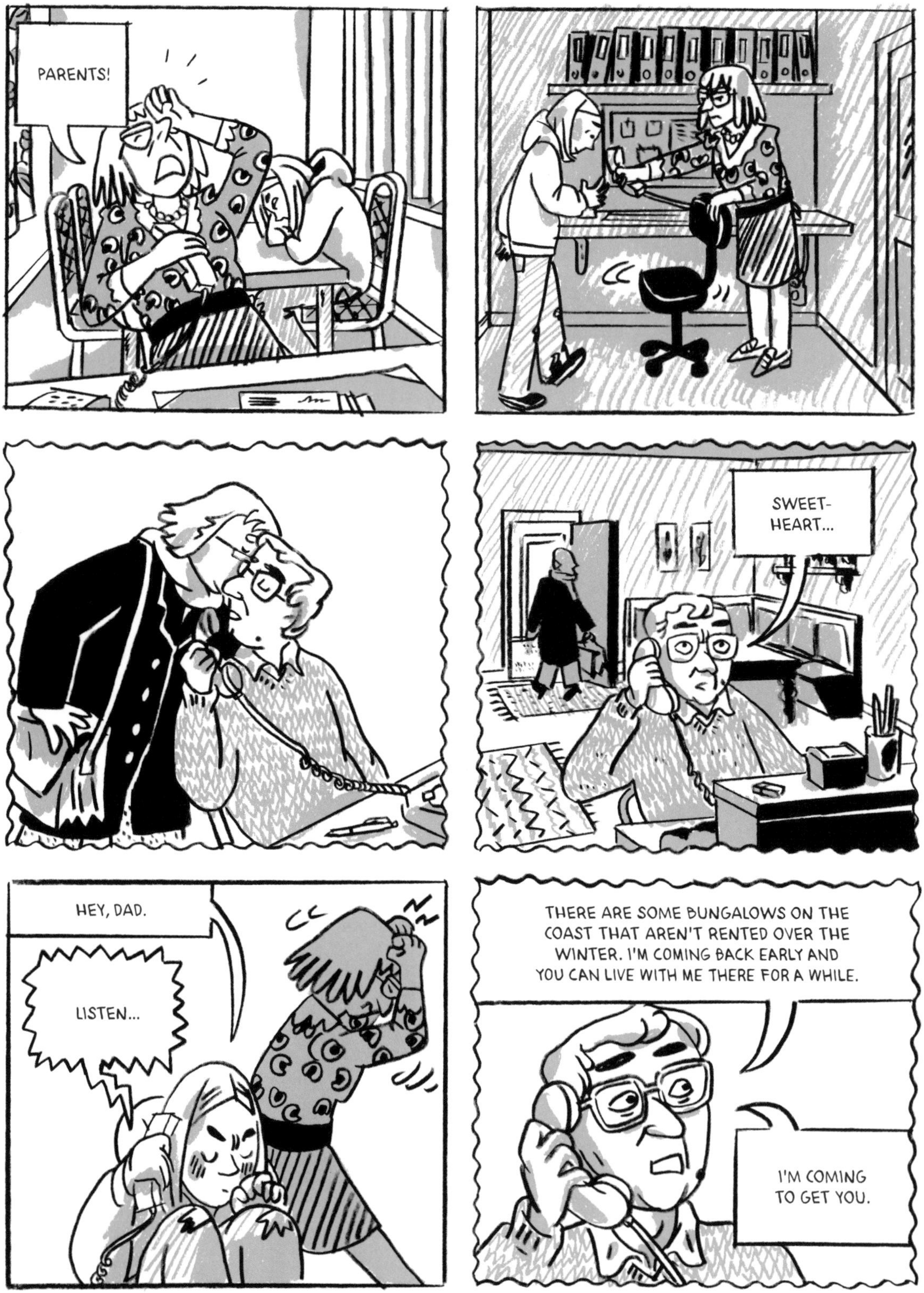
PARENTS!
SWEET-HEART...
HEY, DAD.
LISTEN...
THERE ARE SOME BUNGALOWS ON THE COAST THAT AREN'T RENTED OVER THE WINTER. I'M COMING BACK EARLY AND YOU CAN LIVE WITH ME THERE FOR A WHILE.
I'M COMING TO GET YOU.

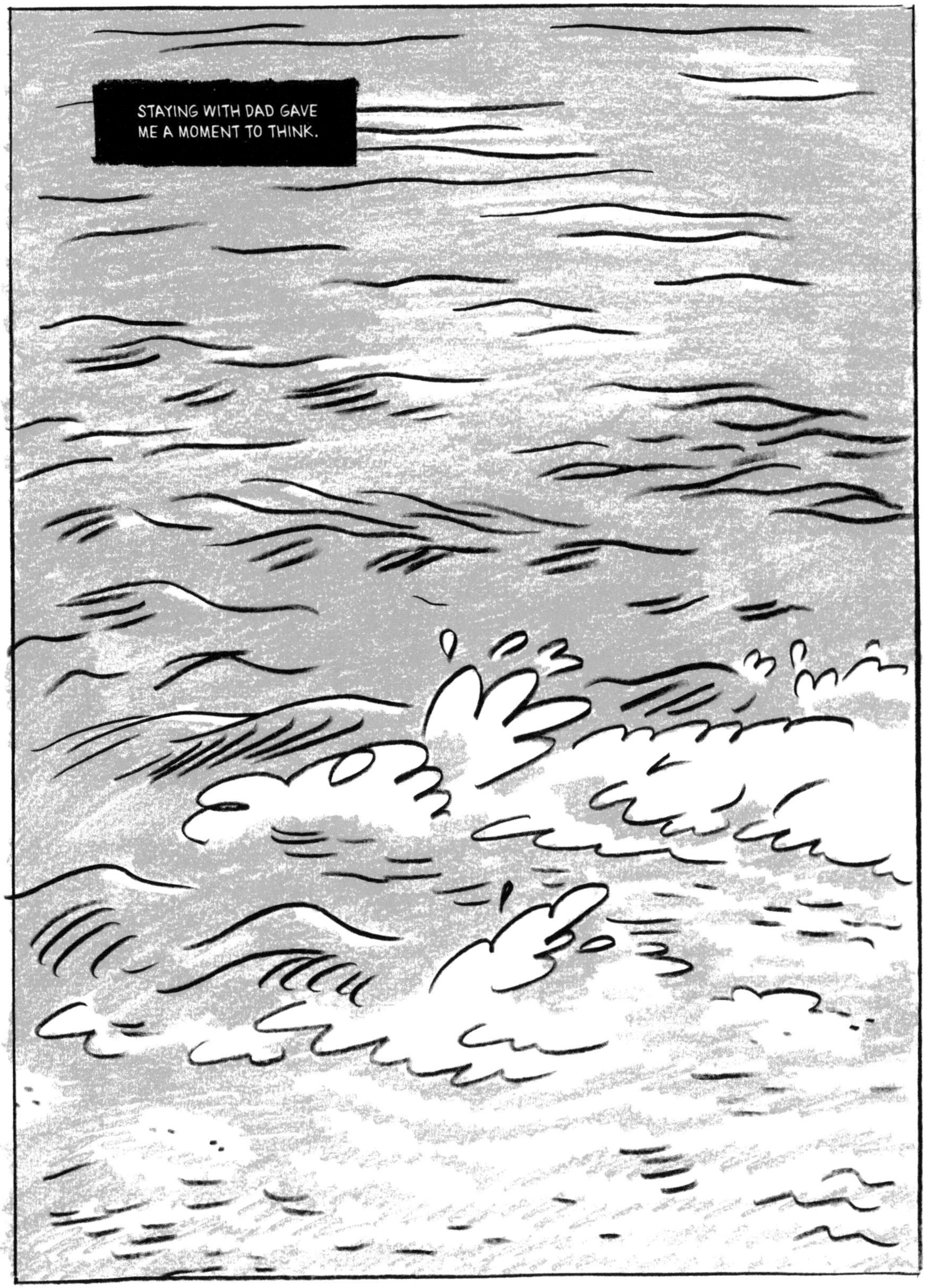
STAYING WITH DAD GAVE ME A MOMENT TO THINK.

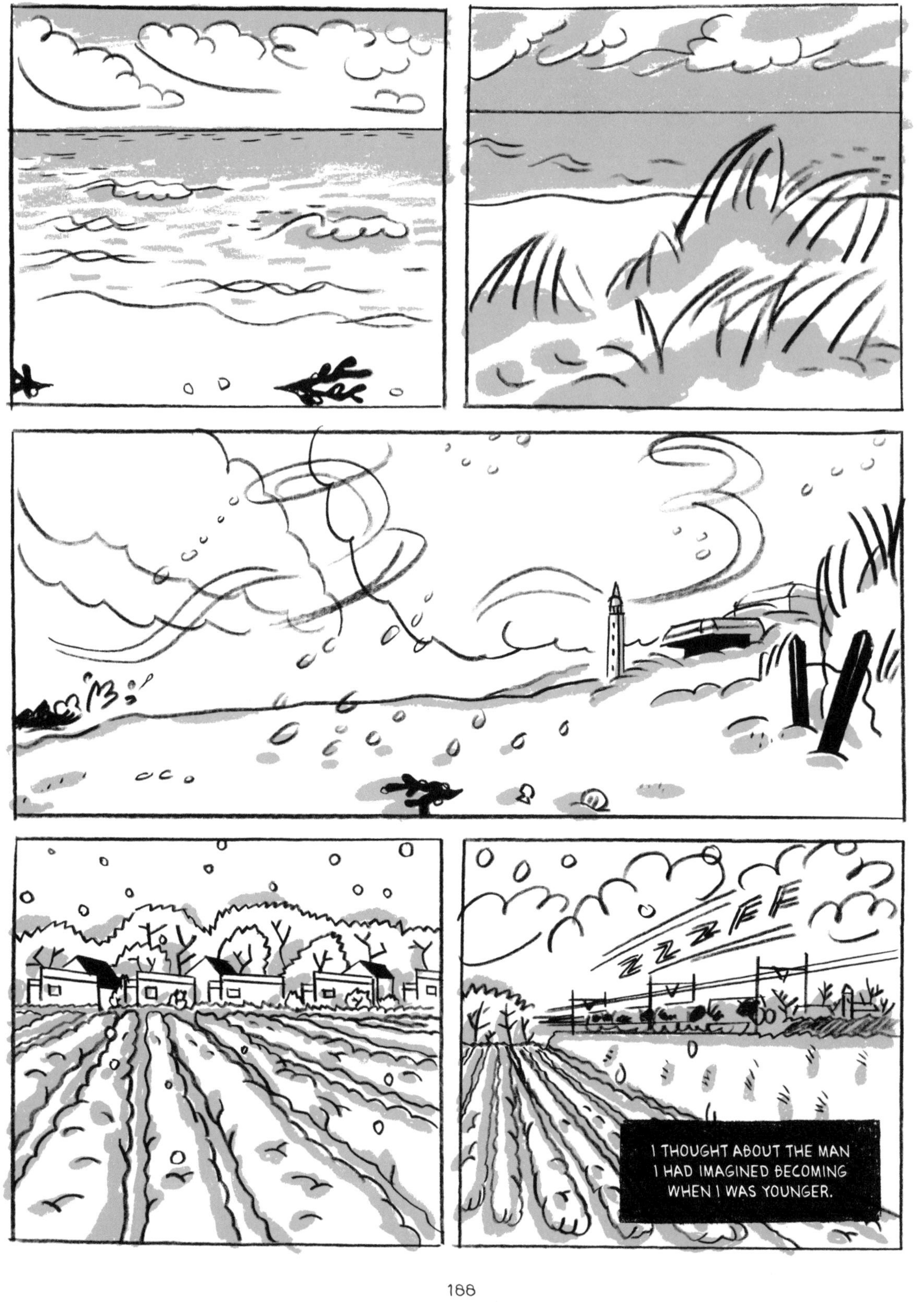
I THOUGHT ABOUT THE MAN
I HAD IMAGINED BECOMING
WHEN I WAS YOUNGER.

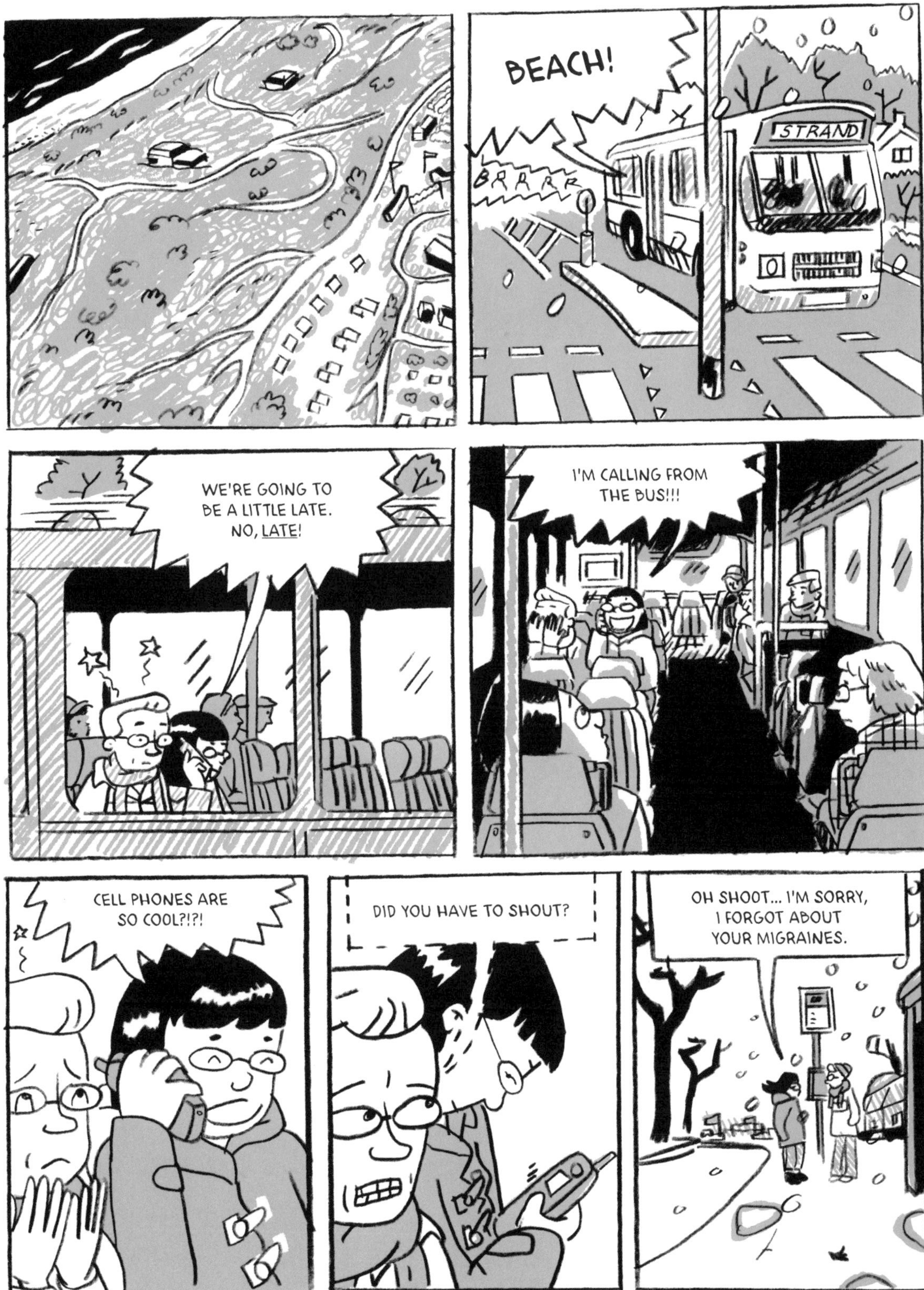
BEACH!
BRRRR
STRAND
WE'RE GOING TO BE A LITTLE LATE. NO, LATE!
I'M CALLING FROM THE BUS!!!
CELL PHONES ARE SO COOL?!?!
DID YOU HAVE TO SHOUT?
OH SHOOT... I'M SORRY, I FORGOT ABOUT YOUR MIGRAINES.

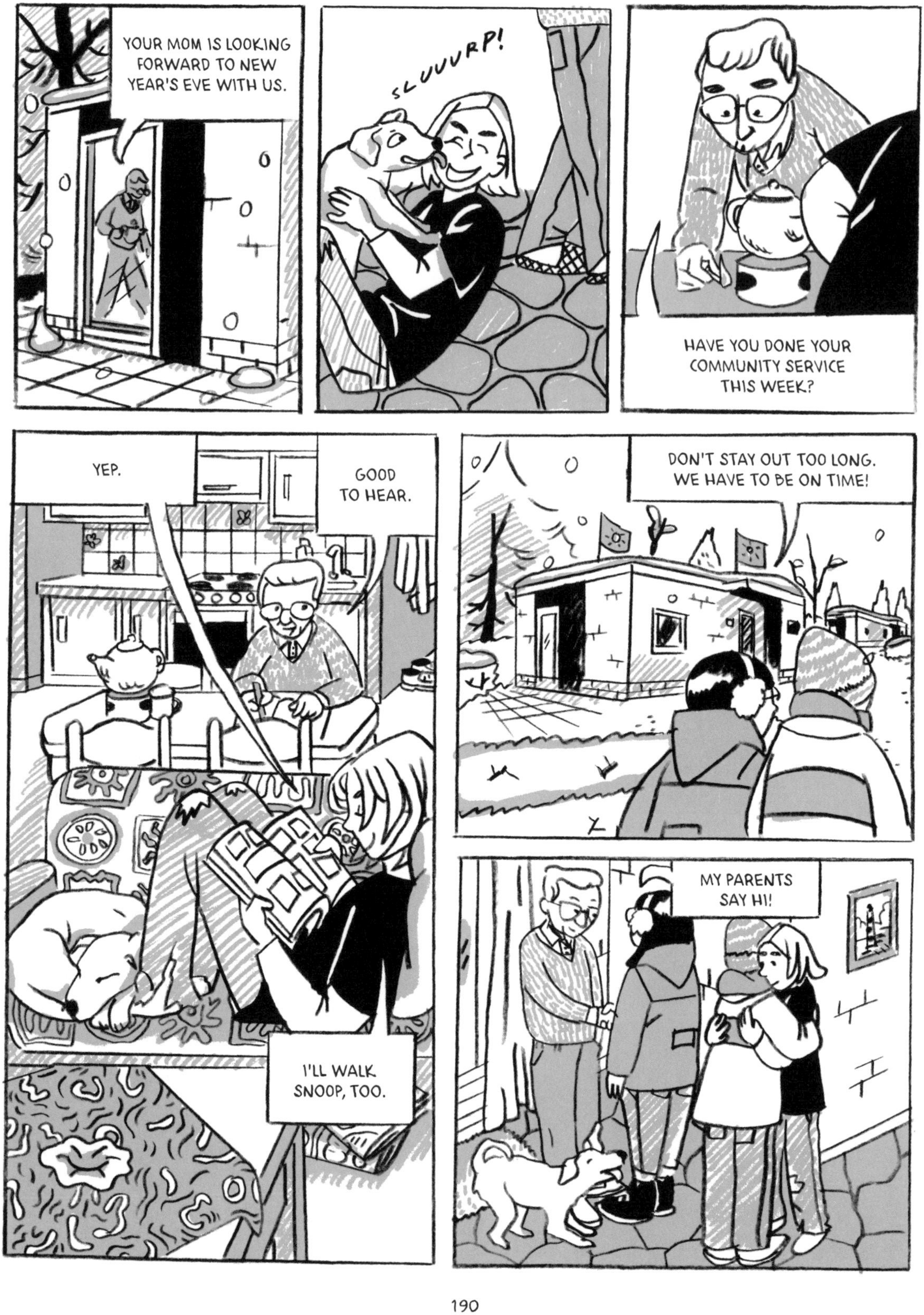
YOUR MOM IS LOOKING FORWARD TO NEW YEAR'S EVE WITH US.
SLUUURP!
HAVE YOU DONE YOUR COMMUNITY SERVICE THIS WEEK?
YEP.
GOOD TO HEAR.
I'LL WALK SNOOP, TOO.
DON'T STAY OUT TOO LONG. WE HAVE TO BE ON TIME!
MY PARENTS SAY HI!

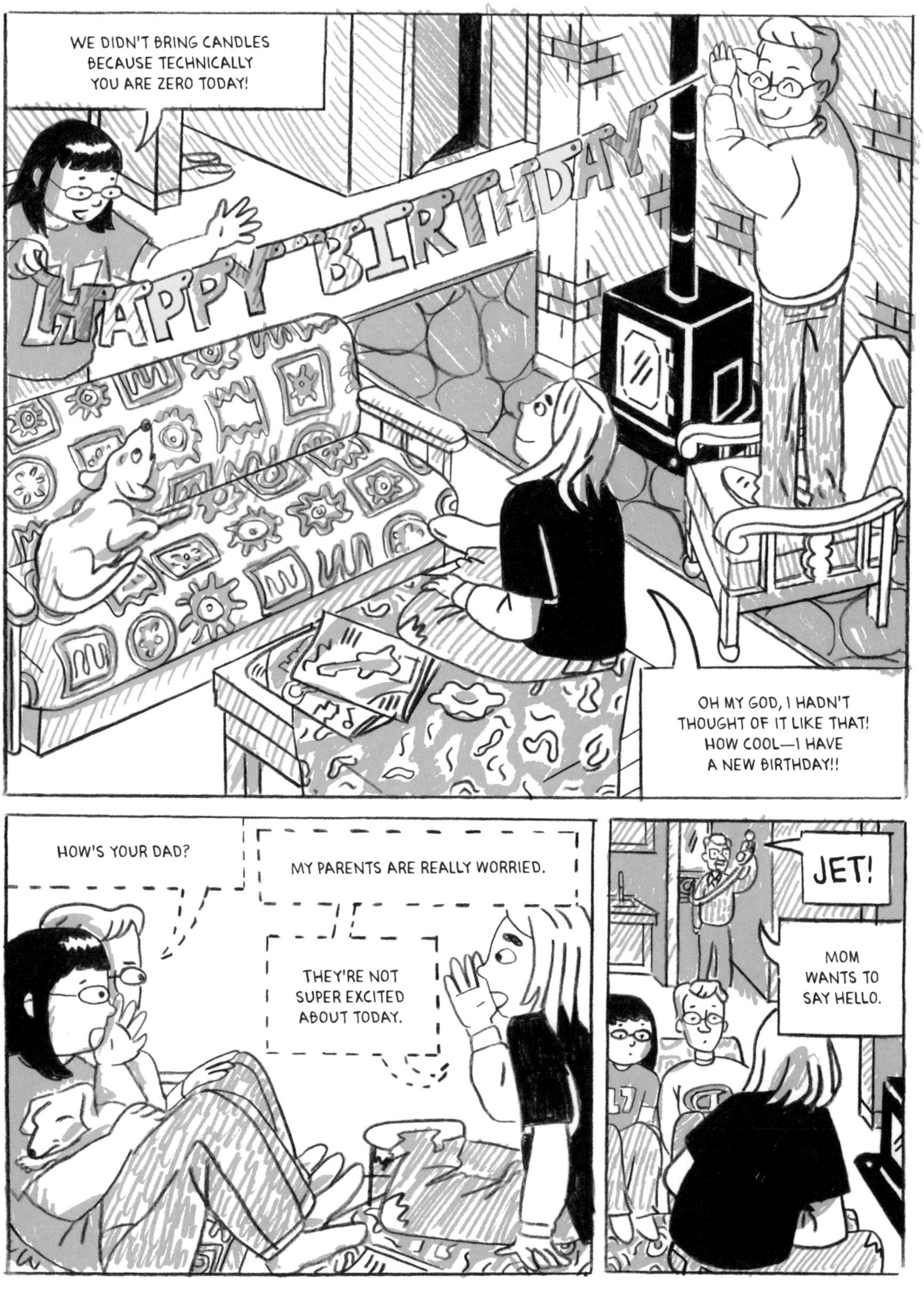
WE DIDN'T BRING CANDLES BECAUSE TECHNICALLY YOU ARE ZERO TODAY!
HAPPY BIRTHDAY
OH MY GOD, I HADN'T THOUGHT OF IT LIKE THAT! HOW COOL—I HAVE A NEW BIRTHDAY!!
HOW'S YOUR DAD?
MY PARENTS ARE REALLY WORRIED.
THEY'RE NOT SUPER EXCITED ABOUT TODAY.
JET!
MOM WANTS TO SAY HELLO.

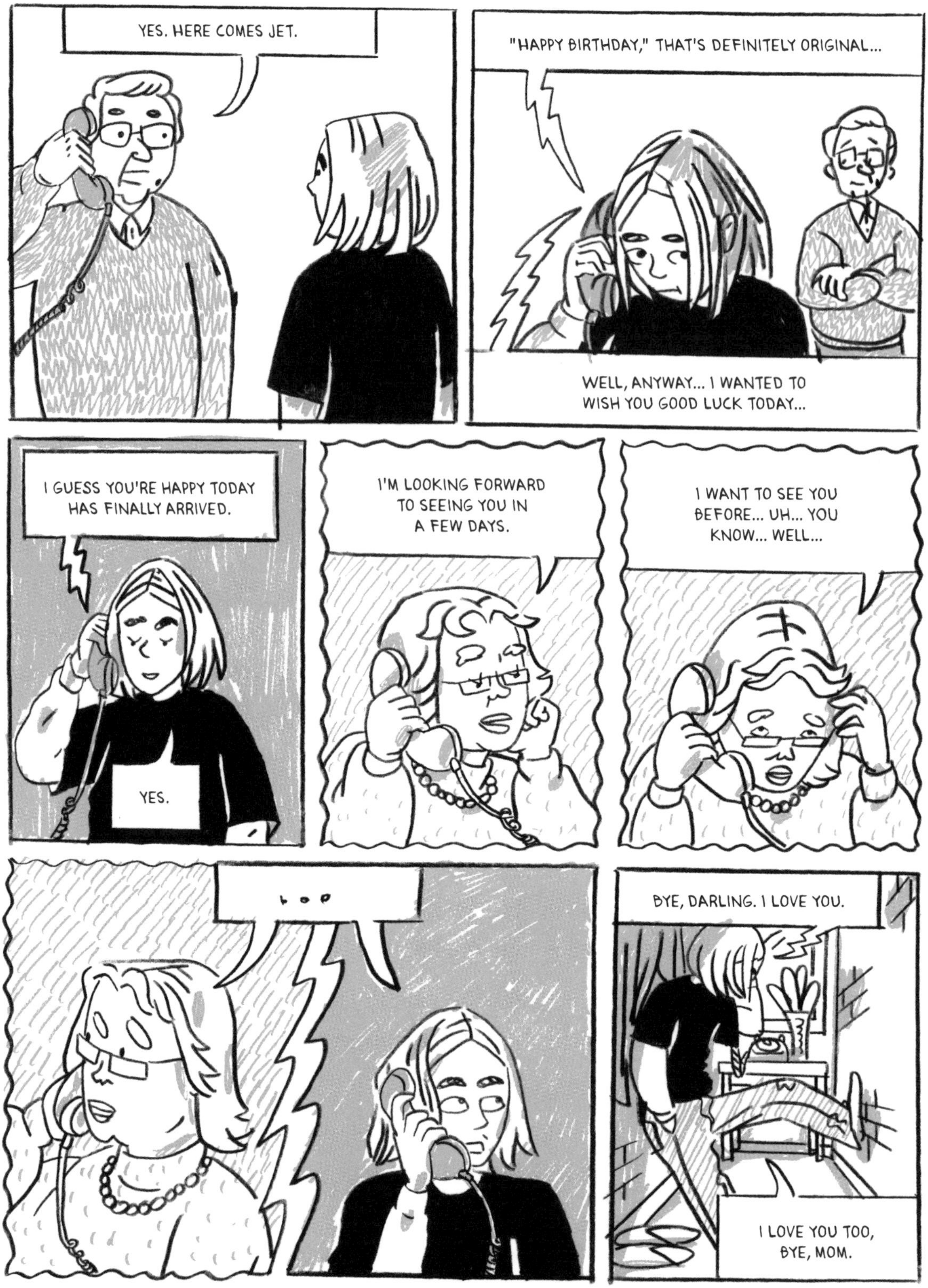
YES. HERE COMES JET.
"HAPPY BIRTHDAY," THAT'S DEFINITELY ORIGINAL...
WELL, ANYWAY... I WANTED TO WISH YOU GOOD LUCK TODAY...
I GUESS YOU'RE HAPPY TODAY HAS FINALLY ARRIVED.
YES.
I'M LOOKING FORWARD TO SEEING YOU IN A FEW DAYS.
I WANT TO SEE YOU BEFORE... UH... YOU KNOW... WELL...
BYE, DARLING. I LOVE YOU.
I LOVE YOU TOO, BYE, MOM.

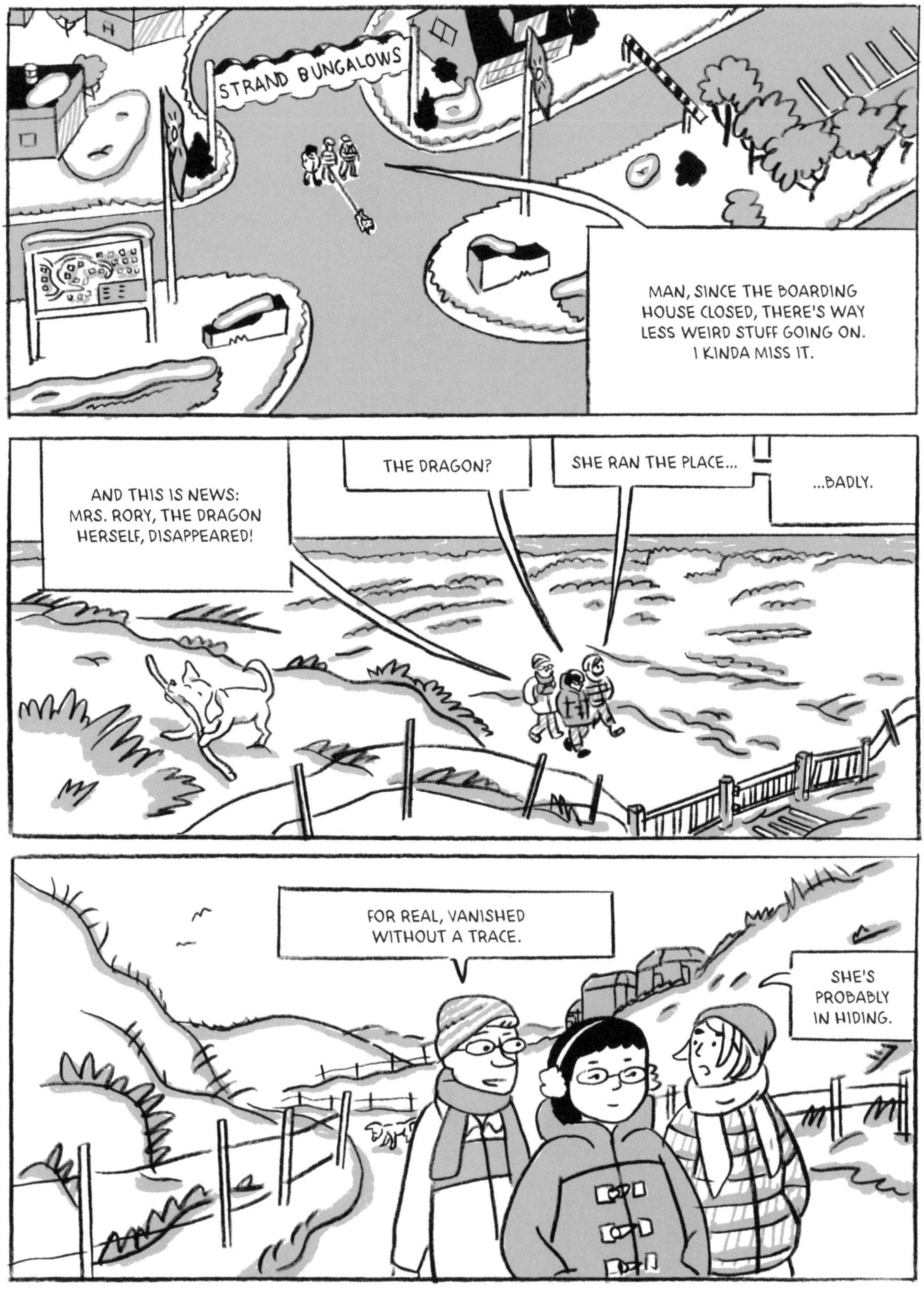
STRAND BUNGALOWS
MAN, SINCE THE BOARDING HOUSE CLOSED, THERE'S WAY LESS WEIRD STUFF GOING ON. I KINDA MISS IT.
AND THIS IS NEWS: MRS. RORY, THE DRAGON HERSELF, DISAPPEARED!
THE DRAGON?
SHE RAN THE PLACE...
...BADLY.
FOR REAL, VANISHED WITHOUT A TRACE.
SHE'S PROBABLY IN HIDING.

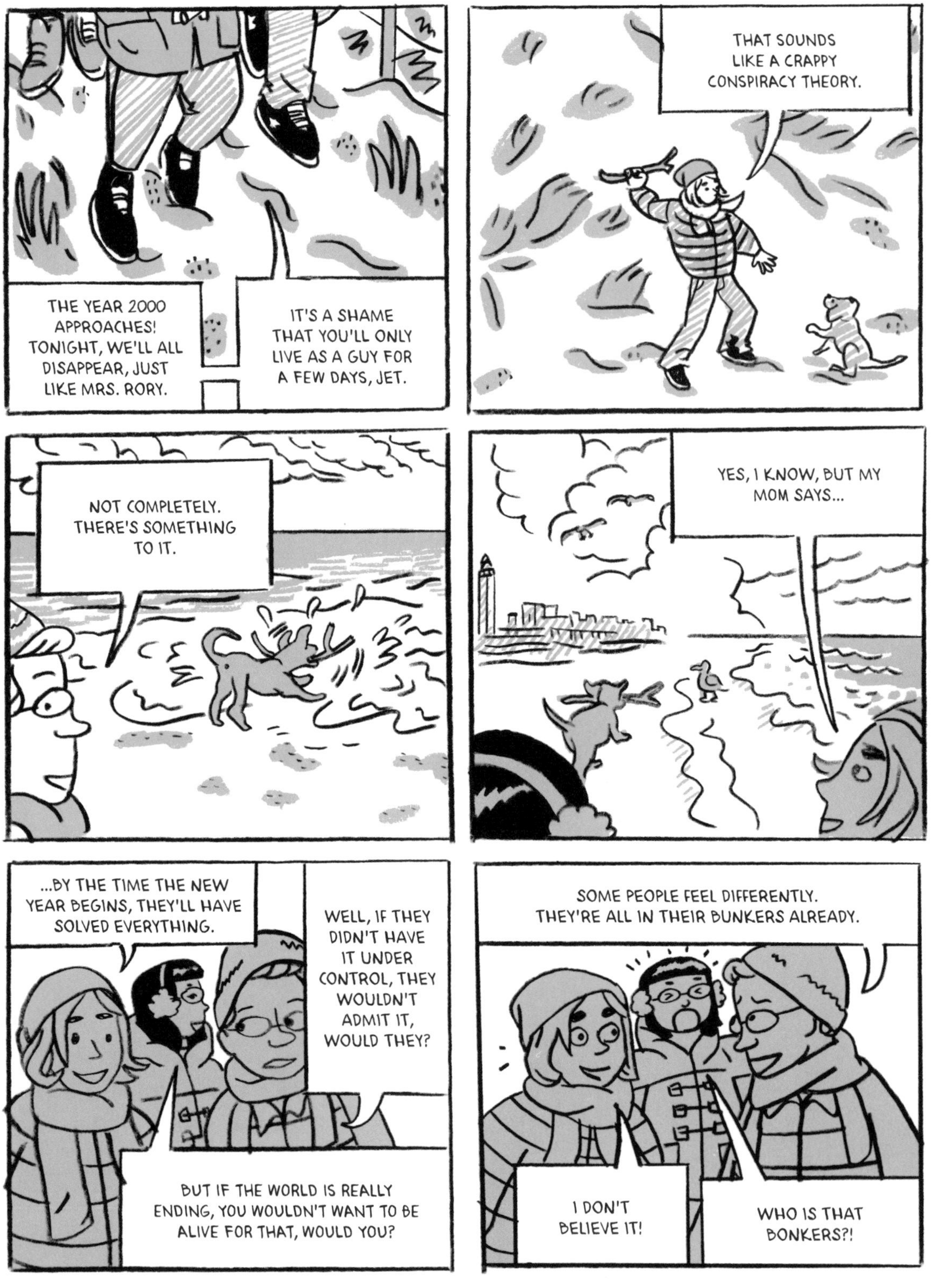
THE YEAR 2000 APPROACHES! TONIGHT, WE'LL ALL DISAPPEAR, JUST LIKE MRS. RORY.
IT'S A SHAME THAT YOU'LL ONLY LIVE AS A GUY FOR A FEW DAYS, JET.
THAT SOUNDS LIKE A CRAPPY CONSPIRACY THEORY.
NOT COMPLETELY. THERE'S SOMETHING TO IT.
YES, I KNOW, BUT MY MOM SAYS...
...BY THE TIME THE NEW YEAR BEGINS, THEY'LL HAVE SOLVED EVERYTHING.
WELL, IF THEY DIDN'T HAVE IT UNDER CONTROL, THEY WOULDN'T ADMIT IT, WOULD THEY?
BUT IF THE WORLD IS REALLY ENDING, YOU WOULDN'T WANT TO BE ALIVE FOR THAT, WOULD YOU?
SOME PEOPLE FEEL DIFFERENTLY. THEY'RE ALL IN THEIR BUNKERS ALREADY.
I DON'T BELIEVE IT!
WHO IS THAT BONKERS?!

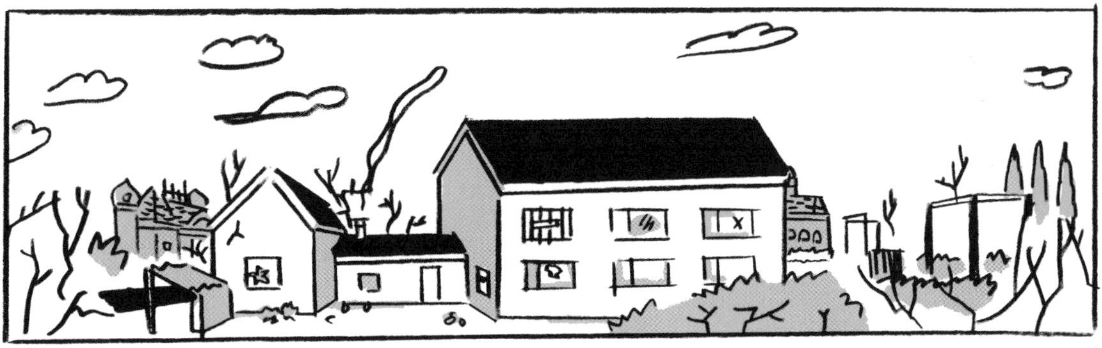

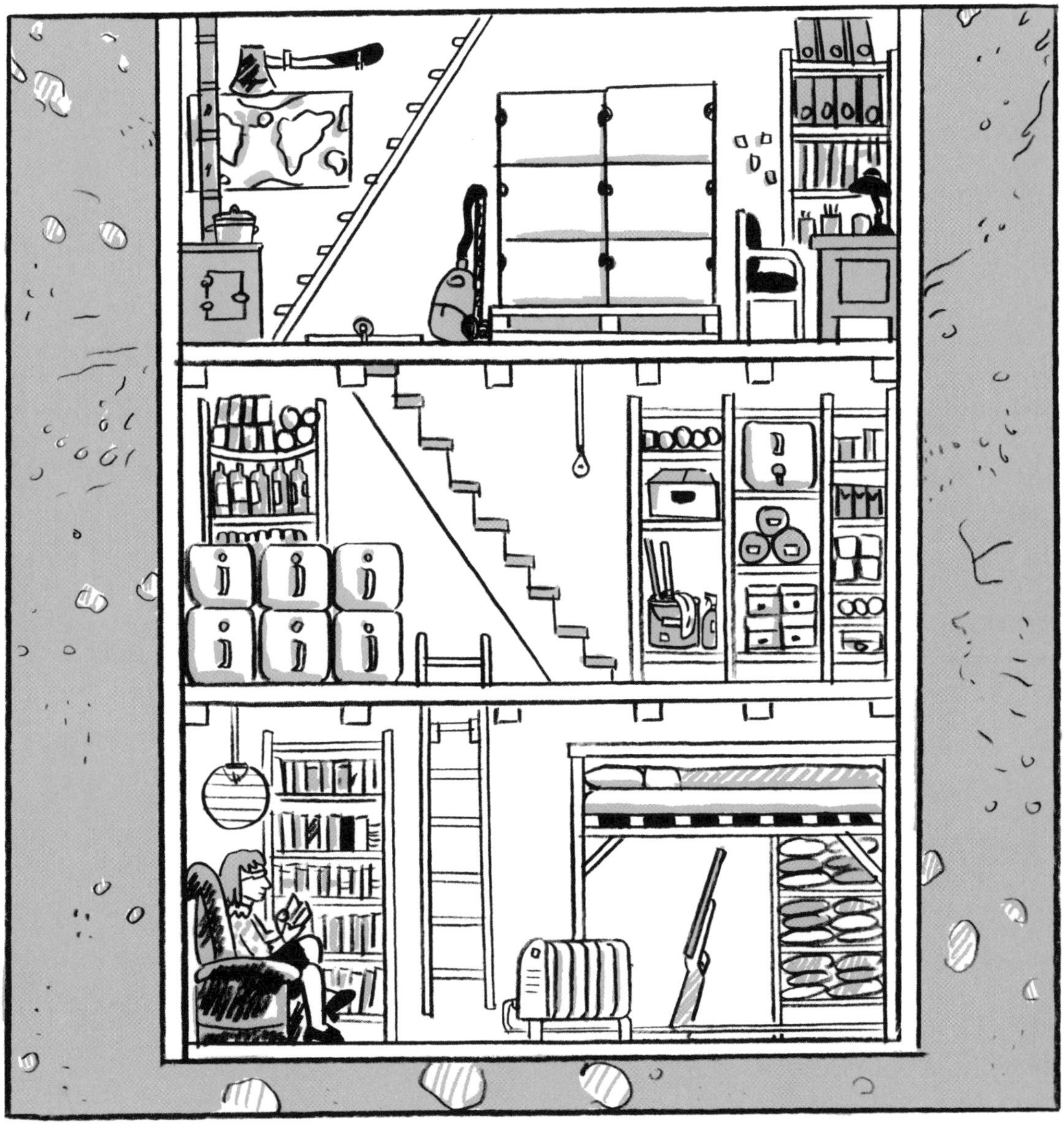

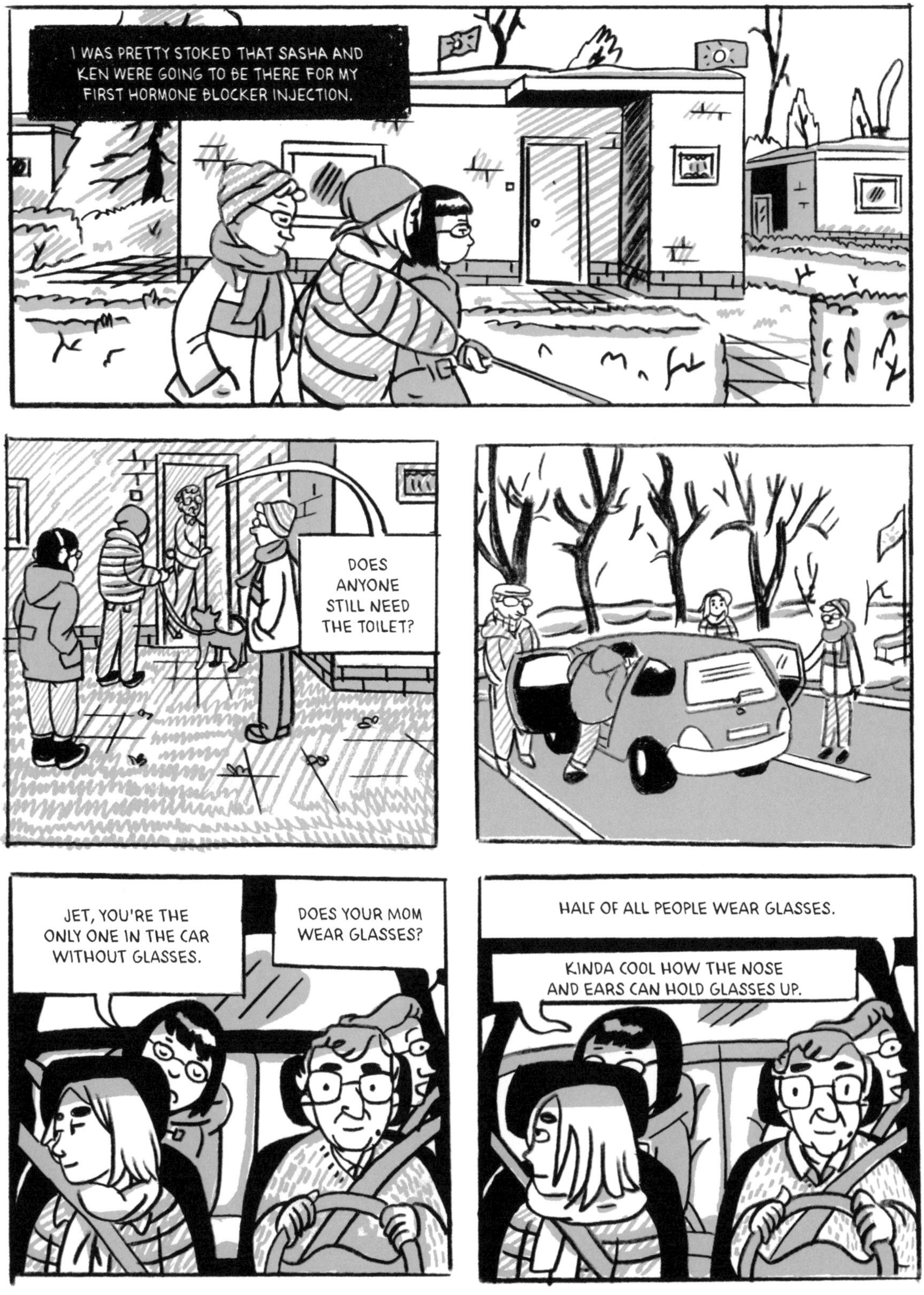
I WAS PRETTY STOKED THAT SASHA AND KEN WERE GOING TO BE THERE FOR MY FIRST HORMONE BLOCKER INJECTION.
DOES ANYONE STILL NEED THE TOILET?
JET, YOU'RE THE ONLY ONE IN THE CAR WITHOUT GLASSES.
DOES YOUR MOM WEAR GLASSES?
HALF OF ALL PEOPLE WEAR GLASSES.
KINDA COOL HOW THE NOSE AND EARS CAN HOLD GLASSES UP.

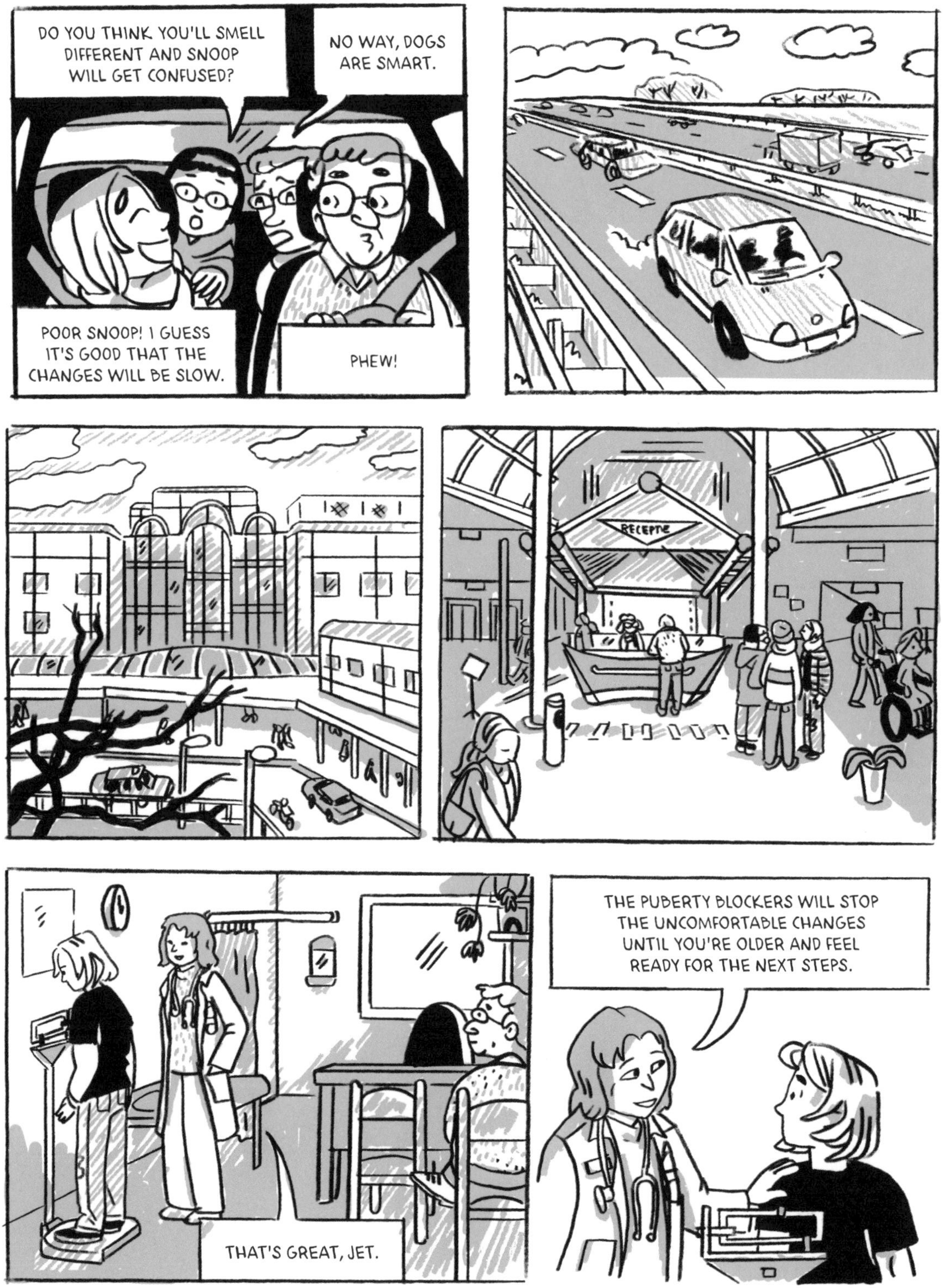
DO YOU THINK YOU'LL SMELL DIFFERENT AND SNOOP WILL GET CONFUSED?
NO WAY, DOGS ARE SMART.
POOR SNOOP! I GUESS IT'S GOOD THAT THE CHANGES WILL BE SLOW.
PHEW!
RECEPTIE
THAT'S GREAT, JET.
THE PUBERTY BLOCKERS WILL STOP THE UNCOMFORTABLE CHANGES UNTIL YOU'RE OLDER AND FEEL READY FOR THE NEXT STEPS.

SINCE YOUR WIFE HAD THE BRILLIANT IDEA TO SEND HER SIGNATURE AHEAD BY MAIL, WE CAN PROCEED TODAY.

THIS IS NURSE MARTHA, SHE'LL GIVE YOU THE FIRST SHOT.

YOU CAN CALL YOUR FRIENDS IN NOW IF YOU LIKE.

YOUR MOM IS GOING TO BE LIKE, "WHERE'S JET? WHO IS THIS GUY?"

AAAH, CAN YOU IMAGINE?

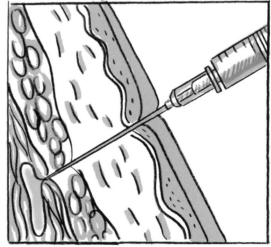

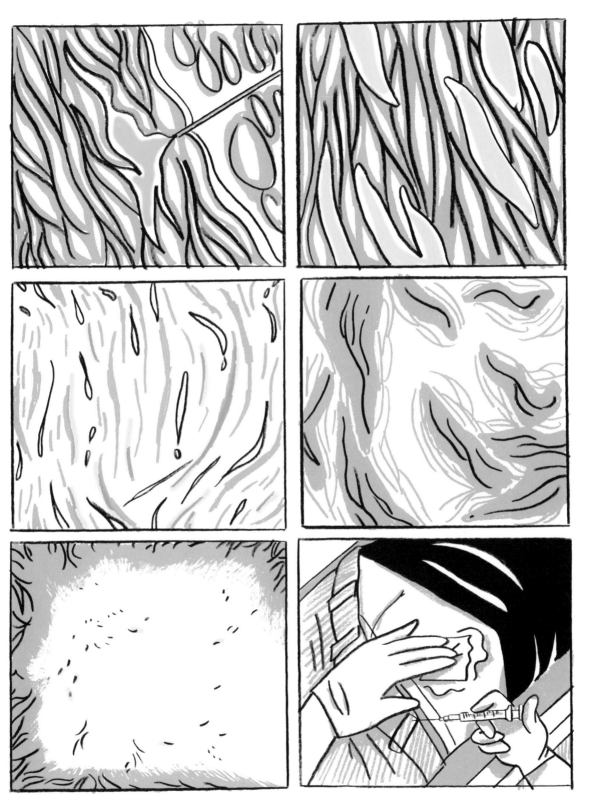

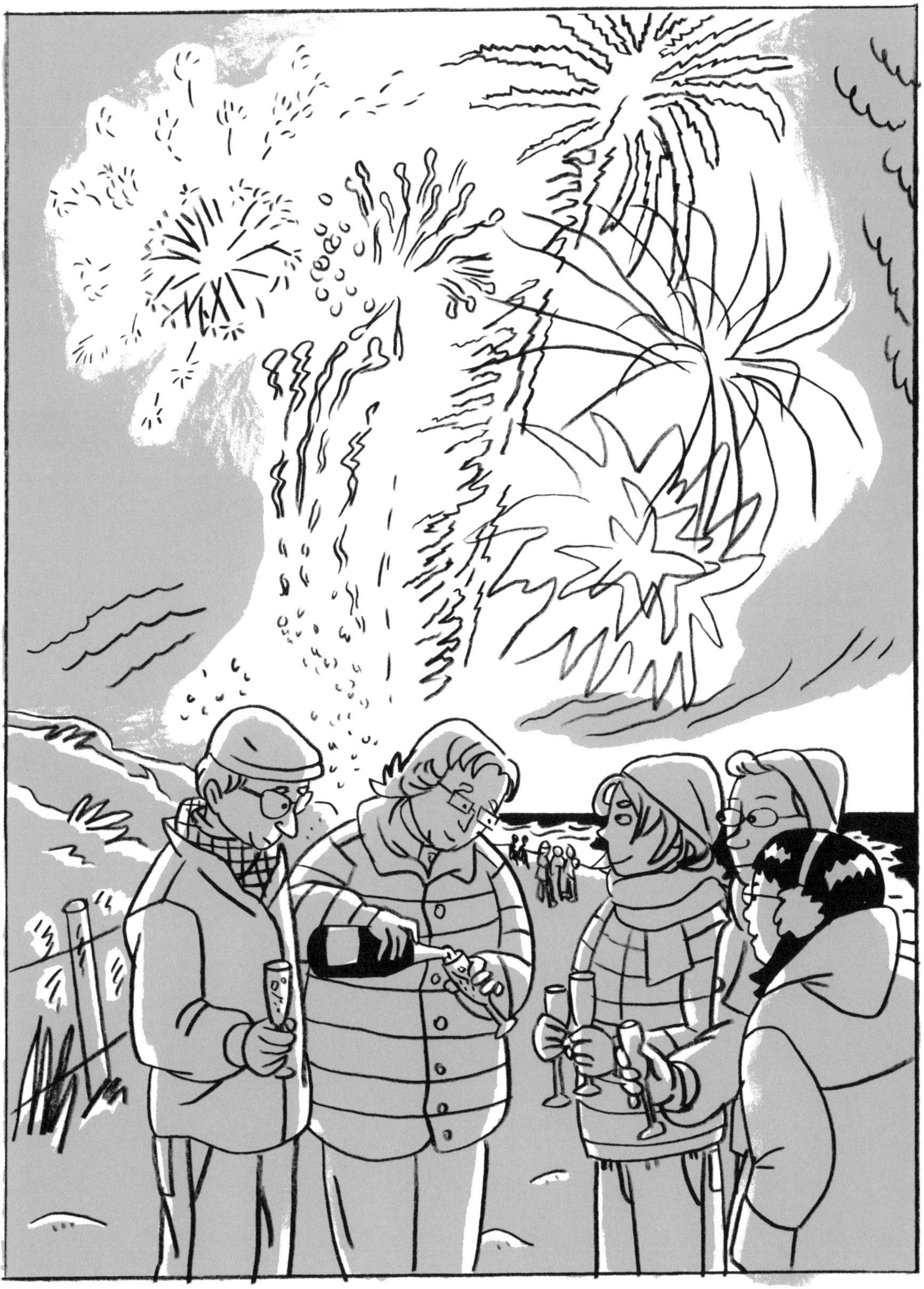

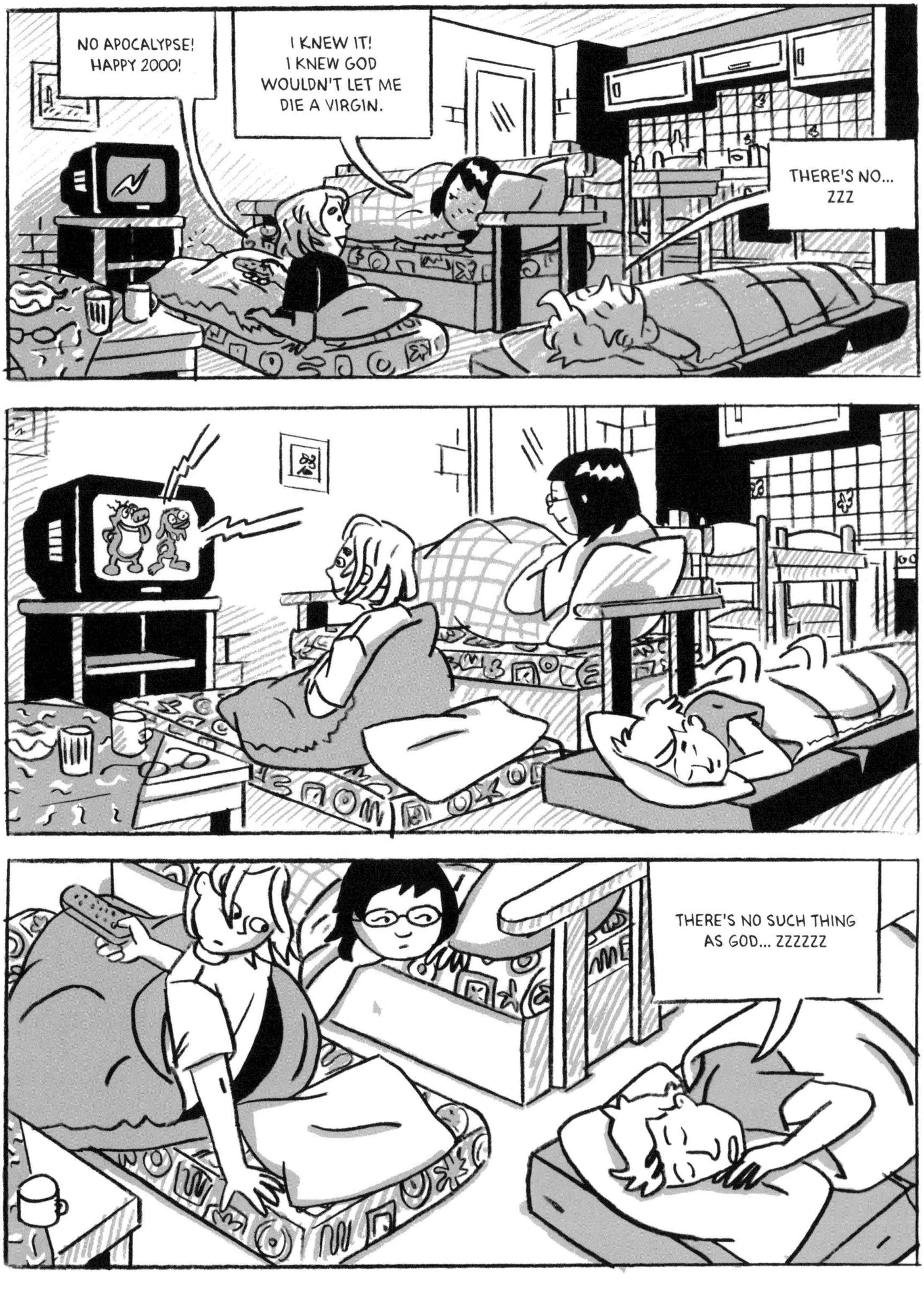
NO APOCALYPSE! HAPPY 2000!
I KNEW IT! I KNEW GOD WOULDN'T LET ME DIE A VIRGIN.
THERE'S NO... ZZZ
THERE'S NO SUCH THING AS GOD... ZZZZZZ

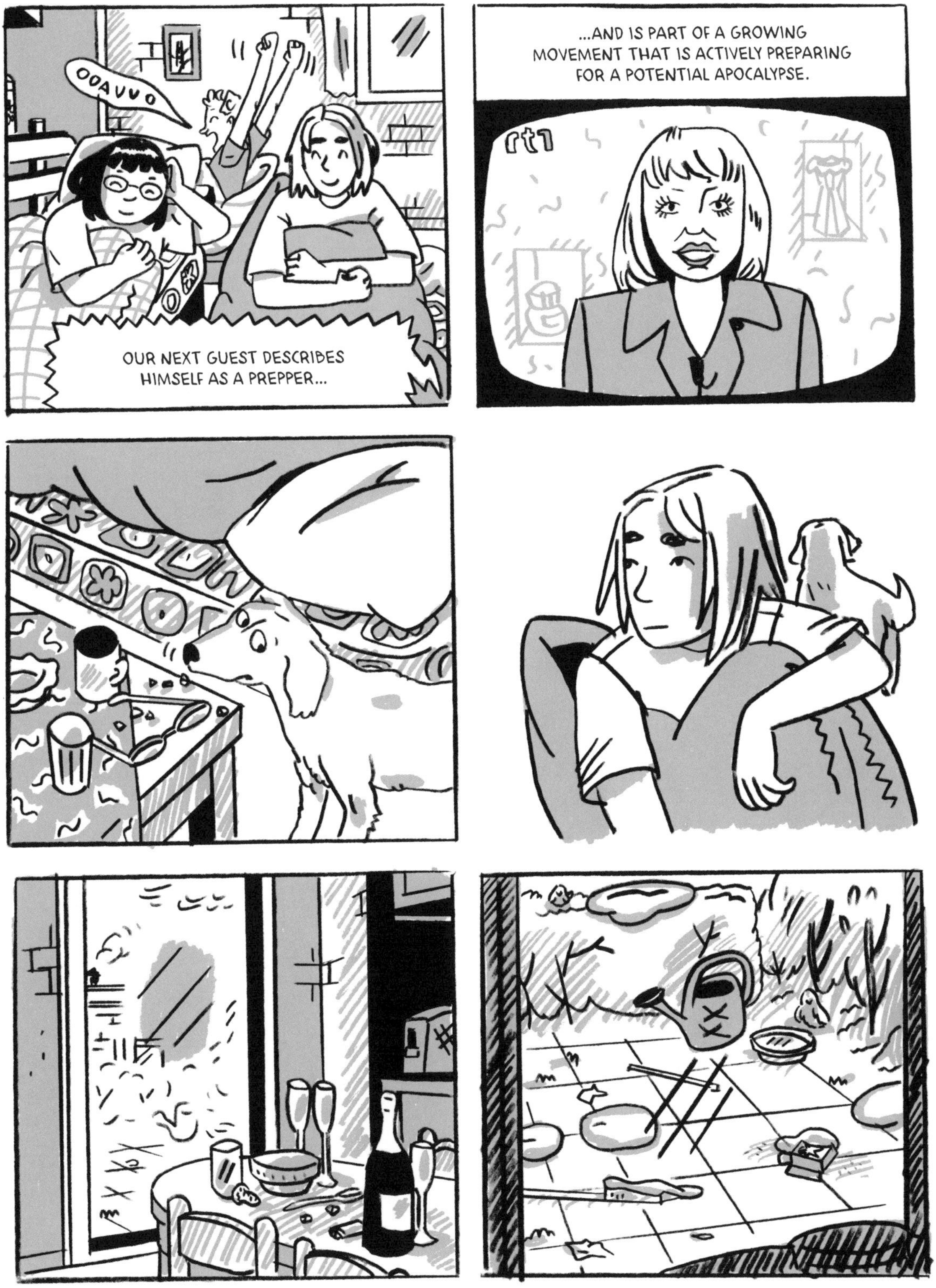
OOAVVO
OUR NEXT GUEST DESCRIBES HIMSELF AS A PREPPER...
...AND IS PART OF A GROWING MOVEMENT THAT IS ACTIVELY PREPARING FOR A POTENTIAL APOCALYPSE.
rt1

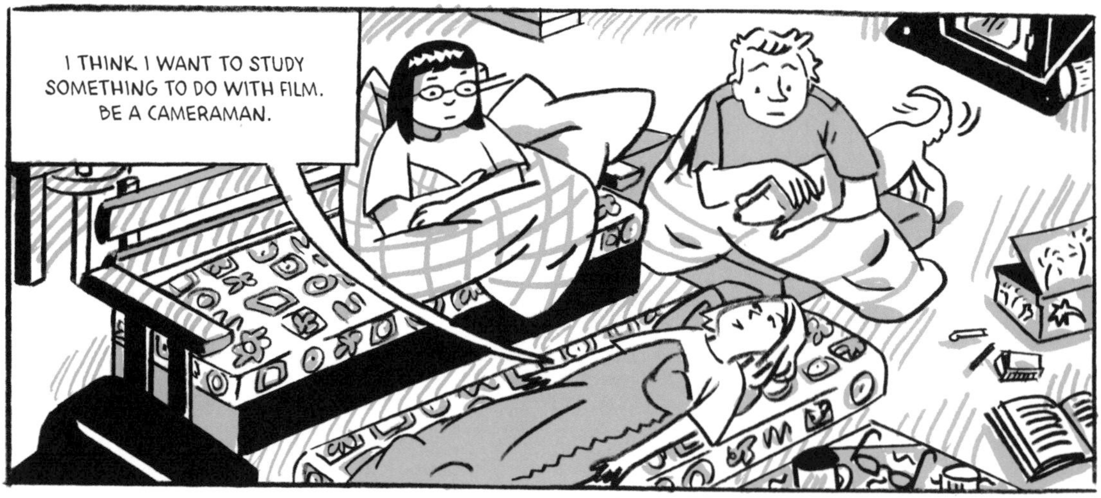
I THINK I WANT TO STUDY SOMETHING TO DO WITH FILM. BE A CAMERAMAN.

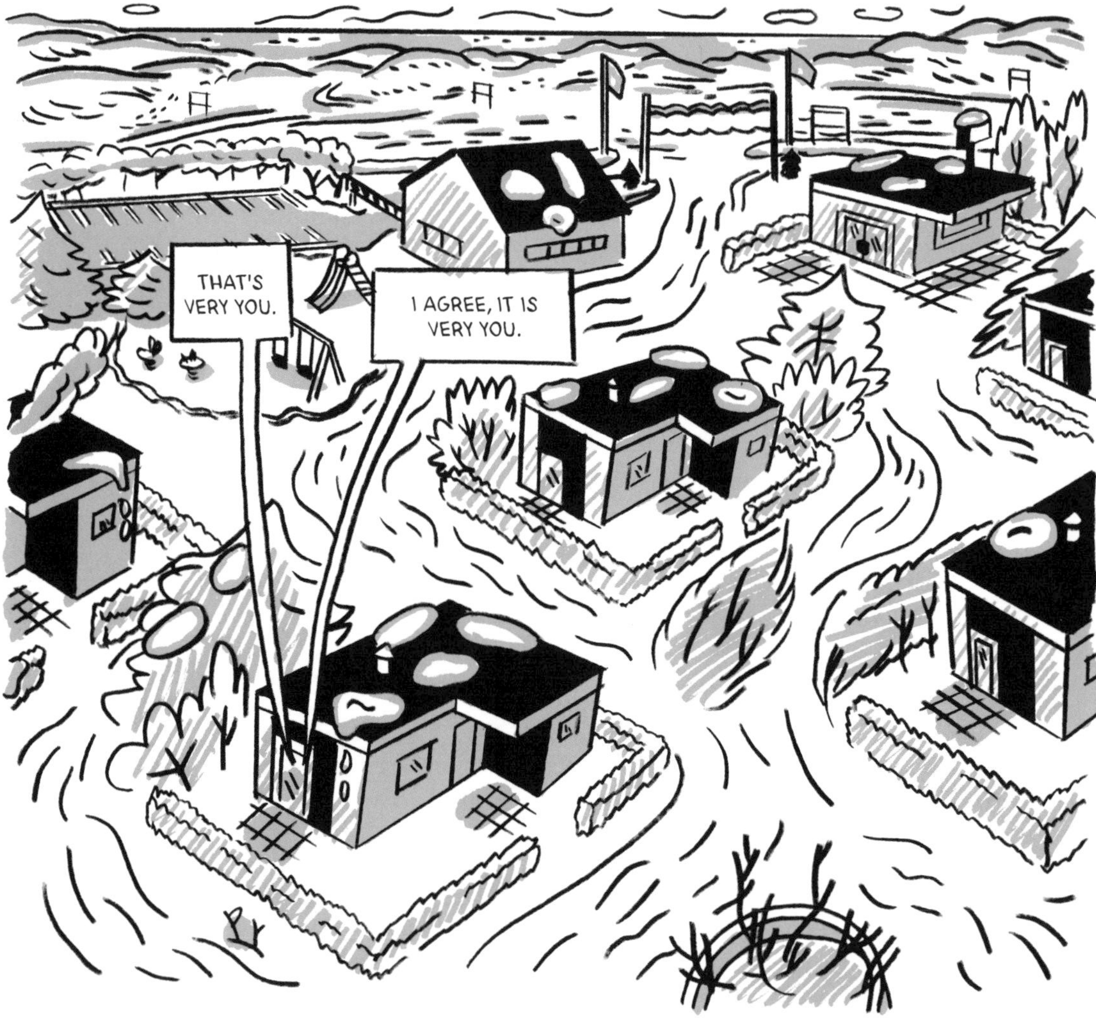
THAT'S VERY YOU.
I AGREE, IT IS VERY YOU.

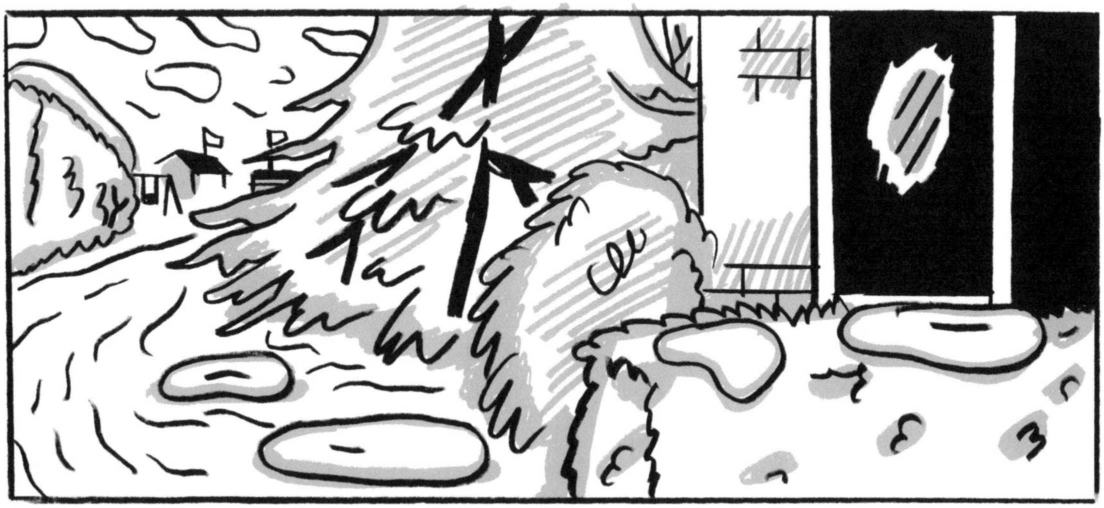

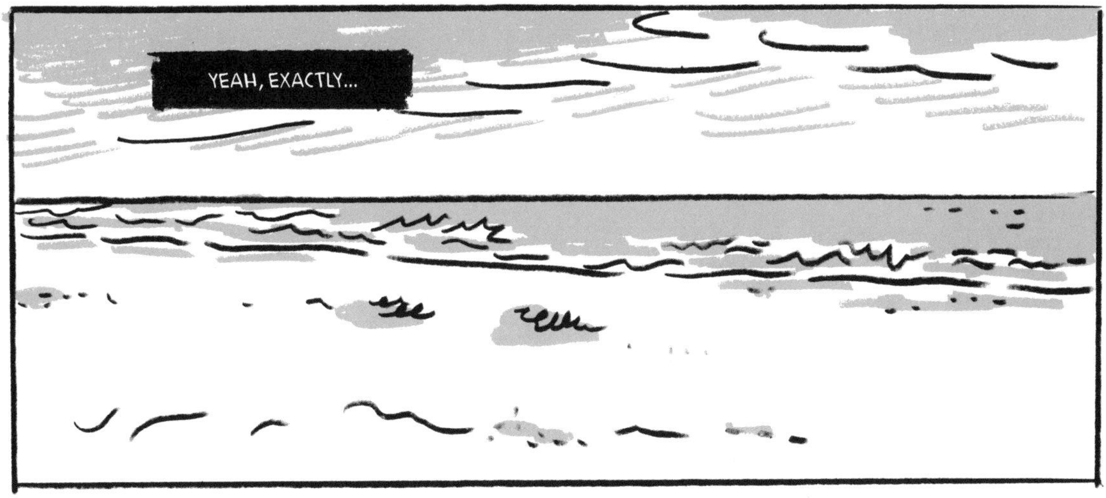
YEAH, EXACTLY...

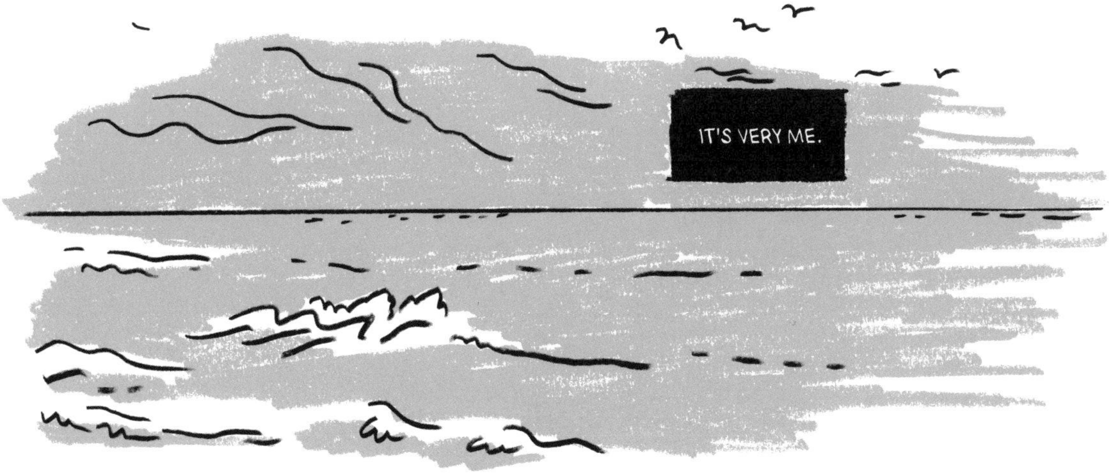
IT'S VERY ME.

KÜSSE
FÜR JET

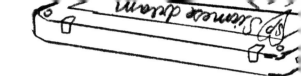

JORIS BAS BACKER WAS BORN ONLY A SHORT BIKE RIDE AWAY FROM THE COAST IN THE HAGUE AND GREW UP IN BUCHAREST, NEW YORK, AND LEIDEN. UNTIL 2003, HE STUDIED FINE ARTS AT THE GERRIT RIETVELD ACADEMIE IN AMSTERDAM. SINCE THEN, JORIS HAS BEEN LIVING IN BERLIN WORKING AS A COMIC ARTIST AND ILLUSTRATOR.

HE IS A CO-FOUNDER OF THE ARTIST COLLECTIVES PALATTI AND CHICKS ON COMICS. IN 2018, TOGETHER WITH NETTMANN, HE PUBLISHED THE CARTOON COLLECTION *FAMILIENJUWELEN*, AT JAJA PUBLISHING AND A SHORT STORY IN THE COMIC ANTHOLOGY, *WE'RE STILL HERE* (STACKED PRESS, USA), WHICH WON THE 2019 IGNATZ AWARD IN THE OUTSTANDING ANTHOLOGY CATEGORY.

JORIS WOULD LIKE TO THANK:

THANKS A LOT TO EVERYONE WHO READ ALONG, LISTENED TO ME, PUT UP WITH ME, STOOD BEHIND ME, BABYSAT MY KID AND GAVE ME TIPS, NUDGES AND THE COURAGE TO KEEP GOING. IN PARTICULAR TO: ULLI, AMELIA, JUTTA, JAJA PUBLISHING, SABINE, ELKE, HENNA, ULRIKA, THE AHOJ'S, CHICKS ON COMICS, MENG, DAD, MOM, NETTMANN, CALVIN, ANNA, MAARTEN, TEUNIS, FRANKIE, SARA, MAARTJE AND KELLY.

B
Random Mix for Jet

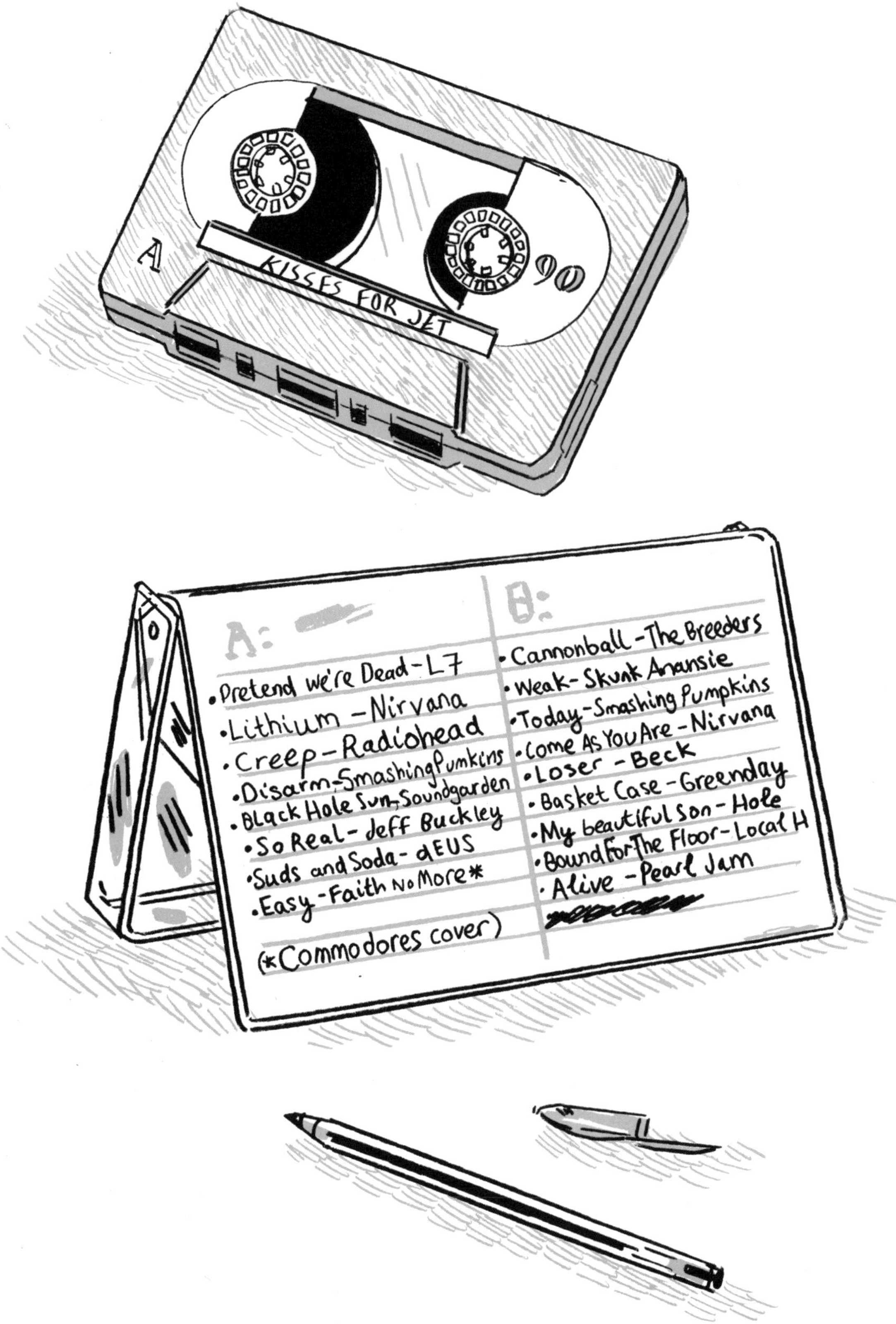
A
KISSES FOR JET
90
A:
• Pretend We're Dead – L7
• Lithium – Nirvana
• Creep – Radiohead
• Disarm – Smashing Pumkins
• Black Hole Sun – Soundgarden
• So Real – Jeff Buckley
• Suds and Soda – dEUS
• Easy – Faith No More*
(*Commodores cover)
B:
• Cannonball – The Breeders
• Weak – Skunk Anansie
• Today – Smashing Pumpkins
• Come As You Are – Nirvana
• Loser – Beck
• Basket Case – Greenday
• My beautiful Son – Hole
• Bound For The Floor – Local H
• Alive – Pearl Jam